SOUS VIDE COOKBOOK

600 Easy Foolproof Recipes to Cook Meat, Seafood and Vegetables in Low Temperature for Everyone, from Beginner to Advanced

Sophia Marchesi

IPPOCERONTE
publishing

CONTENTS

CHAPTER 4: 65
LUNCH RECIPES

INTRODUCTION

Cooking is something that runs in my blood, most of my food memories are of my Nan cooking Sunday dinners - lasagna and cannelloni to share with the whole family. When I was young I've never liked to be stuck in a classroom, I started culinary school at a very young age, and the only thing I really wanted was to be out cooking. You could say I wasn't a very good student but I have always been really passionate about food.

I have been working in a professional kitchen since I was seventeen years old and I'm running my own restaurant since I was 23. The past thirty years have been a rewarding, yet arduous journey that I spent learning the basics and mastering the different cuisines and techniques by taking the best out of each of them. It was last year, during the lockdown, that I realized that I was starting to lose my passion. Preparing a dish had become an aseptic and mechanical where perfection was king.

I wanted to go back to my roots, cooking has always been about my family; preparing a dish together with the people I love gives me time to connect and create precious memories. Setting aside a time where the entire family can work together to create a meal gives us a chance to pause, catch up and just connect with each other.

What I would like to share with you in this book is my renewed passion and a technique that I learned during my time in France, the Sous Vide. This innovative cooking method is something my grandmother never thought existed and creates the perfect opportunity to spend some time in the kitchen with my family. For these reasons, I think the Sous Vide is the perfect combination of my professional and domestic life.

Sous Vide is the French term that translates to "under vacuum" and it is the method for preparing a dish at a specifically controlled temperature and time; your food should be prepared at the temperature at which it will be eaten. Put simply, this procedure involves placing food in vacuum seal bags and boiling it in a specially-built bath of water for longer than average cooking times (usually 1 to 7 hours, up to 48 or more in some cases). Cooking at an exact temperature takes the guesswork out of the equation that defines a perfect meal.

You can easily prepare your steak, chicken, lamb, pork, etc., exactly the way you like it, every single time.

It's easy to use and leads to great results every time. You'll end up with food that's more tender and juicier than anything else you've ever made. This technique will help you to take your everyday cooking to a higher level. To do a top dish, most of the time, you don't need exotic ingredients, it is just a matter to get the best from the ingredients you already know.

The greatest part of Sous Vide cooking is that it does not require your constant presence in the kitchen. When the food is sealed in a bag and placed in the water bath, you can leave it at a low temperature, and it will cook on its own without asking much of your attention. The Sous Vide Cookers that are nowadays available in the market are efficient at regulating the perfect temperature to cook food according to its texture while maintaining the minimum required temperature. So, while your food is in the water, your hands are practically free to work on other important tasks or spend some quality time with your family.

It is an artful skill that is definitely worth trying. If it is just your first time, don't feel bad if you don't get the results you wanted to achieve. You will get better by gaining experience with this cookbook! The key is having patience, the right information, and consistency.

The meals prepared with Sous Vide are tasty and healthy, since this technique does not use added fats during the preparation of your dish also, using low temperature ensures that the perfect cooking point is reached.

Dishes included in this cookbook are simple, delicious, and provide you with so many options that you'll be preparing them for years to come. These recipes are made to be shared with the people you love and to build new precious food memories as I did with my Nan.

CHAPTER 1:
Benefits of Cooking and Why Certain Recipes Are Better Cooked with Sous Vide

Anyone who has ever cooked their meal in a pot on the stove or in the oven can tell you that it is not very efficient. Not only is it difficult to monitor the food, but it also requires constant attention, which isn't always possible when you are cooking.

Cooking Sous Vide means there is no presumption involved as to whether the ingredients are cooked or not. You can use this technique to prepare pasta, meat, fish, vegetables, eggs and so much more.

You can assemble meals ahead of time and cook them when you are ready to eat without stressing about overcooking or undercooking your food. It allows you to get the most out of your meal by knowing exactly how much time each ingredient will take to cook.

Even though your ingredients will be sealed in a bag for longer periods of time than they would normally, you don't have to worry about any bacteria causing contamination. When you use this technique, you know exactly what's going into your food and what's coming out of it.

The Sous Vide cooker provides many benefits for the modern cook. This method is suited to cook at temperatures between 0- and 122-° F. You will have perfectly cooked food every time.

When you use this method, you can seal your food in a vacuum-sealed bag. This will not only make your food safe from air, but it will also help with consistent cooking times and temperatures.

OTHER BENEFITS OF COOKING SOUS VIDE

1. It promotes healthy eating habits because the food can be cooked slowly with gentle heat. In higher temperatures, there is an increase in the loss of vitamins and nutrients in foods such as meats, fish, and vegetables.

2. It is a perfect way to cook for busy families or in restaurants because you don't have to cook large amounts of food at once.

3. It allows you to use different types of foods in your meals. For instance, you can make chicken breasts in one session

and then create a spinach salad for the next meal by using some of the same ingredients and simply reheating them following the same directions for the chicken breast cooking process.

4. It is easy to prepare for even beginners because it provides you with a larger variety of recipes than other cooking methods such as grilling or frying foods.

5. It is an affordable way to create gourmet meals.

6. The recipes are extremely methodical. You will always know exactly what temperature your food is being cooked at all times.

7. It is not affected by changes in the humidity of the kitchen. This allows you to cook Sous Vide even in the winter, or when it's hot outside.

8. The recipes can be adjusted perfectly to your taste. Certain parts of a recipe can be added or removed to get exactly the results you want.

9. It is an incredibly versatile tool that can be used for many different kinds of cooking. It's perfect for braises, stews, and even bread-based recipes, to name a few.

When it comes to cooking, the Sous-vide method offers a number of advantages over other techniques that are commonly used. If you've never used a Sous Vide device before, be prepared for some initial bumps in the road-but once you've come up with a few simple recipes, you'll find that your time spent preparing meals is much shorter and more efficient.

WHY CERTAIN RECIPES ARE BETTER COOKED WITH SOUS VIDE?

Certain dishes are better cooked Sous Vide than others. Some foods contain harmful fat that can lead to harmful bacteria growing, and others can quickly become dry and spoil. This is why Sous Vide cooking is thought to be so much better.

I've tested and retested thousands of recipes to find the best way to cook them. One of the main things I look at when selecting a recipe is what type of food it is. Is the food something that needs heat or water to be cooked? A prime example of this is a tuna steak—tuna is raw fish, so unless it's marinated, it shouldn't be cooked with a traditional method. So, if we want to cook a tuna steak in a traditional manner, using freshly caught tuna, we'd normally need to purchase the fish and marinate it ourselves. However, it can provide a suitable alternative way to prepare this meal by allowing us to cook food at our own convenience without needing to go out of our way to fish and prepare the dish ourselves.

CHAPTER 2:
Appetizer and Snack Recipes

🔪 Preparation Time | 🍲 Cooking Time | ✖ Servings

1. BUFFALO CHICKEN WINGS

Cal.: 344 | Fat: 21g | Protein: 19g   ⟍ 11 min | 🍲 30 min | ✗ Servings 4

INGREDIENTS

- 2 pounds whole chicken wings
- 1/2 cup butter
- 1 cup hot sauce (add another ½ cup if you like it hot)
- 1 teaspoon Worcestershire sauce
- 1 teaspoon garlic salt
- 1 teaspoon freshly ground black pepper
- 1/2 cup all-purpose flour

DIRECTIONS

Cut the chicken wings into 3 pieces. Keep the drumettes and wingettes (flats), but throw away the wing tips. Fill the water bath with water. Set your machine temperature to 176°F/80°C. Place the chicken wing pieces in a food-safe bag and vacuum seal the bag. Make sure they are lined up side by side and not stacked or piled. Use multiple bags if necessary. Place the chicken wings in the water bath and cook for 3 hours. To make the buffalo sauce, melt the butter in a medium saucepan over medium heat. Add all the remaining ingredients, except the flour, and simmer for about 10 minutes, stirring often. Prepare a Dutch oven or deep fryer with oil; preheat oil to 350°F. Remove the chicken wings from the bag and pat dry with a paper towel. Dredge the wings in flour. Shake off excess flour and deep-fry the chicken in 350°F oil for about 8–10 minutes. Place the wings on paper towels to remove the excess oil and then toss them with buffalo sauce.

2. HONEY GARLIC CHICKEN WINGS

Cal.: 381 | Fat: 25g | Protein: 19g   ⟍ 11 min | 🍲 33 min | ✗ Servings 4

INGREDIENTS

- 2 pounds whole chicken wings
- 1/3 cup butter
- 8–10 garlic cloves, minced
- 1/2 cup soy sauce
- 1 cup honey
- 2 teaspoons water
- 1 teaspoon cornstarch
- 1/2 cup all-purpose flour

DIRECTIONS

Cut the chicken wings into 3 pieces. Keep the drumettes and wingettes (flats), but throw away the wing tips. Fill the water bath with water. Set your machine temperature to 176°F/80°C. Place the chicken wing pieces in a food-safe bag and vacuum seal the bag. Make sure they are lined up side by side and not stacked or piled. Use multiple bags if necessary. Place the wings in the water bath and cook for 3 hours.

To make the sauce, melt the butter in a medium saucepan over medium heat. Add the minced garlic and cook for 2–3 minutes to release the flavor. Add the soy sauce and honey and bring to a boil. Lower the heat to a simmer. In a small bowl, whisk together the water and cornstarch to make a slurry. Whisk the slurry into the honey sauce and continue to stir as the sauce thickens over the next 3–4 minutes. Prepare a Dutch oven or deep fryer with oil; preheat oil to 350°F. Remove the chicken wings from the bag and pat dry with a paper towel. Dredge the wings in flour. Shake off the excess flour and deep-fry the wings in 350°F oil for about 8–10 minutes. Place the wings on paper towels to remove the excess oil and toss them with the honey garlic sauce.

3. HUMMUS

Cal.: 244 | Fat: 11g | Protein: 9g   11 min | 3 hours | Servings 6

INGREDIENTS

- ½ cup dried chickpeas
- 2 cups water, divided
- 2 garlic cloves, divided
- 1 tablespoon lemon juice
- 2 tablespoons tahini
- ½ teaspoon sea salt
- 2 tablespoons extra-virgin olive oil
- 1 teaspoon ground cumin

DIRECTIONS

Fill the water bath with water. Set your machine temperature to 195°F/91°C. Place the chickpeas, 1½ cups water, and 1 garlic clove in a large food-safe zip-top bag. Slowly lower the zip-top bag into the water and, using the water displacement method, the air will escape from the bag. Continue to lower the bag until it is about 1" from being fully Immersed. Once the bag has been lowered, zip it shut with your fingers. Cook for 3½ hours. Check to see if chickpeas are tender and cook longer if needed. Drain the chickpeas and let them cool until they come to room temperature. Using a food processor, pulse the chickpeas, lemon juice, remaining garlic clove, tahini, salt, oil, and cumin. While the food processor is running, slowly pour in the remaining water. Check the texture and thickness of the hummus. If needed, add more water to reach the desired consistency. When ready to serve, scoop the hummus into a small serving bowl and serve with pita bread, crackers, or fresh vegetables.

4. LEMON HUMMUS

Cal.: 225 | Fat: 6g | Protein: 6g   15 min | 3 hours | Servings 12

INGREDIENTS

- ½ cup tahini, see our homemade tahini recipe
- 1/3 cup fresh lemon juice
- 1/4 cup extra-virgin olive oil
- 1 teaspoon cayenne pepper
- Salt and black pepper, to taste
- 1 pound chickpeas
- 1 teaspoon onion powder
- 2 garlic cloves, smashed

DIRECTIONS

In a deep and large bowl filled with water, put the chickpeas and leave to soak through the night. Strain the chickpeas. Prepare your sous-vide water bath to a temperature of 183°F/84°C. Transfer the chickpeas into a cooking pouch with 4 cups of water. Seal the pouch and immerse it in the preheated water bath. Cook for 3 hours and 9 minutes. Once done, transfer the cooked chickpeas to a food blender and blend them together with the remaining ingredients. Serve and enjoy chilled!

5. WHITE BEAN AND ARTICHOKE DIP

Cal.: 304 | Fat: 20g | Protein: 13g   10 min | 4 hours | Servings 6

INGREDIENTS

- 1/2 cup dried cannellini beans
- 1½ cups water
- 2 garlic cloves, divided
- 1 (14-ounce) can artichoke hearts, drained
- 2 tablespoons lemon juice
- 2 tablespoons extra-virgin olive oil
- 1/2 teaspoon sea salt
- 1/3 cup grated Parmesan cheese

DIRECTIONS

Fill the water bath with water. Set your machine temperature to 195°F/91°C. Place the beans, 1½ cups water, and 1 garlic clove in a large food-safe zip-top bag. Slowly lower the zip-top bag into the water and, using the water displacement method, the air will escape from the bag. Continue to lower the bag until it is about 1" from being fully Immersed. Once the bag has been lowered, zip it shut with your fingers. Cook for 3 ½ hours. Check to see if the beans are tender and cook a little longer if needed. Drain the beans and let them cool until they come to room temperature. Using a food processor, pulse the beans, artichoke hearts, lemon juice, remaining garlic clove, oil, salt and Parmesan cheese. Process until smooth and creamy. If a thinner consistency is desired, add a little extra water while processing. Serve.

6. SHRIMP AND AVOCADO SALSA

Cal.: 249 | Fat: 26g | Protein: 15g   📐 11 min | 🍲 46 min | 🍴 Servings 6

INGREDIENTS

- 1-pound raw medium shrimp, peeled and deveined
- 1 tablespoon olive oil
- 2 medium avocados, peeled, cored, and cubed
- 3 medium tomatoes, diced
- 2 medium jalapeño peppers, cored and minced
- 1/4 cup chopped fresh cilantro
- Juice of 2 medium limes
- 1/2 teaspoon sea salt

DIRECTIONS

Fill the water bath with water. Set your machine temperature to 140°F/60°C. Place the shrimp and olive oil in a food-safe bag and vacuum seal the bag. Place the shrimp in the water bath and cook for 30 minutes. Remove the shrimp from the bag and cut each into 2–3 pieces. In a large mixing bowl, combine all the ingredients and toss. Let the salsa marinate, in the refrigerator, for 10–15 minutes before serving.

7. TOMATO AND MANGO SALSA

Cal.: 264 | Fat: 20g | Protein: 13g   📐 11 min | 🍲 16 min | 🍴 Servings 6

INGREDIENTS

- 2 tablespoons extra-virgin olive oil
- 3 medium tomatoes, diced
- 2 large ripe mangos, peeled, pitted, and diced
- 1 medium red onion, diced
- 2 tablespoons chopped fresh cilantro
- 1 tablespoon minced fresh mint
- Juice of 1 medium lime
- 1 tablespoon granulated sugar
- 1/2 teaspoon sea salt

DIRECTIONS

Fill the water bath with water. Set your machine temperature to 150°F/65°C. Place the oil, tomatoes, mangos and red onion in a food-safe bag and vacuum seal the bag. Place the bag in the water bath and cook for 1 hour. Quick chill the bag by placing it in an ice bath. Empty the bag into a large bowl and toss well with the remaining ingredients. Let the salsa marinate, in the refrigerator, for 10–15 minutes before serving.

8. SHRIMP AND JALAPEÑO QUESADILLA

Cal.: 294 | Fat: 29g | Protein: 19g   📐 12 min | 🍲 50 min | 🍴 Servings 8

INGREDIENTS

- 1-pound raw medium shrimp, peeled and deveined
- 1 tablespoon olive oil
- 2 jalapeño peppers, cored and minced
- 3 green onions, sliced
- 3 tablespoons minced fresh cilantro
- 2 tablespoons lime juice
- ½ teaspoon sea salt
- 6-8 (8") soft flour tortillas
- 1 cup grated Cheddar cheese
- 1 cup grated Monterey jack cheese

DIRECTIONS

Fill the water bath with water. Set your machine temperature to 140°F/60°C. Place the shrimp and olive oil in a food-safe bag and vacuum seal the bag. Place the shrimp in the water bath and cook for 30 minutes. Preheat the oven to 350°F/176°C. Remove the shrimp from the bag and cut each into 2-3 pieces. Place the shrimp and the jalapeño, green onions, cilantro, lime juice, and salt in a large bowl and toss to combine. To make the quesadillas: scoop some of the shrimp mixtures onto half of a soft tortilla. Evenly sprinkle some of each cheese onto the shrimp mixture and then fold the soft tortilla over, covering the shrimp and cheese. Repeat with all the quesadillas. Bake the quesadillas in the oven until the cheese melts and the tortillas are brown, about 10 minutes. Cut each quesadilla into 4 wedges and serve with salsa.

9. TOMATO CONFIT AND PROVOLONE GRILLED CHEESE SANDWICH WEDGES

Cal.: 464 | Fat: 26g | Protein: 13g   🔪 9 min | 🍲 5 hours | 🍴 Servings 6

INGREDIENTS

- 2 pints cherry tomatoes
- 1/4 cup olive oil
- 1½ tablespoons balsamic vinegar
- ½ teaspoon sea salt
- ½ teaspoon black pepper
- 1/4 cup butter or margarine, softened
- 8 slices fresh bread
- 8 slices provolone or mozzarella cheese
- 1/3 cup thinly sliced fresh basil

DIRECTIONS

Fill the water bath with water. Set your machine temperature to 150°F/65°C. Place the tomatoes, olive oil, vinegar, sea salt and black pepper in a food-safe bag and vacuum seal the bag. Place the tomatoes in the water bath and cook for 4 hours. Remove the tomatoes from the water bath and cool to room temperature. Strain the oil and peel the skins off the tomatoes. The skins should peel off easily. Butter 1 side of each slice of bread. Assemble the sandwiches by laying out a slice of bread buttered side down. Place a slice of cheese on the bread. Put some tomatoes on top of the cheese and sprinkle with fresh basil. Add another slice of cheese and finish the sandwich with another bread slice, buttered side on the outside. Place the sandwiches in a large skillet over medium heat. Cook until golden brown on each side, about 4 minutes per side. Cut the sandwiches into wedges and serve.

10. FLANK STEAK, APRICOT, AND BRIE BITES

Cal.: 549 | Fat: 31g | Protein: 16g   🔪 13 min | 🍲 18 hours | 🍴 Servings 6

INGREDIENTS

- 1 flank steak (about 2 pounds)
- 1 teaspoon sea salt
- 1 teaspoon freshly ground black pepper
- 1 teaspoon paprika
- 1 medium wheel Brie
- 10–12 dried apricots
- 20–24 fresh mint leaves

DIRECTIONS

Fill the water bath with water. Set your machine temperature to 135°F/57°C. Rub the flank steak all over with salt, pepper and paprika. Place the steak in a food-safe bag and vacuum seal the bag. Place the steak in the water bath and cook for 12–18 hours. Remove from the water bath and immediately place in an ice bath to chill the steak. Cut the flank steak, against the grain, into thin slices. Cut the Brie cheese into small slices and cut the dried apricots in half. Assemble the bites by placing a mint leaf and dried apricot half on a piece of sliced Brie. Wrap with a slice of flank steak and pierce with a toothpick. Keep them in the fridge until ready to serve.

11. SZECHUAN BROCCOLI

Cal.: 414 | Fat: 36g | Protein: 19g   🔪 19 min | 🍲 2 hours | 🍴 Servings 4

INGREDIENTS

- 3 cups small broccoli florets
- 2 tablespoons olive oil
- 3 garlic cloves, minced
- 1 teaspoon grated fresh ginger root
- 3 tablespoons soy sauce
- 2 tablespoons rice vinegar
- 2 tablespoons granulated sugar
- 2 tablespoons ketchup
- ½ teaspoon dried red pepper flakes
- 2 tablespoons toasted sesame seeds

DIRECTIONS

Fill the water bath with water. Set your machine temperature to 183°F/83°C. Place the broccoli in a large food-safe bag and vacuum seal the bag. Make sure the broccoli is placed side by side and not stacked. Use multiple bags if necessary. Place the bag in the water bath and cook for 1-1½ hours. Heat the oil in a medium saucepan over medium heat. Add the garlic and ginger and cook for 2–3 minutes. Add the soy sauce, rice vinegar, sugar, ketchup and red pepper flakes. Let the sauce simmer for 7–9 minutes. It should thicken slightly. Remove the bag from the water bath. Place the broccoli in a medium bowl and toss with the Szechuan sauce and toasted sesame seeds.

12. PORK TENDERLOIN, TOMATO, AND BOCCONCINI CANAPÉS

Cal.: 564 | Fat: 36g | Protein: 19g   13 min | 3 hours | Servings 4

INGREDIENTS

- ½ teaspoon sea salt
- ½ teaspoon freshly ground black pepper
- 1 pork tenderloin (about 1 pound)
- 1 tablespoon oil with a high smoke point (like peanut, sunflower, corn, vegetable, or safflower oil)
- 1 baguette, sliced and lightly toasted
- 3–4 plum or Roma tomatoes, sliced
- 1 (8-ounce) container Bocconcini, drained and sliced
- 1 bunch fresh basil
- 2 tablespoons balsamic vinegar (optional)

DIRECTIONS

Rub the salt and pepper all over the tenderloin. Fill the water bath with water. Set your machine temperature to 140°F/60°C. Place the pork tenderloin in a food-safe bag and vacuum seal the bag. Place the pork in the water bath and cook for 3 hours. Remove the pork tenderloin from the bag and pat dry with a paper towel. Heat the oil in a large skillet over high heat. Sear the tenderloin in the skillet for 45–60 seconds per side. Slice the pork into ½" medallions. Assemble the canapés by layering each baguette slice with a slice of pork tenderloin, tomato, Bocconcini, and a fresh basil leaf. If desired, drizzle with a little balsamic vinegar.

13. GREEN BEAN ALMONDINE

Cal.: 294 | Fat: 20g | Protein: 13g   8 min | 1 hour | Servings 4

INGREDIENTS

- 3–4 cups trimmed fresh green beans
- 2 tablespoons olive oil
- 1 tablespoon lemon zest
- 2 tablespoons lemon juice
- 1 teaspoon sea salt
- ½ cup roughly chopped toasted almonds

DIRECTIONS

Fill the water bath with water. Set your machine temperature to 183°F/84°C. Place the green beans, oil and lemon zest in a food-safe bag and vacuum seal the bag. Make sure the beans are lined up side by side and not stacked or piled. Use multiple bags if necessary. Place the beans in the water bath and cook for 45–60 minutes. Remove the green beans from the bag and place on a serving plate. Drizzle with lemon juice and sprinkle with salt. Top with chopped almonds and serve.

14. HONEY GINGER CARROTS

Cal.: 389 | Fat: 31g | Protein: 22g   13 min | 90 min | Servings 4

INGREDIENTS

- 1-pound whole baby carrots, peeled
- 2 tablespoons butter
- 2 tablespoons honey
- 2 teaspoons grated fresh ginger root
- 1 teaspoon sea salt

DIRECTIONS

Fill the water bath with water. Set your machine temperature to 183°F/84°C. Place the carrots, butter, honey and ginger in a food-safe bag and vacuum seal the bag. Make sure the carrots are lined up side by side and not stacked or piled. Use multiple bags if necessary. Place the carrots in the water bath and cook for 60–90 minutes. Remove the carrots from the bag and place on a serving plate. Sprinkle with sea salt and serve.

15. MASHED POTATOES

Cal.: 494 | Fat: 29g | Protein: 13g 19 min | 2 hours | Servings 4

INGREDIENTS

- 2 pounds potatoes (white, Yukon Gold, or other), peeled and cut into 1" chunks
- 1/4 cup butter
- 1/4 cup heavy cream
- ½ cup whole milk
- ½ teaspoon sea salt
- ½ teaspoon freshly ground black pepper

DIRECTIONS

Fill the water bath with water. Set your machine temperature to 183°F/84°C. Place the chopped potatoes and butter in a food-safe bag and vacuum seal the bag. Make sure the potatoes are lined up side by side and not stacked or piled. Use multiple bags if necessary. Place the potatoes in the water bath and cook for 1½-2 hours. Drain the potatoes in a large bowl. Add the butter, milk, salt and pepper. Mash the potatoes with a potato masher or a hand blender.

16. MAPLE BUTTERNUT SQUASH PURÉE

Cal.: 414 | Fat: 29g | Protein: 10g 9 min | 3 hours | Servings 4

INGREDIENTS

- 1 medium butternut squash
- 1/3 cup maple syrup
- 1/4 cup butter
- 1/2 teaspoon sea salt

DIRECTIONS

Cut the squash into quarters. Scoop out all the seeds from the inner part of the squash and discard. Peel or cut off the outer skin and discard. Slice the squash flesh into 1" chunks. Fill the water bath with water. Set your machine temperature to 183°F/84°C. Place the squash chunks, maple syrup, butter and salt in a large food-safe bag and vacuum seal the bag. Make sure that the squash is in a single layer and not stacked. Use multiple bags if necessary. Place the bag in the water bath and cook for 3 hours. Remove the bag from the water bath and let cool slightly. Pour the squash and any liquid into a food processor or blender and purée until smooth.

17. LEEK AND CAULIFLOWER PURÉE

Cal.: 398 | Fat: 34g | Protein: 21g 13 min | 3 hours | Servings 4

INGREDIENTS

- 2 tablespoons butter
- 2/3 cup sliced leeks
- 1 medium head cauliflower
- 2/3 cup heavy cream
- 1/2 teaspoon sea salt

DIRECTIONS

In a small saucepan, melt the butter over medium heat. Add the leeks and cook until soft, about 5 minutes. Cool to room temperature. Fill the water bath with water. Set your machine temperature to 183°F/84°C. Cut the cauliflower into ½" slices. Place the cauliflower in a large food-safe bag and vacuum seal the bag. Make sure the cauliflower is placed side by side and not stacked. Use multiple bags if necessary. Place the bag in the water bath and cook for 2–3 hours. Remove the bag from the water bath and let cool slightly. Place the cauliflower, leeks, heavy cream and salt into a food processor or blender and purée until smooth.

18. BUTTERED CORN ON THE COB

Cal.: 294 | Fat: 21g | Protein: 13g   14 min | 3 hours | Servings 4

INGREDIENTS

- 4 cobs of corn, shucked and cleaned
- 2 tablespoons butter
- 1 teaspoon sea salt

DIRECTIONS

Fill the water bath with water. Set your machine temperature to 183°F/84°C. Place the corn and butter in a food-safe bag and vacuum seal the bag. Make sure the cobs are lined up side by side and not stacked or piled. Use multiple bags if necessary. Place the corn in the water bath and cook for 1½-3 hours. Remove the corn from the bag. Sprinkle with sea salt and serve.

19. RATATOUILLE

Cal.: 411 | Fat: 34g | Protein: 23g   11 min | 3 hours | Servings 4

INGREDIENTS

- 2 tablespoons olive oil
- 1 medium sweet onion, diced
- 1 medium green bell pepper, cored and diced
- 2 garlic cloves, minced
- 2 cups peeled and cubed eggplant, no larger than ½" pieces
- 2 cups cubed zucchini, no larger than ½" pieces
- 2 medium tomatoes, diced
- 1 teaspoon sea salt
- 1 teaspoon dried marjoram or tarragon
- ½ teaspoon freshly ground black pepper

DIRECTIONS

In a medium skillet, heat oil over medium heat. Add the onion, pepper and garlic. Cook until the onions are transparent and the peppers are soft, about 5–7 minutes. Cool to room temperature. Fill the water bath with water. Set your machine temperature to 183°F/84°C. In a large bowl, toss together the sautéed onion and pepper with all the remaining ingredients. Dump the mixture into a food-safe bag and vacuum seal the bag. Make sure the ratatouille is an even thickness within the bag, about 1–1½" thick. Use multiple bags if necessary. Place the bag in the water bath and cook for 3 hours. Remove from the water bath and serve hot.

20. A BED OF VEGETABLES

Cal.: 398 | Fat: 26g | Protein: 19g   9 min | 48 min | Servings 4

INGREDIENTS

- 1 cucumber
- 3 carrots
- 1 sweet potato
- 1 red, green and yellow pepper each
- 1 leek
- 1 pinch each of chili powder, salt and pepper
- 1 tbsp. olive oil

DIRECTIONS

Clean all vegetables, peel them if necessary, and cut them into bite-sized pieces. Marinate in a bowl with the oil, chili, pepper and salt. Vacuum seal in a suitable bag. Preheat the water bath to 185°F/85°C and let the vegetables cook for 40 minutes. This also works in the steamer. Once removed from the bag, the vegetables are ready to be served on the plate. Drape meat or fish on top and let the vegetables turn into a bed.

21. SAUERKRAUT

Cal.: 294 | Fat: 21g | Protein: 10g   9 min | 46 min | Servings 4

INGREDIENTS
- 500 g sauerkraut
- 2 red onions
- 2 tbsp. butter
- 1 tsp. sugar
- 2 tbsp. apple cider vinegar
- 2 bay leaves
- Juniper berries
- Optional: diced bacon and apple

DIRECTIONS
Preheat the water bath to 194°F/90°C. Sweat the onions cut into small pieces in butter and let them cool again. Sauerkraut, if you like diced apples, onions, vinegar, sugar and spices, put them in a Sous-vide bag and close under vacuum. Cook for 45 minutes in a water bath.
Remove from the bag and season to taste. Serve as a side dish with a delicious Sous Vide meat or fish. The recipe can also be modified regionally.

22. ASPARAGUS

Cal.: 313 | Fat: 26g | Protein: 13g   11 min | 24 min | Servings 4

INGREDIENTS
- 500 g white asparagus
- 30 g butter
- Zest of one lemon
- ½ teaspoon each of sugar and salt

DIRECTIONS
Peel the asparagus, cut off the woody end. Put the asparagus in the vacuum bag and vacuum seal together with the lemon zest, butter, salt and sugar. Preheat the water bath to 185°F/85°C and add the asparagus for 30 minutes. This also works with the steamer. When you open the bag, the buttery asparagus is ready. A hollandaise sauce with boiled potatoes goes well with it.

23. HOLLANDAISE SAUCE

Cal.: 314 | Fat: 29g | Protein: 14g   15 min | 75 min | Servings 2

INGREDIENTS
- 8 tablespoons unsalted butter
- 3 large egg yolks, beaten
- 1 tablespoon freshly squeezed lemon juice
- 1/2 teaspoon salt
- 1 generous pinch dry mustard
- Ground white pepper

DIRECTIONS
Set the Sous Vide Machine to 149°F/65° C. Combine butter, egg yolks, lemon juice, salt, and mustard in a wide mouth glass jar with a tight-fitting lid. Seal and place in the water bath. Set the timer for 25 minutes. When the timer goes off, remove the jar from the water bath. Shake well. Return to the water bath and set the timer for 50 minutes. When the timer goes off, remove the jar from thee water bath. Remove lid and process with an immersion blender until smooth, 3 to 4 minutes. (Alternatively, transfer sauce to a standard blender and blend until smooth.) Note: the sauce will look broken and lumpy before blending. Fear not, it will come together!

24. ROSEMARY POTATOES

Cal.: 269 | Fat: 26g | Protein: 14g   9 min | 55 min | Servings 2

INGREDIENTS
- 500 g potatoes
- 1 tbsp. olive oil
- 2 garlic cloves
- 1 bay leaf
- 1 sprig of rosemary
- 1 level teaspoon salt

DIRECTIONS
Peel the potato and cut into smaller cubes. Put the olive oil, salt, bay leaf, peeled garlic cloves and rosemary in a Sous-vide bag and seal it airtight with a vacuum. Preheat the water bath to 185°F/85°C and cook the potatoes for 40 minutes. The cooking time also depends on the size of the potato cubes. After the potatoes have been removed from the bag, they can be browned briefly in the pan until they are golden.

25. HOKKAIDO PUMPKIN

Cal.: 399 | Fat: 31g | Protein: 15g   11 min | 20 min | Servings 2

INGREDIENTS

- 400 g pumpkin meat from Hok-kaido
- 1 tbsp. butter
- Some grated ginger
- 1 tbsp. apple juice
- 1 pinch of salt and pepper each

DIRECTIONS

Cut up the washed pumpkin. Scrape out the seeds with a spoon (these can still be used for other purposes). Cut the Hokkaido with the peel into bite-sized pieces and vacuum seal in a suitable bag with the apple juice, pepper, salt, 1 teaspoon of butter and ginger. Preheat the water bath to 176°F/80°C and cook the pumpkin for 20 minutes using the sous-vide method or in a steam oven. After removing the pumpkin cubes, fry them briefly in hot butter.

26. NAPKIN DUMPLINGS

Cal.: 393 | Fat: 31g | Protein: 17g   12 min | 75 min | Servings 4

INGREDIENTS

- 250 g cubes of dumpling bread
- 250 ml milk
- ½ teaspoon salt
- 1 handful of parsley
- 2 tbsp. butter
- 3 eggs
- Some grated nutmeg

DIRECTIONS

Put the dumpling bread in a bowl. Sauté briefly the parsley in hot butter and mix with the dumpling bread. Separate eggs. Mix the egg yolks with salt, milk and a little nutmeg. Mix this mixture with the dumpling bread. Beat the egg whites until stiff and mix carefully with the dumpling bread. Cover and let rest for ½ hour. Preheat the water bath to 180°F/82°C. Knead the mass quickly and shape into two rolls. The length and thickness depend on the Sous Vide pot used. Seal the rolls individually or side by side in a suitable bag and cook for 60 minutes. Take the dumpling rolls out of the bath and cut into slices for serving.

27. CARROT STICKS

Cal.: 294 | Fat: 21g | Protein: 17g   9 min | 60 min | Servings 4

INGREDIENTS

- 400 g carrots
- 1 tbsp. butter
- 1 teaspoon fennel seeds
- 1 teaspoon grated ginger

DIRECTIONS

Peel finely the washed carrots with a potato peeler and cut into sticks. Place these next to each other in a vacuum bag. Add the fennel seeds and ginger to the bag and close the bag airtight. Preheat the water bath to 176°F/80°C and cook the carrot sticks for 60 minutes. The whole thing also works in the steamer. In the end, rinse the carrots in the bag with cold, preferably ice, water. Finally, toss the carrots through hot butter in a pan.

28. BOLOGNESE SAUCE FOR SPAGHETTI

Cal.: 424 | Fat: 29g | Protein: 14g   8 min | 3 hours | Servings 4

INGREDIENTS

- 250 g ground beef
- 1 garlic clove
- 1 onion
- 300 g tomato purée
- 1 tbsp. rapeseed oil
- 1 teaspoon dried basil
- ½ teaspoon chili flakes
- 1 tablespoon sugar
- Salt

DIRECTIONS

Preheat the water bath to 162°F/72°C. Mix tomato purée and minced meat in a bowl with sugar, basil, chili flakes and 1 teaspoon of salt to form a smooth sauce. Sauté onion cubes and finely chopped garlic clove in hot oil until golden brown. Add to the mince mixture and stir. Divide the sauce between two bags and vacuum seal. Cook for 2 hours and 40 minutes in a water bath. Prepare pasta according to the instructions on the packet. Serve pasta with Bolognese sauce.

29. TOMATOES WITH SHEEP CHEESE

Cal.: 369 | Fat: 23g | Protein: 14g   9 min | 31 min | Servings 2

INGREDIENTS

- 400 g sheep cheese
- 700 g beef tomatoes
- 350 g colorful cocktail tomatoes
- 1 tbsp. olive oil
- 1 handful of basil leaves
- 2 sprigs of thyme and 2 sprigs of rosemary each
- 1 chili pepper
- 2 garlic cloves
- 1 tsp. sugar
- Pepper and sea salt

DIRECTIONS

Place cocktail tomatoes in boiling water for 1 minute, then pour off the water and peel off the skin of the tomatoes. Roast a finely-diced garlic with the same chili in a pan in 1 tablespoon of olive oil. Finely purée the beefsteak tomatoes with garlic, chili and a little sea salt. Obtain the clear tomato stock by pressing the tomato mixture through a paper towel. Put in a suitable vacuum bag: the cherry tomatoes with the tomato stock, the remaining clove of garlic, the herbs, sugar and olive oil. Vacuum seal. Preheat the water bath to 176°F/80°C and cook the tomato bag for 20 minutes. In the meantime, bake the sheep's cheese in an oven preheated to 356°F/180°C until it is soft. This takes about 15 minutes. Then it has a light tan. Open the bag carefully. Spread the sheep's cheese on two plates. Add the cocktail tomatoes with their sauce.

30. WINTER VEGETABLES

Cal.: 384 | Fat: 28g | Protein: 14g   12 min | 58 min | Servings 4

INGREDIENTS

- 2 carrots
- ½ garlic clove
- 10 Brussels sprouts
- 1 small celery
- 2 salsify
- 2 parsnips
- Rosemary and thyme leaves
- Butter-flavored rapeseed oil
- Rock salt

DIRECTIONS

Peel the celery, parsnips, black salsify and carrots and clean the Brussels sprouts. Depending on the firmness of the vegetables, cut them into more or less small pieces, halve the Brussels sprouts so that everything can be cooked at about the same time. Cut the garlic into fine slices. In a large bowl, add the garlic and vegetables and add the spices, oil, salt and herbs. Mix everything together well. Put the seasoned vegetables in a bag and vacuum seal. Preheat the water bath to 185°F/85°C and cook the vegetables for 50 minutes. Quench with ice water at the end. The vegetables can now be kept for 7 days as long as they are in the bag. If it is to be consumed, it is briefly swiveled in a wok or pan.

31. CAULIFLOWER

Cal.: 294 | Fat: 20g | Protein: 9g   ⬊ 8 min | 🍲 50 min | 🍴 Servings 4

INGREDIENTS

- 1 cauliflower
- 10 drops chili oil
- Some chili butter
- Some herb butter
- 2 tbsp. chives rings
- 1 pinch each white pepper, sea salt and nutmeg
- Juice and zest of 1 untreated lemon

DIRECTIONS

Put the cauliflower florets with salt, freshly ground nutmeg, chili oil and lemon juice and zest in a vacuum bag and vacuum seal. Preheat the water bath to 144°F/62°C and cook the cauliflower for 50 minutes. To finish, heat some chili and herb butter in the pan or wok. Take the cauliflower florets out of the bag and toss in the butter. Season if necessary and sprinkle with the chive's rings. This buttery, aromatic cauliflower can be enjoyed as a side dish or as a stand-alone, vegetarian dish.

32. ORANGE FENNEL

Cal.: 294 | Fat: 28g | Protein: 14g   ⬊ 10 min | 🍲 60 min | 🍴 Servings 4

INGREDIENTS

- 3 tender fennel bulbs
- Juice and zest of 1 untreated orange
- 20 g butter
- 1 teaspoon peppercorns (Sancho)
- 1 teaspoon fennel seeds
- Salt

DIRECTIONS

Cut the bulbs lengthways into three slices and brush with butter. Crush peppercorns in a mortar. Season the fennel with pepper, orange peel and salt; and place in a suitable bag. Add the fennel seeds and orange juice and vacuum seal everything well. Preheat the water bath to 194°F/90°C and cook the fennel for 60 minutes. Take out of the bag and serve on plates. Drizzle with the sauce.

33. RICE PUDDING WITH CARAMELIZED APPLES

Cal.: 284 | Fat: 29g | Protein: 18g   ⬊ 9 min | 🍲 80 min | 🍴 Servings 2

INGREDIENTS

- 100 g rice pudding
- 300 ml of milk
- 50 ml apple juice
- 100 ml whipped cream
- 2 ½ tbsp. butter
- 2 apples
- 1 pinch of cinnamon and cardamom each
- 1 teaspoon vanilla paste

DIRECTIONS

Put in a vacuum-sealable bag: rice pudding, cream, milk, apple juice, cardamom, cinnamon, vanilla paste and 1 teaspoon butter. Vacuum seal. Preheat the water bath to 185°F/85°C and cook the rice pudding for 65 minutes. Cut the peeled and cored apple quarters into thin wedges. Stew the apples in hot butter in a pan for 3 minutes. Sprinkle the icing sugar over the apples and let them caramelize until golden brown. Take the rice pudding out of the bag and serve with the caramel apples.

34. PEACH

Cal.: 374 | Fat: 23g | Protein: 14g 9 min | 2 hours | Servings 2

INGREDIENTS

- 2 peaches or apricots
- 60 g cane sugar
- 1 tbsp. freshly roasted almond sticks
- Juice of ½ lemon
- 50 ml of water
- 1 teaspoon cinnamon
- 1 teaspoon vanilla sugar

DIRECTIONS

Melt cane and vanilla sugar, 40 ml water and cinnamon in a pan at 212°F/100°C for 4 minutes to form a sauce. In the meantime, remove the core of the peaches and quarter them. Mix the sauce with the fruit and let it work for a moment. Vacuum the peaches with a little sauce and place them in a water bath that has been heated to 176°F/80°C. Cook the peach pieces for 90 minutes. Divide the peaches between 2 plates, pour the remaining sauce over them and sprinkle with the freshly roasted almond sticks.

35. CREAMY SESAME DRESSING WITH BABY CARROTS

Cal.: 129 | Fat: 1g | Protein: 1g 8 min | 60 min | Servings 6

INGREDIENTS

- 1 tablespoon mint, minced
- 2 teaspoons olive oil
- Sea salt and white pepper, to taste
- 1 ½ pounds baby carrots
- 1 tablespoon fresh parsley, minced

Dressing:

- 1 tablespoon lemon juice
- 1 teaspoon maple syrup
- 1/2 teaspoon mustard powder
- 1 tablespoon fresh dill leaves, chopped
- 1/3 cup sesame seeds, toasted
- 1/3 cup sour cream

DIRECTIONS

Prepare your sous-vide water bath to a temperature of 183°F/84°C. In a cooking pouch, put the carrots, parsley, olive oil, white pepper and mint into the pouch and seal it appropriately. Immerse the pouch into the preheated water bath and let it cook for 55 minutes. To prepare the dressing, mix the ingredients. Dress and serve.

36. BAKED YAM CHIPS

Cal.: 193 | Fat: 9g | Protein: 8g 12 min | 90 min | Servings 4

INGREDIENTS

- Coarse sea salt and freshly ground black pepper, to taste
- 1/3 teaspoon ancho chili powder
- 1 pound yams, peeled and cubed
- ½ teaspoon Hungarian paprika
- 2 tablespoons extra-virgin olive oil

DIRECTIONS

Prepare your sous-vide water bath to a temperature of 183°F/84°C. In a large bowl, sprinkle over yams with pepper and salt. Transfer the yam to a Ziploc bag and seal it after squeezing out the excess air. Immerse the bag into the water bath and cook for 1 hour. Once cooked, remove the bag from the water bath and pat dry the yams using a kitchen towel. Preheat your oven to 350°F/176°C. Place the yams orderly on a parchment-lined baking sheet. Sprinkle over with chili powder and Hungarian paprika and drizzle with olive oil. Bake for 23 minutes and remove. Serve and enjoy!

37. BABA GHANOUJ

Cal.: 194 | Fat: 19g | Protein: 10g   ⟍ 9 min | 🍲 3 hours | ✗ Servings 6

INGREDIENTS
- 1 large eggplant, peeled and cubed
- 1 tablespoon lemon juice
- 2 garlic cloves
- 2 tablespoons tahini
- 1 teaspoon sea salt
- 2 tablespoons extra-virgin olive oil
- 2 tablespoons chopped fresh cilantro

DIRECTIONS
Fill the water bath with water. Set your machine temperature to 185°F/85°C. Place the cubed eggplant in a food-safe bag and vacuum seal the bag. Make sure the eggplant is in only 1–2 layers within the bag. Use multiple bags if necessary. Place the eggplant in the water bath and cook for 2–3 hours. Using a food processor, pulse the cooked eggplant, lemon juice, garlic, tahini, salt and olive oil. Process until smooth and creamy. Add the cilantro and pulse a few times or until it is evenly mixed throughout the dip. Serve.

38. SWEET POTATO FRIES

Cal.: 134 | Fat: 8g | Protein: 2g   ⟍ 9 min | 🍲 75 min | ✗ Servings 4

INGREDIENTS
- 2 tablespoons canola oil
- 1 cup water
- 1 ½ pounds sweet potatoes, peeled and cut into sticks
- 1/4 teaspoon ground allspice
- 1 tablespoon sea salt

DIRECTIONS
Prepare your sous-vide water bath to a temperature of 183°F/84°C. In a cooking pouch, add the potatoes, salt and water and vacuum seal it. Immerse the pouch into the preheated water bath and let it cook for 1 hour. Once done, remove the pouch from the water bath and remove the potatoes. Pat dry the potatoes and toss in a bowl with canola oil. Place the parchment paper on a baking sheet lined with parchment. Preheat the oven to 400°F/205°C and bake for 11 minutes until crispy. Serve and enjoy with a dipping sauce of your choice.

39. GARLIC DIPPING SAUCE WITH ASPARAGUS

Cal.: 232 | Fat: 15g | Protein: 2g   ⟍ 12 min | 🍲 40 min | ✗ Servings 8

INGREDIENTS
- ½ stick butter, melted
- Sea salt and black pepper, to taste
- 1 ½ pounds asparagus spears, halved lengthwise
- 4 garlic cloves, minced
- 1/4 cup sour cream
- 10 garlic cloves, smashed
- Salt and pepper, to taste
- 1/4 cup mayonnaise
- ½ cup plain yogurt

DIRECTIONS
Prepare your sous-vide water bath to a temperature of 183°F/84°C. In a Ziploc bag, put the asparagus spears, black pepper, butter, garlic cloves and salt into and seal it after squeezing out the excess air. Lower the pouch in the water bath and cook for 30 minutes. For the dipping, get a bowl and thoroughly mix all the remaining ingredients. Serve asparagus with dipping sauce.

40. GARLIC CORN AND HERBY

Cal.: 397 | Fat: 37g | Protein: 6g   9 min | 30 min | ✖ Servings 6

INGREDIENTS
- 1 teaspoon granulated garlic
- 1 tablespoon paprika
- 1 tablespoon fresh chives, chopped
- 6 ears corn
- 2 sticks butter, melted
- 1 teaspoon shallot powder
- Flaked sea salt and white pepper, to taste

DIRECTIONS
Prepare your sous-vide water bath to a temperature of 183°F/84°C. Get the corn tossed with the entire ingredients. Put the corn in a cooking pouch and seal after removing the excess air. Immerse the pouch in the water bath and cook for 25 minutes. Sprinkle with seasonings. Serve and enjoy!

41. SIMPLE DIP WITH DELICIOUS ARTICHOKES

Cal.: 314 | Fat: 21g | Protein: 3g   11 min | 50 min | ✖ Servings 6

INGREDIENTS
- 6 garlic cloves, peeled
- 1 ½ sticks butter, room temperature
- 6 artichokes, trimmed and cut into halves
- ½ cup mayonnaise
- 2 teaspoons lemon zest
- ½ cup sour cream
- Sea salt and freshly ground black pepper, to taste

DIRECTIONS
Prepare your sous-vide water bath to a temperature of 183°F/84°C. Put the butter, garlic, lemon zest, salt, trimmed artichokes, salt and black pepper into a pouch and vacuum seal it. Immerse the pouch into the preheated water bath and cook underwater for 50 minutes. Once cooked, remove the pouch from the water bath and pat dry the artichokes. Blowtorch on the artichokes and transfer to a platter. Get a bowl and mix the mayonnaise and sour cream. Serve and enjoy the artichokes with sour cream mayo dip.

42. BÉARNAISE SAUCE

Cal.: 175 | Fat: 12g | Protein: 4g   10 min | 46 min | ✖ Servings 12

INGREDIENTS
- 1 tablespoon fresh tarragon, finely chopped
- ½ cup dry white wine
- 3 tablespoons shallots, finely chopped
- 1 tablespoon fresh lemon juice
- 4 tablespoons Champagne vinegar
- 2 sticks butter, melted
- 5 egg yolks

DIRECTIONS
Prepare your sous-vide water bath to a temperature of 148°F/64°C. Get a pan and add the shallots, wine, vinegar and tarragon. Bring to a boil and then simmer for 12 minutes. Using a fine-mesh strainer, strain the mixture and transfer it to a food blender. Add the egg yolks and blend until completely smooth. Put the sauce into a cooking pouch and immerse it into the preheated water bath. Cook for 25 minutes. Once done, remove the pouch from the water bath and transfer the contents to a bowl. Add the lemon juice and butter and blend until smooth. Serve and enjoy with your choice of roasted vegetable bites.

43. KALE CHEESE

Cal.: 79 | Fat: 6g | Protein: 7g    9 min | 🍲 50 min | ✖ Servings 10

INGREDIENTS

- 1 cup ale
- 4 ounces Colby cheese, shredded
- 1/4 cup Thai fish sauce
- ½ pound Cottage cheese
- 1 cup kale leaves, chopped
- 2 garlic cloves, smashed
- 1 sun-dried Thai chili, finely chopped
- 1 teaspoon mustard powder
- Sea salt and ground black pepper, to taste

DIRECTIONS

Preheat the container with water and set the temperature to 183°F/84°C. In a Ziploc bag, add all the listed ingredients and seal it after removing the excess air. Immerse the bag into the water bath and cook for 45 minutes. Serve and enjoy with vegetable chips, tortilla chips, or breadsticks.

44. ARROWROOT COUNTRY-STYLE RIBS

Cal.: 280 | Fat: 9g | Protein: 42g   26 min | 🍲 18 hours | ✖ Servings 10

INGREDIENTS

- 1 teaspoon mustard powder
- 1 cup stock, preferably homemade
- 1/3 cup tamari sauce
- 4 pounds country-style ribs
- ½ teaspoon onion powder
- ½ teaspoon garlic powder
- ½ teaspoon ground ginger
- 2 tablespoons arrowroot powder
- ½ cup brown sugar, packed

DIRECTIONS

Prepare your Sous-vide water bath to a temperature of 145°F/63°C. Put the stock, ribs, mustard powder, garlic and onion powder into a Ziploc bag and seal it after squeezing out the excess air. Immerse the bag into the water bath and cook for 18 hours. Preheat your oven to 360°F/182°C. Put the ribs and the cooking liquid in a baking pan. Get a bowl and add the tamari, arrowroot, sugar and ground pepper. Mix the sauce and drizzle it over the ribs. Bake the ribs for 20 minutes until crispy.
Serve and enjoy!

45. COCKTAIL MEATBALLS

Cal.: 276 | Fat: 18g | Protein: 24g   10 min | 🍲 3 hours | ✖ Servings 10

INGREDIENTS

- 2 eggs
- ½ pound mild sausage, ground
- ½ cup seasoned breadcrumbs
- 1 pound ground beef
- ½ pound ground pork
- 1 cup leeks, finely chopped
- 1 teaspoon garlic paste
- Salt and ground black pepper, to taste
- ½ teaspoon ancho chili powder
- 1 teaspoon dried basil
- ½ teaspoon dried marjoram
- 1/4 teaspoon ground allspice

DIRECTIONS

Prepare your sous-vide water bath to a temperature of 146°F/63°C. Add all the ingredients to a bowl and mix thoroughly. Using your hand, shape the mixture into balls. Put the balls into a cooking pouch and seal it after removing the excess air. Immerse the pouch into the water bath. Cook for 3 hours. Grease a nonstick pan with cooking spray. Sear the meatballs in batches. Sear each side for 3 minutes.
Serve and enjoy!

46. CARNITAS PORK

Cal.: 405 | Fat: 24g | Protein: 34g   ⟍ 11 min | 🍲 18 hours | ✗ Servings 12

INGREDIENTS

- 1 habanero pepper, deseeded and minced
- 2 garlic cloves, smashed
- 1 cup Pico de Gallo, for garnish
- Sea salt and ground black pepper, to taste
- 3 pounds boneless pork butt
- 1 cup ale
- ½ cup bone broth
- 1 teaspoon dried basil
- 1 cup Queso Manchego, shredded
- 1 teaspoon dried rosemary
- 24 wonton wraps
- 2 bay leaves

DIRECTIONS

Prepare your sous-vide water bath to a temperature of 145°F/63°C. Put the salt, habanero pepper, bone broth, ale, basil, rosemary, garlic, pork and bay leaves in a Ziploc bag. Seal the pouch after removing the excess air. Immerse the pouch into the water bath and let it cook for 18 hours. Once done, remove the bag from the water bath and shred. Preheat your oven to 380°F/195°C. Apply cooking spray to your cooking pan. Using wonton wraps, fill in the shredded pork and add Queso manchego as a topping. Bake in the preheated oven for 9 minutes and keep to cool for 5 minutes. Once done, remove and serve with Pico de gallo. Serve and enjoy!

47. CRISPY POLENTA SQUARES AND CHEESY

Cal.: 225 | Fat: 12g | Protein: 1g   ⟍ 9 min | 🍲 140 min | ✗ Servings 6

INGREDIENTS

- 2 cups broth, preferably homemade
- 2 cups water
- 1 teaspoon paprika
- ½ cup Monterey-Jack cheese, freshly grated
- Salt and pepper, to taste
- ½ pound polenta
- 1 stick butter, diced

DIRECTIONS

Prepare your Sous-vide water bath to a temperature of 185°F/85°C. Put the polenta, butter and water into cooking pouches and vacuum seal them. Lower the pouch into the water bath and let it cook for 2 hours. Once done, remove the pouch and transfer the polenta into a bowl. Add the paprika, shredded cheese, and salt and mix well. Transfer the polenta into a baking pan and keep to cool. Broil for 7 minutes while flipping halfway. Top with polenta squares and more cheese if you wish. Serve and enjoy!

48. TACO CHEESY DIP

Cal.: 195 | Fat: 12g | Protein: 24g   ⟍ 5 min | 🍲 2 hours | ✗ Servings 10

INGREDIENTS

- ½ cup medium-hot taco sauce
- 1 teaspoon taco seasoning
- ½ pound beef, ground
- 1 pound pork, ground
- 1 cup shallots, chopped
- 3 garlic cloves, chopped
- 1 cup processed American cheese
- Sea salt and ground black pepper, to taste
- 12 ounces cream of celery soup

DIRECTIONS

Prepare your sous-vide water bath to a temperature of 144°F/62°C. Put all the ingredients into a cooking pouch and vacuum seal it. Immerse the pouch into the preheated water bath and cook for 2 hours. Sprinkle it with pepper and salt. Serve and enjoy with tortilla chips or vegetable sticks.

49. RICH FRENCH FONDUE AND LUXURY

Cal.: 191 | Fat: 14g | Protein: 16g
11 min | 35 min | Servings 12

INGREDIENTS

- 12 ounces Swiss cheese, shredded
- 3 tablespoons flour
- 1 garlic clove, cut in half
- 1 cup dry white wine
- Salt and ground black pepper, to taste
- 1/4 teaspoon freshly grated nutmeg
- A pinch of paprika
- 3 tablespoons Kirsch
- 12 ounces cheddar cheese

DIRECTIONS

Prepare your sous-vide water bath to a temperature of 170°F/76°C. Brush the garlic halves in your pan. Add the wine to the pan and cook over high heat. Bring the content to a boil and reduce the heat to medium-low. Get a bowl, put and thoroughly combine the flour and cheese and wine. Carefully put the mixture into a cooking pouch and seal after removing all the excess air. Cook underwater for 35 minutes. Serve and enjoy!

50. PINEAPPLE SALSA

Cal.: 58 | Fat: 2g | Protein: 7g
9 min | 36 min | Servings 4

INGREDIENTS

- ½ teaspoon coriander seeds
- 1 jalapeno pepper, stemmed, seeded and finely chopped 1/3 cup white distilled vinegar
- ½ pineapple, peeled, cored and chopped
- Kosher salt and freshly ground black pepper, to taste
- 1 red onion, sliced
- ½ teaspoon mustard seed
- 1 bay leaf, crumbled
- ½ teaspoon whole allspice
- 1 cinnamon stick
- ½ teaspoon ground ginger
- 2 whole cloves

DIRECTIONS

Prepare your sous-vide water bath to a temperature of 145°F/63°C. Distribute the ingredients into a cooking pouch and vacuum seal it. Immerse the pouch into the water bath and cook for 36 minutes. Once done, remove the pouch from the water bath and keep it cool. Transfer and store the content in a glass jar for up to 7 days.

51. LIL SMOKIES

Cal.: 314 | Fat: 24g | Protein: 26g
11 min | 2 hours | Servings 8

INGREDIENTS

- 1 (12-ounce) bottle chili sauce
- 2 pounds cocktail sausages

DIRECTIONS

Prepare your sous-vide water bath to a temperature of 141°F/61°C. Put all the ingredients into a cooking pouch and vacuum seal it. Immerse the pouch into the water bath and cook for 120 minutes. Once done, remove and serve.

52. EASY PIZZA DIP AND RICH

Cal.: 230 | Fat: 17g | Protein: 14g | 12 min | 3 hours 15 min | Servings 12

INGREDIENTS

- 3/4 cup pasta sauce
- 1 cup Romano cheese, shredded
- 2 cups Colby cheese, freshly grated
- ½ teaspoon dried parsley
- 10 ounces Cottage cheese, at room temperature
- 1/4 cup black olives, sliced
- ½ teaspoon dried basil
- 2 tablespoons green pepper, chopped
- 1-ounce pepperoni, sliced
- ½ pound ground pork

DIRECTIONS

Prepare your sous-vide water bath to a temperature of 146°F/63°C. Distribute the ingredients into separate cooking pouches, except for the Colby cheese. Vacuum sealsseal the pouch. Immerse the pouches into the preheated water bath and cook for 3 hours. Preheat your oven to 380°F/193°C. Spray your baking pan with cooking spray and add all the contents from the pouches to the pan. Add the Colby cheese as a topping and bake for 15 minutes. Serve and enjoy!

53. SIRLOIN SLIDERS

Cal.: 314 | Fat: 24g | Protein: 26g | 11 min | 3 hours | Servings 8

INGREDIENTS

- Sea salt and freshly ground black pepper, to taste
- 1 (25-ounce envelope onion soup mix
- ½ pound ground sirloin
- 4 tablespoons mayonnaise
- ½ pound ground pork
- 3/4 pound Gorgonzola cheese
- Crumbled 16 miniature burger buns
- 1 tablespoon Dijon mustard
- 1 banana shallot, chopped

DIRECTIONS

Prepare your sous-vide water bath to a temperature of 146°F/63°C. In a bowl, add the meat, pepper and salt and thoroughly mix well. Using your hands, press and shape the content into 16 meatballs. Press the meatballs on top to flatten into patties of ½ inch in thickness. Carefully put the patties into Ziploc bags. Immerse the bags into the water bath and cook for 3 hours. Grill the burgers in batches over medium heat. Grill each side for 2 minutes. Carefully distribute the shallots, mustard and mayonnaise to the bottom buns. Top with a slider and add gorgonzola cheese. Place the bun on top. Serve and enjoy!

54. APPLE JELLY SAUCE AND KIELBASA BITES

Cal.: 241 | Fat: 12g | Protein: 11g | 6 min | 2 hours | Servings 12

INGREDIENTS

- 2 ½ pounds kielbasa, cut into ½-inch-thick slices
- 4 ounces lager beer
- 2 bay leaves
- 1 teaspoon mixed whole peppercorns
- 1 (18-ounce) jar apple jelly
- 2 tablespoons spicy brown mustard

DIRECTIONS

Prepare your sous-vide water bath to a temperature of 150°F/65°C. Put the beer, bay leaves, kielbasa and peppercorns in a Ziploc bag. Add the mustard and apple jelly and seal it after squeezing out the excess air. Immerse the bag into the water bath and let it cook for 2 hours. Serve and enjoy with cocktail sticks.

CHAPTER 3:
Breakfast Recipes

🔪 Preparation Time | 🍲 Cooking Time | 🍴 Servings

56. EGG

Cal.: 274 | Fat: 21g | Protein: 15g   ✎ 12 min | 🍲 35 min | ✗ Servings 1

INGREDIENTS

- 1 egg
- 1 pinch of salt

DIRECTIONS

Place the whole egg in a water bath heated to 144°F/62°C. Vacuum sealing is not necessary. Cook the egg for 45 minutes. So, the yolk will be very runny. At 155°F/68°C, it becomes more solid. Remove the egg from the water and rinse in cold water. Whip up and place on a plate. Salt and pepper to taste.

55. POACHED EGGS IN HASH BROWN NESTS

Cal.: 384 | Fat: 27g | Protein: 19g   ✎ 11 min | 🍲 60 min | ✗ Servings 3

INGREDIENTS

- 6 large eggs, at room temperature
- 3 cups frozen shredded hash brown, thawed completely
- 1 teaspoon fresh rosemary, chopped, or ¼ teaspoon dried rosemary
- Freshly ground pepper to taste
- Salt to taste
- 2 tablespoons chopped fresh chives
- 1 ½ tablespoons extra-virgin olive oil
- ¼ teaspoon paprika
- 3 thin slices prosciutto, halved crosswise
- Cooking spray

DIRECTIONS

Preheat the Sous Vide machine to 147°F/64°C. Place the eggs on a spoon, one at a time, and gently lower them into the water bath and place on the lower rack. Set the timer for 60 minutes. Meanwhile, grease a 6-count muffin pan with cooking spray. Place hash browns on a kitchen towel. Squeeze out as much moisture as possible. Place the hash browns in a bowl. Add oil, rosemary, pepper, paprika and salt. Mix well. Divide this mixture among the muffin cups. Press down at the bottom and sides of the muffin cups. Spray cooking spray over it. Preheat the oven to 375°F/190°C. Place the muffin tin in the oven and bake for about 30 minutes or until nearly golden brown. Place half slice of prosciutto over each hash brown. Let it hang from the edges of the hash brown nests. Bake for 5 minutes. Remove from the oven and cool for 4 or 5 minutes. Run a knife around the edges of the hash brown nest and gently lift it out from the muffin tin. When the timer of the cooker goes off, immediately remove the eggs. Break 2 cooked eggs in each nest. Garnish with chives and serve immediately.

57. EGG WITH SUNCHOKES VELOUTÉ, CRISPY PROSCIUTTO AND HAZELNUT

Cal.: 434 | Fat: 31g | Protein: 18g 7 min | 49 min | Servings 3

INGREDIENTS

For Sunchokes Velouté:
- 2 tablespoons butter
- 1 small leek, only white part, thinly sliced
- 1 pound Jerusalem artichokes (sunchokes), peeled
- ½ quart milk
- ¼ cup heavy cream (optional)
- 1 medium onion, thinly sliced
- 1 garlic clove, sliced
- ½ quart chicken stock
- ¼ vanilla bean, scraped

For bouquet garni:
- 2 or 3 thyme sprigs
- 2 or 3 fresh sage leaves
- 1 bay leaf
- Leek greens, to wrap

For eggs:
- 3 eggs, at room temperature

For finishing:
- 3 thin slices prosciutto
- Few strips fried Jerusalem artichokes (sunchokes)
- A handful of baby watercress
- 6 hazelnuts, toasted, chopped
- Oil, as required

DIRECTIONS

Preheat the Sous Vide machine to 145°F/63°C. Place the eggs on a spoon and gently lower them into the water bath. Place on the lower rack. Set the timer for 47 minutes. Meanwhile, make the sunchoke velouté as follows: Place a casserole dish over medium flame. Add butter. When butter melts, add onion, garlic, leeks, salt and pepper.

To make bouquet garni, place together thyme, sage, and bay leaf and wrap it with leek greens. Place bouquet garni in the casserole dish. Cook for a few minutes. Stir in the artichokes and cook until slightly tender. Stir occasionally. Add the rest of the ingredients and stir. Once it boils, reduce the flame and let it simmer until tender. Turn off the heat and remove the bouquet garni. Blend the mixture in a blender. Strain the mixture through a wire mesh strainer placed over a saucepan.

To finish: Smear oil over the prosciutto slices and lay them on a lined baking sheet. Bake in a preheated oven at 300°F/150°C until crisp. Remove from the oven and cool. Place a few strips of sunchoke on a nonstick pan. Add a bit of oil. Add sunchoke and cook until crisp. Sprinkle salt. Crack a cooked egg into each of 3 bowls. Spoon the sunchoke velouté over the eggs in each bowl. Serve topped with prosciutto, hazelnuts, watercress and fried sunchoke strips.

58. SMOKED FISH AND POACHED EGG

Cal.: 419 | Fat: 29g | Protein: 15g 14 min | 20 min | Servings 4

INGREDIENTS
- 4 fillets smoked fish
- 2 lemons, cut into slices
- Seasonings of your choice
- 4 large eggs
- 4 tablespoons olive oil

DIRECTIONS

Preheat the Sous Vide machine to 140°F/60°C. Divide all the ingredients, except eggs, into 4 vacuum-seal pouches or Ziploc bags. Seal the pouches, but do not remove the air completely. Immerse both pouches in the water bath and set the timer for 20 minutes. When the timer goes off, remove the pouches and set aside. Increase the temperature to 167°F/75°C. Place the eggs on a spoon, one at a time, and gently lower them into the water bath and place on the lower rack. Set the timer for 15 minutes. Empty each pouch onto individual serving plates. Break an egg over each fillet and serve.

59. EGGS BENEDICT

Cal.: 344 | Fat: 21g | Protein: 19g

🔪 13 min | 🍲 60 min | 🍴 Servings 4

INGREDIENTS

- 4 English muffins, halved, toasted
- 8 slices Canadian bacon
- A handful of fresh parsley, chopped
- 8 eggs
- Butter, as required

For hollandaise sauce:

- 8 tablespoons butter
- 2 teaspoons lemon juice
- 1 shallot, diced
- Salt to taste
- Cayenne pepper to taste
- 2 egg yolks
- 2 teaspoons water

DIRECTIONS

Preheat the Sous Vide machine to 148°F/64°C. Place the eggs in a vacuum-seal pouch or Ziploc bag. Place all the ingredients for hollandaise sauce into another bag. Vacuum seal the pouches. Immerse both pouches in the water bath and set the timer for 1 hour. Meanwhile, cook the bacon in a pan to the desired doneness. Keep warm in an oven along with muffins if desired. Remove the pouches from the water bath. Transfer the contents of the sauce into a blender and blend until smooth. Place muffins on individual serving plates. Crack an egg on each muffin and place on the bottom half of the muffins. Spoon hollandaise over the eggs and garnish with parsley. Cover with the top half of the muffins and serve.

60. BRIOCHE AND EGGS

Cal.: 397 | Fat: 34g | Protein: 19g

🔪 13 min | 🍲 46 min | 🍴 Servings 6

INGREDIENTS

- 6 brioche buns
- 6 large eggs
- 2 scallions, sliced (optional)
- 1 ½ cups grated cheese

DIRECTIONS

Preheat the Sous Vide machine to 149°F/65°C. Place the eggs on a spoon, one at a time, and gently lower them into the water bath and place on the rack. Set the timer for 45 minutes. When the timer goes off, immediately remove the eggs from the water bath. Place the eggs in a bowl of cold water for a few minutes. Place brioche buns on a baking sheet and break a cooked egg on each bun. Sprinkle cheese on top. Set an oven to broil and place the baking sheet in the oven. Broil for a few minutes until the cheese melts.

61. EGG BITES

Cal.: 392 | Fat: 22g | Protein: 13g

🔪 9 min | 🍲 60 min | 🍴 Servings 4

INGREDIENTS

- 5 eggs
- ¼ cup shredded Colby Jack cheese
- 3 tablespoons unsweetened almond milk
- Salt to taste
- Pepper to taste

DIRECTIONS

Preheat the Sous Vide machine to 172°F/78°C. Add a tablespoon of cheese into each of 4 canning jars or Mason jars. Whisk together eggs and milk in a bowl. Divide the egg mixture among the jars. Season with salt and pepper. Fasten the lid lightly, not very tight. Immerse the canning jars in a water bath and adjust the timer for 1 hour or until eggs are set. Remove the jars from the water bath. Serve directly from the jars.

62. PERFECT EGG TOSTADA

Cal.: 354 | Fat: 28g | Protein: 16g   ⟋ 13 min | 🍲 16 min | ✖ Servings 4

INGREDIENTS
- 4 large eggs, at room temperature
- ¼ cup cooked or canned black beans, heated
- 4 sprigs cilantro, chopped
- 4 corn tostadas
- 4 teaspoons salsa taquera or salsa Verde or chili de arbol
- 4 teaspoons Queso fresco, crumbled

DIRECTIONS
Preheat the Sous Vide machine to 162°F/72°C. Place the eggs on a spoon, one at a time, and gently lower them into the water bath and place on the rack. Set the timer for 15 minutes. When the timer goes off, immediately remove the eggs from the water bath. Place the eggs in a bowl of cold water for a few minutes. To assemble: Place the tostadas on 4 serving plates. Spread a tablespoon of beans over it, then salsa, then sprinkle cheese on top and serve.

63. SCRAMBLED EGGS

Cal.: 384 | Fat: 28g | Protein: 13g   ⟋ 9 min | 🍲 12 min | ✖ Servings 4

INGREDIENTS
- 8 large eggs
- Freshly ground pepper to taste
- Salt to taste
- Aleppo pepper to taste (optional)

DIRECTIONS
Preheat the Sous Vide machine to 165°F/74°C. Add eggs, salt, and pepper into a bowl and whisk well. Pour into a large silicone bag and vacuum seal the pouch. Immerse the pouch in the water bath and adjust the timer for 10 minutes. Remove the pouch from the water bath and place the pouch between your palms. Press it and shake it. Place it back in the water bath. Set the timer for 12 minutes. When the timer goes off, remove the pouch from the water bath. Open the pouch and divide into 4 plates. Garnish with Aleppo pepper. Serve immediately.

64. EGGS AND OREGANO

Cal.: 331 | Fat: 7g | Protein: 7g   ⟋ 9 min | 🍲 32 min | ✖ Servings 2

INGREDIENTS
- 1 red bell pepper, chopped
- 2 shallots, chopped
- 4 eggs, whisked
- A pinch of salt and black pepper
- 1 tablespoon oregano, chopped
- ½ teaspoon chili powder
- ½ teaspoon sweet paprika

DIRECTIONS
Prepare your sous-vide water bath to a temperature of 170°F/76°C.
Pour the whisked egg into a cooking pouch and add the other ingredients. Immerse the pouch into the water bath and cook for 30 minutes. Once done, remove the pouch from the water bath and transfer the contents to a serving plate. Serve and enjoy!

65. CINNAMON EGGS

Cal.: 240 | Fat: 12g | Protein: 14g   ⟋ 13 min | 🍲 40 hours | ✖ Servings 2

INGREDIENTS
- 1/3 cup heavy cream
- 2 eggs
- 1 tablespoon stevia
- Pinch of cinnamon powder

DIRECTIONS
Whisk the ingredients together, add to a bag, seal, and add to the prepared water bath for 30 minutes at 167°F/75°C.
When done, divide and enjoy!

66. BRIOCHE AND EGGS

Cal.: 397 | Fat: 34g | Protein: 19g   ✎ 13 min | 🍲 46 min | ✗ Servings 6

INGREDIENTS

- 6 brioche buns
- 6 large eggs
- 2 scallions, sliced (optional)
- 1 ½ cups grated cheese

DIRECTIONS

Preheat the Sous Vide machine to 149°F/65°C. Place the eggs on a spoon, one at a time, and gently lower them into the water bath and place on the rack. Set the timer for 45 minutes. When the timer goes off, immediately remove the eggs from the water bath. Place the eggs in a bowl of cold water for a few minutes. Place brioche buns on a baking sheet and break a cooked egg on each bun. Sprinkle cheese on top. Set an oven to broil and place the baking sheet in the oven. Broil for a few minutes until the cheese melts.

67. EGG BITES WITH EMMENTAL CHEESE

Cal.: 392 | Fat: 22g | Protein: 13g   ✎ 9 min | 🍲 60 min | ✗ Servings 4

INGREDIENTS

- 5 eggs
- ¼ cup shredded Emmental cheese
- 3 tablespoons unsweetened almond milk
- Salt to taste
- Pepper to taste

DIRECTIONS

Preheat the Sous Vide machine to 172°F/78°C. Add a tablespoon of cheese into each of 4 canning jars or Mason jars. Whisk together eggs and milk in a bowl. Divide the egg mixture among the jars. Season with salt and pepper. Fasten the lid lightly, not very tight. Immerse the canning jars in a water bath and adjust the timer for 1 hour or until eggs are set. Remove the jars from the water bath. Serve directly from the jars.

68. BAR-STYLE PINK PICKLED EGGS

Cal.: 166 | Fat: 10g | Protein: 9.3g   ✎ 6 min | 🍲 2 hours 2 min | ✗ Servings 6

INGREDIENTS

- 6 eggs
- 1 cup white vinegar
- 1 can beets Juice
- ¼ cup sugar
- ½ tablespoon salt
- 2 garlic cloves
- 1 tablespoon whole peppercorn
- 1 bay leaf

DIRECTIONS

Preheat the water bath to 170°F/76°C. Place eggs in the bag. Seal the bag and place it in the bath. Cook for 1 hour. After 1 hour, place eggs in the bowl of cold water to cool and carefully peel. In the bag in which you cooked the eggs, combine vinegar, beet juice, sugar, salt, garlic and bay leaf. Replace eggs in the bag with pickling liquid. Replace in the water bath and cook for 1 additional hour. After 1 hour, move eggs with pickling liquid to the refrigerator. Allow cooling completely before eating.

69. HARD-BOILED EGGS

Cal.: 78 | Fat: 5.3g | Protein: 6.29g   ✎ 13 min | 🍲 70 hours | ✗ Servings 3

INGREDIENTS

- 1 ice bath
- 3 large eggs

DIRECTIONS

Set the temperature in the machine at 165°F/74°C. Arrange the eggs in the cooker. Prepare for 1 hour. Once the time has elapsed, place the eggs into an ice bath. When cool, peel and enjoy salads as a meal or just a snack anytime.

70. SMOKED SALMON EGGS BENEDICT

Cal.: 604 | Fat: 49g | Protein: 26.1g   8 min | 2 hours 30 min | Servings 4

INGREDIENTS

- 4 eggs
- 8 ounces smoked salmon
- 2 English muffins, split
- Hollandaise sauce, bagged and uncooked

DIRECTIONS

Preheat the Sous Vide machine to 147°F/64°C. Seal the eggs in a bag. Place the bag of eggs, and the bag of hollandaise into the bath. Cook for 2 hours. 30 minutes before the end of cooking time, toast and butter the English muffins. Remove eggs and sauce from the bath. Pour sauce into a blender and blend until smooth and meanwhile, cold eggs in a bowl of cold water. Arrange 2 ounces of smoked salmon on each English muffin half to form a cup that will hold the poached egg. Carefully crack each egg over a slotted spoon held over a bowl to allow the excess white to drip away. Place one egg in each smoked salmon cup. Top with hollandaise sauce.

71. EGGS WITH ROASTED PEPPERS

Cal.: 144 | Fat: 10.7g | Protein: 9.4g   15 min | 60 min | Servings 6

INGREDIENTS

- 6 large eggs
- ½ cup grated Gouda cheese
- ¼ cup cream cheese
- 3 roasted peppers (peeled and seeded)
- Salt and pepper, to taste

DIRECTIONS

Preheat the Sous Vide machine to 172°F/78°C. In a food blender, blend eggs, Gouda cheese, cream cheese, salt and pepper. Slice the peppers into thin strips. Place the peppers in the bottom of six 4oz. jars, making sure they go up the sides a bit. Pour the egg mixture. Attach two-part canning lids "fingertip tight". Immerse in a water bath and cook for 1 hour. Remove the jars from a water bath. Slide a knife around the peppers and eggs and remove carefully, or invert onto a plate. Serve with warm bread.

72. CRISPY EGG YOLKS

Cal.: 161 | Fat: 6.3g | Protein: 9.5g   11 min | 65 min | Servings 4

INGREDIENTS

- 4 + 1 egg
- 4 tablespoons all-purpose flour
- 1/3 teaspoon baking powder
- ½ cup breadcrumbs
- ½ teaspoon fine salt
- ¾ teaspoon black truffle salt
- Salt and pepper, to taste

DIRECTIONS

Fill and preheat the cooker to 148°F/64°C. Cook four eggs for 60 minutes. Let the eggs cool in cold water for 10 minutes. Carefully peel the eggs, and let the egg white drip out. Reserve egg yolks. Heat 1-inch oil in a skillet over medium heat. While the oil is heating, whisk flour, baking powder, and salt in a bowl. Beat the remaining egg in a small bowl. Dredge egg yolks in flour and dip into beaten egg. Finally, roll in breadcrumbs. Fry in heated oil until golden brown. Drain the egg yolks on a paper towel. Sprinkle with black truffle salt. Serve.

73. DEVILS EGGS NICOISE

Cal.: 160 | Fat: 12.38g | Protein: 9.33g   🔪 31 min | 🍲 60 min | 🍴 Servings 6

INGREDIENTS

- 6 eggs
- 2 tablespoons black olives, minced
- 1 small tomato, seeded and minced
- 1 teaspoon Dijon mustard
- Juice of 1 lemon
- 1 tablespoon olive oil
- 1 tablespoon plain Greek yogurt
- 2 tablespoons fresh parsley, minced, plus more for garnish

DIRECTIONS

Preheat the water bath to 170°F/76°C. Place eggs in the bag. Seal with water method, then place in the bath. Cook for 1 hour. Place eggs in a bowl of cold water to cool. Peel carefully, then cut each egg in half lengthwise. Scoop egg yolks into a bowl. Stir in olives, tomato, mustard, lemon, oil, yogurt, and parsley. Fill egg whites with the egg yolk mixture. Garnish with parsley.

74. EGG AND CHOPPED SCALLION

Cal.: 62 | Fat: 2g | Protein: 9g   🔪 11 min | 🍲 30 min | 🍴 Servings 6

INGREDIENTS

- ½ finely chopped roasted red bell pepper
- 2 tbsp. finely chopped scallions
- Salt and freshly ground black pepper, to taste
- 6 egg whites
- ¼ cup shredded Monterey Jack cheese
- 1 tsp. arrowroot starch
- Dash of hot sauce
- ¼ cup finely chopped fresh spinach
- ¼ cup shredded cottage cheese
- 1 tbsp. unsalted butter

DIRECTIONS

Prepare your sous-vide water bath to a temperature of 173°F/78°C. Set up a rack in the bath. Grease 6 of 4oz mason jars. Add egg whites in a deep bowl and beat thoroughly and add all the other ingredients. Distribute mixture in equal proportion over the 6 mason jars. Seal the jars and gently such that steam can escape during cooking. Cook underwater for 1 hour. Remove the bag from the bath. Remove food from the sous bag and serve warm!

75. SWEET EGG BITES

Cal.: 202 | Fat: 17g | Protein: 12g   🔪 14 min | 🍲 56 min | 🍴 Servings 4

INGREDIENTS

- 3 tbsp. softened cream cheese
- 1/3 cup grated Gruyere cheese
- 2 cooked and halved pancetta slices
- Salt and freshly ground black pepper, to taste
- 4 large eggs

DIRECTIONS

Prepare your sous-vide water bath to a temperature of 173°F/78°C. Set up a rack inside the container. Apply grease to 4oz of mason glass jars. Add all the ingredients in a food processor, except the pancetta. Press and hold the pulse until the mixture becomes smooth. Place half the sliced pancetta into each jar and carefully pour the egg mixture. Seal the jars. Place the jars in the water bath and cook for 56 minutes. Remove content from the jars and serve.

76. TURKEY WITH ARUGULA AND EGGS

Cal.: 391 | Fat: 22g | Protein: 41g   11 min | 16 min | Servings 6

INGREDIENTS

- 1½ tbsp. melted butter
- 2 large eggs
- 1 pound of cooked and shredded turkey
- Salt and freshly ground black pepper, to taste
- 3 tsp. butter
- ¼ cup heavy cream
- 2 cups of fresh baby arugula

DIRECTIONS

Fill water in 6 ramekins. Fill water halfway up the height of the ramekins. Apply butter to your clean ramekins. Preheat the water to 168°F/75°C. Whisk 1 egg over each ramekin and add cream, butter, black pepper and salt. Place the ramekins on the baking rack and cook for 14 minutes. Serve with cooked turkey. Enjoy!

77. CINNAMON AND EGG MIX

Cal.: 240 | Fat: 12g | Protein: 14g   10 min | 30 min | Servings 2

INGREDIENTS

- 2 tablespoons sugar
- ½ teaspoon cinnamon powder
- 1 teaspoon ginger powder
- 1/3 cup heavy cream
- 4 eggs, whisked

DIRECTIONS

Prepare your sous-vide water bath to a temperature of 167°F/75°C. Vacuum seal the entire ingredients in a cooking pouch. Lower the pouch into the preheated water bath and cook for 30 minutes. Remove the pouch from the water bath and transfer the contents into serving bowls. Serve and enjoy!

78. CHERRY TOMATOES WITH EGGS

Cal.: 210 | Fat: 6g | Protein: 12g   10 min | 40 min | Servings 4

INGREDIENTS

- 1 cup cherry tomatoes, cubed
- 1 tablespoon ginger, grated
- 4 eggs, whisked
- A drizzle of olive oil
- 1 red onion, chopped
- Salt and black pepper to the taste
- A pinch of red pepper, crushed
- 1 garlic clove, minced
- 1 tablespoon chives, chopped

DIRECTIONS

Prepare your sous-vide water bath to a temperature of 170°F/76°C. Pour oil in a pan and place it over medium to high heat. Add the above-listed ingredients in the pan except for the eggs. Thoroughly stir the mixture and cook for 10 minutes. Remove the pan from the heat and combine the ginger mixture with the eggs in a bowl. Pour the mixture in a Ziploc bag and vacuum seal it after squeezing out the excess air. Lower the bag into the water bath and cook for 30 minutes. Once done, remove the bag from the water bath and serve.

79. MUSHROOMS

Cal.: 429 | Fat: 34g | Protein: 18g   9 min | 30 min | Servings 8

INGREDIENTS

- 2 pounds mushrooms of your choice
- 4 tablespoons extra-virgin olive oil
- 4 teaspoons minced fresh thyme
- 1 teaspoon salt or to taste
- 1 teaspoon freshly ground pepper, or to taste
- 4 tablespoons soy sauce
- 2 tablespoons vinegar of your choice

DIRECTIONS

Preheat the Sous Vide machine to 176°F/80°C. Place mushrooms in a bowl. Add the rest of the ingredients and stir until well coated. Transfer into a large vacuum-seal pouch or Ziploc bag. Vacuum seal the pouch. Immerse the pouch in the water bath. Set the timer for 30 minutes. When the timer goes off, remove the pouch from the water bath. Set aside to cool. Open the pouch and transfer into a bowl. Serve right away.

80. CORN

Cal.: 244 | Fat: 27g | Protein: 13g   12 min | 30 min | Servings 2

INGREDIENTS

- 2 ears corn
- Kosher salt to taste
- 1 tablespoon butter + extra to serve
- Aromatics (optional, to taste):
- Handful cilantro, chopped
- 1 or 2 scallions, chopped
- Dried red chilies to taste
- 4 or 5 garlic cloves, minced

DIRECTIONS

Preheat the Sous Vide machine to 183°F/84°C. Add all the ingredients including the aromatics into a vacuum-seal pouch or Ziploc bag. Vacuum seal the pouch. Immerse the pouch in the water bath and fix on the edge of the water bath with clips. Set a timer for 30 minutes. Remove corn from the pouch and discard the rest of the ingredients. Brush with more butter and serve.

81. MEATBALLS

Cal.: 417 | Fat: 21g | Protein: 17g   9 min | 3 hours | Servings 10

INGREDIENTS

- 2 pounds ground beef
- 4 to 6 ounces milk
- ½ teaspoon pepper
- 1 shallot minced
- 2 tablespoons dried oregano
- 6 tablespoons grated parmesan cheese
- ½ cup dried breadcrumbs
- 1 teaspoon salt, or to taste
- 2 large eggs, beaten
- 1/3 cup chopped parsley
- 2 tablespoons garlic powder
- Dip of your choice, to serve
- A little oil to seas (optional)

DIRECTIONS

Add all the ingredients into a large bowl and mix with your hands until just incorporated. Do not mix for long, as the meat will tend to get tough. Make 1-inch balls of the mixture. Place on a tray and freeze until firm. Fill the water bath with water. Preheat it to 135°F/57°C. Transfer the meatballs into 1 or 2 large vacuum-seal pouches or Ziploc bags. Vacuum seal the pouches. Immerse the pouches in the water bath. Set the timer for 3 hours. When the timer goes off, remove the pouch from the water bath. Set aside to cool. Open the pouch and transfer into a bowl. Serve with a dip of your choice. If you want to sear the meatballs: Place a non-stick pan over medium heat and add a bit of oil. When the oil is heated, add meatballs and cook until browned. Serve.

82. OVERNIGHT OATMEAL

Cal.: 284 | Fat: 20g | Protein: 9g   ⟍ 11 min | 🍲 10 hours | ✗ Servings 4

INGREDIENTS

- 2/3 cup rolled oats
- 2/3 cup pinhead oatmeal
- 1 1/3 cups milk or cream
- 4 teaspoons raisins
- 2 cups water
- 2 teaspoons maple syrup or honey

DIRECTIONS

Preheat the Sous Vide machine to 140°F/60°C. Take 4 Mason jars or glass jam jars with lids. Divide the oats and pinhead oatmeal (you can also use quick-cook steel-cut oats) among the jars. Divide the milk and pour over the oats. Pour ½ cup water in each jar. Add a teaspoon of raisins to each jar. Fasten the lids lightly, not tight. Immerse the filled jars in the water bath. The lids of the jars should be above the level of water in the cooker. This is important. Set the timer for 9 to 10 hours. When done, stir and serve with some butter, if desired.

83. OVERNIGHT OATMEAL WITH STEWED FRUIT COMPOTE

Cal.: 364 | Fat: 32g | Protein: 19g   ⟍ 9 min | 🍲 6 hours | ✗ Servings 4

INGREDIENTS

For oatmeal:
- 2 cups quick-cooking rolled oats
- ¼ teaspoon ground cinnamon
- 6 cups water
- A pinch salt

For Stewed Fruit Compote:
- 1½ cups mixed dried fruit of your choice—cherries, apricots, cranberries, etc.
- 1 cup water
- Zest of an orange, finely grated
- Zest of a lemon, finely grated
- ¼ cup white sugar
- ¼ teaspoon vanilla extract

DIRECTIONS

Preheat the Sous Vide machine to 155°F/68°C. Place oatmeal, water, salt, and cinnamon in a vacuum-seal pouch or Ziploc bag. Place all the ingredients of the fruit compote in another similar pouch and vacuum seal both. Immerse both pouches in the water bath and set the timer for 6 to 10 hours. Remove the pouches and shake them well. Divide the oatmeal into 4 bowls. Top with fruit compote and serve.

84. CURED SALMON

Cal.: 344 | Fat: 21g | Protein: 19g   ⟍ 9 min | 🍲 60 min | ✗ Servings 2

INGREDIENTS

- 2 salmon fillets (6 ounces each)
- 8 tablespoons sugar
- 8 tablespoons salt
- 2 teaspoons smoke flavor powder (optional)

DIRECTIONS

Take 2 bowls and place a fillet in each bowl. Divide the sugar, salt and smoke flavor powder among the bowls. Mix well. Set aside for 30 minutes. Rinse the fillets in water. Place in a large Ziploc bag. Vacuum seal the pouch. Immerse the pouch in the water bath at 104°F/40°C and adjust the timer for 30 minutes. Just before the timer goes off, make an ice water bath by filling a large bowl with water and ice. When done, remove the pouch from the water bath and immerse it in the ice water bath. When cooled, remove the pouch from the water bath. Remove the fillets from the pouch and serve.

85. TOMATO SUSHI

Cal.: 514 | Fat: 36g | Protein: 19g   7 min | 4 hours | Servings 24

INGREDIENTS

For tomatoes:
- 6 Roma tomatoes
- 2 tablespoons soy sauce
- 2 cups water
- 6 nori sheets
- ½ teaspoon salt

For sushi rice:
- 2 cups uncooked glutinous white rice, rinsed
- ½ cup rice vinegar
- ½ teaspoon salt
- 3 cups water
- 4 tablespoons sugar

DIRECTIONS

For tomatoes

Preheat the Sous Vide machine to 140°F/60°C. Add 4 nori sheets, soy sauce, water, and salt in a large saucepan over medium heat. Simmer until it has reduced to half its original quantity. Turn off the heat. Cut off a slice from the top of the tomatoes. Make cuts in the shape of an "X" with a paring knife. Place a pan with water over high heat. When it begins to boil, add the tomatoes and let it cook for about 30 to 60 seconds. Remove the tomatoes and place in a bowl filled with ice and water. Peel the tomatoes. Cut each into quarters. Discard the seeds. Place the tomatoes in the nori water. Transfer into a vacuum-seal pouch or Ziploc bag. Vacuum seal the pouch. Immerse the pouch in a water bath and adjust the timer for 4 hours.

To make sushi rice

Add vinegar, salt, and sugar into a saucepan over medium heat. Stir frequently until sugar dissolves. Turn off the heat. Add rice and water into a pot over high heat. When it begins to boil, reduce the heat and cover with a lid. Simmer until all liquid is absorbed. Add sugar solution and mix well. Turn off the heat.

To assemble

Cut the remaining nori sheets into 24 strips. Remove the pouch from the water bath. When the rice is cool enough to handle, divide the rice into 24 equal portions and shape into sushi. Place a piece of tomato on each sushi. Wrap the sushi along with the tomato with a nori strip and place on a serving platter. Serve.

86. LEMON-BUTTER SHRIMP

Cal.: 534 | Fat: 20g | Protein: 13g   9 min | 30 min | Servings 8

INGREDIENTS

- 2 pounds large shrimp, peeled, deveined
- 16 strips (½ inch each) lemon zest
- 4 ounces chilled butter, cut into 8 slices
- 1 teaspoon creole seasoning or to taste + extra to serve
- 6 sprigs of fresh thyme

DIRECTIONS

Preheat the Sous Vide machine to 135°F/57°C. Place shrimp in a bowl. Sprinkle creole seasoning on top and toss well. Transfer into a large Ziploc bag or vacuum-seal pouch. Spread the shrimp in a single layer. Use 2 pouches, if required. Scatter lemon zest, butter, and thyme all over the shrimp. Vacuum seal the pouch. Immerse the pouch in a water bath and adjust the timer for 30 minutes. When the timer goes off, remove the pouch from the water bath. Transfer the shrimp onto a serving platter. Sprinkle some more creole seasoning on top and serve.

87. HUEVOS RANCHEROS

Cal.: 554 | Fat: 34.6g | Protein: 28.5g   11 min | 150 min | Servings 3

INGREDIENTS

- ½ can (7 ounces) crushed tomatoes
- ½ small yellow onion, minced
- 2 garlic cloves, minced
- ¼ teaspoon dried oregano
- ¼ teaspoon ground cumin
- ½ lime juice
- 1 canned chipotle adobo chili, minced
- ½ can refried beans
- 6 eggs
- 6 corn tortillas
- ¼ cup fresh cilantro, chopped
- ½ cup crumbled cotija cheese or grated Monterey Jack

DIRECTIONS

Preheat the water bath to 147°F/64°C. Combine tomatoes, onion, garlic, oregano, cumin, lime and chili in a bag. Seal using the water method. Pour refried beans into a second bag and seal using the water method. Place eggs in a third bag and seal using the water method. Place all three bags into the water bath. Cook for 2 hours. When the other components have 20 minutes left to cook, heat tortillas in a pan. Place 2 on each plate. Top the tortillas with salsa, followed by the shelled eggs, cheese and cilantro. Serve with refried beans.

88. STEAMED ASPARAGUS WITH HOLLANDAISE SAUCE

Cal.: 109 | Fat: 10.1g | Protein: 4.8g   21 min | 31 min | Servings 4

INGREDIENTS

- 20 spears white asparagus, trimmed
- 2 tablespoons butter
- ¼ cup orange juice
- 2 orange slices
- 1 teaspoon salt

Hollandaise sauce:

- 2 eggs
- ¼ cup butter
- ½ tablespoon lemon juice
- Salt and pepper, to taste

DIRECTIONS

Preheat the Sous Vide machine to 185°F/85°C. Place the asparagus, butter, orange juice, orange slices, and salt in a vacuum seal bag. Seal the bag and immerse in a water bath. Cook for 25 minutes. Heat a large skillet over medium-high heat. Remove the asparagus from the bag and transfer to the skillet. Cook for 30 seconds and remove. Make the sauce; place the egg yolks in a heat-proof bowl. Set the bowl over simmering water. Melt butter over medium heat. Gradually add butter to egg yolks, whisking rapidly. Continue until all butter is incorporated. Stir in the lemon juice. Season to taste. Serve asparagus and drizzle with sauce.

89. BEEF TRI-TIP WITH BBQ SAUCE

Cal.: 163 | Fat: 5.6g | Protein: 18.2g   11 min | 6 hours | Servings 6

INGREDIENTS

- 2 ½ lb. beef tri-tip
- 2 teaspoons kosher salt
- 1 teaspoon freshly ground black pepper
- ½ cup barbecue sauce, divided
- 2 teaspoons light brown sugar

DIRECTIONS

Preheat the Sous Vide machine to 130°F/55°C. Season beef with 1 teaspoon salt and ½ teaspoon black pepper. Transfer meat to a Ziploc bag and add ¼ cup barbecue sauce. Seal the bag using the water immersion technique and place in a water bath for 6 hours. When the timer goes off, remove the bag from the water bath. Take out the meat and pat dry with kitchen towels. Preheat the broiler to medium heat and place the meat on the foil-lined broiler-safe baking sheet. Brush the meat with remaining sauce and sprinkle with sugar, remaining salt and pepper. Broil for 5 minutes or until caramelized. Place the meat on the serving platter and let it rest for 10 minutes. Slice before serving.

90. SHRIMP AND MUSHROOMS

Cal.: 340 | Fat: 23g | Protein: 17g   ⊿ 11 min | 🍲 30 min | ✘ Servings 4

INGREDIENTS

- 1 cup shrimp, peeled and deveined
- 3 spring onions, chopped
- 1 cup mushrooms, sliced
- 4 eggs, whisked
- ½ teaspoon coriander, ground
- Salt and black pepper to the taste
- ½ cup coconut cream
- ½ teaspoon turmeric powder
- 4 bacon slices, chopped

DIRECTIONS

Prepare your sous-vide water bath to a temperature of 140°F/60°C. Vacuum seal all the listed ingredients and lower the pouch in the water bath. Cook for 30 minutes. Serve and enjoy!

91. GARLIC MUSHROOMS WITH TRUFFLE OIL

Cal.: 322 | Fat: 34.1g | Protein: 1.5g   ⊿ 9 min | 🍲 75 min | ✘ Servings 2

INGREDIENTS

- 10 media to large button mushrooms
- 2 garlic cloves, minced
- 3 tablespoons of olive oil
- 2 tablespoons of truffle oil
- 1 tablespoon fresh thyme, chopped

DIRECTIONS

Prepare your water bath by attaching the immersion circulator and setting the temperature to 185°F/85°C. Mix the olive oil with the truffle oil and the rest of the ingredients. Add the mushrooms and make sure that they are well coated with the oil mixture. Place the mushrooms into a sealable plastic pouch and seal using a vacuum sealer or the water displacement method. Place into the water bath and cook for 1 hour. Once the mushrooms are cooked, remove from the bag, drain and toss in a grilling pan to sear, until golden brown. Serve hot and garnish optionally with some extra thyme on top.

92. OLIVES SQUASH

Cal.: 263 | Fat: 23g | Protein: 15g   ⊿ 9 min | 🍲 50 min | ✘ Servings 4

INGREDIENTS

- 1 tablespoon butter, melted
- 1 butternut squash, peeled and cubed
- 4 eggs, whisked
- 1 cup black olives, pitted and cubed
- Salt and black pepper to the taste
- ½ cup tomatoes, chopped
- 2 garlic cloves, minced
- ½ teaspoon Italian seasoning
- 3 ounces Italian salami, chopped
- 1 tablespoon oregano, chopped

DIRECTIONS

Prepare your sous-vide water bath to a temperature of 170°F/76°C. Get a cooking pouch and add the eggs and the other ingredients listed above. Shake the pouch to combine thoroughly, then vacuum seal it. Immerse the pouch in the water bath and cook for 40 minutes. Remove the pouch once done and transfer the contents to a serving platter. Serve and enjoy!

93. SAUSAGE SCRAMBLE

Cal.: 384 | Fat: 34g | Protein: 21g   11 min | 20 min | Servings 3

INGREDIENTS

- 16 large eggs, well beaten
- 8 ounces breakfast sausages, crumbled
- 4 tablespoons butter
- Salt and pepper, as per taste
- ½ cup Mexican cheese, grated

DIRECTIONS

Preheat the Sous Vide machine to 165°F/74°C. Place a skillet over medium heat and cook the sausages until they are browned. Transfer the cooked sausages to a bowl lined with paper towels and allow them to cool. Once the sausages cool, place them in a Ziploc bag. Add the eggs, butter, cheese, salt and pepper and vacuum seal the bag. Immerse and cook in the cooker for around 20 minutes. Take the pouch out occasionally and shake the contents well before submerging again. Cook until the eggs are as per your liking. Remove from the water bath and serve.

94. CHILI OREGANO SAUSAGE

Cal.: 297 | Fat: 25g | Protein: 18g   15 min | 3 hours | Servings 4

INGREDIENTS

- ½ teaspoon oregano
- 1 teaspoon paprika
- 1 teaspoon salt
- ¼ teaspoon chili flakes
- 1 teaspoon dried basil
- 1-pound breakfast sausages
- 1 teaspoon cilantro
- 1 teaspoon turmeric
- 1 tablespoon butter

DIRECTIONS

In a deep bowl, add the breakfast sausage and the other ingredients except for the butter and mix thoroughly. Put the ingredients into a Ziploc bag, remove all air and seal the bag. Set the temperature to 153°F/67°C. Transfer the sealed bag into the preheated water and cook for 3 hours. Remove the bag and set aside. Spoon the butter into a skillet and melt it over high heat. Transfer the sausages to the skillet and roast them for 2 minutes and 30 seconds. Remove the sausages and place them on a platter. Serve immediately.

95. SAUSAGE TOMATO

Cal.: 250 | Fat: 12g | Protein: 18g   9 min | 43 min | Servings 4

INGREDIENTS

- 1 cup baby spinach
- 1 tablespoon avocado oil
- 2 pork sausage links, sliced
- 1 cup cherry tomatoes, halved
- 1 cup kalamata olives, pitted and halved
- 2 tablespoons lemon juice
- 2 tablespoons basil pesto
- Salt and black pepper to the taste

DIRECTIONS

Prepare your sous vide water bath to a temperature of 180°F/82°C. Get a cooking pouch and add all the listed ingredients. Immerse the pouch into the water bath and let it cook for 40 minutes. Once done, remove the pouch from the water bath. Transfer the contents into two serving bowls. Serve and enjoy!

96. TOMATO SORBET AND VEGETABLES

Cal.: 229 | Fat: 11g | Protein: 5.3g   ⟍ 7 min | 🍲 28 min | ✗ Servings 4

INGREDIENTS

- 8 carrots, halved
- 12 spears green asparagus
- 1 cup fresh peas
- 3 tablespoons olive oil
- Salt and pepper, to taste

Sorbet:

- ¼ cup water
- 2 tablespoons sugar
- 4 ripe tomatoes, peeled
- 2 tablespoons fresh lemon juice
- 1 tablespoon tomato paste
- Salt and black pepper, to taste

DIRECTIONS

Make the sorbet; in a food blender, blend the tomatoes until pureed. Bring water, sugar and basil to a boil in a saucepan. Remove from heat and allow to cool. Pour in the tomatoes and add tomato paste. Stir to combine. Season to taste with salt and pepper. Place the sorbet into a freezer. Freeze 2–4 hours or until firm. Make the vegetables; peel and trim asparagus. Place the asparagus in one sous-vide bag and add 1 tablespoon olive oil. In a separate bag, place carrots and peas. Drizzle with olive oil. Vacuum seal both bags. Set the water bath to 190°F/88°C. Cook the carrots and peas for 12 minutes in heated water. After the carrots have been cooked for 8 minutes, add asparagus. Remove the bags from the water bath. Unpack the bags and arrange veggies onto a serving plate. Season to taste. Serve veggies with a scoop of tomato sorbet.

97. BUTTERED ROOT VEGETABLES

Cal.: 244 | Fat: 9.65g | Protein: 38.7g   ⟍ 7 min | 🍲 3 hours 30 min | ✗ Servings 2

INGREDIENTS

- 1 small turnip
- 4 small carrots
- 1 small parsnip
- ½ small red onion
- 1 small rutabaga
- 1 sprig of fresh rosemary
- 2 garlic cloves, crushed
- A pinch of salt and pepper
- 1 tablespoon butter
- 1 tablespoon extra-virgin olive oil

DIRECTIONS

Preheat a water bath to 185°F/85°C. Add rosemary, vegetables and olive oil to a vacuum bag and seal. Cook for three hours. Then pour the mixture from the bag into a sauté pan and sprinkle with salt and pepper. Cook for 4 minutes at a high temperature—the liquid should turn into a sauce. Add butter and stir slowly. When the veggies turn brown, set aside. Serve warm.

98. BEET SIDE SALAD

Cal.: 188 | Fat: 4g | Protein: 5g   ⟍ 9 min | 🍲 70 min | ✗ Servings 4

INGREDIENTS

- 1 bunch Yellow beets, trimmed into wedges
- 1 bunch of Radishes, trimmed into wedges
- 1 bunch Red beets, trimmed into wedges
- 10 oz. rocket/arugula leaves
- 2 ½ tablespoons balsamic vinegar
- 2/3 cup toasted walnuts
- 2/3 cup olive oil
- 1 pkg. stevia
- To Your Liking: Pepper and salt

DIRECTIONS

Combine the beets, some of the oil, pepper and salt in the bags. Toss and close the bag, removing the air. Place in the prepared water bath for 1 hour at 180°F/82°C. In a mixing container, whisk the rest of the oil, vinegar, stevia, pepper and salt. When the beets are cooked, add all of the fixings in a mixing container. Serve and enjoy!

99. POTATO SALAD

Cal.: 108 | Fat: 1.6g | Protein: 3.7g   ⬛ 11 min | 🍲 90 min | ✖ Servings 6

INGREDIENTS

- 1 ½ pounds yellow potatoes or red potatoes (waxy potatoes work best)
- ½ cup chicken stock
- Salt and pepper to taste
- 4 oz. thick cut bacon, sliced into about ¼-inch slices
- ½ cup chopped onion
- 1/3 cup cider vinegar
- 4 scallions, thinly sliced

DIRECTIONS

Set the cooker to 185°F/85°C. Cut potatoes into ¾-inch-thick cubes. Place potatoes and chicken stock to the Ziploc bag, making sure they are in a single layer; seal using the immersion water method. Place potatoes in a water bath and cook for 1 hour 30 minutes. Meanwhile, in the last 15 minutes, heat the non-stick skillet over medium-high heat. Add bacon and cook until crisp; remove bacon and add chopped onions. Cook until softened for 5-7 minutes. Add vinegar and cook until reduced slightly. Remove potatoes from the water bath and place them in a skillet, with the cooking water. Continue cooking for a few minutes until the liquid thickens. Remove potatoes from the heat and stir in scallions; toss to combine. Serve while still hot.

100. ROSEMARY FAVA BEANS

Cal.: 333 | Fat: 9.8g | Protein: 19.7g   ⬛ 11 min | 🍲 70 min | ✖ Servings 4

INGREDIENTS

- 1.25 pounds Fava beans, cleaned
- ½ teaspoon salt
- 2 sprigs rosemary
- ¼ teaspoon caraway seeds
- 1 pinch black pepper
- 3 tablespoons cold butter

DIRECTIONS

Preheat the Sous Vide machine to 176°F/80°C. Blanche the fava beans in simmering water for 1 minute. Drain and divide between two bags. Season the beans with salt, pepper, and caraway seeds. Add 1 tablespoon of butter per bag, and vacuum seals the bags. Immerse the bags in water and cook for 70 minutes. Remove the veggies from the bag. Heat remaining butter in a skillet. Toss in the beans and coat the beans with butter. Serve warm.

101. THYME LARD BROAD BEANS

Cal.: 265 | Fat: 21.6g | Protein: 4.1g   ⬛ 11 min | 🍲 60 min | ✖ Servings 4

INGREDIENTS

- 1.5 pounds Broad beans
- 4 sprigs thyme
- 3oz. lard
- 1 pinch red pepper flakes

DIRECTIONS

Preheat the Sous Vide machine to 176°F/80°C. Trim the beans and blanch in simmering water for 30 seconds. Rinse the beans under cold water. Divide the beans between two bags. Add two sprigs of thyme per bag. Chop the lard and sprinkle over the beans, along with red pepper flakes. Vacuum seal the bag and Immerse in a water bath. Cook the beans for 60 minutes. Remove the beans from the cooker and immerse in ice-cold water for 2–3 minutes. Open the bags and serve the beans.

102. TOMATO CONFIT

Cal.: 30 | Fat: 0.3g | Protein: 1.3g   📐 15 min | 🍲 20 min | 🍴 Servings 4

INGREDIENTS

- 1.25 lb. Cherry tomatoes (red, orange, yellow)
- 1 pinch Fleur de sel
- 6 black peppercorns
- 1 teaspoon cane sugar
- 2 tablespoons Bianco Aceto Balsamico
- 2 sprigs rosemary

DIRECTIONS

Preheat the Sous Vide machine to 126°F/52°C. Heat water in a pot and bring to a simmer. Make a small incision at the bottom of each tomato. Place the tomatoes into simmering water and simmer for 30 seconds. Remove from the water and peel their skin. Divide the tomatoes between two sous-vide bags. Sprinkle the tomatoes with salt, peppercorns, sugar and Aceto Balsamico. Add 1 sprig of rosemary per bag. Vacuum-seal the bags, but just to 90%. Tomatoes are soft, and they can turn into mush. Immerse tomatoes in water and cook for 20 minutes. Remove the tomatoes from the cooker and immerse in ice-cold water for 5 minutes. Transfer the tomatoes to a bowl and serve with fresh mozzarella.

103. HONEY GINGER CHICORY

Cal.: 127 | Fat: 1.2g | Protein: 6.6g   📐 11 min | 🍲 20 min | 🍴 Servings 4

INGREDIENTS

- 1.25lb chicory
- 1 cup fresh orange juice
- 1-inch ginger, sliced
- 1 tablespoon honey
- Salt and pepper, to taste

DIRECTIONS

Preheat the Sous Vide machine to 185°F/85°C. Remove the chicory outer leaves and place in a bag. Add the orange juice, ginger slices, and honey. Season to taste with salt and pepper, and vacuum seals the bag. Immerse the chicory in water and cook for 20 minutes. Remove the chicory from the cooker. Open the bag and serve chicory with toasted bread.

104. SALTY CUSTARD

Cal.: 168 | Fat: 12.5g | Protein: 12.9g   📐 11 min | 🍲 30 min | 🍴 Servings 4

INGREDIENTS

- 8 large eggs
- 2 cups chicken stock
- 2 teaspoons sesame oil
- Salt and pepper, to taste
- Soy sauce, chopped green onion

DIRECTIONS

Fill and preheat the sous-vide cooker to 180°F/82°C. In a blender, blend eggs, chicken stock, sesame oil, salt, and pepper until smooth. Strain through a fine-mesh sieve to remove any foam. If needed, strain again and transfer into the vacuum bag. Seal the bag and immerse into the water bath. Cook for 20 minutes. Remove from the water bath and shake or massage gently. Cook 10 minutes additional. Remove from the water bath and place into an ice-cold bath for 20 minutes. Serve in a bowl, and top with a splash of soy sauce and chopped green onion.

105. BREAKFAST ROLLS WITH VANILLA EXTRACT

Cal.: 310 | Fat: 13g | Protein: 4g   13 min | 62 min | Servings 6

INGREDIENTS

- 1 1/3 cups of all-purpose flour
- 1¼ tsp. baking powder
- ½ cup plus 1 tbsp. whole milk
- 1½-ounce of softened cream cheese
- ½ cup confectioner's sugar
- Salt, to taste
- ¼ cup melted unsalted butter, divided
- ¾ tsp. vanilla extract, divided
- 2 tbsp. warm milk
- 1/3 cup dark brown sugar
- 3 tbsp. granulated sugar, divided
- 1½ tsp. ground cinnamon
- 2 tsp. active dry yeast

DIRECTIONS

Prepare your sous-vide water bath to a temperature of 196°F/91°C. Set up a rack in the water bath. Grease 6 mason jars of 8oz. In a bowl, add the cinnamon, salt, 2 tbsp. of granulated sugar and brown sugar, and mix thoroughly. Add the vanilla extract and butter and beat till well combined. In a separate bowl, mix the milk, ½ tsp. of granulated sugar and yeast. Set aside for 4 minutes. Get another bowl and mix the flour, baking powder, 1/3 tsp. of salt, and 2 ½ tsp. of granulated sugar. Stir well to combine. Add 1 tbsp. of butter, ½ cup milk and yeast to the mixture and mix very well until a shaggy dough forms. Knead the dough on a well-floured surface until soft dough forms. Roll the dough carefully into a ¼-inch-thick and 10x6-inch rectangle. Coat the dough with 1 tbsp. of butter. Sprinkle the top with brown sugar and roll into logs. Next, cut the dough into 6 rolls and distribute each roll into each prepared jar. Cover the top of the jars with a kitchen towel for 30 minutes. Seal the jars tightly and transfer them into the water bath.
Cook for 2 hours 57 minutes. For the glaze, get a bowl and add 1 tbsp. of butter, ¼ tsp. of vanilla, 1 tbsp. of milk, salt and cream cheese. Beat until the mixture is smooth. Add the confectioner's sugar and mix thoroughly until well combined. Gently remove the jars from the water bath and place them on the wire rack for 4 minutes. Remove the food content from the jars and keep to cool. Lightly top with prepared glaze and serve!

106. MEXICAN BREAKFAST

Cal.: 554 | Fat: 34.6g | Protein: 28.5g   31 min | 2 hours | Servings 3

INGREDIENTS

- ½ can (7 ounces) crushed tomatoes
- ½ small yellow onion, minced
- 2 garlic cloves, minced
- ¼ teaspoon dried oregano
- ¼ teaspoon ground cumin
- Juice of ½ lime
- 1 canned chipotle adobo chili, minced
- ½ can refried beans
- 6 eggs
- 6 corn tortillas
- ¼ cup fresh cilantro, chopped
- ½ cup crumbled cotija cheese or grated Monterey Jack

DIRECTIONS

Preheat the water bath to 147°F/64°C. Combine tomatoes, onion, garlic, oregano, cumin, lime and chili in a bag. Seal using the water method. Pour refried beans into a second bag and seal using the water method. Place eggs in a third bag and seal using the water method. Place all three bags into the water bath. Cook for 2 hours. When the other components have 20 minutes left to cook, heat tortillas in a pan. Place 2 on each plate. Top the tortillas with salsa, followed by the shelled eggs, cheese and cilantro. Serve with refried beans.

107. BREAKFAST YOGURT

Cal.: 134 | Fat: 4g | Protein: 3g   🔪 10 min | 🍲 3 hours 10 min | 🍴 Servings 6

INGREDIENTS
- 1 qt. almond milk
- ½ cup coconut yogurt
- ½ tablespoon lime, zest and grated
- ½ tablespoon orange, zest and grated
- ½ tablespoon lemon, zest and grated

DIRECTIONS
Warm up the milk and mix with the yogurt in a bowl. Whisk and add the rest of the fixings. Pour the mixture into canning jars. Add to a water bath with the cooker and cover the tops with some foil. Cook for 3 hours at 113°F/45°C.
Serve and enjoy!

108. OKRA AND SPICED YOGURT

Cal.: 186 | Fat: 10.5g | Protein: 7.2g   🔪 8 min | 🍲 75 min | 🍴 Servings 6

INGREDIENTS
- 2.5 lbs. fresh okra
- 4 tablespoons olive oil
- 1 ½ tablespoon lime zest
- 2 garlic cloves, crushed
- Salt and white pepper, to taste

Yogurt:
- 1 cup Greek yogurt
- 2 teaspoons chili powder
- ¼ cup chopped cilantro

DIRECTIONS
Preheat your cooker to 178°F/81°C. Divide the fresh okra among two cooking bags. Drizzle the okra with 2 ½ tablespoons olive oil (divided per bag), lime zest and season to taste. Add one garlic clove per pouch. Vacuum seal the bags and immerse in water. Cook the okra for 1 hour. Remove from a water bath and drain the accumulated liquid in a bowl. Place the okra in a separate bowl. In a medium bowl, combine Greek yogurt, chili powder, cilantro and accumulated okra water. Stir to combine. Heat remaining vegetable oil during a skillet over medium-high heat. Fry okra in the heated oil for 2 minutes.
Serve warm, with chili yogurt.

109. CITRUS YOGURT

Cal.: 394 | Fat: 20g | Protein: 14g   🔪 12 min | 🍲 3 hours | 🍴 Servings 8

INGREDIENTS
- 1 cup yogurt
- 8 cups full cream milk
- 1 tablespoon grated orange zest
- 1 tablespoon grated lime zest
- 1 tablespoon grated lemon zest

DIRECTIONS
Preheat the Sous Vide machine to 113°F/45°C. Pour milk into a saucepan and place over medium heat. When the temperature of the milk reaches 180°F/82°C, turn off the heat. Let the milk cool to 110°F/43°C. Add 2 tablespoons of yogurt in each of 8 canning jars. Divide the milk among the jars, then divide the zests among the jars and stir. Fasten the lid on the jars. Immerse the filled jars in the water bath. The lids of the jars should be above the level of water in the cooker. Set the timer for 3 hours. Remove from the water bath and cool completely. Refrigerate for a few hours before use.

110. BLACKBERRY HIBISCUS DELIGHT

Cal.: 149 | Fat: 0.6g | Protein: 1.6g   11 min | 90 min | Servings 4

INGREDIENTS
- 1lb. fresh blackberries
- ½ cup red wine vinegar
- ½ cup caster sugar
- 2 teaspoons crushed hibiscus flowers
- 3 bay leaves

DIRECTIONS
Preheat the Sous Vide machine to 140°F/60°C. In a saucepot, combine red wine vinegar, caster sugar, hibiscus, and bay leaves. Heat until the sugar is dissolved. Allow cooling. Place the blackberries and cooled syrup in a bag. Vacuum seal and immerse in water. Cook for 1 hour 30 minutes. Remove the bag from the cooker and place in ice-cold water for 10 minutes. Open carefully and transfer the content to a bowl. Serve.

111. PEARS IN POMEGRANATE JUICE

Cal.: 268 | Fat: 0.3g | Protein: 0.8g   21 min | 30 min | Servings 8

INGREDIENTS
- 8 pears
- 5 cups pomegranate juice
- ¾ cup sugar
- 1 cinnamon stick
- ¼ teaspoon nutmeg
- ¼ teaspoon ground cloves
- ¼ teaspoon allspice

DIRECTIONS
Preheat the Sous Vide machine to 176°F/80°C. Combine all ingredients, except the pears. Simmer until the liquid is reduced by half. Strain and place aside. Gently scrub the pears or peel if desired. Place each pear in a bag, and pour in some poaching liquid. Make sure each pear has the same level of poaching liquid. Vacuum seal the pears and Immerse in water. Cook for 30 minutes. Open bags and remove pears carefully. Slice the pears and place onto a plate. Cook the juices in a saucepan until thick. Drizzle over pears. Serve warm.

112. COCONUT AND ALMOND PORRIDGE

Cal.: 260 | Fat: 12g | Protein: 16g   11 min | 3 hours | Servings 1

INGREDIENTS
- ½ cup ground almonds
- ¾ cup coconut cream
- 1 teaspoon Cinnamon powder
- 1 teaspoon Stevia
- 1 pinch ground cardamom
- 1 pinch ground cloves
- 1 pinch Nutmeg

DIRECTIONS
Combine all of the ingredients in a vacuum-sealed bag. Immerse the bag to the preheated water bath for 3 hours at 180°F/82°C. Remove from the bag, serve, and enjoy.

113. PORRIDGE WITH CHIA AND FLAX SEEDS

Cal.: 230 | Fat: 12g | Protein: 13g   11 min | 3 hours 3 min | Servings 1

INGREDIENTS
- 2 tablespoons flax seeds
- 1 cup almond milk
- 1 tablespoon Stevia
- 1 tablespoon Chia seeds
- ½ cup hemp hearts
- ½ teaspoon cinnamon powder
- ¾ teaspoon vanilla extract
- ¼ cup almond flour

DIRECTIONS
Prepare the water bath. Combine all of the ingredients in a mixing container. Pour into a vacuum-sealable baggie and cook for 3 hours at 180°F/82°C in the prepared cooker. Add to your plate and enjoy it!

114. CHICKEN WINGS

Cal.: 361 | Fat: 29.8g | Protein: 14.7g   ⟍ 19 min | 🍲 7 hours | ✖ Servings 4

INGREDIENTS

- 12 chicken wings
- ¼ cup vegetable oil
- 4 sprigs thyme
- 2 teaspoons crushed red pepper flakes
- Salt, to taste

DIRECTIONS

Preheat the Sous Vide machine to 167°F/75°C. In a bag, combine the chicken wing with the remaining ingredients. Shake gently to coat the chicken and vacuum seal the bag. Immerse in water and cook for 7 hours. Remove the bag with chicken from the cooker. Heat some oil in a large skillet. Place the wings into a skillet and cook until the skin is crispy. Serve.

115. CHICKEN SKEWERS

Cal.: 298 | Fat: 12.1g | Protein: 35g   ⟍ 13 min | 🍲 1 hour 45 min | ✖ Servings 2

INGREDIENTS

- 2 (4 oz.) chicken breasts, cubed
- Salt, to taste
- Black pepper, to taste
- 1 teaspoon cayenne pepper
- ½ teaspoon mustard powder
- ½ cup yogurt
- 1 tablespoon vegetable oil

DIRECTIONS

Prepare and preheat the water bath at 150°F/65°C. Mix chicken cubes with yogurt and all the spices in a bowl. Thread the chicken onto wooden skewers. Place the skewers in two zipper-lock bags. Seal the zipper-lock bags using the water immersion method. Immerse the sealed bag in the water. Cover the water bath and cook for 1 hour, 15 minutes. Once done, remove the chicken skewers from the bag. Grill the chicken skewers with oil in a grill pan for 1 minute per side. Serve warm.

116. EASY CHICKEN BREAST—NO-SEAR

Cal.: 164 | Fat: 6.48g | Protein: 24.8g   ⟍ 8 min | 🍲 65 min | ✖ Servings 3

INGREDIENTS

- 1 lb. chicken breasts
- 1 teaspoon garlic powder
- To Taste: Salt and pepper

DIRECTIONS

Make the water bath and set the cooker to 150°F/65°C. Remove the bones from the chicken and pat the breasts dry. Add the seasonings and place them in a vacuum bag. Close the bag and add it to the cooker for 1 hour. When the time is completed, remove the chicken and store it in the fridge until mealtime.

117. PORK MEDALLIONS

Cal.: 317 | Fat: 10.6g | Protein: 52.1g   ⟍ 11 min | 🍲 60 min | ✖ Servings 4

INGREDIENTS

- 1 tablespoon olive oil
- 1 pinch salt
- 1 pinch black pepper
- 1 teaspoon ground cumin
- ¼ cup chopped fresh parsley
- 1 ¾ lb. pork tenderloin

DIRECTIONS

Preheat the Sous Vide machine to 145°F/63°C. Cut the pork tenderloin in medallions. Season with salt, pepper, and cumin. Place the seasoned pork into the bag and add parsley. Vacuum seal the bag and immerse in water. Cook the medallions for 1 hour. Heat olive oil in a large skillet. Remove the medallions from the cooker. Sear on both sides. Serve warm.

118. SMOKY SOLE FISH

Cal.: 298 | Fat: 22.9g | Protein: 22.4g   ⟍ 11 min | 🍲 30 min | ✖ Servings 2

INGREDIENTS

- 2 5oz. sole fish fillets
- 2 tablespoons olive oil
- 2 slices bacon
- ½ tablespoon lemon juice
- Salt and pepper, to taste

DIRECTIONS

Preheat the Sous Vide machine to 132°F/56°C. Cook the bacon in a non-stick skillet and cook bacon until crispy. Remove the bacon and place aside. Season fish fillets with salt, pepper and lemon juice. Brush the fish with olive oil. Place the fish in a bag. Top the fish with the bacon. Vacuum seal the bag. Immerse in a water bath and cook for 25 minutes. Remove the fish from the bag. Serve while warm.

119. FLAX SEEDS MIX

Cal.: 230 | Fat: 12g | Protein: 13g   ⟍ 3 min | 🍲 60 min | ✖ Servings 2

INGREDIENTS

- 1 tablespoon sugar
- 2 tablespoons flax seeds
- 1 tablespoon sunflower seeds
- 1 cup almond milk
- ½ cup heavy cream
- ½ teaspoon cinnamon powder
- ¾ teaspoon vanilla extract

DIRECTIONS

Prepare your sous-vide water bath to a temperature of 180°F/82°C. Thoroughly mix the listed ingredients in a bowl. Transfer the mixture to a Ziploc bag and seal the bag after squeezing out the excess air. Lower the bag into the water bath and let it cook for 1 hour. Once cooked, remove the bag from the water bath. Transfer the porridge into serving bowls. Serve and enjoy!

120. PERSIMMON BUTTER TOASTS

Cal.: 129 | Fat: 9g | Protein: 4g   ⟍ 10 min | 🍲 3 hours 50 min | ✖ Servings 6

INGREDIENTS

- 2 teaspoon orange juice
- 1 oz. French toasts
- 3 tablespoon sugar
- ½ teaspoon vanilla extract
- ¼ teaspoon salt
- 4 persimmon
- ½ teaspoon ground cinnamon

DIRECTIONS

Add the chopped persimmons, vanilla extract, salt, orange juice and sugar in a Ziploc bag. Remove the excess and seal the bag. Turn the temperature to 154°F/67°C. Immerse the bag into the preheated water bath. Cook for 3 hours 50 minutes Remove the Ziploc bag from the water bath. Blend the Persimmons in a food blender until the mixture becomes smooth. Remove the persimmon mixture from the blender and pour it over the French toast. Serve and enjoy!

121. NICE BREAD

Cal.: 200 | Fat: 7g | Protein: 7g   🥄 7 min | 🍲 58 min | 🍴 Servings 10

INGREDIENTS

- ½ cup milk
- 1½ tsp. active dry yeast
- 1 tbsp. melted butter
- 1½ cups plus
- 2 tbsp. all-purpose flour
- 3 tbsp. water
- 2 tbsp. granulated sugar
- ½ tsp. salt
- 1 tsp. ground cinnamon
- ½ cup light brown sugar
- 1 tbsp. butter

DIRECTIONS

In a saucepan, mix ½ cup milk, 1 tbsp. of butter and 3 tbsp. of water and bring to a boil over medium heat. Cook and stir frequently until butter melts. Transfer the mixture into a deep bowl. Add salt and sugar and stir well. Keep the mixture aside for 4 minutes. Add yeast to the milk mixture and beat until thoroughly combined. Add flour to the mixture and stir until dough forms. Transfer the dough to a clean surface and knead until the dough becomes soft. Roll the dough into a ball and transfer into a greased bowl. Cover the greased bowl and keep until the dough size rises. Prepare your sous-vide water bath to a temperature of 194°F/90°C. Grease butter over 5 canning jars of 4.4 oz. Add the melted butter to a bowl. In a separate bowl, mix the cinnamon and the brown sugar. On an even surface, sprinkle flour on the surface and press the dough into about a 9-inch square. Cut the kneaded square into equal quarters. Cut each of the divided quarters into 7 to 8 evenly sized proportions. Roll the pieces into a ball and dip into the butter medium. Then coat with brown sugar. Distribute the coated balls into the jars. Cover the jars using a paper towel and keep for 45 minutes until the size of the balls rises. Using a paper towel, wipe off the sides and the tops of the jars. Seal the lids tightly and place jars into a bath. Cook for 3 hours and remove jars from hot water. Place them on a wire rack for 4 to 6 minutes. Remove the lids and set the jars to cool over the wire rack. Gently remove from the jars and transfer on a platter. Serve and enjoy!

122. GOOD AND SIMPLE BREAD

Cal.: 380 | Fat: 5g | Protein: 4g   🥄 14 min | 🍲 68 min | 🍴 Servings 12

INGREDIENTS

- 2¼ tsp. dry yeast
- 4 cups whole wheat flour
- 3 cups warm water, divided
- 1 beaten egg
- ¼ cup melted butter
- Salt, to taste
- ½ cup plus
- 1 tbsp. sugar, divided
- 4 cups unbleached white flour

DIRECTIONS

Get a large bowl and add ½ cup of water, one tbsp. of sugar and yeast. Mix thoroughly until well combined. Set aside for ten minutes. Then add the remaining ½ cup of sugar, 2 ½ cups of water and butter, egg and salt into the bowl and stir well. In the same bowl, add 4 cups of flour and mix until it forms to the dough. Using your hands, knead the flour mixture for 9 minutes. Set aside for 80 to 90 minutes until the dough rises. Prepare your sous-vide water bath to a temperature of 190°F/88°C. Press down the dough and make three loaves out of it. In a cooking pouch, put the dough loaves. Vacuum seal the pouch and cook in a water bath for 1 ½ hours. Remove the pouch from the water bath and cut each loaf on a platter according to choice.

123. AMAZING MORNING BREAD

Cal.: 219 | Fat: 11g | Protein: 16g 16 min | 43 min | Servings 6

INGREDIENTS

- 3-ounce of cooked and shredded chicken
- 2-ounce of grated Sharp Cheddar cheese
- 1 tbsp. honey
- ¾ tsp. minced fresh rosemary
- 1 cup half-and-half
- Salt, to taste
- 1 cup water
- 2/3 cup cornmeal
- 1½ tbsp. melted butter
- 2 eggs (separated)

DIRECTIONS

Set up a baking rack. Fill 6 ramekins with water and carefully place each ramekin over the baking rack. Add water halfway up the ramekins. Remove the ramekins from the water bath. Completely remove the water from the ramekins and dry it using a paper towel. Prepare your water bath to a temperature of 196°F/91°C. In a saucepan, add the rosemary and honey and bring it to a boil over medium heat. Gently add the cornmeal to the pan and stir regularly. Reduce the heat from medium to low and cook for extra 2 minutes. Remove the pan from heat and add the cheese, stirring until it melts completely. Add the egg yolk, stir and combine well. Fold and set the shredded chicken aside. Take the turkey into a deep bowl. In a separate bowl, add and thoroughly mix the egg whites until stiff peak forms. Carefully fold egg whites in the turkey mixture. Fold in three batches. Evenly pour the mixture into the prepared ramekins and place them on the baking rack. Cook for 24 minutes. Remove ramekins and let them cool for 9 minutes. Serve and enjoy!

124. CLASSIC TOAST

Cal.: 217 | Fat: 16g | Protein: 11g 7 min | 70 min | Servings 4

INGREDIENTS

- 2 tbsp. unsalted butter
- 2 large day-old challah pieces
- 8 large eggs
- Pinch of salt
- ¾ cup milk
- 1/8 tsp. vanilla extract

DIRECTIONS

Prepare your sous-vide water bath to a temperature of 148°F/64°C. In a deep bowl, whisk the eggs together with the vanilla extract, salt and milk. Beat thoroughly until the mixture is well combined. Transfer the mixture to a Ziploc bag and add the challah pieces. Remove the excess air from the bag and seal the bag. Place the bag in the water bath container. Let it cook for 70 minutes. When ready, remove the Ziploc bag from the water bath. Add butter to a skillet placed over high heat. Transfer the food content from the bag to the skillet and cook until it turns golden brown. Divide each piece into half and serve immediately.

125. FRENCH TOAST

Cal.: 404 | Fat: 29g | Protein: 13g 13 min | 60 min | Servings 8

INGREDIENTS

- 8 slices bread
- 1 cup heavy cream
- 1 teaspoon ground cinnamon
- 4 eggs
- 2 teaspoons vanilla extract

For finishing:
- ½ cup butter

DIRECTIONS

Preheat the Sous Vide machine to 147°F/64°C. Add eggs, vanilla, cream, and cinnamon into a bowl and whisk well. Dip the bread slices in the egg mixture, one at a time, and place in a large vacuum-seal pouch or Ziploc bag. Use 2 bags, if desired. Place in a single layer. Vacuum seal the pouch. Immerse the pouch in the water bath. Set the timer for 60 minutes. Remove the pouch from the water bath and remove the bread slices from the pouch. For finishing: Place a large skillet over medium heat. Add 1 or 2 tablespoons butter. When butter melts, place 2 or 3 bread slices on the pan and cook to desired doneness.

126. COCONUT CONGEE

Cal.: 609 | Fat: 35g | Protein: 9g   20 min | 75 min | Servings 3

INGREDIENTS
- 2 cups water
- Salt
- ½ tbsp. pumpkin pie spice
- ½ cup sugar
- 2 cups coconut milk
- ½ cup short-grain rice

DIRECTIONS
Prepare your sous-vide water bath to a temperature of 190°F/88°C. In a large Ziploc bag, add the coconut milk, pumpkin, water and rice, and seal tightly. Ensure the excess air is properly removed from the bag, then seal. Immerse the bag into the water bath and cook for 1 hour 25 minutes. Remove the bag from the water bath and transfer the content to a platter. Sprinkle with salt. Serve and enjoy!

127. CHOCOLATE CARAMEL BITES

Cal.: 180 | Fat: 8g | Protein: 3g   10 min | 30 min | Servings 1

INGREDIENTS
- 2 tablespoons granulated sugar
- 2 teaspoon cinnamon powder
- 1 tablespoon coconut oil
- 2 bananas
- 1/4 cup melted chocolate

DIRECTIONS
Cut the bananas into slices. In a pan, add the granulated sugar and bring to a boil over low to medium heat until it melts and caramelizes. Prepare your water bath to a temperature of 133°F/56°C. Put the banana slices into the Ziploc bag and add the caramel mixture. Shake the bag carefully for a thorough combination. Remove the excess air and gently immerse the bag in the preheated water bath. Cook for 30 minutes and remove the bag from the water. Remove the slices from the Ziploc bag and sprinkle the banana slices with sugar and cinnamon mixture. Serve and enjoy!

128. OATMEAL WITH DRIED APRICOTS

Cal.: 248 | Fat: 2g | Protein: 7g   10 min | 7 hours 55 min | Servings 4

INGREDIENTS
- ¼ cup dried apricots
- 1 tablespoon butter
- ¼ teaspoon salt
- 3 tablespoon prunes
- 2 cup milk
- 1 tablespoon cream
- 2 cup oatmeal
- 2 tablespoon white sugar
- 1 teaspoon vanilla extract
- 1 tablespoon raisins

DIRECTIONS
Put oatmeal into a large Ziploc bag and combine it with dried apricots, chopped prune, white sugar and raisins. Add the butter, cream, salt and vanilla extract into the Ziploc bag. Shake the bag well to combine. Pour milk into the bag. Ensure that excess air is removed, then seal the bag. Set the temperature to 180°F/82°C. Put the bag into the preheated water and cook for 7 hours 55minutes. Remove the bag from the water bath and place the oatmeal on a platter. Serve and enjoy!

129. MUFFINS AND ROSEMARY

Cal.: 329 | Fat: 19g | Protein: 16g   11 min | 60 min | Servings 12

INGREDIENTS

- 3 tbsp. olive oil
- ¼ tsp. crushed dried rosemary
- 6 halved crosswise thin prosciutto slices
- ½ tsp. smoked paprika
- 6 cups of thawed and squeezed frozen shredded hash browns
- 3 tbsp. minced fresh chives
- Salt and freshly ground black pepper, to taste
- 12 large eggs

DIRECTIONS

Prepare your sous-vide water bath to a temperature of 148°F/64°C Cook the eggs in the bags and cook for 1 hour. When cooked, remove the bag and keep it cool. Preheat your oven to 374°F/190°Cand grease 12 nonstick tins. In a deep bowl, add and mix the salt, black pepper, rosemary, oil and hash brown. Evenly pour the hash brown mixture into the 12 muffin cups. Slightly apply pressure on the harsh brown mixture. Bake the mixture for 30 minutes. Then top each cup with 1 prosciutto and bake for another 5 minutes. Remove the muffin cups from the oven and allow them to cool for 5 minutes. Gently remove the content from the cups. Crack and pour 1 single egg over each nest. Sprinkle the nest lightly with chives. Serve and enjoy!

130. WONDERFUL FLAN

Cal.: 159 | Fat: 17g | Protein: 9g   11 min | 55 min | Servings 4

INGREDIENTS

- 1 tsp. minced fresh chives
- ¼ cup crumbled feta cheese
- Salt and freshly ground black pepper, to taste
- ½ tbsp. olive oil
- 1 chopped small onion
- 1 tbsp. melted butter
- 4 eggs
- ½ cup cream
- 4 trimmed and halved asparagus spears

DIRECTIONS

Put your baking rack in the bath. Prepare your water bath to a temperature of 185°F/85°C. Prepare 4 ramekins by brushing with melted butter and set aside. Pour oil in a frying pan and heat it over medium heat. Add chopped onion in a pan and sauté for 10 minutes. Remove from the heat and keep aside to cool slightly. Get a deep bowl, crack and whisk eggs and black pepper thoroughly. Evenly distribute the onion into ramekins and top with asparagus, egg mixture and cheese. Place a foil over each ramekin and carefully carry them over to the baking rack. Cook for 40 to 45 minutes and remove. Serve and enjoy!

131. CHIVES VEGGIES

Cal.: 100 | Fat: 3g | Protein: 6g   10 min | 30 min | Servings 4

INGREDIENTS

- ½ tablespoon red pepper flakes
- 1 red onion, chopped
- 2 tablespoons chives, chopped
- A drizzle of olive oil
- 1 cup white mushrooms, halved
- 1 bunch bok Choy, chopped
- 1 cup cherry tomatoes, halved
- Salt and black pepper to the taste
- 2 tablespoons balsamic vinegar
- 2 tablespoons Worcestershire sauce
- 1 cup kalamata olives, pitted and halved

DIRECTIONS

Prepare your sous-vide water bath to a temperature of 170°F/76°C. Mix the listed ingredients in a bowl and transfer the mixture into a cooking pouch. Vacuum seal the pouch using a vacuum sealer. Immerse the pouch into the water bath and cook for 20 minutes. Once done, remove the pouch from the water bath. Divide the contents into bowls and serve.

132. AMAZING HAM

Cal.: 146 | Fat: 9g | Protein: 19g   25 min | 8 hours | Servings 4

INGREDIENTS

- 1/3 teaspoon salt
- 1 teaspoon chili flakes
- 1 teaspoon butter
- 1-pound ham
- ½ teaspoon ground black pepper
- 1 tablespoon apple cider vinegar
- 1 tablespoon honey

DIRECTIONS

In a bowl, thoroughly mix all the ingredients except the ham and the butter. Apply the vinegar mixture over the ham. Transfer the ham into a Ziploc bag, remove the excess air and seal the bag. Prepare your water bath to a temperature of 142°F/61°C. Then transfer the sealed bag into the preheated water bath and cook for 8 minutes. Once cooked, remove the cooked ham and apply butter all over it. Preheat your oven to 488°F. Place the cooked ham in an oven pan and cook for 10 minutes. Remove the ham and shred on a platter. Serve and enjoy immediately!

133. SWEET PAPRIKA WITH ZUCCHINI PROSCIUTTO

Cal.: 200 | Fat: 3g | Protein: 10g   9 min | 32 min | Servings 4

INGREDIENTS

- 1 teaspoon sweet paprika
- ½ teaspoon rosemary, dried
- 2 zucchinis, cubed
- Salt and black pepper to the taste
- 4 prosciutto slices, chopped
- 8 eggs, whisked
- ¼ cup chives, chopped

DIRECTIONS

Prepare your sous-vide water bath to a temperature of 170°F/76°C. Put the eggs in a cooking pouch together with the other listed ingredients and shake to mix. Vacuum seal the pouch and immerse it into the preheated water bath. Cook for 30 minutes. Remove the pouch from the water bath once cooked and transfer the contents to a platter. Serve and enjoy!

134. FRESH VEGETABLES CONFIT

Cal.: 387 | Fat: 31g | Protein: 19g   8 min | 2 hours | Servings 10

INGREDIENTS

- 1 cup peeled pearl onions
- 1 cup peeled garlic cloves
- 6 cups olive oil
- 2 cups halved, deseeded mini peppers

Garnish:

- 10 to 12 ounces spreadable goat cheese
- Ciabatta bread slices, as required, toasted
- Salt to taste
- Fresh herbs of your choice

DIRECTIONS

Preheat the Sous Vide machine to 185°F/85°C. Place garlic in a Ziploc bag or vacuum-seal pouch. Pour 1½ cups oil into the pouch. Add mini peppers into a second Ziploc bag. Pour 3 cups of oil into the pouch. Add pearl onions into a third Ziploc bag. Pour 1½ cups oil into the pouch. Vacuum seal the pouches. Immerse the pouches in a water bath and adjust the timer for 1½ hours. When the timer goes off, remove the pouches from the water bath and place in chilled water for 30 minutes. Spread goat cheese over toasted ciabatta slices. Top with vegetables from each pouch. Garnish with fresh herbs and serve.

CHAPTER 4:
Lunch Recipes

Preparation Time | Cooking Time | Servings

135. MIXED VEGETABLES

Cal.: 244 | Fat: 13.2g | Protein: 3.5g   15 min | 3 hours | Servings 4

INGREDIENTS

- 1 potato, peeled and diced
- 1 butternut squash, peeled and diced
- ½ cauliflower head, diced into florets
- 6 carrots, peeled and diced
- 1 parsnip, peeled and diced
- ½ red onion, peeled and diced
- 4 garlic cloves, crushed
- 4 sprigs of fresh rosemary
- 2 tablespoons olive oil
- Salt and black pepper, to taste
- 2 tablespoons butter

DIRECTIONS

Prepare and preheat the water bath at 185°F/85°C. Add vegetables and all the ingredients to a zipper-lock bag. Seal the zipper-lock bag using the water immersion method. Place the sealed bag in the bath and cook for 3 hours. Once done, transfer the vegetables along with the sauce to a plate. Serve.

136. BUTTERY MAPLE CARROTS

Cal.: 89 | Fat: 7.7g | Protein: 0.1g   15 min | 2 hours | Servings 6

INGREDIENTS

- 6 baby carrots
- 2 tablespoons maple syrup
- Salt, to taste
- Black pepper, to taste
- 4 tablespoons butter, melted

DIRECTIONS

Prepare and preheat the water bath at 180°F/82°C. Add carrots and all the ingredients to a zipper-lock bag. Seal the zipper-lock bag using the water immersion method. Place the sealed bag in the bath and cook for 2 hours. Once done, transfer the carrots along with the sauce to a plate. Serve.

137. BACON ASPARAGUS

Cal.: 190 | Fat: 8.1g | Protein: 8.6g   15 min | 45 min | Servings 2

INGREDIENTS

- ½ lb. asparagus, chopped
- Salt, to taste
- Black pepper, to taste
- 2 bacon slices, cooked and chopped
- 2 tablespoons honey
- 1 teaspoon lemon juice

DIRECTIONS

Prepare and preheat the water bath at 190°F/88°C. Add asparagus and all the ingredients to a zipper-lock bag. Seal the zipper-lock bag using the water immersion method. Place the sealed bag in the bath and cook for 45 minutes. Once done, transfer the asparagus to a plate. Serve.

138. BUTTER-GLAZED SWEET POTATOES

Cal.: 198 | Fat: 9.5g | Protein: 1.7g   10 min | 60 min | Servings 4

INGREDIENTS

- 1 lb. sweet potatoes, peeled and halved
- 2 tablespoons butter
- 1 tablespoon olive oil
- 1 tablespoon fresh thyme, minced
- 2 teaspoons salt
- 1 teaspoon black pepper

DIRECTIONS

Prepare and preheat the water bath at 190°F/88°C. Add potatoes and all the ingredients to a zipper-lock bag. Seal the zipper-lock bag using the water immersion method. Place the sealed bag in the bath and cook for 1 hour. Once done, transfer the potatoes along with the sauce to a plate. Serve.

139. FINGERLING POTATOES WITH ROSEMARY

Cal.: 85 | Fat: 2.7g | Protein: 1.8g   10 min | 2 hours | Servings 12

INGREDIENTS

- 2 tablespoons olive oil
- 4 garlic cloves, peeled
- 1 sprig fresh rosemary, chopped
- 12 fingerling potatoes, washed
- Salt, to taste
- Black pepper, to taste

DIRECTIONS

Prepare and preheat the water bath at 194°F/90°C. Add potatoes and all the ingredients to a zipper-lock bag. Seal the zipper-lock bag using the water immersion method. Place the sealed bag in the bath and cook for 2 hours. Once done, transfer the potatoes along with the sauce to a plate. Serve.

140. SESAME EGGPLANT

Cal.: 200 | Fat: 7.2g | Protein: 4.5g   20 min | 3 hours 5 min | Servings 2

INGREDIENTS

- 1 eggplant, cut into ½-inch slices
- 1/4 cup Worcestershire sauce
- 2 tablespoons red wine
- 1 tablespoon soy sauce
- 1 tablespoon sugar
- 1 teaspoon sesame oil
- Salt, to taste
- 2 tablespoons sesame seeds, toasted
- 2 tablespoons scallions, sliced

DIRECTIONS

Prepare and preheat the water bath at 185°F/85°C. Add sliced eggplant to a zipper-lock bag. Seal the zipper-lock bag using the water immersion method. Place the sealed bag in the bath and cook for 3 hours. Once done, transfer the eggplant to a plate. Mix the remaining sauce ingredients, except sesame seeds in a bowl and pour over the eggplant. Spread the eggplant in a baking tray and broil for 5 minutes. Garnish with sesame seeds. Serve.

141. MAPLE BUTTERNUT SQUASH

Cal.: 160 | Fat: 8.1g | Protein: 6.5g   20 min | 1 hour | Servings 2

INGREDIENTS

- 1 butternut squash, peeled and diced
- 1 tablespoon maple syrup
- 1 teaspoon fresh thyme, chopped
- ½ teaspoon garlic powder
- 1 tablespoon pancetta, chopped
- Salt and black pepper, to taste
- 2 tablespoons pumpkin seeds, toasted, to garnish

DIRECTIONS

Prepare and preheat the water bath at 172°F/78°C. Add butternut squash and all the ingredients to a zipper-lock bag. Seal the zipper-lock bag using the water immersion method. Place the sealed bag in the bath and cook for 1 hour. Once done, transfer the squash along with the sauce to a plate. Serve.

142. ZUCCHINI MEDALLIONS

Cal.: 133 | Fat: 11.9g | Protein: 2.5g   15 min | 30 min | Servings 2

INGREDIENTS

- 2 zucchinis, sliced
- 2 tablespoons butter
- Salt and black pepper, to taste

DIRECTIONS

Prepare and preheat the water bath at 185°F/85°C. Add zucchini and all the ingredients to a zipper-lock bag. Seal the zipper-lock bag using the water immersion method. Place the sealed bag in the bath and cook for 30 minutes. Once done, transfer the zucchini along with the sauce to a plate. Serve.

143. GARLICKY RATATOUILLE

Cal.: 264 | Fat: 18.6g | Protein: 5.3g   15 min | 2 hours | Servings 4

INGREDIENTS

- 2 teaspoons red pepper flakes
- 1 yellow bell pepper, cored and sliced
- 1 eggplant, sliced
- 1 red bell pepper, cored and sliced
- 3 zucchinis, sliced
- 1 onion, peeled and sliced
- ½ cup tomato purée
- Salt, to taste
- 10 garlic cloves, peeled and minced
- 5 tablespoons avocado oil
- 5 sprigs fresh basil, chopped

DIRECTIONS

Prepare and preheat the water bath at 185°F/85°C. Add veggies and all the ingredients to a zipper-lock bag. Seal the zipper-lock bag using the water immersion method. Place the sealed bag in the bath and cook for 2 hours. Once done, transfer the veggies along with the sauce to a plate. Serve.

144. BACON-BRUSSELS SPROUTS

Cal.: 259 | Fat: 16.3g | Protein: 18.1g   15 min | 60 min | Servings 2

INGREDIENTS

- 4 slices bacon, cooked
- 2 garlic cloves
- ½ lb. Brussels sprouts

DIRECTIONS

Prepare and preheat the water bath at 172°F/78°C. Add Brussels sprouts and all the ingredients to a zipper-lock bag. Seal the zipper-lock bag using the water immersion method. Place the sealed bag in the bath and cook for 1 hour. Once done, transfer the Brussels sprouts mixture to a plate. Serve.

145. CIDER DIPPED FENNEL

Cal.: 67 | Fat: 0.4g | Protein: 2.2g   15 min | 60 min | Servings 2

INGREDIENTS

- ½ lb. fennel bulbs, chopped
- Salt, to taste
- 2 tablespoons apple cider vinegar
- Black pepper, to taste

DIRECTIONS

Prepare and preheat the water bath at 190°F/88°C. Add fennel and all the ingredients to a zipper-lock bag. Seal the zipper-lock bag using the water immersion method. Place the sealed bag in the bath and cook for 1 hour. Once done, transfer the fennel along with the sauce to a plate. Serve.

146. GARLIC BROCCOLI

Cal.: 240 | Fat: 25.5g | Protein: 1.6g

 15 min | 20 min | Servings 2

INGREDIENTS

- 1 broccoli head, cut into florets
- 3 garlic cloves, peeled
- 1/4 cup olive oil
- 1 teaspoon dried rosemary
- Salt, to taste
- Black pepper, to taste

DIRECTIONS

Prepare and preheat the water bath at 194°F/90°C. Add broccoli and all the ingredients to a zipper-lock bag. Seal the zipper-lock bag using the water immersion method. Place the sealed bag in the bath and cook for 20 minutes. Once done, transfer the broccoli along with the sauce to a plate. Serve.

147. ALLSPICE POACHED PEAR

Cal.: 245 | Fat: 1.1g | Protein: 1.1g

 15 min | 30 min | Servings 2

INGREDIENTS

- 4 oz. red wine
- 10 oz. Sugar
- 3/4 oz. cinnamon stick, whole
- 1/4 oz. nutmeg, ground
- 1/6 oz. mace, whole
- 1/4 oz. clove
- 1/6 oz. allspice, whole
- 8 pears

DIRECTIONS

Prepare and preheat the water bath at 176°F/80°C. Add pears and all the ingredients to a zipper-lock bag. Seal the zipper-lock bag using the water immersion method. Place the sealed bag in the bath and cook for 30 minutes. Once done, transfer the pears to a plate and slice them. Strain the remaining sauce and pour over the pears. Serve.

148. VANILLA PEARS

Cal.: 160 | Fat: 0.2g | Protein: 0.5g

 15 min | 30 min | Servings 2

INGREDIENTS

- 2 Comice pears
- 1/4 cup sugar syrup
- 1 vanilla pod, cracked

DIRECTIONS

Prepare and preheat the water bath at 170°F/76°C. Add pears and all the ingredients to a zipper-lock bag. Seal the zipper-lock bag using the water immersion method. Place the sealed bag in the bath and cook for 30 minutes. Once done, transfer the pears to a plate and slice them. Strain the remaining sauce and pour over the pears. Serve.

149. JUICY RASPBERRIES

Cal.: 75 | Fat: 0.5g | Protein: 0.8g

 15 min | 2 hours | Servings 4

INGREDIENTS

- 2 cups fresh raspberries
- 2 tablespoons elderflower cordial
- 1 tablespoon apple juice
- 1 teaspoon cornstarch

DIRECTIONS

Prepare and preheat the water bath at 150°F/65°C. Add raspberries and all the ingredients to a zipper-lock bag. Seal the zipper-lock bag using the water immersion method. Place the sealed bag in the bath and cook for 2 hours. Once done, transfer the raspberries to a plate and slice them. Serve.

150. STRAWBERRIES WITH BALSAMIC VINEGAR

Cal.: 72 | Fat: 0.4g | Protein: 1g   15 min | 2 hours | Servings 4

INGREDIENTS
- 2 cups strawberries, quartered
- 2 tablespoons balsamic vinegar
- 1 tablespoon sugar

DIRECTIONS
Prepare and preheat the water bath at 158°F/69°C. Add strawberries and all the ingredients to a zipper-lock bag. Seal the zipper-lock bag using the water immersion method. Place the sealed bag in the bath and cook for 2 hours. Once done, transfer the strawberries to a plate. Serve.

151. PINEAPPLE IN MALIBU

Cal.: 110 | Fat: 0.1g | Protein: 0.5g   15 min | 2 hours | Servings 4

INGREDIENTS
- 1 pineapple, peeled and sliced
- 4 tablespoons of Malibu
- 1 teaspoon coriander seeds, toasted
- 1/4 cup brown sugar

DIRECTIONS
Prepare and preheat the water bath at 185°F/85°C. Add pineapple and all the ingredients to a zipper-lock bag. Seal the zipper-lock bag using the water immersion method. Place the sealed bag in the bath and cook for 2 hours. Once done, transfer the pineapple to a plate. Serve.

152. SWEET PLUMS

Cal.: 69 | Fat: 0.2g | Protein: 0.7g   20 min | 60 min | Servings 6

INGREDIENTS
- 6 red plums, halved and deseeded
- 2 tablespoons Tamarind liquid
- 1/4 teaspoon Chinese five spices
- 2 tablespoons sugar
- 1 tablespoon honey
- Zest of ½ orange

DIRECTIONS
Prepare and preheat the water bath at 154°F/67°C. Add plums and all the ingredients to a zipper-lock bag. Seal the zipper-lock bag using the water immersion method. Place the sealed bag in the bath and cook for 1 hour. Once done, transfer the plums to a plate. Serve.

153. STRAWBERRY WATERMELON

Cal.: 33 | Fat: 0.1g | Protein: 0.2g   15 min | 30 min | Servings 1

INGREDIENTS
- 1/4 cup strawberry vodka
- 1/4 watermelon, peeled and cubed

DIRECTIONS
Prepare and preheat the water bath at 185°F/85°C. Add watermelon and vodka to a zipper-lock bag. Seal the zipper-lock bag using the water immersion method. Place the sealed bag in the bath and cook for 30 minutes. Once done, transfer the watermelon to a plate. Serve.

154. GLAZED BABY CARROTS

Cal.: 68 | Fat: 3.9g | Protein: 0.5g   10 min | 10 min | Servings 6

INGREDIENTS
- 1 pound baby whole baby carrots
- 2 tablespoons unsalted butter
- 1 tablespoon granulated sugar
- Salt
- Freshly ground black pepper

DIRECTIONS
Set your immersion circulator to 183°F/83.8°C. In a vacuum-sealed bag, combine the carrots, butter, sugar and ½ teaspoon salt and seal. Immerse the bag in the water bath for one hour. When the carrots are almost finished, heat a pan over high heat. Empty the carrots into the pan and cook until the liquid from the bag thickens and becomes a glaze.

155. SAFFRON CLEMENTINE

Cal.: 300 | Fat: 12.5g | Protein: 4g

 20 min | 6 hours | Servings 8

INGREDIENTS

- 4 whole clementines, peeled
- 3/4 cup honey
- 1/4 teaspoon allspice, ground
- 2 crushed cardamom seeds
- 1 pinch saffron
- Zest of 2 clementines
- 2 bay leaves
- ½ cinnamon stick
- 1 cup brown sugar
- 2 cups double cream
- 2 ½ cups milk
- 1/4 teaspoon ground nutmeg
- ½ cup sugar

DIRECTIONS

Prepare and preheat the water bath at 185°F/85°C. Add clementines and all the ingredients to a zipper-lock bag. Seal the zipper-lock bag using the water immersion method. Place the sealed bag in the bath and cook for 6 hours. Once done, transfer the clementines to a plate and cut them in half. Strain the remaining liquid and pour it over the clementines. Serve.

156. AGNOLOTTI WITH ARTICHOKE SAUCE

Cal.: 525 | Fat: 27.6g | Protein: 475g

 15 min | 30 min | Servings 4

INGREDIENTS

Sauce:
- 1 (9-ounce) package frozen artichoke hearts, thawed and coarsely chopped
- 1 cup frozen peas (do not thaw)
- 1 cup half-and-half
- 1 garlic clove, smashed
- 1/8 teaspoon red pepper flakes
- 1 teaspoon finely grated lemon zest
- 2 teaspoons fresh lemon juice
- Salt

Pasta:
- 1 pound refrigerated cheese Agnolotti (or ravioli)
- 1 cup grated parmesan cheese
- 1/4 cup fresh basil leaves, chopped

DIRECTIONS

Sauce
Combine the artichokes, half-and-half, garlic, red pepper flakes and 1/4 teaspoon salt in a vacuum-sealed bag. Set your immersion circulator to 165°F/73.8°and put the bag in the water bath for 30 minutes

Pasta
While the sauce is cooking, bring a pot of water to a boil and add the agnolotti. Drain the pasta, but retain ½ of the pasta water. Heat a pan over medium heat, and when the sauce is finished in the immersion circulator, remove the bag from the water and pour the contents into the skillet. Add the pasta and ½ cup pasta water and stir to coat. Then add the parmesan cheese and stir. Serve topped with the chopped basil.

157. FRITTATA WITH ASPARAGUS

Cal.: 383 | Fat: 31g | Protein: 23g | 10 min | 1 hour | Servings 3

INGREDIENTS

- 6 large eggs
- 2 tablespoons whipping cream
- 1/4 teaspoon freshly ground black pepper
- 1 tablespoon olive oil
- 1 tablespoon butter
- 12 ounces asparagus, trimmed, cut into 1/4 to ½-inch pieces
- 1 tomato, seeded, diced
- 2 teaspoons salt
- 3 ounces fontina, diced

DIRECTIONS

Heat your immersion circulator to 176°F/80°C. While the water is coming up to temperature, heat a pan over medium heat adding the olive oil. When oil is hot, add the asparagus, salt, pepper and tomato. Sauté until the asparagus is tender and remove from heat. Beat the eggs and pour into a vacuum-sealed bag. Add the contents of the pan along with the butter and diced fontina. Immerse the bag into the water and try to keep it flat on the bottom of the container. Cook for 1 hour, and remove from the water bath. Cut the bag open and serve.

158. CURRIED POTATOES AND CHICKPEAS

Cal.: 322 | Fat: 7.9g | Protein: 13.3g | 20 min | 2 hours | Servings 8

INGREDIENTS

- 1 ½ pounds Yukon gold potatoes, peeled and cut into 3/4-inch chunks
- 3 tablespoons unsalted butter
- 1 ½ teaspoons curry powder
- 1/4 teaspoon cayenne pepper
- 1 (15-ounce) can chickpeas, drained and rinsed
- 2 cups fried onions
- ½ cup plain Greek yogurt
- 1/4 cup chopped fresh cilantro, plus leaves for topping
- 2 tablespoons fresh lime juice
- 1 jalapeno pepper, thinly sliced
- Salt

DIRECTIONS

Set your immersion circulator to 200°F/93.3°while the water is heating, heat 2 tablespoons of butter in a saucepan and fry the onions. Add the cut potatoes, curry powder, cayenne pepper, chickpeas and onions to a vacuum-sealed bag. Immerse the bag in the water bath and cook for at least 2 hours and not more than 4. In a small bowl, combine the yogurt, cilantro and lime juice. Remove the bag from the water bath and divide among small bowls. Top with the yogurt sauce and sliced jalapenos to serve.

159. SPICY BUTTER POACHED ASPARAGUS

Cal.: 78 | Fat: 9g | Protein: 0.2g | 10 min | 12 min | Servings 4

INGREDIENTS

- 1 bunch of asparagus, trimmed
- 3 tablespoons unsalted butter
- ½ teaspoon cayenne pepper
- Pinch of salt

DIRECTIONS

Set your immersion circulator for 185°F/85°C. Trim the bottoms of the asparagus and place them flat in a vacuum-sealed bag. Melt the butter and add the cayenne pepper. Drizzle the spiced butter over the asparagus and use a vacuum sealer to seal the bag. When the water bath has reached the proper temperature, place the bag in the water and cook for 10 to 12 minutes. Remove the bag from the water and sprinkle a pinch of salt on the asparagus before serving.

160. SUMMER SALSA

Cal.:155 | Fat: 0.6g | Protein: 5.6g   10 min | 30 min | Servings 10

INGREDIENTS

- 2 cans of sweet corn (yellow or white)
- 1 can of black beans
- ½ red onion, chopped
- 1 red bell pepper, chopped
- ½ cup sugar
- ½ cup rice wine vinegar (red wine or champagne vinegar will also work)
- Salt

DIRECTIONS

Set your immersion circulator to 125°F/51.6°and combine all the ingredients in a vacuum-sealed bag. Seal the bag and immerse in the water bath for 30 minutes. Remove the bag from water and chill in the refrigerator for 1 hour before serving.

161. BALSAMIC BEETS

Cal.: 74 | Fat: 4.8g | Protein: 0.8g   10 min | 2 hours | Servings 6

INGREDIENTS

- 6 medium beets (2 bunches, or about 3-½ pounds)
- 1 teaspoon salt
- 2 tablespoons extra virgin olive oil
- 1/3 cup inexpensive balsamic vinegar
- 1 tablespoon maple syrup
- Freshly ground black pepper, to taste

DIRECTIONS

Set your immersion circulator to 185°F/85°. Place the chopped beets, olive oil, salt and 2 tablespoons of balsamic vinegar into a vacuum-sealed bag. Immerse the bag in the water bath and cook for 2 hours. While the beets are cooking, combine the remaining balsamic vinegar and maple syrup in a small saucepan. Heat on medium until the mixture has reduced slightly, making sure not to burn the vinegar. Remove the beets from the water bath and transfer to a medium bowl. Pour balsamic reduction over the beets and stir to coat.

162. ROOT VEGETABLES

Cal.: 114 | Fat: 8.9g | Protein: 0.9g   30 min | 3 hours | Servings 6

INGREDIENTS

- 1 turnip, peeled and cut into pieces
- 8 baby carrots, peeled and cut into pieces
- 1 medium parsnip, peeled and cut into pieces
- ½ medium red onion, peeled and cut into pieces
- 4 garlic cloves, crushed
- 4 sprigs of fresh rosemary, on the stem
- 2 tablespoons extra-virgin olive oil
- 2 tablespoons butter
- Salt and freshly ground pepper

DIRECTIONS

Set your immersion circulator to 185°F/85°C. Combine all ingredients in a large vacuum-sealed bag. Immerse the bag in the water bath and cook for 3 hours. Remove the bag from the water bath and strain out the cooking liquid. Heat a saucepan over medium heat and add the cooking liquid, reducing until it slightly thickens. Pour the liquid over the vegetables to serve.

163. BOURBON CHICKEN

Cal.: 566 | Fat: 23.9g | Protein: 67.2g   ⬥ 20 min | 🍲 1 hour 10 min | ✖ Servings 4

INGREDIENTS

- 2 pounds boneless chicken breasts, cut into bite-size pieces
- 2 tablespoons olive oil
- 1 garlic clove, crushed
- 1/4 teaspoon ginger
- 3/4 teaspoons crushed red pepper flakes
- 1/4 cup apple juice
- 1/3 cup light brown sugar
- 2 tablespoons ketchup
- 1 tablespoon cider vinegar
- ½ cup water
- 1/3 cup soy sauce

DIRECTIONS

Set your immersion circulator to 150°F/65.5°C. In a medium pan, heat the oil until hot but not smoking. Add the chicken and cook just until lightly browned. Remove chicken from heat. Add the remaining ingredients and chicken to a vacuum-sealed bag. Place the bag into the water bath and cook for one hour. This will give the ingredients time to combine into a flavorful sauce and finish cooking the chicken. Remove the bag from the water bath and serve with steamed white or brown rice, or your choice of vegetables that can be cooked in a separate bag at the same time.

164. BARBECUE CHICKEN

Cal.: 123 | Fat: 4.8g | Protein: 18.1g   ⬥ 10 min | 🍲 60 min | ✖ Servings 4

INGREDIENTS

- 1 ½ pounds Yukon gold potatoes, peeled and cut into 3/4-inch chunks
- 3 tablespoons unsalted butter
- 1 ½ teaspoons curry powder
- 1/4 teaspoon cayenne pepper
- 1 (15-ounce) can chickpeas, drained and rinsed
- 2 cups fried onions
- ½ cup plain Greek yogurt
- 1/4 cup chopped fresh cilantro, plus leaves for topping
- 2 tablespoons fresh lime juice
- 1 jalapeno pepper, thinly sliced
- Salt

DIRECTIONS

Set your immersion circulator for 141°F/60°C. Season the chicken with salt and pepper and place them in a vacuum-sealed bag. Add the rosemary and thyme to the bag and seal. Place the bag in the water bath and cook for at least 1 ½ hours and not more than 2 ½. When the chicken is almost finished cooking, heat either your grill or broiler too high. Remove the chicken from the bag and pat dry with paper towels. Slather with BBQ sauce and place them on the grill or under the broiler for just long enough to char the sauce. Serve immediately.

165. CURRIED ACORN SQUASH

Cal.: 99 | Fat: 1.2g | Protein: 6.1g   ⬥ 30 min | 🍲 2 hours | ✖ Servings 4

INGREDIENTS

- 1 acorn squash, seeded and cut into wedges
- 2 tbsp. butter
- 1 tbsp. curry powder or garam masala
- ¼ tsp. salt

DIRECTIONS

Preheat the water bath to 185°F/85°C. Combine squash, butter, spice mix, and salt in a bag. Seal and place in a water bath. Cook for 1½ to 2 hours.

166. TEQUILA LIME CHICKEN

Cal.:131 | Fat: 3.4g | Protein: 12.8g   20 min | 1 hour | Servings 4

INGREDIENTS

- 3 tablespoons olive oil
- 3 tablespoons tequila
- 1 tablespoon lime zest, from about 2 limes
- 4 garlic cloves, minced
- 1 1/4 teaspoons ancho chili powder
- ½ teaspoon ground coriander
- 1/4 teaspoon dried oregano
- 1 1/4 teaspoons salt
- ½ teaspoon freshly ground black pepper
- 2 teaspoons honey
- 4 boneless skinless chicken breasts
- 1 lime, sliced into wedges, for serving

DIRECTIONS

Set your immersion circulator for 150°F/65.5°C. Season the chicken with salt and pepper and set aside. Combine all of the other ingredients in a bowl and stir. Place the chicken breasts in a vacuum-sealed bag, add 2/3 of the seasoning mixture, and seal. The vacuum-sealed bag will marinate the meat as it cooks. Place in the water bath and cook for at least 1 hour and not more than 2. When you are almost finished cooking, heat your broiler to high. Remove the chicken from the bag and pat dry with paper towels. Place on a baking sheet and baste with the remaining seasoning mixture. Cook under the broiler for just long enough for the chicken to char. Flip the chicken over and char that side. Serve immediately. This dish goes well with a fresh corn salad.

167. MID-WEEK CHICKEN

Cal.: 146 | Fat: 6g | Protein: 16g   11min | 30 min | Servings 4

INGREDIENTS

- 4 (6-ounce) skinless, boneless chicken breasts
- Salt and freshly ground black pepper, to taste
- 3 tbsp. butter
- 1 sliced crosswise large leek
- ½ cup panko breadcrumbs
- 1-ounce shredded sharp cheddar cheese
- 2 tbsp. chopped fresh parsley
- 1 tbsp. olive oil

DIRECTIONS

Fill and preheat the bath to 145°F/63°C. Season the chicken breasts with salt and pepper evenly. In a cooking pouch, place the chicken breasts. Seal the pouch tightly after squeezing out the excess air. Place the pouch in the bath and cook for about 45 minutes. Meanwhile, in a skillet, melt 2 tbsp. of butter on medium heat. Stir in leeks, salt and black pepper. Reduce heat to low and cook for about 10 minutes. Remove from the heat and keep aside. In a frying pan, melt the remaining butter on medium heat. Add the panko and toast till golden, stirring continuously. Transfer the toasted panko in a bowl with cheddar and parsley and toss to coat well. Remove the pouch from the bath. Remove the chicken breasts from the pouch and discard the cooking liquid. With paper towels, gently pat dry the chicken breasts. In a skillet, heat olive oil on high heat and sear the chicken breasts for about 1 minute per side. Divide the cooked leek into serving plates and top each with 1 chicken breast. Sprinkle with toasted panko mixture and serve immediately.

168. WHISKEY INFUSED APPLES

Cal.: 99 | Fat: 0.2g | Protein: 0.5g   11 min | 60 min | Servings 4

INGREDIENTS

- 4 Gala apples
- 2 tablespoons brown sugar
- 2 tablespoons maple whiskey

DIRECTIONS

Preheat the Sous Vide machine to 175°F/79°C. Peel, core, and slice apples. Place the apple slices, sugar, and whiskey into a bag. Vacuum seal and immerse in water. Cook for 1 hour.

169. SPECIAL DINNER CHICKEN

Cal.: 568 | Fat: 36.1g | Protein: 57g   ⟍ 8 min | 🍲 46 min | ✗ Servings 2

INGREDIENTS

- 1 (12-ounce) butterflied skinless, boneless chicken breast
- ¼ cup prepared pesto
- 4 mozzarella cheese slice
- 1 tbsp. extra-virgin olive oil

DIRECTIONS

Fill and preheat the bath to 140°F/60°C. With a meat mallet, flatten the chicken breast into ¼-1/3-inch thickness. Spread the pesto across the breast evenly and top with the mozzarella slices. Tightly roll the chicken breast in a cylinder. In a cooking pouch, place the chicken roll. Seal the pouch tightly after squeezing out the excess air. Place the pouch in the bath and cook for about 1¼ hours. Remove the pouch from the bath. Remove the roll from the pouch and discard the cooking liquid. With paper towels gently pat dry the chicken roll. In a medium skillet, heat oil on high heat and sear the chicken roll till golden brown from both sides. With a sharp knife, cut the roll into desired slices and serve.

170. AMAZING CHICKEN

Cal.: 198 | Fat: 10.4g | Protein: 20.6g   ⟍ 15 min | 🍲 60 min | ✗ Servings 2

INGREDIENTS

- 2 (6-ounce) skinless, boneless chicken breasts
- Salt and freshly ground black pepper, to taste
- 2 thin prosciutto slices
- 1 tbsp. extra-virgin olive oil

DIRECTIONS

Fill and preheat the bath to 145°F/63°C. Cut each breast in half lengthwise and season with salt and pepper evenly. Arrange a plastic wrap onto a cutting board. Place 1 slice of prosciutto in the center of the plastic wrap. Place 2 chicken strips side-by-side in the center of the prosciutto to form an even rectangle. Roll prosciutto around the chicken to form a cylinder. Wrap tightly in the plastic wrap and with butcher's twine, tie off the ends. Repeat with remaining prosciutto and chicken. In a cooking pouch, place the chicken cylinders. Seal the pouch tightly after squeezing out the excess air. Place the pouch in the bath and cook for about 1 hour. Remove the pouch from the bath. Remove the chicken cylinders from the pouch and discard the cooking liquid. With paper towels, gently pat dry the chicken cylinders and season with salt and pepper. In a large non-stick skillet, heat the oil on medium-high heat and sear the chicken cylinders till golden brown from all sides. With a sharp knife, cut the roll into desired slices and serve.

171. FAVORITE THAI DINNER

Cal.: 477 | Fat: 32.8g | Protein: 24.9g   ⟍ 14 min | 🍲 76 min | ✗ Servings 2

INGREDIENTS

- 1 skinless, boneless chicken breast
- Salt and freshly ground black pepper, to taste
- 2 tbsp. vegetable oil
- ½ cup cashews
- 2 cut into 1-inch segments scallions
- 2 tbsp. sweet chili sauce
- 1 tbsp. hoisin sauce
- 1 tsp. light soy sauces
- 1 tsp. chopped fresh cilantro

DIRECTIONS

Fill and preheat the bath to 140°F/60°C. Season the chicken breast with salt and pepper slightly. In a cooking pouch, place the chicken breast. Seal the pouch tightly after squeezing out the excess air. Place the pouches in the bath and cook for about 1¼ hours. Remove the pouch from the bath. Remove the chicken breast from the pouch and discard the cooking liquid. Cut the chicken breast into bite-sized pieces. In a skillet, heat the oil on medium heat and stir fry the cashews and scallions for about 2 minutes. Stir in all sauces and chicken breast; and fry for about 1 minute. Serve hot with the garnishing of cilantro.

172. SUPER-FLAVORED CHICKEN

Cal.:495 | Fat: 29.3g | Protein: 23.8g   🔪 16 min | 🍲 85 min | 🍴 Servings 3

INGREDIENTS

- 2 skinless, boneless chicken thighs
- 1/3 cup olive oil, divided
- 4 minced garlic cloves
- 2 tsp. grated fresh ginger
- 1 cup chopped fresh pineapple
- ½ cup chopped Chinese cabbage
- 1 seeded and roughly chopped red bell pepper
- ½ of peeled and chopped carrot
- 1 roughly chopped small onion
- 1 tbsp. roughly chopped dried Thai chilies
- ¼ cup plus 1 tbsp. cornstarch, divided
- 1 cup cold water
- 2 tbsp. juice from canned tomatoes
- 2 tbsp. tomato paste
- 2 tbsp. light brown sugar
- 2 tbsp. apple cider vinegar
- 1 tbsp. light soy sauce
- 2 beaten large eggs
- 1 tsp. sesame seeds

DIRECTIONS

Fill and preheat the bath to 140°F/60°C. In a cooking pouch, place the chicken thighs and 1 tbsp. oil. Seal the pouch tightly after squeezing out the excess air. Place the pouches in the bath and cook for about 2 hours. Meanwhile in a large skillet, heat 1 tbsp. oil on medium-high heat and sauté the garlic and ginger for about 1 minute. Add pineapple, cabbage, bell pepper, carrot, onion and dried chilies and cook for about 5-10, stirring occasionally. Meanwhile, dissolve 1 tbsp. cornstarch in the cold water. In the skillet, add the cornstarch mixture, tomato juice, tomato paste, brown sugar, vinegar and soy sauce and stir to combine. Reduce the heat to low and cover to keep warm. Remove the pouch from the bath. Remove the chicken thighs from the pouch and discard the cooking liquid. Cut the chicken thighs into bite-sized pieces. Coat the chicken with the remaining ¼ cup of cornstarch and then with beaten eggs. In a large pan, heat the remaining ¼ cup of oil on medium-high heat and fry the chicken pieces for about 2–3 minutes or till golden and crisp. Transfer the chicken pieces onto a paper towel-lined plate to drain. Place the chicken pieces onto a serving platter and top with the sauce. Serve with a garnishing of sesame seeds.

173. FRENCH DUCK CONFIT

Cal.: 272 | Fat: 15.3g | Protein: 30g   🔪 20 min | 🍲 15 hours | 🍴 Servings 4

INGREDIENTS

- 16 oz. duck legs
- 1 teaspoon thyme
- 1 teaspoon coriander
- 1 teaspoon lime zest
- 2 tablespoon kaffir leaves
- 1 teaspoon palm sugar
- 1 teaspoon salt
- 1 tablespoon orange peel
- 1 teaspoon ground paprika
- 2 teaspoon sesame oil

DIRECTIONS

Wash the duck legs carefully and dry them with the help of the paper towel. After this, combine the thyme, coriander, palm sugar, salt and ground paprika together. Stir the spices gently with the help of the fork. After this, wash the kaffir leaves and place them in the blender. Add the kaffir leaves and orange peel. Blend the mixture until it is smooth. Transfer the dried duck legs in the plastic bag. Then add the mixed spices and blended lemon zest mixture. Close the plastic bag and shake it well. After this, seal the plastic bag. Set the water bath to 160°F/71°C and place the sealed plastic bag with the duck legs there. Cook the dish for 15 hours. After this time, you will get totally tender duck legs. When the time is over, transfer the duck legs in the serving plates or use one serving plate for everyone. Serve it!

174. JUICY ORANGE DUCK BREAST

Cal.: 155 | Fat: 4.2g | Protein: 18g

⬒ 18 min | 🍲 10 hours | ✗ Servings 6

INGREDIENTS

- 19 oz. duck breast, with skin
- 1 oz. fresh rosemary
- 1 teaspoon salt
- 1 teaspoon ground black pepper
- ½ cup orange juice
- 2 tablespoon honey
- 1 tablespoon ghee
- ½ teaspoon fennel seeds
- ¼ teaspoon ground cardamom

DIRECTIONS

Cut the duck breast into 2 parts. Then chop the fresh rosemary. Sprinkle the duck breasts with salt, ground black pepper and ground cardamom from each side. After this, sprinkle the duck breasts with fresh rosemary. Then rub the duck breasts with honey and put them in the plastic bags. Use 2 bags to make the taste of every part of the duck breast wonderful. Then add the orange juice. Seal the plastic bags and put them in the preheated to 158°F/69°C water batch. Cook the duck breasts for 10 hours. After this, open the plastic bags and discard the duck breast. Leave the orange juice sauce in the plastic bag. Toss the ghee into the saucepan and melt it. When the ghee starts to boil, add the duck breasts and roast them on high heat for 2 minutes from each side. After this, add the orange juice from the plastic bags. Then add the fennel seeds and reduce the heat to the medium level. Simmer the duck breast for 5 minutes with the closed lid. Then serve the duck breasts with a small amount of the orange juice sauce. Enjoy!

175. GROUND DUCK CUTLETS WITH BBQ SAUCE

Cal.: 152 | Fat: 10.8g | Protein: 11g

⬒ 25 min | 🍲 51 min | ✗ Servings 8

INGREDIENTS

- 1 egg
- 1-pound ground duck
- 2 tablespoon dried parsley
- 1 teaspoon salt
- 1 teaspoon ground black pepper
- ½ teaspoon turmeric
- 1 teaspoon tomato sauce
- 3 oz. BBQ sauce
- 1 tablespoon almond flour
- 1 teaspoon sesame seeds
- 1 teaspoon nutmeg
- 1 teaspoon sesame oil

DIRECTIONS

Crack the egg into the big mixing bowl. Whisk it with the help of the hand whisker. When you get the smooth egg mass, add the dried parsley, salt, ground black pepper, turmeric, almond flour and nutmeg. Whisk it gently. After this, add the ground duck and stir it carefully with the help of the spoon. After this, make the small round cutlets with the help of the fingertips. Then put every cutlet in the separated plastic bag and seal it. Preheat the water bath to 152°F/66°C and put the sealed plastic bags there. Cook the duck cutlets for 51 minutes. When the duck cutlets are cooked, remove them from the plastic bag. Preheat the skillet well and pour the sesame oil there. Preheat the sesame oil and then toss the duck cutlets there. Fry the duck cutlets for 1 minute from each side on high heat. Then dry the duck cutlets with the help of the paper towel and serve the dish with the BBQ sauce. Enjoy!

176. CAULIFLOWER ALFREDO

Cal.: 78 | Fat: 1.3g | Protein: 5.8g

⬒ 16 min | 🍲 2 hours | ✗ Servings 4

INGREDIENTS

- 2 cups (400g) chopped cauliflower florets
- 2 garlic cloves, crushed
- 2 tablespoons butter
- ½ cup double-strength chicken stock
- 2 tablespoons milk
- Salt and pepper

DIRECTIONS

Preheat the Sous Vide machine to 185°F/85°C). Place all your ingredients into a Ziploc or vacuum-seal bag. Squeeze out some air and then fold the edge of the bag over to seal. Place the bag into the prepared water bath and clip the edge to the container or pot. Cook for 2 hours. When ready, pour the contents of the bag into a food processor and blend until smooth and creamy.

177. CHOPPED DUCK WITH HONEY

Cal.:229 | Fat: 13.3g | Protein: 15g   18 min | 4 hours | Servings 6

INGREDIENTS
- 4 tablespoon liquid honey
- 1 teaspoon nutmeg
- 1 tablespoon ground paprika
- 18 oz. duck fillet
- 1 teaspoon ground cinnamon
- 1 teaspoon fresh dill

DIRECTIONS
Pour the liquid honey into the plastic bag. Add the nutmeg and ground paprika. Then add the ground cinnamon and fresh dill. Close the plastic bag and massage it to make the homogenous mixture. After this, chop the duck fillet and add it to the plastic bag too. Close the plastic bag again and massage it with the help of the fingers to make the homogenous meat mixture. Leave the chopped duck mixture for 10 minutes to marinate. After this, preheat the water bath to 147°F/64°C. Seal the plastic bag with the chopped duck and put it in the water bath. Cook the chopped duck for 4 hours. When the dish is cooked, transfer it directly to the serving plates. Enjoy the dish immediately!

178. BACON BRUSSELS SPROUTS

Cal.: 230 | Fat: 4g | Protein: 20.2g   20 min | 65 min | Servings 4

INGREDIENTS
- Brussels sprouts (1 lb., trimmed, halved)
- 2 tbsp. butter
- 2 ounces thick-cut bacon, fried and chopped
- 2 garlic cloves, minced
- ¼ tsp. salt
- ¼ tsp. pepper

DIRECTIONS
Preheat the water bath to 183°F/84°C. Combine all your ingredients in a large Ziploc bag. Seal and place in a water bath. Cook for 1 hour. Meanwhile, preheat the oven to 400°F/205°C. After 1 hour has passed, transfer Brussels sprouts onto a lined baking tray. Set to bake until nicely roasted (about 5 minutes). Enjoy!

179. INDIAN STYLE PORK

Cal.: 363 | Fat: 12.7g | Protein: 19.5g   15 min | 2 hours | Servings 4

INGREDIENTS
- 1.5lb. Pork tenderloin, sliced
- 2 cups yogurt
- 1 cup sour cream
- 2 tablespoons tandoori paste
- 1 tablespoon curry paste
- 1-inch ginger, minced
- 2 garlic cloves, minced
- Salt and pepper, to taste

DIRECTIONS
In a large bowl, combine yogurt, sour cream, tandoori paste, curry paste, garlic, and ginger. Add sliced pork. Cover and marinate for 20 minutes in a fridge. Preheat your cooker to 135°F/57°C. Remove the pork from the marinade and place into the bag. Vacuum seal the bag. Immerse pork in the water bath and cook for 2 hours. Remove the bag from water and open carefully. Heat 1 tablespoon olive oil in a large skillet. Sear the pork for 3 minutes per side. Serve warm.

180. GARLIC CONFIT

Cal.: 52 | Fat: 1.1g | Protein: 2.9g   11 min | 4 hours | Servings 8

INGREDIENTS
- Garlic (1 cup, cloves, peeled, minced)
- Olive oil (1/4 cup, extra virgin)
- Salt (1 tbsp.)

DIRECTIONS
Preheat the Sous Vide machine to 190°F/88°C. Add your ingredients to a vacuum seal bag. Seal and set to cook in your water bath for 4 hours. To finish, transfer to an airtight container and set to refrigerate for about a month.

181. SWEET POTATO SALAD

Cal.: 597 | Fat: 20.1g | Protein: 52.8g   ➘ 11 min | 🍲 4 hours | 🍴 Servings 4

INGREDIENTS

- 1 ½ lbs. sweet potatoes
- ½ cup chicken stock
- Salt and pepper to taste
- 4 oz. thick cut bacon, sliced
- ½ cup chopped onion
- 1/3 cup cider vinegar
- 4 scallions, thinly sliced

DIRECTIONS

Preheat the Sous Vide machine to 185°F/85°C. Cut potatoes into ¾-inch-thick cubes. Place potatoes and chicken stock in the Ziploc bag, making sure they are in a single layer; seal using the immersion water method. Place potatoes in a water bath and cook for 1 hour 30 minutes. Meanwhile, in the last 15 minutes, heat a non-stick skillet over medium heat. Once hot, add bacon, then allow to cook until the fat renders and the bacon gets crisp; set the bacon aside and add chopped onions to the remaining fat. Cook until softened for 5–7 minutes. Add vinegar and cook until reduced slightly. Remove potatoes from the water bath and place them in a skillet, with the cooking water. Continue cooking for a few minutes until the liquid thickens. Remove potatoes from the heat and stir in scallions; toss to combine. Serve while still hot.

182. CHICKEN MARSALA

Cal.: 365 | Fat: 1.3g | Protein: 23.2g   ➘ 11 min | 🍲 4 hours | 🍴 Servings 2

INGREDIENTS

- 2 boneless, skinless chicken breasts
- 1 teaspoon salt
- 1 teaspoon pepper
- 1 lb. fresh mushrooms, sliced
- 1 shallot or ½ small onion, diced
- 2 garlic cloves, minced
- 1 cup chicken stock
- 1 cup marsala wine
- ½ tablespoon flour
- 1 tablespoon butter
- Cooked pasta for serving

DIRECTIONS

Preheat the water bath to 140°F/60°C. Salt and pepper the chicken breasts. Place in a bag and add mushrooms. Cook for 2 hours. When chicken is almost cooked, prepare the sauce. Melt butter in a pan and cook garlic for 30 seconds. Add flour and cook until bubbling subsides, then pour in the stock and wine. Cook until sauce reduces by half. Season to taste. Remove the cooked chicken from the bag then slice and stir chicken and mushrooms into sauce.

183. WARM ASSORTED BROCCOLI SALAD

Cal.: 93 | Fat: 3.4g | Protein: 5.6g   ➘ 11 min | 🍲 47 min | 🍴 Servings 4

INGREDIENTS

- 3 heads broccoli, washed, chopped into florets
- 3 heads cauliflower, washed, chopped into florets
- ½ cup extra virgin olive oil, divided
- 20 cherry tomatoes, quartered
- 6 anchovy fillets, rinsed, cut into pieces
- Salt to taste
- Pepper powder to taste

DIRECTIONS

Fill and preheat the water bath to 183°F/84°C according to the operating instructions. Place the cauliflower and broccoli in a bowl. Sprinkle half the olive oil, salt and pepper. Toss well. Transfer into a Ziploc bag and vacuum-seal it. Immerse the bag in the water bath and cook for 45 minutes. Meanwhile, place the tomatoes in a bowl. Add olives and anchovies and set aside. When the vegetables are cooked, discard any liquid remaining in the pouch and transfer the vegetables into the bowl of anchovies. Sprinkle the remaining olive oil. Add some salt and pepper. Toss well and serve.

184. BEET SALAD

Cal.: 77 | Fat: 6.1g | Protein: 2.4g 🔪 9 min | 🍲 16 min | 🍴 Servings 4

INGREDIENTS

- Beets (2 large, sliced, peeled)
- Carrots (2 large, peeled, sliced)
- Onion (½, large, peeled, sliced)
- Potato (1 small, peeled and sliced)
- Red cabbage (¼ head, shredded)
- Stock (2 quarts)
- Dill (½ cup, chopped)
- Red wine vinegar (3 tbsp.)
- Salt and pepper to taste
- Sour cream, to serve
- Fresh dill, to serve

DIRECTIONS

Set your machine to 182°F/83°C. Put the beets, carrots, and onions into a vacuum-seal bag and remove all the air. Do the same with the cabbage in a separate pouch. Place the bags in the cooker for at least 1 hour. They can stay in for up to 2. Remove the vegetables. Leave the cabbage to the side. Bring the stock to the boil, adding the pureed vegetables, cabbage, dill, vinegar, salt and pepper. Let the soup simmer until you are ready to eat. Serve the soup with a spoonful of sour cream and some fresh dill.

185. PUMPKIN PURÉE

Cal.: 30 | Fat: 1.2g | Protein: 0.12g 🔪 11 min | 🍲 18 min | 🍴 Servings 3

INGREDIENTS

- 1 pumpkin, peeled and chopped
- 2 parsnips, peeled and chopped
- 1 large sweet potato, peeled and chopped
- 2 tbsp. butter
- ½ tsp. sage
- ¼ tsp. salt
- ¼ tsp. pepper

DIRECTIONS

Preheat the water bath to 185°F/85°C. Combine vegetables, butter, sage, salt and pepper in a bag. Seal and place in a water bath. Cook for 3 hours. Pour the contents of the bag into a pan. Reduce liquid to a syrup. Pour the vegetables into a bowl and mash thoroughly. Season to taste with additional salt, pepper, and butter if desired.

186. CAULIFLOWER PURÉE

Cal.: 60 | Fat: 0.9g | Protein: 5.6g 🔪 11 min | 🍲 16 min | 🍴 Servings 8

INGREDIENTS

- 3 heads cauliflower, chopped
- 2 tbsp. butter
- ½ tsp. oregano
- ¼ tsp. salt
- ¼ tsp. pepper

DIRECTIONS

Preheat the water bath to 185°F/85°C. Combine vegetables, butter, sage, salt, and pepper in a bag. Seal and place in a water bath. Cook for 3 hours. Pour the contents of the bag into a pan. Reduce liquid to a syrup. Pour the vegetables into a bowl and mash thoroughly. Season to taste with additional salt, pepper and butter if desired.

187. ASPARAGUS WITH HOLLANDAISE

Cal.: 347 | Fat: 5.5g | Protein: 34.9g 🔪 21 min | 🍲 30 min | 🍴 Servings 4

INGREDIENTS

- 1 bunch asparagus, trimmed
- Hollandaise

DIRECTIONS

Preheat the water bath to 145°F/63°C. Place bagged sauce in the bath. Set a timer for 30 minutes. When the timer has 12 minutes remaining, bag and seal asparagus. Place in a water bath and cook for the remaining 10–12 minutes. Remove cooked asparagus from the bath. Arrange on a plate. Blend sauce until smooth. Pour over asparagus.

188. FRENCH HERB OMELET

Cal.: 279 | Fat: 8.9g | Protein: 25.6g   9 min | 20 min | Servings 1

INGREDIENTS
- Eggs (3 large)
- Butter (1 tbsp., unsalted, melted)
- Chives (¼ tbsp., minced)
- Parsley (¼ tbsp., minced)
- Tarragon (¼ tbsp., minced)
- Rosemary (¼ tsp., minced)
- Greek yogurt (1 tbsp., plain)
- Salt (¼ tsp.)
- Pepper (¼ tsp.)

DIRECTIONS
Set your machine to preheat to 165°F/74°C. Add your eggs, herbs, yogurt and butter to a bowl, whisk to combine, then season to taste. Transfer the mixture to a vacuum seal bag and add to your water bath. Allow the eggs to cook for 10 minutes. Press your eggs gently into the shape of an omelet. Add the bag back into the water bath and continue to cook for another 10 minutes. Transfer to a serving plate and enjoy!

189. CORN ON THE COB

Cal.: 568 | Fat: 36.1g | Protein: 57g   9 min | 60 min | Servings 4

INGREDIENTS
- Corn (4 ears, shucked, washed)
- Salt, to taste
- Pepper, to taste
- Butter (4 tbsp.)
- Cilantro (1 handful, chopped)

DIRECTIONS
Set your machine to preheat with water to 182°F/83°C. Season your corn to taste then add it to your vacuum seal bag with cilantro and butter. Seal, and set to cook in your bath for about 40 minutes. Serve immediately.

190. SPICY GINGER TOFU

Cal.: 95 | Fat: 4.3g | Protein: 3.6g   12 min | 60 min | Servings 4

INGREDIENTS
- 1 lb. firm tofu, cut into 12 pieces
- ¼ cup soy sauce
- ¼ cup sugar
- 2 tablespoons mirin
- 2 tablespoons water
- 2 tablespoon crushed ginger
- 1 tablespoon crushed garlic
- 1 small red chili, thinly sliced

DIRECTIONS
Set your Sous Vide machine to 180°F/82°C. Shallow-fry the tofu pieces until the outsides are golden brown. Combine all other ingredients over medium heat until the sugar is dissolved. Place all ingredients into a Ziploc or vacuum-sealed bag and seal using the water displacement method or a vacuum-sealed.

191. BUTTER GARLIC ARTICHOKES

Cal.: 269 | Fat: 6.7g | Protein: 20.2g   31 min | 2 hours | Servings 4

INGREDIENTS
- Artichokes (4 whole, trimmed, halved)
- Butter (8 tbsp., unsalted)
- Garlic (8 cloves, peeled)
- Lemon zest (1 tbsp.)
- Salt
- Black pepper
- Lemon (wedges, to serve)

DIRECTIONS
Set your Sous Vide machine to 180°F/82°C. Fill each artichoke half with a garlic clove and a tablespoon of butter. Season to taste and sprinkle with lemon zest. Transfer to a vacuum-sealed bag and set to cook in your machine for 2 hrs. Remove from the bag, season to taste and enjoy!

192. CREAMY CAULIFLOWER SOUP

Cal.: 36 | Fat: 0.2g | Protein: 3.6g   16 min | 23 min | Servings 4

INGREDIENTS

- 1 large head cauliflower, break into florets
- 2 shallots, chopped
- 4 cups of vegetable stock
- ½ cup white wine
- ½ cup sour cream
- 1 ½ cups cream
- Juice of a lemon
- 1 teaspoon Ras el Hanout
- Zest of 2 lemons, grated
- A few slices of roasted caraway bread
- 1 teaspoon ground cumin
- Cooking spray
- 1 cup grated cauliflower to serve
- Extra virgin olive oil to serve

DIRECTIONS

Place a skillet over medium heat. Spray with cooking spray. Add shallot and sauté for a couple of minutes. Set your machine to 167°F/75°C. Place shallots, cauliflower, stock, wine, sour cream, cream and lemon juice into a Ziploc or a vacuum-sealed bag and remove all the air with the water displacement method or a vacuum-sealed. Seal and immerse the bag in the water bath. Meanwhile, mix together the grated cauliflower, Ras el Hanout and half of the lemon zest. Remove the pouch from the cooker and transfer into the blender and blend until smooth. Season with salt and pepper. Pulse a couple of times to mix well. Place the grated cauliflower mixture on bread slices. Drizzle some oil over it. Sprinkle salt, cumin and the remaining lemon zest. Ladle into individual soup bowls.

193. BUTTER-POACHED ASPARAGUS WITH FRESH MINT

Cal.: 150 | Fat: 5.7g | Protein: 11.8g   9 min | 13 min | Servings 2

INGREDIENTS

- White asparagus (1 bunch, trimmed)
- Butter (3 tbsp., unsalted, chopped)
- Salt
- Mint (julienned)

DIRECTIONS

Set your Sous Vide machine to preheat to 185°F/85°C. Add asparagus to your vacuum seal or Ziploc bag in a flat layer then top evenly with your remaining ingredients. Seal and set to cook for about 10 minutes. Carefully remove from bag and serve.

194. GREEN SESAME SALAD

Cal.: 115 | Fat: 8.3g | Protein: 5.8g   16 min | 23 min | Servings 4

INGREDIENTS

- 2 cups broccoli, snapped into small florets
- 1 cup green beans, topped and tailed
- 1 cup asparagus stems, cut in half
- 2 tablespoons soy sauce
- 1 teaspoon sesame oil
- 1 tablespoon vegetable oil
- 1 teaspoon fish sauce
- 1 handful sesame seeds
- ¼ cup scallions, finely chopped

DIRECTIONS

Set your machine to 180°F/82°C. Place the vegetables into a vacuum-seal bag and seal. Immerse the bag in the water bath and cook for 10 minutes, and up to 20 if you prefer a more tender texture. While vegetables are cooking, whisk together the soy sauce, sesame oil, vegetable oil and fish sauce in a small bowl. Put the vegetables into a large bowl and pour the dressing over, using your hands to mix everything through.

CHAPTER 5:
Dinner Recipes

🔪 Preparation Time | 🍲 Cooking Time | 🍴 Servings

195. TENDER PORK CHOPS

Cal.: 378 | Fat: 32g | Protein: 18g   ⟍ 5 min | 🍲 2 hours | 🍴 Servings 2

INGREDIENTS
- 2 pork chops
- 1 tbsp. canola oil
- 1 tbsp. butter
- 4 garlic cloves
- Rosemary
- Thyme
- Pepper
- Salt

DIRECTIONS
Preheat the Sous Vide machine to 140°F/60°C. Season the pork with pepper and salt. Place pork chops into the Ziploc bag. Remove all the air from the bag before sealing. Place the bag into the hot water bath and cook for 2 hours. Remove pork from the bag and pat dry with a paper towel. Heat oil and butter in a pan over high heat with rosemary, thyme, and garlic. Place pork chops in a pan, sear until lightly brown, about 1 minute on each side. Serve and enjoy!

196. PORK CHOPS WITH MUSHROOMS

Cal.: 392 | Fat: 31.8g | Protein: 21g   ⟍ 10 min | 🍲 2 hours 10 min | 🍴 Servings 4

INGREDIENTS
- 4 pork chops, boneless
- 4 tbsp. butter
- 2 garlic cloves, minced
- 1 tbsp. flour
- 1 cup chicken broth
- 8 oz. crimini mushrooms, sliced
- 1 large shallot, sliced
- Pepper
- Salt

DIRECTIONS
Preheat the Sous Vide machine to 140°F/60°C. Place the chops into a Ziploc bag. Place the bag into a water bath and cook for 2 hours. Remove the pork chops from the bag and pat dry with a paper towel. Season the chop with salt and pepper. Heat 2 tbsp. of butter in a pan. Sear the chops on both sides. Add remaining 2 tbsp. of butter in a pan. Add sliced mushrooms to the pan and cook for 4–5 minutes stirring occasionally. Add shallots, cook for 2 minutes until tender, add garlic and stir for 1 minute constantly, then add flour. Stir well until mixture is evenly coated over mushrooms, add chicken broth, stir for 1 minute. Season with salt and pepper. Serve and enjoy!

197. PORK TENDERLOIN

Cal.: 440 | Fat: 20.7g | Protein: 59.6g   ⟍ 10 min | 🍲 2 hours 10 min | 🍴 Servings 2

INGREDIENTS
- 16 oz. pork tenderloin
- 1 tbsp. olive oil
- 1 tbsp. butter
- 2 small shallots, sliced
- 2 garlic cloves
- 8 sprigs of fresh herbs
- Black pepper
- Kosher salt

DIRECTIONS
Preheat the Sous Vide machine to 150 °F/66°C. Season the pork with salt and pepper. Place the pork into a Ziploc bag. Remove all the air from the bag before sealing. Place the bag into the hot water bath and cook for 2 hours. Remove pork from the Ziploc bag and pat dry with a paper towel. Heat olive oil in a pan over medium heat. Add pork and cook for 2 minutes until lightly browned. Add butter with fresh thyme, shallots, and garlic. Cook for 1 minute. Serve and enjoy!

198. HERB RUB PORK CHOPS

Cal.: 383 | Fat: 33.1g | Protein: 18.6g   10 min | 2 hours 10 min | Servings 4

INGREDIENTS
- 4 pork chops, bone-in
- 1/4 cup olive oil
- 1 tsp. black pepper
- 1 tbsp. balsamic vinegar
- 1 lemon zest
- 2 garlic cloves, minced
- 6 thyme sprigs, remove stems
- 1/4 cup chives
- 1/4 cup rosemary
- 10 basil leaves
- 1/4 cup parsley
- ½ tsp. salt

DIRECTIONS
Preheat the Sous Vide machine to 140 F/ 60 C. Add herbs to the food processor and process until chopped. Add garlic, olive oil, pepper, salt, vinegar, and lemon zest and blend until a smooth paste. Rub herb mixture over pork chops. Place pork chops into the Ziploc bag and remove all the air from the bag before sealing. Place the bag into the hot water bath and cook for 2 hours. Remove pork chops from the water bath and boil for 3-4 minutes. Serve and enjoy!

199. BONE-IN PORK CHOP

Cal.: 276 | Fat: 22.2g | Protein: 18g   5 min | 2 hours 10 min | Servings 2

INGREDIENTS
- 2 pork chops, bone-in
- 1 tsp. olive oil
- 1/8 tsp. tarragon
- 1/8 tsp. thyme
- Black pepper
- Salt

DIRECTIONS
Preheat the Sous Vide machine to 145°F/62°C. Season pork chops with pepper and salt. Rub tarragon, olive oil and thyme over pork chops. Place pork chops into the Ziploc bag and remove all the air from the bag before sealing. Place the bag into the hot water bath and cook for 2 hours. Remove pork chops from the bag and sear until lightly brown. Serve and enjoy!

200. PORK LOIN

Cal.: 487 | Fat: 21.9g | Protein: 65.1g   5 min |  4 hours | Servings 4

INGREDIENTS
- 2 lbs. pork loin roast
- 2 tbsp. sweet and sour sauce
- 1 tsp. black pepper
- 1 tsp. garlic powder
- ½ tsp. chipotle powder
- 1 tsp. salt

DIRECTIONS
Preheat the Sous Vide machine to 153°F/67°C. In a small bowl, mix together chipotle powder, garlic powder, black pepper, and salt. Rub spice mixture over the pork loin roast. Place pork into the Ziploc bag and remove all the air from the bag before sealing. Place the bag into the hot water bath and cook for 4 hours. Remove pork from the bag and coat outside with sweet and sour sauce. Broil pork for 5 minutes until lightly brown. Serve and enjoy!

201. LEMON PORK CHOPS

Cal.: 286 | Fat: 23.4g | Protein: 18g   5 min | 6 hours | Servings 4

INGREDIENTS
- 4 pork chops, bone in
- 1 lemon, sliced
- 4 fresh thyme sprigs, chopped
- 1 tbsp. olive oil
- Pepper
- Salt

DIRECTIONS
Preheat the Sous Vide machine to 138°F/59°C. Season pork chops with pepper and salt. Place pork chops into the Ziploc bag with thyme and lemon slices. Drizzle with olive oil. Remove all air from the bag before sealing. Place the bag into the hot water bath and cook for 6 hours. Remove pork chops from the bag and pat dry with a paper towel. Using a kitchen torch, sear the pork chops until caramelizing. Serve and enjoy!

202. BBQ PORK RIBS

Cal.: 663 | Fat: 19g | Protein: 10g   5 min | 18 hours | Servings 2

INGREDIENTS
- 1 rack back ribs, cut into rib portions
- 2 tbsp. Worcestershire sauce
- 1/3 cup brown sugar
- 1 ½ cups BBQ sauce

DIRECTIONS
Preheat the Sous Vide machine to 160°F/75°C. Whisk brown sugar in 1 cup BBQ sauce and Worcestershire sauce. Place ribs into the large mixing bowl then pour marinade over ribs and toss well. Place ribs into the Ziploc bag and remove all the air from the bag before sealing. Place the bag into the hot water bath and cook for 18 hours. Remove ribs from the bag and place on a baking tray. Brush ribs with remaining BBQ sauce and broil for 5 minutes. Serve and enjoy!

203. FIVE SPICE PORK

Cal.: 549 | Fat: 32g | Protein: 54g   5 min | 48 hours | Servings 4

INGREDIENTS
- 1 lb. pork belly
- 1 bacon slice
- 1 tsp. Chinese 5 spice powder
- Black pepper
- Salt

DIRECTIONS
Preheat the Sous Vide machine to 140°F/60°C. Add pork belly into the Ziploc bag with bacon slice and seasoning. Remove all the air from the bag before sealing. Place the bag into the hot water bath and cook for 48 hours. Remove pork from bag and broil until crisp. Serve and enjoy!

204. BBQ BABY BACK RIBS

Cal.: 850 | Fat: 48g | Protein: 45g   5 min | 24 hours | Servings 2

INGREDIENTS
- 1 rack baby back pork ribs
- 6 tbsp. Chipotle BBQ sauce
- Pepper
- Salt

DIRECTIONS
Preheat the Sous Vide machine to 143 °F/ 61 °C. Cut the rib rack in half and season with pepper and salt. Brush BBQ sauce over the pork ribs. Place ribs into the Ziploc bag and remove all the air from the bag before sealing. Place the bag into the hot water bath and cook for 24 hours. Remove ribs from bag and grill for 1 minute. Serve and enjoy!

205. PORK CARNITAS

Cal.: 729 | Fat: 51g | Protein: 55g   10 min | 2 hours 10 min | Servings 12

INGREDIENTS

- 6 lb. pork shoulder
- 2 tbsp. anise
- 2 bay leaves
- 2 cinnamon sticks
- 3 tbsp. garlic, minced
- 4 bacon slices
- 1/3 cup brown sugar
- 2 orange juices
- 1 onion, chopped
- 1 tbsp. sea salt

DIRECTIONS

Preheat the Sous Vide machine to 175°F/79°C. In a small bowl, mix together anise, sugar, salt, garlic and orange juice. Place pork into the Ziploc bag then pours orange juice mixture over pork. Add cinnamon, bay leaves, bacon and onions into the bag. Seal the bag and place into the hot water bath and cook for 20 hours. Heat a large pan over medium-high heat. Remove pork from bag and place on pan and shred using a fork. Cook shredded pork until crispy. Serve and enjoy!

206. PULLED PORK

Cal.: 733 | Fat: 48g | Protein: 53g   10 min | 18 hours 35 min | Servings 4

INGREDIENTS

- 2 lb. pork shoulder, boneless
- ½ cup taco seasoning
- 1 onion, diced
- 1/4 cup cilantro, chopped

DIRECTIONS

Preheat the Sous Vide machine to 165°F/73°C. Season pork with half taco seasoning. Place pork into the Ziploc bag and remove all the air from the bag before sealing. Place the bag into the hot water bath and cook for 18 hours. Remove pork from the bag and pat dry with a paper towel. Season pork with remaining taco seasoning. Place pork in a preheated 350°F/176°C oven and cook for 30 minutes. Remove pork from the oven and use a fork to shred the pork. Garnish with cilantro and serve.

207. SIMPLE SLICED PORK BELLY

Cal.: 374 | Fat: 25g | Protein: 27g   10 min | 3 hours 10 min | Servings 2

INGREDIENTS

- 4 oz. pork belly, sliced
- 3 bay leaves
- 1 tbsp. garlic salt
- 1 tbsp. whole black peppercorns
- 1 ½ tbsp. olive oil

DIRECTIONS

Preheat the Sous Vide machine to 145°F/62°C. Add sliced pork belly, bay leaves, garlic salt, peppercorns, and 1 tbsp. of olive oil into the large Ziploc bag. Remove all the air from the bag before sealing. Place the bag into the hot water bath and cook for 3 hours. Heat remaining oil in a pan over medium heat. Remove pork from bag and sear in hot oil for 2 minutes on each side. Serve and enjoy!

208. PERFECT PORK CHOP

Cal.: 731 | Fat: 48g | Protein: 69g   5 min | 50 min | Servings 2

INGREDIENTS

- 20 oz. pork rib chop, bone in
- 2 tbsp. butter
- Black pepper
- Salt

DIRECTIONS

Preheat the Sous Vide machine to 140°F/60°C. Season pork chops with pepper and salt. Place pork chops into the Ziploc bag and remove all the air from the bag before sealing. Place the bag into the hot water bath and cook for 45 minutes. Heat butter into the pan over medium heat. Remove pork chop from the bag and pat dry with a paper towel. Sear pork chops in hot butter until lightly brown from both sides. Serve and enjoy!

209. SWEET AND SPICY PORK RIBS

Cal.: 880 | Fat: 56g | Protein: 56g   5 min | 20 hours 10 min | Servings 6

INGREDIENTS

- 2 full racks baby back pork ribs, cut in half
- ½ cup jerk seasoning mix

DIRECTIONS

Preheat the Sous Vide machine to 145°F/62°C. Season pork rib rack with half jerk seasoning and place in a large Ziploc bag. Remove all the air from the bag before sealing. Place the bag into the hot water bath and cook for 20 hours. Remove meat from bag and rub with remaining seasoning and place on a baking tray. Broil for 5 minutes. Slice and serve.

210. ROSEMARY GARLIC LAMB CHOPS

Cal.: 349 | Fat: 29g | Protein: 19.2g   5 min | 2 hours 30 min | Servings 4

INGREDIENTS

- 4 lamb chops
- 1 tbsp. butter
- 1 tsp. fresh thyme
- 1 tsp. fresh rosemary
- 2 garlic cloves
- Pepper
- Salt

DIRECTIONS

Preheat the Sous Vide machine to 140°F/60°C. Season lamb chops with pepper and salt. Sprinkle lamb chops with garlic, thyme and rosemary. Add butter to the Ziploc bag then place lamb chops into the bag. Remove all air from the bag before sealing. Place the bag in a hot water bath and cook for 2 ½ hours. Once it's done, sear it on high heat until lightly brown. Serve and enjoy!

211. LAMB CHOPS WITH BASIL CHIMICHURRI

Cal.: 435 | Fat: 44.8g | Protein: 8.4g   10 min | 2 hours | Servings 4

INGREDIENTS

- 2 rack of lamb, drenched
- 2 garlic cloves, crushed
- Pepper
- Salt

For basil Chimichurri:

- 3 tbsp. red wine vinegar
- ½ cup olive oil
- 1 tsp. red chili flakes
- 2 garlic cloves, minced
- 1 shallot, diced
- 1 cup fresh basil, chopped
- 1/4 tsp. pepper
- 1/4 tsp. sea salt

DIRECTIONS

Preheat the Sous Vide machine to 132°F/56°C. Season lamb with pepper and salt. Place lamb in a large Ziploc bag with garlic and remove all air from the bag before sealing. Place the bag into the hot water bath and cook for 2 hours. Add all chimichurri ingredients to the bowl and mix well. Place in the refrigerator for minutes. Remove lamb from the bag and pat dry with a paper towel. Sear lamb in hot oil. Slice lamb between the bones. Place seared lamb chops on a serving dish and top with chimichurri. Serve and enjoy!

212. GARLIC BUTTER LAMB CHOPS

Cal.: 662 | Fat: 29.8g | Protein: 92g   10 min | 2 hours | Servings 4

INGREDIENTS
- 4 lamb chops
- ½ tsp. onion powder
- 1 garlic clove, minced
- 2 tbsp. butter
- 1 tsp. dried rosemary
- Pepper
- Salt

DIRECTIONS
Preheat the Sous Vide machine to 140°F/60°C. Season chops with rosemary, pepper and salt. Place lamb chops into the Ziploc bag and remove all air from the bag before sealing. Place the bag in a hot water bath and cook for 2 hours. Remove lamb chops from the bag and pat dry with a paper towel. In a microwave-safe bowl, add butter and microwave until butter is melted. Make sure butter doesn't burn it. Add onion powder and garlic into the melted butter and stir well. Baste lamb chops with butter mixture and sear until golden brown. Serve and enjoy!

213. SIMPLE RACK OF LAMB

Cal.: 494 | Fat: 32.8g | Protein: 46.2g   5 min | 2 hours | Servings 4

INGREDIENTS
- 2 lbs. rack of lamb
- 2 tbsp. butter
- 2 tbsp. canola oil
- Black pepper
- Salt

DIRECTIONS
Preheat the Sous Vide machine to 140°F/60°C. Season lamb with pepper and salt and place in a large Ziploc bag. Remove all air from the bag before sealing. Place the bag in a hot water bath and cook for 2 hours. Remove lamb from the bag and pat dry with paper towels. Heat canola oil in a pan over medium heat. Spread butter over lamb and sear lamb in hot oil until lightly brown. Serve and enjoy!

214. HERB GARLIC LAMB CHOPS

Cal.: 663 | Fat: 29.8g | Protein: 92.1g   10 min | 2 hours | Servings 4

INGREDIENTS
- 4 lamb chops, bone in
- 2 tbsp. butter
- 8 black peppercorns
- 1 tsp. fresh oregano
- 1 tbsp. fresh parsley
- 1 bay leaf
- 4 fresh thyme sprigs
- 2 tsp. garlic, sliced
- Sea salt

DIRECTIONS
Preheat the Sous Vide machine to 132°F/56°C. Add lamb, butter, peppercorns, herbs and garlic into the large Ziploc bag and remove all the air from the bag before sealing. Place the bag into the hot water bath and cook for 2 hours. Remove lamb chops from the bag and pat dry with paper towels. Heat pan over high heat and sear lamb chops for 30 seconds on each side. Serve and enjoy!

215. BONELESS STRIP STEAK

Cal.: 541 | Fat: 36g | Protein: 57g   🔪 31 min | 🍲 2 hours 30 min | 🍴 Servings 2

INGREDIENTS

- 1 14-16-ounce boneless strip steak, 1½-2 inches thick
- ¼ tsp. garlic powder
- ¼ tsp. onion powder
- 1 tsp. kosher salt, plus more
- ¼ tsp. freshly ground black pepper, plus more
- 3 sprigs rosemary
- 3 sprigs thyme
- 1 tbsp. grape seed or other neutral oil

DIRECTIONS

Preheat your water bath to 130°F/54.5°C for a medium-rare steak. Change the temperature to 5°F in either direction to adjust wellness. Mix garlic powder, onion powder, 1 tsp. of salt, ¼ tsp. of pepper in a bowl. Rub the mixture all over all 4 sides of the steak. Smack the sprigs of herbs against a cutting board. Place the steak in the bag you're going to use to sous, along with the sprigs of herbs and seal the bag. Place the bag in your preheated water. Set a timer for 2 hours and 30 minutes. When the steak is ready, allow it to rest for 15 minutes. Take the steak out of the bag and let it rest for a few more minutes. While it's resting, season it with salt and pepper to taste. Heat a skittle (ideally cast-iron) on high heat. When it gets really hot, pour in the oil and put in the steak. Let the steak sear for 1 to 2 minutes total, flipping it on all four sides. The steak should form a very nice crust on all sides. Serve immediately.

216. KOREAN KALBI SHORT RIBS

Cal.: 508 | Fat: 30g | Protein: 56g   🔪 19 min | 🍲 2 hours 30 min | 🍴 Servings 4

INGREDIENTS

- 16 Korean Style crosscut beef short ribs

Marinade:

- 2 tbsp. sesame oil
- 2 tbsp. brown sugar
- 1 ½ tsp. chili flakes
- 1 tbsp. chopped garlic
- ½ cup soy sauce
- ¼ cup chopped green onions
- ¼ Cup orange juice

DIRECTIONS

Heat a pan on medium-high heat and add in the sesame oil and garlic. Allow the garlic to cook for 2 minutes then take the pan off the heat. Add the rest of the marinade ingredients to the pan while it's still warm and stir the mixture until well combined. Place the ribs in a baking dish and pour in the marinade. Place the dish in the refrigerator, covered for 1 hr. Turn the meat every 15 min. Preheat the Sous Vide machine to 138°F/59°C. Save the marinade for later. Place the steak in the bag you're going to use to sous. Seal the bag. Place the bag in your preheated water and set the timer for 3 hours. While the meat is cooking, put the marinade in a pot and allow it to come to a boil. Allow the sauce to cook for 15 to 20 minutes until it starts to reduce a little. When the ribs are almost done, preheat your broiler. When the steaks are cooked, use a brush to coat them with the marinade. Place the ribs on an aluminum foil-rimmed baking sheet or pan. Put the baking sheet under the broiler and allow the meat to cook for 1 to 2 minutes per side. You just want the sauce to caramelize. Serve the ribs immediately.

217. HANGER STEAK

Cal.: 577 | Fat: 32g | Protein: 50g   6 min | 4 hours | Servings 4

INGREDIENTS

- 4 (8 oz.) pieces of hanger steak
- Kosher or truffle salt
- Freshly ground black pepper
- 12 sprigs thyme
- 2 garlic cloves
- 2 shallots, peeled and thinly sliced
- 2 tbsp. high-smoke point oil

DIRECTIONS

Preheat the Sous Vide machine to 130°F/54.5°C for a medium-rare steak. Change the temperature to 10°F in either direction to adjust wellness. Season the steak with salt and pepper to taste. Place the steak in the bag you're going to use to sous along with the sprigs of thyme, garlic and shallots. Divide the herbs, garlic, and shallots among the 4 steaks. Place thyme sprigs, and shallots slices on both sides, and seal the bag. Place the bag in your preheated water and set the timer for 4 hours. When the steak is ready, allow it to rest for a few minutes. While it's resting, heat a skittle (ideally cast-iron) on high heat. When it gets really hot, pour in the oil and put in the steak. Let the steak sear for 1 minute per side. Should form a nice crust on both sides. Serve immediately.

218. SPICE RUBBED SHORT RIBS

Cal.: 428 | Fat: 26.1g | Protein: 67g   11 min | 48 hours | Servings 6

INGREDIENTS

- 1 tbsp. ground cumin
- 1 tbsp. ancho chili powder
- 1/4 tsp. ground cloves
- 1 tsp. Kosher salt
- 1 tsp. freshly ground black pepper
- 3 lbs. beef short ribs

DIRECTIONS

Preheat the Sous Vide machine to 140°F/60°C. Combine the spices in a bowl. Coat the beef ribs with the spice rub. Place the steak in the bag or bags you're going to use to sous and seal the bag or bags. Place the bag in your preheated water and set the timer for 48 hours. When the ribs are almost ready, preheat your broiler. Place the cooked ribs on an aluminum foil-rimmed baking sheet or pan. Broil for about 5 minutes, until you see the edges char. Serve immediately.

219. BEEF SHOGAYAKI

Cal.: 498 | Fat: 41.1g | Protein: 67g   11 min | 12 hours | Servings 3

INGREDIENTS

- 18 oz. Beef Stew Meat
- 3 tbsp. Soy Sauce
- 3 tbsp. Mirin
- 3 tbsp. Water
- 1 Thumb-Sized Piece Ginger grated
- 1 tbsp. high-smoke point oil

DIRECTIONS

Preheat the Sous Vide machine to 140°F/60°C. Mix together the soy, water, ginger and mirin in a bowl. Add the beef, and toss it in the mixture to coat. Place the beef in the bag you're going to use to sous along with the sauce and seal the bag. Place the bag in your preheated water and set the timer for 12 hours. When the beef is ready, heat a skittle (ideally cast-iron) on high heat. When it gets really hot, pour in the oil and put in the beef. Let the steak sear for 1 minute, flipping halfway through. The steak should form a nice crust on both sides.

220. BEEF MEATBALLS

Cal.: 508 | Fat: 46.1g | Protein: 58g   🔪 11 min | 🍲 60 min | 🍴 Servings 3

INGREDIENTS
- 11 oz. ground beef
- 1 egg
- 4 garlic cloves, minced
- 1 piece shallot, minced
- 1/4 cup bread crumbs
- 1/4 tsp. granulated ginger
- 1/4 tsp. garlic powder
- 1/4 tsp. cumin powder
- 1/4 tsp. black pepper powder
- ½ tsp. paprika powder
- 2 tbsp. yogurt
- 1 tsp. salt
- 1 tsp. liquid smoke
- 1 tbsp. high-smoke point oil

DIRECTIONS
Preheat the Sous Vide machine to 140°F/60°C. Mix all the ingredients together in a bowl. Use your hands to make the mixture into 8 equal size balls. Put the balls on a baking sheet and cover with plastic wrap or aluminum foil. Place the baking sheet in the refrigerator for 10 minutes. Place the beef in the bag you're going to use to sous and seal the bag. Place the bag in your preheated water and set the timer for 1 hour. When the meatballs are ready, heat a skittle (ideally cast-iron) on high heat. When it gets really hot, pour in the oil and put in the beef. Let the meatballs sear for 1 minute, flipping halfway through. The meatballs should brown on both sides.

221. ROAST BEEF

Cal.: 498 | Fat: 46.1g | Protein: 61g   🔪 16 min | 🍲 24 hours | 🍴 Servings 8

INGREDIENTS
- 3 ½ lb. beef roast
- 2 garlic cloves minced
- 1 tbsp. rosemary minced
- ½ tbsp. Worcestershire sauce
- 1 tsp. smoked paprika
- ½ tsp. mustard powder
- ½ tsp. onion powder
- 2 ½ tsp. salt
- ½ tsp. pepper

DIRECTIONS
Preheat the Sous Vide machine to 136°F/58°C. Combine all the ingredients, except for the beef and Worcestershire sauce in a bowl. Rub the Worcestershire sauce all over the beef then coat the beef with the spice mixture. Place the beef in the bag you're going to use to sous and seal the bag. Place the bag in your preheated water and set the timer for 24 hours. When the beef is almost ready, preheat your oven to 350°F/176°C. Place the cooked roast on a broiler pan. Place the roast in the oven and allow it to cook for 15 minutes.

222. TUSCAN RIB-EYE STEAK

Cal.: 488 | Fat: 29.1g | Protein: 60g   🔪 11 min | 🍲 30 min | 🍴 Servings 4

INGREDIENTS
- 4 tbsp. extra virgin olive oil
- 2 tbsp. finely chopped garlic
- 1 tbsp. ground black pepper
- 1 tbsp. ground fennel
- 2 tbsp. chopped anchovies
- 2 tbsp. chopped parsley
- 1 tbsp. chopped rosemary
- 4, 10 to 12 oz. natural boneless rib-eye steaks
- 2 tbsp. olive oil
- Kosher salt

DIRECTIONS
Preheat the Sous Vide machine to 168°F/75.5°C Heat a skillet on medium heat and add in the olive oil and garlic. Allow the garlic to cook until it browns, about 4 min. Then put in the anchovies, rosemary, fennel, parsley and black pepper. Take the skillet off the heat. Season the rib eyes with a little kosher salt. Coat both sides of the steaks with the rosemary mixture. Rub the Worcestershire sauce all over the beef then coat the beef with the spice mixture. Place each steak in its own bag and seal the bags. Place the bag in your preheated water and set the timer for 30 min. When the steaks are ready heat a skittle (ideally cast-iron) on high heat and get the skillet really hot. Place a little oil in the skillet. Place the cooked steaks in the skillet. Sear for about 1 min. per side. Serve the steaks immediately.

223. BURGERS

Cal.: 578 | Fat: 39g | Protein: 52g   6 min | 60 min | Servings 2

INGREDIENTS

- 10 oz. freshly ground beef
- 2 hamburger buns
- 2 slices American cheese
- Salt
- Pepper
- Condiments and toppings of choice

DIRECTIONS

Preheat the Sous Vide machine to 137°F/58.3°C. Use your hands to form the burgers into 2 equal-sized 1-inch-thick patties. Place the patties in the bag you're going to use to sous and seal the bag. Place the bag in your preheated water and set the timer for 1 hour. When the patties are ready, heat a skittle (ideally cast-iron) on high heat. When it gets really hot, put in the patties. Let the patties sear for 1 minute, flipping halfway through. When you flip the burgers, top with cheese slices, so the cheese melts. Serve on buns with the condiments of your choice.

224. SMOKED BRISKET

Cal.: 538 | Fat: 33g | Protein: 50g   2 hours 15 min | 38 hours | Servings 10

INGREDIENTS

- 2 oz. coarsely ground black peppercorns
- 2 1/4 oz. kosher salt
- 1/4 oz. pink salt
- 1, 5 lb. flat-cut or point-cut brisket
- 1/4 tsp. liquid smoke

DIRECTIONS

Mix together the different salts and pepper in a bowl. Coat the brisket with about 2/3 of the mixture. Then cut the brisket in half crosswise. Place the 2 briskets in 2 bags, put in 4 drops of liquid smoke in each bag, and seal the bags. Allow the bags to marinate in your refrigerator for 2 to 3 hours. Preheat the Sous Vide machine to 155°F/68°C. Place the bag in your preheated water and set the timer for 36 hours. When the brisket is almost ready, move one of your oven racks to the lower-middle position. Preheat your oven to 300°F/150°C. Use a paper towel to pat the cooked brisket dry. Coat the brisket with the remaining seasoning mixture. Put a wire rack on a baking sheet and place the brisket on top of it with the fat side up. Place the brisket in the oven for about 2 hours. The brisket is done when a dark bark forms on the outside. Place the brisket on a cutting board and use aluminum foil to tent it. Allow the brisket to rest for 30 min. You want the internal temperature to be between 145°F/63°C and 165°F/74°C. Cut the brisket against the grain into desired size pieces and serve.

225. ASIAN MARINATED PORK BELLY

Cal.: 468 | Fat: 46g | Protein: 67g   6 min | 8 hours | Servings 4

INGREDIENTS

- 1 lb. Pork Belly
- 1/4 Cup Soy Sauce
- 1/4 Cup Mirin or 1/4 cup white wine and 1 tbsp. sugar
- 1/4 Cup Sugar

DIRECTIONS

Preheat the Sous Vide machine to 170°F/76.7°C. Place all the ingredients in the bag you're going to use to sous and seal the bag. Place the bag in the preheated water and set the timer for 8 hours. When the pork belly is almost done preheat your broiler. Place the marinade from the bag into a saucepan and cut the pork belly into ¼-inch-thick pieces. Line a rimmed baking sheet or broiler pan with aluminum foil and place the pork belly on it. Place the baking sheet or pan under the broiler and cook for 3 to 5 minutes. The pork belly should be crispy when done. Bring the marinade liquid to a boil on high heat, then lower the temperature to medium-low to simmer. Reduce the sauce and allow it to thicken. Pour the reduced sauce over the pork belly to serve.

226. MISO SOY GLAZED PORK CHOPS

Cal.: 568 | Fat: 36.1g | Protein: 57g   ✎ 75 min | 🍲 60 min | 🍴 Servings 2

INGREDIENTS

- 4 whole pork chops, bone-in
- 1/3 cup mirin japanese cooking wine
- 1/3 cup low sodium soy sauce
- 2 tbsp. white miso paste
- 2 garlic cloves, minced
- 2 tbsp. brown sugar
- 2 tbsp. butter, cubed
- Green onion, chopped (garnish)
- Sesame seeds, for garnish

DIRECTIONS

Place the mirin, miso, soy sauce, sugar and garlic in a bowl. Use a whisk to mix the ingredients until the miso and sugar dissolve. Divide the pork chops between 2 large resealable plastic bags. Pour in half the sauce to each bag. Place the sealed bag in your refrigerator for at least 1 hour. Then preheat the Sous Vide machine to 140°F /60°C. Remove the air from the plastic bags and place them in your preheated water. Set the timer for 1 hour. While the pork chops are cooking, preheat a grill to high heat. Use a paper towel to pat the cooked pork chops dry. Put the sauce from the bag in a saucepan. Bring the sauce to a simmer. Once simmering, cook for 8 to 10 minutes. Then use a whisk to mix in the butter. Remove the pan from the heat. Put the pork chops on the preheated grill. Sear the pork chops for about 1 to 2 minutes per side. Top the seared pork chops with the thicken sauce and top with green onions and sesame seeds to serve.

227. SPICE-RUBBED BBQ BABY BACK RIBS

Cal.: 508 | Fat: 30g | Protein: 51g   ✎ 16 min | 🍲 24 hours 10 min | 🍴 Servings 8

INGREDIENTS

- Two 2½-pound racks baby back ribs, cut in half crosswise
- 1 cup BBQ sauce

Rub:
- 2 tbsp. kosher salt
- 2 tbsp. smoked paprika
- 2 tbsp. light brown sugar
- 1 tbsp. ground cumin
- 1 tbsp. ground cayenne
- 1 tbsp. ground coriander

DIRECTIONS

Preheat the Sous Vide machine to 155°F/68.3°C. Place the rub ingredients in a bowl and use a whisk to mix them together. Coat the ribs with rub. Place the ribs in the bags you're going to use and seal the bags. Place the bags in your preheated water and set the timer for 24 hours. When the ribs are almost ready, preheat a grill on medium-high heat. Baste the ribs with BBQ sauce and place them on the grill. Continue to baste the ribs with BBQ sauce as they cook. Cook for 6 to 8 minutes, flipping frequently. The ribs are done when they start to char. Serve the ribs immediately.

228. BACON

Cal.: 568 | Fat: 36.1g | Protein: 57g   ✎ 11 min | 🍲 8 hours | 🍴 Servings 4

INGREDIENTS

- 1 lb. pork bacon

DIRECTIONS

Preheat the Sous Vide machine to 145°F/63°C. Place the bacon in the bag you're going to use to sous and seal the bag. Place the bag in the preheated water and set the timer for 8 hours. When the bacon is almost done, heat a skillet on medium-high heat for a minimum of 5 minutes. Place the bacon in the skillet and press down on it with a spatula to ensure it stays flat. Cook the bacon for around 2 minutes, until the bacon browns and becomes crispy. Then flip the bacon and cook it for an additional 15 seconds. Place the bacon on a plate that has been lined with paper towels. Allow the excess grease to drain. Serve while still hot.

229. SPICE-RUBBED PULLED PORK

Cal.: 458 | Fat: 32g | Protein: 51g   11 min | 19 hours 30 min | Servings 12

INGREDIENTS

Rub:
- 1/4 cup paprika
- 1/4 cup dark brown sugar
- 3 tbsp. kosher salt
- ½ tsp. Prague Powder #1, optional
- 1 tbsp. whole yellow mustard seed
- 1 tsp. freshly ground black pepper
- 2 tbsp. granulated garlic powder
- 1 tbsp. dried oregano
- 1 tbsp. whole coriander seed
- 1 tsp. red pepper flakes

Pork:
- 1 whole boneless or bone-in pork butt (shoulder), 5 to 7 lbs.
- ½ tsp. liquid smoke, optional
- Kosher salt

DIRECTIONS

Preheat the Sous Vide machine to 165°F/74°C. Mix all the spice rub ingredients in a bowl and grind them into a powder using a spice grinder in batches. Season the pork lightly with kosher salt. Coat the pork with half of the spice rub and save the other half for later. Place the pork in the bag used to sous, add in the liquid smoke and seal the bags. Place the bags in your preheated water and set the timer for 18 hours. When the pork is almost ready preheat your oven to 300°F/150°C. Use a paper towel to pat the pork dry. Coat the pork with the remaining spice rub. Line a baking sheet or broiler pan with aluminum foil, and put a wire rack on top of it. Place the pork on the wire rack. Place the broiler pan or baking sheet in the oven and cook for 90 minutes. The pork is done when a beautiful, dark bark forms on the outside. Slice the pork and serve it immediately.

230. SWEET AND SPICY PORK TENDERLOIN

Cal.: 468 | Fat: 26.9g | Protein: 47g   11 min | 65 min | Servings 3

INGREDIENTS

Rub:
- 5 fresh thyme sprigs
- 1 pork tenderloin
- 1 tbsp. canola or vegetable oil

Pork:
- 1 tbsp. decaf Coffee Grounds
- 1 scant tsp. Cayenne Pepper
- 1 ½ tbsp. Brown Sugar
- 1 tsp. Cinnamon
- 1 scant TBS Cumin
- 1 tsp. Garlic Powder
- 1 tsp. smoked Paprika
- 1 tsp. Salt
- ½ tsp. black pepper

DIRECTIONS

Preheat the Sous Vide machine to 134.6°F/57°C. Place the rub ingredients in a bowl and whisk them together. Coat the pork with the rub mixture. Place pork in the bag you're going to use to sous. Put the thyme sprigs on both sides of the pork, and seal the bag. Then place the bag in the preheated water and set the timer for 1 hour and 5 min. When the pork is done, use a paper towel to pat it dry. Heat a skittle (ideally cast-iron) on high heat. When it gets really hot, pour in the oil and put in the pork. Let the pork sear for 30 seconds to 1 min. on all sides. The pork should form a nice crust on all sides. Allow the pork to rest for about 3 minutes. Slice and serve the pork.

231. CHIPOTLE APPLE PORK LOIN

Cal.: 548 | Fat: 34g | Protein: 51g   📐 11 min | 🍲 4 hours | 🍴 Servings 6

INGREDIENTS

- 1 tsp. salt
- 1 tsp. black pepper
- ½ tsp. chipotle powder
- ¼ tsp. ground cloves
- ¼ tsp. ground nutmeg
- 2 lbs. pork loin
- 2 tbsp. apple concentrate
- 1 tbsp. maple syrup
- 1 tbsp. coconut oil

DIRECTIONS

Preheat the Sous Vide machine to 134°F /56.7°C. Place the rub ingredients in a bowl and mix them together. Coat the pork with the rub mixture. Place the pork in the bag you're going to use to sous, pour in the apple concentrate, maple syrup and coconut oil, and seal the bag. Place the bag in the preheated water and set the timer for 4 hours. When the pork is done allow it to rest for 5 minutes. Slice and serve the pork.

232. SOUTHWESTERN PORK TENDERLOIN

Cal.: 538 | Fat: 39g | Protein: 51g   📐 11 min | 🍲 3 hours | 🍴 Servings 3

INGREDIENTS

Rub:

- 1 tsp. chili powder
- ½ tsp. garlic powder
- 1/4 tsp. chipotle
- 1 tsp. salt
- ½ tsp. pepper

Rub:

- 1 lb. pork tenderloin
- 2 tsp. lemon juice
- 1 tbsp. olive oil

DIRECTIONS

Preheat the Sous Vide machine to 133°F/56.1°C. Place the rub ingredients in a bowl and whisk them together. Cut any excess fat off the tenderloin. Coat the pork with the lemon juice and then the rub mixture. Place the pork in the bag you're going to use to sous and seal. Place the bag in the preheated water and set the timer for 3 hours. When the pork is done, use a paper towel to pat it dry. Heat a skittle (ideally cast-iron) on high heat. When it gets really hot, pour in the oil and put in the pork. Let the pork sear for 3-4 minutes per side. The pork should form a nice crust on all sides. Allow the pork to rest for about 3 minutes.

233. PAPRIKA AND BROWN SUGAR RUBBED PORK CHOPS

Cal.: 568 | Fat: 36.1g | Protein: 51g   📐 15 min | 🍲 2 hours 10 min | 🍴 Servings 2

INGREDIENTS

Rub:

- 1 tsp. salt
- ½ tsp. pepper
- 1/4 tsp. roasted garlic powder
- 3/4 tsp. smoked paprika
- ½ tsp. mustard powder
- ½ tsp. brown sugar

Pork:

- 2 bone in pork chops

DIRECTIONS

Preheat the Sous Vide machine to 134°F/56.7°C. Mix together the rub ingredients in a bowl. Coat the pork chops with the rub mixture. Place the pork chops in the bag you're going to use to sous, and seal the bag. Place the bag in the preheated water and set the timer for 2 hours. When the pork chops are almost done, preheat a grill to high heat. Grill the pork chops for around 2 minutes per side. The pork chops should caramelize on both sides when they're ready. Serve the pork chops immediately.

234. FRESH HERB RUBBED PORK CHOPS

Cal.: 518 | Fat: 31g | Protein: 52g   ⟍ 11 min | 🍲 3 hours | ✕ Servings 3

INGREDIENTS

Rub:
- 1/4 cup parsley
- 10 large basil leaves
- 1/4 cup rosemary, stems removed
- 1/4 cup chives
- 6 sprigs thyme, remove stems
- 2 garlic cloves, minced
- 1 zest of 1 lemon
- 1 tbsp. white balsamic vinegar
- ½ tsp. salt
- 1 tsp. fresh cracked pepper
- 1/4 cup extra virgin olive oil

Pork:
- 4 bone in pork chops about 1 ½ inches thick

DIRECTIONS

Preheat the Sous Vide machine to 140°F/60°C. Place the basil, rosemary, chives and thyme in a food processor or blender, and pulse until finely chopped. Add the remaining rub ingredients and blend until the ingredients form a paste. Coat the pork chops with the rub mixture. Place the pork chops in the bag or bags you're going to use to sous, and seal the bag or bags. Place the bag in the preheated water and set the timer for 2 hours. When the pork chops are almost done, preheat your broiler. Coat a rimmed baking sheet with olive oil and place the cooked pork chops on it. Let the pork cook under the broiler for 3 to 4 minutes per side. The pork chops should have a nice brown color and a lightly crisp texture. Serve the pork chops immediately.

235. EASY CHICKEN CORDON BLEU

Cal.: 276 | Fat: 14g | Protein: 34.2g   ⟍ 6 min | 🍲 90 min | ✕ Servings 4

INGREDIENTS
- 2 boneless, skinless chicken breasts
- 1 teaspoon sea salt
- 1 teaspoon black pepper
- 4 Swiss cheese slices
- 2 slices of uncured ham
- Binding string

DIRECTIONS

Prepare the water bath to 140°F/60°C. Butterfly chicken breasts and place them between two sheets of plastic wrap. Tenderize flat using a meat tenderizer. Remove plastic wrap and season the chicken with salt and pepper. Lay Swiss cheese in a single layer down the middle of each chicken breast. Place a layer of uncured ham on top of the cheese. Roll each chicken breast up like a jelly roll, beginning at the narrowest edge. Use a binding string on each end to hold together. Place the chicken rolls in a vacuum bag, seal and cook for 1 hour 30 minutes. Allow chicken to rest for 5 minutes, and slice to serve warm.

236. HARISSA CHICKEN

Cal.: 643 | Fat: 50g | Protein: 43.5g   ⟍ 31 min | 🍲 2 hours | ✕ Servings 2

INGREDIENTS
- 2 boneless, skinless chicken breasts
- 1 tablespoon harissa, powdered; or ½ tablespoon harissa paste
- ½ teaspoon cayenne pepper
- 2 garlic cloves, minced
- Sea salt, to taste
- 1 preserved lemon, chopped
- 4 tablespoons olive oil, divided

DIRECTIONS

Add all ingredients to a resealable bag and marinate for 30 minutes. Use only half the olive oil. Preheat the water bath to 141°F/61°C. Seal the bag and add chicken to the water bath and cook for 2 hours. Heat remaining olive oil in a frying pan on medium-high. Remove chicken from the water bath and sear on both sides for 2 minutes. Serve with juices over couscous and enjoy!

237. MOIST DELICIOUS THANKSGIVING TURKEY

Cal.: 1960 | Fat: 68.9g | Protein: 310.9g   61 min | 2 hours 30 min | Servings 6

INGREDIENTS

- 14 lbs. turkey
- Salt
- 1 stick unsalted butter
- 8 garlic cloves, minced
- 4 sprigs sage
- 4 sprigs thyme
- 4 sprigs rosemary

DIRECTIONS

Defrost turkey according to the instructions on the packaging. Preheat the water bath 149°F/65°C. Remove the packaged gizzards inside the turkey cavity. Remove the thighs and drumsticks with a boning knife, then remove the wings of the turkey. Cut out the rib cage, with kitchen shears, and save for stock or gravy. Cut the breast in half, down the middle with a boning knife, and keep the bone in. Place the thighs and wings in a one-gallon vacuum bag and do not overlap. Place drumsticks in another bag, turkey breast in a third and fourth bag. Add 2 smashed garlic cloves, 1 sprig of each herb, and two tablespoons of butter to each bag. Seal with a vacuum sealer or use the water displacement method. Take care that the turkey pieces inside the bags are completely Immersed while cooking. Cook for 2 hours 30 minutes; legs will be most tender when cooked at 4 to 6 hours. Here, you can crisp in a cast-iron skillet for 3 minutes on each side and serve immediately with your favorite trimmings.

238. RICH AND TASTY DUCK À ORANGE

Cal.: 205 | Fat: 9.3g | Protein: 18.7g   21 min | 2 hours 30 min | Servings 4

INGREDIENTS

- 2 small duck breasts
- 1 orange, sliced
- 4 garlic cloves, smashed
- 1 shallot, smashed
- 4 thyme sprigs
- ½ tablespoon black peppercorns
- 1 tablespoon sherry vinegar
- 1/4 cup red wine, like Merlot
- 2 tablespoons butter
- Sea salt, to taste

DIRECTIONS

Preheat the water bath to 135°F/57°C. Add the duck breasts with slices of orange, garlic, shallots, thyme and peppercorns to a vacuum bag. Seal and cook for 2 hours 30 minutes. Preheat a frying pan to medium-high heat. Remove duck from the bag and set the bag aside. Fry the duck breast, skin side down, for 30 seconds. Remove the duck breast from the pan and keep warm. Add vinegar and red wine to a frying pan to deglaze leftover fat. Add the contents of the vacuum bag and cook for about 6 minutes over medium heat. Fold in the butter and season with salt and pepper. Slice the duck breast into 2-inch medallions, top with sauce, and serve.

239. TEMPTING TERIYAKI CHICKEN

Cal.: 300 | Fat: 4.1g | Protein: 27.1g    6 min | 2 hours | Servings 1

INGREDIENTS

- 1 skinless, boneless chicken breast
- ½ teaspoon ginger juice
- 2 tablespoons sugar, plus 1 teaspoon
- ½ teaspoon salt
- 2 tablespoons soy sauce
- 2 tablespoons sake or mirin

DIRECTIONS

Dry the chicken with a paper towel and then coat with ginger juice. Mix 1 teaspoon sugar and salt in a small bowl, and sprinkle on both sides of the chicken. Add the chicken to a vacuum bag and seal; set aside to marinate for 30 minutes or overnight. Preheat water bath to 140°F/60°C. Add chicken and cook for 1 hour 30 minutes. Combine the remaining sugar, soy sauce and sake in a small saucepan, bring to a boil, and cook until the sauce is thick, forming large shiny bubbles. Remove sauce and place on warm until the chicken is done. Plate chicken, top with teriyaki sauce, and serve!

240. SPICY HONEY SRIRACHA WINGS

Cal.: 195 | Fat: 9.3g | Protein: 22.3g   6 min | 46 hours | Servings 4

INGREDIENTS

Rub:

- 1 lb. chicken wings
- ½ teaspoon sea salt
- ½ teaspoon paprika
- ½ teaspoon garlic
- ½ teaspoon ginger
- ½ teaspoon black pepper

For the glaze:

- 1 tablespoon sesame oil
- 2 tablespoons soy sauce
- 2 tablespoons honey
- 2 tablespoons Sriracha

DIRECTIONS

Preheat the water bath to 140°F/60°C. Mix spices in a mixing bowl and toss wings to coat. Add wings to a vacuum bag. Cook the wings for 40 minutes. Combine glaze ingredients in a large mixing bowl. Transfer chicken wings in an ice bath. For crispy wings, fry in a cast-iron skillet on high heat for 1 to 2 minutes, or until golden. Toss the wings in the glaze and serve hot.

241. AROMATIC ROSEMARY CHICKEN

Cal.: 195 | Fat: 9.3g | Protein: 22.3g   60 min | 2 hours | Servings 4

INGREDIENTS

- 4 chicken breasts

Rub:

- 2 cups of chicken stock
- 4 tablespoons salt
- 2 tablespoons brown sugar

For the glaze:

- 1 stick of butter
- 2 teaspoons rosemary, chopped
- 1 teaspoon garlic powder
- ½ teaspoon paprika
- ½ teaspoon sea salt
- ½ teaspoon black pepper
- 1 tablespoon olive oil

DIRECTIONS

Add chicken to a shallow dish with brine, cover, and refrigerate for 60 minutes. Preheat the water bath to 141°F/61°C. Combine rosemary sauce ingredients in a mixing bowl. Add chicken breasts to a vacuum bag and seal. Add to the bath and cook for 2 hours. Add rosemary sauce to a pan on medium-high heat and brown for 5 minutes. Remove chicken from bags, coat with butter, and brown in a frying pan on medium-high, on both sides, for 2 minutes. Serve drizzled with sauce and enjoy!

242. ITALIAN-STYLE CHICKEN MARSALA

Cal.: 550 | Fat: 23.6g | Protein: 46.6g   15 min | 3 hours | Servings 4

INGREDIENTS

- 4 chicken breasts
- 2 sprigs of fresh thyme
- Sea salt
- Black pepper

Rub:

- 1 cup unbleached flour
- Olive oil
- 3 cups sliced baby portabella mushrooms
- 3/4 cup Marsala wine
- 3/4 cup chicken stock
- 3 tablespoons butter
- 4 tablespoons chopped Italian parsley

DIRECTIONS

Preheat the water bath to 141°F/61°C. Lightly salt and pepper the chicken breasts and place in a vacuum bag with thyme and seal. Add to the water bath and cook for 2 hours. Heat olive oil in a sauté pan over high heat. Preheat the oven to warm. Remove the chicken breasts from the bath, pat dry with a paper towel and dredge them in the flour. Sear the chicken breasts for 1 minute per side. Remove and place on a baking sheet in the warm oven. Turn heat to medium-high for the sauté pan and melt 1 tablespoon butter. Add mushrooms and cook until they brown and release their liquid; about 4 to 6 minutes. Turn heat down to medium and add the Marsala wine to the pan; simmer for 1 minute, scraping the bottom of the pan to dislodge the browned bits. Add the chicken stock and simmer for 10 minutes to reduce the sauce. Fold the remaining 2 tablespoons of butter into the sauce and plate the seared chicken breasts. Spoon the Marsala sauce evenly over the chicken breasts. Garnish with Italian parsley and serve.

243. CHICKEN BREAST WITH CREAMY MUSHROOM SAUCE

Cal.: 653 | Fat: 47.2g | Protein: 2.7g   26 min | 1 hour 35 min | Servings 2

INGREDIENTS

- 2 boneless, skinless chicken breasts
- 1/8 teaspoon sea salt
- For the mushroom cream sauce:
- 3 shallots, finely chopped
- 2 large garlic cloves, minced
- 1 teaspoon olive oil
- 2 tablespoons butter
- 1 cup button mushrooms, sliced
- 2 tablespoons port wine
- ½ cup chicken stock
- 1 cup heavy cream
- 1/4 teaspoon fresh ground black pepper

DIRECTIONS

Preheat the water bath to 140°F/60°C. Salt chicken breasts evenly, place in a vacuum bag, and seal. Cook for 1 hour 30 minutes. Add the olive oil to a frying pan on medium heat. Add shallots and cook for 3 minutes. Add the butter and garlic and stir for 1 minute. Turn the stove up to medium-high and add the mushrooms; cook until they release liquid and it evaporates. Add the port wine and cook until it's nearly evaporated. Add the stock and cook for 2 minutes, then fold in the cream until well incorporated. Cook over medium heat until the sauce thickens and finish with pepper. Remove chicken from the bath and plate. Top with mushroom sauce and enjoy!

244. DUCK BREAST WITH AMARENA CHERRY SAUCE

Cal.: 373 | Fat: 20.9g | Protein: 35.5g   16 min | 60 min | Servings 4

INGREDIENTS

- 4 duck breasts
- 1 small jar of Amarena cherries in syrup
- 1 cup red wine
- 4 sprigs thyme
- 5 tablespoons butter

DIRECTIONS

Preheat the Sous Vide machine to 145°F/63°C. Wash and dry the duck, and then cut the skin off of it. Salt and pepper the duck to taste. Place the duck in the bag with 1 tablespoon butter and 1 sprig of thyme on each breast. Seal the bag, then place in the preheated container and set the timer for 1 hour. Place cherries and wine in a pan and bring to a boil over high heat. Reduce the temperature to medium heat and simmer until the sauce becomes thick. Take the pan off the heat. When the duck is cooked, pat it dry and heat a skillet on medium heat with a tablespoon of butter. Once the skillet is hot, add in the duck and sear it for about a minute per side. Serve topped with the cherry sauce.

245. DUCK LEG CONFIT

Cal.: 351 | Fat: 20.5g | Protein: 35.8g   6 hours 11 min | 8 hours 3 min | Servings 2

INGREDIENTS

- 2 duck legs
- 2 teaspoons salt
- Bay leaf
- Sprig of thyme
- 2 thin orange slices
- 1 garlic clove
- Salt and pepper
- 2 tablespoons duck fat or olive oil

DIRECTIONS

Place all the ingredients in a medium-size bowl and mix until the salt dissolves. Place the duck in the bowl and refrigerate for 6 hours covered. Preheat the Sous Vide machine to 176°F/80°C. Take the duck out of the mixture and pat it dry using a paper towel. Salt and pepper the duck to taste and place it in the bag with the oil or fat. Seal the bag and place it in your preheated container and set your timer for 8 hours. When the duck is almost done cooking, preheat your broil to high. When the duck is done cooking, broil it until the skin side becomes crispy.

246. LEMON HERB TURKEY BREAST

Cal.: 639 | Fat: 7.9g | Protein: 78.8g   6 min | 4 hours | Servings 2

INGREDIENTS

- 2 lbs. boneless, skinless turkey breast
- 1/4 cup honey
- 1/4 cup lemon juice
- 1 teaspoon dried dill or 1 tablespoon fresh
- 1 teaspoon dried parsley or 1 tablespoon fresh
- 1 teaspoon dried basil or 1 tablespoon fresh
- 1/4 teaspoon black pepper
- 1 teaspoon salt
- 2 tablespoons flour

DIRECTIONS

Preheat the Sous Vide machine to 143°F/62°C. Combine all the ingredients except for the turkey and flour in a bowl. Place the turkey in the bag along with the marinade mixture. Seal the bag and place in the water bath. Cook for 4 hours. When the turkey is cooked, put the flour in a small saucepan along with 1 tablespoon oil. Heat the mixture over medium heat, stirring constantly for about 1 minute. Pour in the juices from the bag and use a whisk to remove any lumps from the gravy. Slice the turkey thin and serve with the gravy.

247. FILIPINO ADOBO CHICKEN

Cal.: 376 | Fat: 21.5g | Protein: 36.8g   🔪 15 min | 🍲 4 hours | 🍴 Servings 4

INGREDIENTS

- 1-½ lbs. chicken thighs and drumstick
- 6 pieces dried bay leaves
- 1 cup soy sauce
- 1 head garlic crushed
- 1 tablespoon whole peppercorn
- 1/4 cup vinegar
- ½ cup chicken broth

DIRECTIONS

Preheat the Sous Vide machine to 155°F/68°C. Place the chicken and all of the other ingredients in the bag. Place the bag in your preheated container and set your timer for 4 hours. Serve chicken with the sauce from the bag.

248. SPICY CURRIED CHICKEN THIGHS

Cal.: 510 | Fat: 42g | Protein: 39.2g   🔪 15 min | 🍲 2 hours | 🍴 Servings 4

INGREDIENTS

- 8 pieces boneless, skinless chicken thighs
- 8 garlic cloves
- 6 tablespoons olive oil
- 2 tablespoons cumin
- 2 tablespoons coriander
- 2 teaspoons kosher salt
- 2 teaspoons allspice
- 2 teaspoons turmeric
- 1 teaspoon curry
- 1 teaspoon ground ginger
- 1 teaspoon ground pepper
- 1/4 teaspoon cayenne

DIRECTIONS

Preheat the Sous Vide machine to 165°F/74°C. Place all the ingredients except for the chicken thighs in a blender or food processor. Blend until the ingredients form a thick paste. Coat the chicken with the paste. Place in a bag and seal. Put the chicken in the water bath for 2 hours. Towards the end of the cooking process, preheat your broiler. When the chicken is cooked, take it out of the bag and place it under the broiler. Broil each side until it browns, no more than 2 minutes per side.

249. CHICKEN TIKKA MASALA

Cal.: 370 | Fat: 12.3g | Protein: 30.5g   🔪 15 min | 🍲 2 hours | 🍴 Servings 2

INGREDIENTS

- 4 boneless, skinless chicken breasts
- 2 tablespoons butter
- Pinch of salt and pepper
- 2 cups crushed or strained tomatoes
- 2 cups heavy cream
- 1-inch piece peeled ginger cut into chunks
- 4 garlic cloves
- 1-½ tablespoons honey
- 1 tablespoon paprika
- 1 tablespoon cumin
- 3 teaspoons turmeric
- 2 teaspoons coriander
- 1-½ teaspoons salt

DIRECTIONS

Preheat the Sous Vide machine to 146°F/63°C. Cut the ginger into chunks. Salt and pepper the chicken to taste and place it in the bag with the butter and seal. Blend all the remaining ingredients in a blender until smooth. Place the sauce in another bag. Place both bags in your preheated container and set your timer for 2 hours. When the chicken is cooked, remove from the bag and slice it. Then, top the chicken with the sauce and serve.

250. LEMONGRASS AND GARLIC PORK BELLY ROLL

Cal.: 439 | Fat: 28.9g | Protein: 35.5g   🔪 11 min | 🍲 8 hours | 🍴 Servings 6

INGREDIENTS

- 1 lb. pork belly, leave whole
- 3-½ teaspoons sea salt
- ½ teaspoon pepper
- 1/4 cup olive oil
- 4 stalks lemongrass, white part only
- 1 whole garlic bulb, peeled
- 2 bell peppers, sliced into strips
- Cooking string to secure belly closed

DIRECTIONS

Preheat the water bath to 165°F/74°C. Generously season pork belly with salt all over. Lay skin side down. Add lemongrass, bell pepper, and garlic, in a line in the belly's center, and drizzle with a little olive oil. Roll belly into a log and tie shut with a cooking string. Add pork belly to a large bag. Seal the bag and place in the preheated container. Cook for 8 hours. Slice into 1-inch-thick medallions and serve warm with your favorite sides.

251. HERB CRUSTED PORK CHOPS

Cal.: 508 | Fat: 12.4g | Protein: 29.7g   🔪 6 min | 🍲 4 hours 5 min | 🍴 Servings 4

INGREDIENTS

- 4 bone-in pork chops
- 3 eggs, beaten
- 1 teaspoon whole milk

Rub:

- 1-½ cups all-purpose flour
- 1-½ cups panko
- 2 tablespoons fresh basil, finely chopped
- 1 tablespoon fresh oregano, finely chopped
- 1/4 cup Parmesan, finely grated
- 1 lemon, quartered

DIRECTIONS

Preheat a water bath to 140°F/60°C. Add pork to the vacuum bag, seal and cook for 4 hours. Remove pork chops. Whisk milk and egg together to make an egg wash. Combine herb crust ingredients together in a large mixing bowl. Dip a pork chop into the egg wash and fully coat. Dip in the herb crust to coat evenly and transfer to a greased baking sheet; repeat until all pork chops are coated. Broil for 2-3 minutes on each side until golden brown. Transfer to plates and top with salt and pepper to serve. Squeeze fresh lemon juice over the chops for added zing.

252. HONEY MUSTARD GLAZED PORK LOIN

Cal.: 234 | Fat: 12.9g | Protein: 21.9g   🔪 11 min | 🍲 90 min | 🍴 Servings 6

INGREDIENTS

- 1 pork loin
- 4 tablespoons French mustard, grainy
- 2 tablespoons honey
- 1 tablespoon chopped tarragon
- 2 tablespoons olive oil
- 1 onion, sliced in thin roundels
- Salt and pepper

DIRECTIONS

Preheat the Sous Vide machine to 140°F/60°C. Mix all ingredients except pork loin in a bowl. Pour this mixture into a zipper-lock gallon bag. Add the pork loin and seal; turn the bag a few times so that loin is covered in marinade. Immerse in the bath and cook for 90 minutes. If a sear is desired, place loin in a very hot cast-iron sauté pan with butter, turning a few times to brown. Serve sliced, pouring a few spoons of the cooking juices with onions on the loin.

253. PULLED PORK WITH CHILI PEPPER BBQ SAUCE

Cal.: 344 | Fat: 24.4g | Protein: 26.5g   ➘ 6 min | 🍲 20 hours | 🍴 Servings 8

INGREDIENTS

- 2 lbs. pork shoulder meat, removed from the bone
- 1 tablespoon brown sugar
- 1 teaspoon chili powder
- 1 teaspoon garlic powder
- 2 teaspoons kosher salt
- 1 teaspoon hot red pepper flakes
- BBQ sauce, for serving

DIRECTIONS

Preheat the water bath to 165°F/74°C. Add all ingredients, except sauce, to a large bag. Seal the bag and place in the preheated container. Cook for 12 to 20 hours. Transfer pork from bag to a plate and pull apart with two forks. Add pork to a large mixing bowl and fold in BBQ sauce until well-covered. Serve with bread to make sandwiches or with your favorite sides as the main dish.

254. JUICY BEER-INFUSED SAUSAGES

Cal.: 125 | Fat: 9.5g | Protein: 4.8g   ➘ 21 min | 🍲 4 hours | 🍴 Servings 8

INGREDIENTS

- 3 lbs. natural-casing raw bratwurst sausage links
- 6 ounces craft beer
- Dijon mustard
- Sliced tomatoes
- Sliced pickles
- Chopped onions
- Buns

DIRECTIONS

Preheat the water bath to 160°F/71°C. Add sausages to a vacuum bag in a single layer. Add beer to the bag. Seal the bag, but not airtight, so the sausages are not squeezed. Add sausages to a water bath and cook for 4 hours. Remove sausages from bags and discard beer. Dry sausages carefully on a paper towel-lined plate. Here, you can grill for 3 minutes each to sear or serve immediately on buns with your favorite toppings.

255. SPICED LAMB KEBABS

Cal.: 667 | Fat: 27.7g | Protein: 92.8g   ➘ 16 min | 🍲 2 hours | 🍴 Servings 4

INGREDIENTS

- 2 garlic cloves, minced
- Sea salt
- Freshly ground black pepper
- 1 teaspoon dried oregano
- 1 tablespoon olive oil
- 4 lamb steaks cut into 2-inch chunks
- 2 red peppers, deseeded and cut into chunks
- 1 large onion, cut into chunks
- 2 lemons, cut into wedges
- 6 steel or bamboo skewers

DIRECTIONS

Set your Sous Vide Machine to 140°F/60°C. In a large bowl, combine the garlic, salt, pepper, oregano, olive oil and lamb chunks. Stir thoroughly to coat. Spoon the lamb into a vacuum-sealed bag. Immerse in the water bath and cook for 1-½ hours. When the lamb is almost finished cooking, heat your oven to 500°F/260°C. Remove the bag from the water and pat lamb dry with a paper towel. Skewer the lamb, alternating lamb, pepper and onion chunks. Arrange the skewers on a baking sheet and cook in the oven for 5 minutes. Remove from the oven, turn the skewers and cook for an additional 5 minutes. The high heat of the oven should give the kebabs a nice sear. Serve with lemon wedges.

256. TANDOORI LAMB CHOPS

Cal.: 308 | Fat: 12.7g | Protein: 42.9g   60 min | 🍲 3 hours | 🍴 Servings 8

INGREDIENTS

- 8 lamb rib chops (2-½ pounds)
- 3/4 cups Greek yogurt
- 1/4 cup heavy cream
- 3 tablespoons fresh lemon juice
- 1 (3-inch piece) fresh ginger, peeled and minced
- 4 large garlic cloves, minced
- 1 tablespoon malt vinegar
- 1 tablespoon garam masala
- 1 tablespoon ground cumin
- 1 tablespoon paprika
- ½ teaspoon cayenne pepper
- Salt

DIRECTIONS

Set your Sous Vide Machine to 135°F/57.2°C. In a large bowl, whisk the yogurt with heavy cream, lemon juice, ginger, garlic, malt vinegar, garam masala, cumin, paprika, cayenne and 1 teaspoon salt. Place lamb chops in a large vacuum-sealed bag or place two to three chops in smaller bags. Pour the yogurt marinade over the lamb and seal using your vacuum-sealed. Place the bag in the refrigerator to marinate for 2 hours. When your water bath is ready, Immerse the bag and cook for at least 2 hours and not more than 3 hours. When the lamb is almost finished, heat your oven to 450°F/230°C. Remove the lamb from the bag and transfer to a baking sheet. Cook in the oven for 6 minutes and turn the chops over. Cook an additional 6 minutes and serve.

257. SHAWARMA LEG OF LAMB

Cal.: 864 | Fat: 45.2g | Protein: 107g   11 min | 🍲 14 hours | 🍴 Servings 6

INGREDIENTS

- 1 (5-pound) bone-in leg of lamb,
- Salt, freshly ground pepper
- 2 tablespoons cumin seeds
- 2 teaspoons caraway seeds
- 2 teaspoons coriander seeds
- 2 Thai chilies, very finely chopped
- 4 garlic cloves, finely grated
- ½ cup olive oil
- 1 tablespoon paprika
- ½ teaspoon ground cinnamon

DIRECTIONS

Set your Sous Vide Machine to 143°F/62°C. In a large bowl combine, salt, pepper, cumin, caraway, coriander, chilies, garlic, olive oil, paprika and cinnamon. Rub the mixture all over the lamb and place in a vacuum-sealed bag. Seal the bag with your Foodsaver or any vacuum sealer available and place in the refrigerator for 2 hours. Immerse the lamb in the water bath and cook for 12 hours. For an even more tender texture, cook an additional 6 hours.

258. HERBED LAMB CHOPS

Cal.: 205 | Fat: 11.1g | Protein: 24.1g   60 min | 🍲 4 hours | 🍴 Servings 6

INGREDIENTS

- 4 large garlic cloves, pressed
- 1 tablespoon fresh thyme leaves, lightly crushed
- 1 tablespoon fresh rosemary leaves, lightly crushed
- 1 teaspoon cayenne pepper
- 2 teaspoons coarse salt
- 2 tablespoons extra-virgin olive oil, divided
- 6 (1-1/4-inch thick) lamb loin chops

DIRECTIONS

Set your Sous Vide Machine to 135°F/57.2°C. In a vacuum-sealed bag combine the herbs, cayenne pepper, salt, pepper, oil and lamb chops. Seal the bag and allow it to marinate in the refrigerator for 1 hour. Immerse in the water bath and cook for at least 2 hours and not more than 4 hours. When chops are almost finished, heat a skillet over high heat. Remove the chops from the bag and sear for 3 minutes per side before serving. These chops pair well with a roasted garlic mashed potato.

259. LAMB CASSEROLE

Cal.: 434 | Fat: 14.7g | Protein: 50g   🔪 21 min | 🍲 4 hours | 🍴 Servings 6

INGREDIENTS

- 2 tablespoons flour
- Salt and pepper
- 1-½ pounds lamb neck fillet, diced
- 2 tablespoons vegetable oil
- 1 medium onion
- 1 carrot, peeled and diced
- 1 teaspoon ground cinnamon
- 28 ounces chopped tomatoes
- 2 teaspoons honey
- 2 cups chicken or lamb stock
- ½ pound small red potatoes
- 1 package frozen peas

DIRECTIONS

Set your Sous Vide Machine to 180°F/82.2°C. Combine the salt, pepper and flour and toss the lamb pieces to coat. Then, in a medium skillet heat the oil. Brown the lamb on all sides and remove from heat. Add the onion and carrots to the pan and cook for 5 minutes, until lightly browned. Toss in the cinnamon. Transfer the lamb, vegetables and all remaining ingredients to a vacuum-sealed bag. Immerse the bag in the water bath and cook for at least 2 and not more than 4 hours. Remove the bag from the water and pour contents into a casserole dish. The liquid in the bag should have thickened into a nice smooth gravy.

260. LAMB LOIN WITH CHERRY-BALSAMIC SAUCE

Cal.: 691 | Fat: 28.7g | Protein: 65g   🔪 11 min | 🍲 4 hours | 🍴 Servings 2

INGREDIENTS

- 1 (1-pound) boneless lamb loin roast
- Salt and freshly ground black pepper
- 1 tablespoon chopped plus 2 whole sprigs of fresh rosemary
- 2 tablespoons unsalted butter
- 1 medium red onion, thinly sliced
- ½ pound fresh cherries, pitted and chopped
- 1/4 cup balsamic vinegar

DIRECTIONS

Set your Sous Vide Machine to 134°F/57°C. Season the lamb with salt, pepper and one sprig of rosemary, seal in a vacuum-sealed bag and Immerse in the water bath for at least 2 hours and not more than 4. While the lamb cooks, combine the butter, onion, cherries and vinegar in another vacuum-sealed bag. An hour before the lamb has finished, add the sauce bag to the water bath and cook until the lamb is done. Remove both bags from the water bath. Slice the lamb into 3/4-inch-thick pieces and top with sauce.

261. SIMPLE RACK OF LAMB

Cal.: 224 | Fat: 12g | Protein: 23.1g   🔪 60 min | 🍲 4 hours | 🍴 Servings 3

INGREDIENTS

- 2 racks of lamb, trimmed
- 1 garlic clove, minced
- 2 teaspoons salt
- 1/3 cup fresh rosemary leaves
- ½ teaspoon freshly ground black pepper
- 2 teaspoons extra-virgin olive oil

DIRECTIONS

Set your Sous Vide Machine to 134°F/56.5°C. Combine the garlic, salt, rosemary leaves and pepper, and rub all over the racks. Place the racks into separate vacuum-sealed bags. Marinate the bags in the refrigerator for 1 hour before submerging in the water bath. Cook the racks in the water bath for between 2 to 4 hours. When the lamb is almost done, heat your oven to 450°F/230°C. Remove the racks from the vacuum-sealed bags and place on a baking sheet or roasting pan. Roast in the oven for about 10 minutes. Remove from the oven and serve immediately.

262. SLOW COOKED LAMB SHANKS

Cal.: 319 | Fat: 12.3g | Protein: 46.4g   11 min | 48 hours | Servings 4

INGREDIENTS
- 2 bone-in lamb shanks
- Salt and black pepper
- 6 sprigs of fresh thyme
- 2 garlic cloves, crushed

DIRECTIONS
Set your Sous Vide Machine for 143°F/62°C. Rub the lamb shanks all over with the salt and pepper and place into separate vacuum-sealed bags. Add three sprigs of thyme and one clove of crushed garlic to each bag. Seal the bags and Immerse in the water bath for 48 hours. When the lamb is nearly finished in the water bath, heat your oven to 500°F/260°C. Remove the lamb from the bags and place on a baking sheet or roasting pan. Cook in the oven for 10 minutes to achieve a nice sear. At this point, the lamb should be crispy on the outside and fall-off-the-bone tender on the inside.

263. SLOW COOKED LAMB SHOULDER

Cal.: 329 | Fat: 19.9g | Protein: 35.3g   11 min | 8 hours | Servings 4

INGREDIENTS
- 1 whole lamb shoulder, deboned
- Salt and pepper
- 3 tablespoons olive oil
- 1 clove of garlic, crushed
- Large sprig for each thyme, rosemary and mint

DIRECTIONS
Set your Sous Vide Machine to 182°F/83.3 C. Rub the lamb with salt and pepper, and place inside a vacuum-sealed bag. Add the garlic, oil and herbs. Seal the bag and Immerse in the water bath for 8 hours. When the lamb is almost finished cooking, heat your broiler to high temperature. Remove the lamb from the water bath and place on a baking sheet, Fat: side up. Broil for 8 to 10 minutes or until the fat side is crispy.

264. SPICED LAMB CHOPS

Cal.: 679 | Fat: 29.8g | Protein: 95.7g   11 min | 2 hours | Servings 2

INGREDIENTS
- 1-½ teaspoons chopped fresh rosemary
- ½ teaspoon salt
- 1/4 teaspoon freshly ground black pepper
- 1 garlic clove, minced
- 8 (3-ounce) lamb rib chops, trimmed
- 2 teaspoons olive oil

DIRECTIONS
Set your Sous Vide Machine to 140°F/60°C. Place the lamb chops in a vacuum-sealed bag with the rosemary, salt, and pepper and seal. Immerse in the water bath and cook for 2 hours. When the lamb is almost finished, heat a skillet over medium heat, and brown the garlic. Add the lamb and cook until the chops have browned. Remove from heat and serve immediately.

265. CAROLINA PULLED PORK

Cal.: 603 | Fat: 41.3g | Protein: 41.9g

 21 min | 24 hours | Servings 8

INGREDIENTS

For the pork:
- 1 (2-3 pounds) pork shoulder
- 1 teaspoon mild paprika
- 2 teaspoons light brown sugar
- 1-½ teaspoons hot paprika
- ½ teaspoon celery salt
- ½ teaspoon garlic salt
- ½ teaspoon dry mustard
- ½ teaspoon freshly ground black pepper
- ½ teaspoon onion powder
- 1/4 teaspoon salt

For the Sauce:
- 1-½ cups yellow mustard
- ½ cup brown sugar
- 3/4 cups cider vinegar
- 3/4 cups beer
- 1 teaspoon fresh ground pepper
- ½ teaspoon cayenne pepper
- 1-½ teaspoons Worcestershire sauce
- 2 tablespoons butter, melted
- 1-½ teaspoons liquid smoke

DIRECTIONS

Set your Sous Vide Machine to 140°F/60°C. Combine all the spices for the pork in a small bowl and rub the mixture all over the pork shoulder. Place the pork shoulder in a vacuum-sealed bag. Immerse the bag in the water and cook for 24 hours. To make the sauce, combine all sauce ingredients in a medium saucepan and heat over low heat until just bubbling. Remove the pork from the water bath and place in a large bowl. Pour in the sauce, and with two forks, shred the pork and mix with the sauce. Serve on soft buns and top with your favorite coleslaw.

266. SIMPLE RACK OF LAMB

Cal.: 326 | Fat: 14.9g | Protein: 29g

21 min | 12 hours | Servings 4

INGREDIENTS

- 2 racks of St. Louis or baby back ribs
- 1 teaspoon liquid hickory smoke
- 1/3 cup paprika
- 1/3 cup dark brown sugar
- 1/4 cup salt
- 2 tablespoons whole yellow mustard seed
- 1 teaspoon freshly ground black pepper
- 2 teaspoons granulated garlic powder
- 1 tablespoon dried oregano

DIRECTIONS

Set your Sous Vide Machine to 165°F/74°C. Combine the paprika, sugar, salt, mustard seed, pepper, garlic powder and oregano. Remove the silver skin on the back of the ribs and cut into three or four rib sections. Coat the ribs in the spice mix and place in vacuum-sealed bags. Place in the water bath and cook for 12 hours. Remove from the water bath and pat dry with paper towels. Heat your oven to 300°F and coat the racks with your favorite barbecue sauce. Cook ribs in the oven for about 30-40 minutes. A nice coating of sauce will form.

Note: Feel free to add more sauce while the ribs are in the oven for even more flavor.

267. ADOBO PORK RIBS

Cal.: 520 | Fat: 12.3g | Protein: 90g   21 min | 12 hours | Servings 4

INGREDIENTS

- 1 cup apple cider vinegar
- 1 tablespoon soy sauce
- 3 bay leaves
- 1 large jalapeño chili, chopped
- 1 side baby-back pork ribs, cut into individual ribs
- 2 teaspoons sea salt
- 6 garlic cloves, peeled
- 2 teaspoons black peppercorns

DIRECTIONS

Set your Sous Vide Machine to 165°F/74°C. In a bowl, combine the vinegar, soy sauce, bay leaves, and chilies. Season the ribs with salt and place inside a vacuum-sealed bag with the garlic, pepper and vinegar mixture. Seal the bag and Immerse in the water bath for 12 hours. When the ribs are nearly finished in the water bath, preheat your oven to 400°F/205°C. Remove the ribs from the bag and pour 1/4 cup of the liquid over the ribs. Place in the oven for 10-15 minutes, or until browned. Serve with steamed rice and the remaining cooking liquid.

268. SPICY KOREAN PORK RIBS

Cal.: 536 | Fat: 14.3g | Protein: 89.7g   11 min | 12 hours | Servings 4

INGREDIENTS

- 3 pounds baby back pork ribs, separated into individual ribs
- ½ cup gochujang
- 2 tablespoons dark brown sugar
- 2 tablespoons soy sauce
- 2 tablespoons rice vinegar
- 2 teaspoons toasted sesame oil
- Salt to taste

DIRECTIONS

Set your Sous Vide Machine to 165°F/74°C. In a bowl, combine the gochujang, brown sugar, soy sauce, vinegar and sesame oil. Season the ribs with salt and place in a vacuum-sealed bag. Add the marinade to the bag and seal. Immerse the bag in the water bath and cook for 12 hours. When the ribs are nearly finished, heat your oven to 450°F/230°C. Remove the ribs from the bag and reserve the marinade. Place the ribs on a baking sheet and brush with the reserved marinade. Cook in the oven for 15 minutes and baste again with marinade. Cook for an additional 10 minutes.

269. ROSEMARY LAMB CHOPS

Cal.: 679 | Fat: 29.8g | Protein: 95.7g   11 min | 2 hours | Servings 2

INGREDIENTS

- 8 (3-ounce) lamb rib chops, trimmed
- 1-½ teaspoons chopped fresh rosemary
- ½ teaspoon salt
- 1/4 teaspoon freshly ground black pepper
- 1 garlic clove, minced
- 2 teaspoons olive oil

DIRECTIONS

Set your Sous Vide Machine to 140°F/60°C. Place the lamb chops in a vacuum-sealed bag with the rosemary, salt and pepper, and seal. Immerse in the water bath and cook for 2 hours. When the lamb is almost finished, heat a skillet over medium heat, and brown the garlic. Add the lamb and cook until the chops have browned. Remove from heat and serve immediately.

270. HERBED PORK CHOPS

Cal.: 370 | Fat: 32.5g | Protein: 18.2g

🔪 11 min | 🍲 60 min | 🍴 Servings 4

INGREDIENTS

- 4 bone-in pork chops
- 4 sprigs of fresh rosemary
- 2 garlic cloves, crushed
- 2 tablespoons olive oil
- 2 tablespoons butter
- Salt and pepper

DIRECTIONS

Heat your Sous Vide Machine to 140°F/60°C for medium-rare chops. For medium-well, set your Sous Vide Machine to 150°F/66°C. Place the chops, herbs, salt, pepper, and butter in a vacuum-sealed bag. Immerse in the water bath for at least 1 hour and not more than 4. When the chops are nearly finished, heat a skillet (preferably cast-iron) on high heat with olive oil. Remove chops from the bag and sear quickly on both sides until a nice crust is achieved. Remove from the pan and serve immediately.

271. COCHINITA PIBIL

Cal.: 405 | Fat: 34.6g | Protein: 97.9g

🔪 15 min | 🍲 24 hours | 🍴 Servings 6

INGREDIENTS

- 1 boneless pork shoulder
- 3/4 cups crumbled achiote paste
- 3 tablespoons orange juice
- 1 tablespoon white wine vinegar
- 2 garlic cloves, minced
- 1/4 teaspoons dried oregano
- 3 medium yellow onions, quartered
- ½ cup water

DIRECTIONS

Set your Sous Vide Machine to 158°F/70°C. Combine the achiote paste, orange juice, vinegar, garlic and oregano in a bowl and mix well. Season the pork shoulder with the mixture so that it is fully coated. Place the pork in a vacuum-sealed bag with the quartered onions, water and remaining seasoning mixture. Seal the bag and Immerse in the water bath for 12 to 24 hours. Remove the pork from the water bath, pour the entire contents into a large bowl. Using forks, shred the pork and onions, and mix with the cooking liquid. The pork should be so tender that it falls apart easily. Serve with salsa and corn tortillas.

272. HERBED PORK ROAST

Cal.: 989 | Fat: 52.6g | Protein: 103.6g

🔪 11 min | 🍲 4 hours | 🍴 Servings 6

INGREDIENTS

- 1 (5 pounds) boneless pork loin
- 1 teaspoon rubbed sage
- ½ teaspoon salt
- 1/4 teaspoon pepper
- 1 garlic clove, crushed
- ½ cup sugar
- 1 tablespoon cornstarch
- 1/4 cup vinegar
- 1/4 cup water
- 2 tablespoons soy sauce

DIRECTIONS

Set your Sous Vide Machine to 140°F/60°C. In a bowl, combine the sage, salt, pepper and garlic. Rub the mixture liberally on the pork and place in a vacuum-sealed bag. Immerse the bag in the water bath and cook for at least 2 hours and not more than 4. When the pork is nearly finished, heat your oven to 450°F/230°C. In a saucepan, combine the sugar, cornstarch, vinegar, water and soy sauce. Cook over medium heat until the sauce has reduced and slightly thickened. Remove the pork from the water bath and place on a baking sheet or roasting pan. Baste with the mixture and place in the oven for 20 minutes. Remove roast from the oven and slice into ½-inch-thick pieces.

273. ESPRESSO-CHILI RIBS

Cal.: 482 | Fat: 11.3g | Protein: 80g ⟍ 11 min | 🍲 12 hours | ✗ Servings 6

INGREDIENTS

- 4 pounds baby back pork ribs
- 2 tablespoons cayenne pepper
- 1 tablespoon paprika
- 1 tablespoon ground cumin
- 1-½ teaspoons salt
- 3/4 teaspoons ground black pepper
- 1 (12-ounce) bottle dark beer
- Your favorite barbecue sauce
- ½ cup water
- 2 tablespoons light brown sugar
- 1 tablespoon instant espresso powder

DIRECTIONS

Set your Sous Vide Machine to 165°F/74°C. In a small bowl, combine the cayenne pepper, paprika, cumin, salt and pepper. Rub the spice mix on the ribs, covering completely. Place the ribs in a vacuum-sealed bag, but don't seal it yet. In a small saucepan, reduce the beer by about half and pour into the bag with the ribs and then seal. Immerse the bag in the water bath and cook for 12 hours. When the ribs are nearly finished cooking, combine the barbecue sauce, water, brown sugar and espresso powder in a medium saucepan over low heat. Remove the ribs from the water bath and pat dry with paper towels. Heat your oven to 400°F and brush the barbecue sauce mixture over the ribs. Place the ribs on a baking sheet and cook in the oven for 10 minutes. Brush another coating of sauce onto the ribs and cook for an additional 10 minutes. **Note:** Serve ribs with the remaining barbecue sauce on the side.

274. PORK MEDALLIONS WITH FENNEL

Cal.: 385 | Fat: 25.4g | Protein: 32.2g ⟍ 11 min | 🍲 2 hours | ✗ Servings 6

INGREDIENTS

- 1-½ pounds pork loin, cut into medallions
- Salt and ground pepper
- 4 tablespoons olive oil, plus more for serving
- 2 fennel bulbs, trimmed and thinly sliced
- Juice of ½ lemon
- 1 sprig of fresh thyme
- 1 sprig fresh oregano
- 2 garlic cloves, peeled and lightly crushed
- Chopped fresh parsley, for serving

DIRECTIONS

Set your Sous Vide Machine to 140°F/60°C. Rub the pork with salt and pepper, and 1 tablespoon oil, and place in one vacuum-sealed bag. In another vacuum-sealed bag, combine 1 tablespoon oil, fennel, lemon juice, thyme, oregano and garlic. Immerse both bags in the water bath and cook for 2 hours. Just before removing the bags from the water bath, heat a large skillet on medium heat and add the remaining oil. Place the pork medallions and the fennel mixture in the pan and cook the pork for 2 minutes per side. Remove from heat and garnish with fresh parsley.

275. PHILLY CHEESESTEAK

Cal.: 680 | Fat: 33g | Protein: 46g   🔪 5 min | 🍲 60 min | 🍴 Servings 4

INGREDIENTS

- 500g sirloin steak
- 4 Part baked rustic bread roll
- 1 red onion
- 1 red pepper
- 1 green pepper
- For the cheese sauce:
- 100g cheese grated
- 1 tablespoon flour
- 25g butter
- Half teaspoon of ground Nutmeg
- Milk to pour

DIRECTIONS

Preheat your Sous vide machine at 126°F/52°C. Place the steaks in a vacuum bag and vacuum seal. Transfer to the water bath and cook for 1 hour. Cut the onions and peppers into strips and pan fry in oil and butter until soft. Add half a beef stock cube by crumbling direct onto the vegetables, stir through until combined and a slight sauce is formed coating the vegetables. Prepare a roux for the cheese sauce: melt the butter in a pan, sprinkle over the flour and stir until foaming, then add the milk gradually until a thick white sauce is made. Now add the cheese and nutmeg then stir until thick and sticky. Place the part-baked bread rolls in the oven to crisp up and warm through just in time for the steak to end its cooking. Slice the steak into strips and place inside the pre-cut bread rolls with the vegetable mix. Smother in that unctuous cheesy sauce before grilling on high for a minute to just catch the sauce for extra flavor.

276. BEEF & ALE CUPCAKE PIES

Cal.: 923 | Fat: 54g | Protein: 60g   🔪 30 min | 🍲 16 hours | 🍴 Servings 8

INGREDIENTS

For the Filling:

- 3 tbsp olive oil
- Sprig of Thyme
- 500g Scotch Braising Beef
- 2 onions, peeled and diced
- 6 Chestnut Mushrooms diced
- 1 garlic clove, grated
- 2 tbsp tomato paste
- 500ml beef stock/broth
- 2 tbsp miso paste
- 2 tbsp beef Bovril
- 1/2 bottle of Newcastle Brown Ale
- 2 dried bay leaves
- 1 1/2 tsp salt, plus more to taste
- 2 tsp black pepper
- 3 tbsp cornstarch (cornflour)

For the Pastry:

- 1 egg yolk, lightly beaten
- Ready to roll Shortcrust
- Ready to Roll Puff Pastry

DIRECTIONS

Sear the meat in a hot pan with oil and thyme. Place the beef in the vacuum bag within 1 tbsp of miso, 1 tbsp of the Bovril. Seal the bag and leave it to marinate for 4 hours in the fridge. Preheat your Sous Vide machine to 140°F/60°C. When the machine is ready place the beef in the water bath and cook for 16 hours. To make the sauce: In a frying pan, cook the onions, pepper with some oil, and salt. Let this sweat down then add to the pan the mushrooms and garlic. Once slightly browning on the edges add the miso, Bovril, and tomato paste mixing all the ingredients to get a good coating. While cooking stir in the stock and ale allowing all the liquid to come to the boil. Once at boiling point turn down to a slow rumble and let the liquid reduce by half. As the consistency starts to get a glossier mix together the cornstarch with 2 tbsp of cold water, reduce the heat and stir in the mixture until it starts to thicken. Leave to cool. Grease a cupcake tin, cut the shortcrust pastry to size, and place into the tin leaving an overlapping edge at the top. Take your meat from the sous vide and drain away the juices, take the meat, and put it in the pan with the sauce, and coat evenly starting to break up the chunks. Take the combined filling and start to spoon into the shortcrust lined tin until just at the top. Make an egg wash up and start to put around the overlap edges and with a cutter cut a lid from the puff pastry and place the lids on top of the filling, gently pressing to try to join the top with the casing. Pierce the lids 2 times with a small knife. Brush with egg wash. Bake in the oven at 350°F/176°C for 20 to 25 minutes until a deep golden brown.

277. SMOKED OXTAIL BAU BUNS

Cal.: 513 | Fat: 19.3g | Protein: 53.3g  2 hours | 12 hours | Servings 4

INGREDIENTS

- 1 oxtail
- 1 tbsp. Bovril
- 1 tbsp. chopped thyme
- 2-star anise, crushed

For the onion Jam:
- 2kg white onions or regular onions
- 4 garlic cloves
- 130g butter
- 4 tbsp. oil
- 140g golden caster sugar
- 1 tbsp. fresh thyme leaf
- pinch of chili flakes (optional)
- 75cl bottle white wine
- 350ml white wine vinegar
- 250ml sake
- 150g soy sauce
- 100g oyster sauce

For the Bau Buns:
- 525g plain flour, plus extra for dusting
- 1½ tbsp. caster sugar, plus a pinch
- 1 tsp fast-action dried yeast
- 50ml milk
- 200ml tepid water
- 1 tbsp. sunflower oil
- 1 tbsp. rice vinegar
- 1 tsp baking powder

DIRECTIONS

Sear the oxtail in a hot pan then rub with Bovril, chopped thyme, and 2 crushed star. Season. Vacuum seal and cook at 176°F/80°C for 12 hours. Once cooked, allow cooling then pick the meat off the bone. Place into a bowl and season. Reserve for next step. To make the onion jam, place all onions and garlic in the pan and sweat out until soft and translucent. Add the rest of the ingredients add cook until the texture is syrup-like. Season and cool. Add the onion to the oxtail mix. For the Bau Buns, mix together the flour, sugar, and 1/2 tsp of salt in a mixer. Dissolve the yeast and a pinch of salt in 1 tbsp. warm water. Add it to the bowl along with the oil, vinegar, baking powder, and 200ml water. Mix into a dough, adding a little extra water if needed. The dough should be nice and gelatinous Place in a lightly oiled bowl, cover with a damp cloth and leave to rise for 1 ½ hour, or until doubled in size.

Tip the dough out onto a clean work surface and knock the air out. Divide into 12-15 portions then flatten the doughs with your hands, and place a tbsp. of the oxtail/jam mix inside and roll each piece of dough into a ball and leave to rest for 2-3 minutes. Transfer the prepared buns to a steamer basket lined with baking parchment. Cover with a clean tea towel or lightly oiled cling film and leave to prove in a warm place for 1 hour 30 minutes, or until doubled in size. To finish, place the oxtail mix into the proved buns and place the steamer basket over medium-high heat. Steam the buns for 8 minutes until puffed up (you'll need to do this in batches) and sprinkle with the chili, spring onion, and coriander and serve.

CHAPTER 6:
Side Recipes

🔪 Preparation Time | 🍲 Cooking Time | ✖ Servings

278. GARLICKY BRUSSELS SPROUTS

Cal.: 326 | Fat: 26g | Protein: 8.3g   ⬛ 21 min | 🍲 60 min | ✖ Servings 2

INGREDIENTS
- 1 lb. Brussels sprouts, trimmed
- 1/4 cup premium olive oil
- 2 tablespoons garlic, minced
- 1 tablespoon sea salt

DIRECTIONS
Preheat a water bath to 185°F/85°C. Add all ingredients to a bag and seal airtight. Add to the water bath and cook for 1 hour.
Serve immediately with your favorite dish.

279. ARTICHOKES

Cal.: 368 | Fat: 25.7g | Protein: 10.6g   ⬛ 21 min | 🍲 60 min | ✖ Servings 2

INGREDIENTS
- 4 artichokes, trimmed down to their hearts
- 1/4 cup premium olive oil
- 1 tablespoon sea salt

DIRECTIONS
Preheat a water bath to 185°F/85°C. Toss artichokes with all ingredients until well-coated in a large mixing bowl. Place in a vacuum sealable bag and vacuum airtight. Add to the water bath and cook for 1 hour. Serve immediately with your favorite dish.

280. TENDER GARLIC ASPARAGUS

Cal.: 50 | Fat: 2.5g | Protein: 2.8g   ⬛ 6 min | 🍲 60 min | ✖ Servings 4

INGREDIENTS
- 1 lb. asparagus, cleaned and dried with a paper towel
- 2 teaspoons olive oil
- 1 tablespoon garlic powder
- 1 teaspoon sea salt

DIRECTIONS
Preheat the Sous Vide machine to 135°F/57°C. Toss asparagus with all ingredients until well-coated in a large mixing bowl. Place asparagus, lined flat, in a vacuum sealable bag and vacuum airtight. Cook for 1 hour. Serve immediately with your favorite dish.

282. RICH AND CREAMY POLENTA

Cal.: 176 | Fat: 10.7g | Protein: 15.8g   ⬛ 5 min | 🍲 60 min | ✖ Servings 6

INGREDIENTS
- ½ cup dry yellow polenta
- 2 cups chicken or vegetable stock
- 1/4 cup butter, unsalted
- Sea salt
- 1/4 cup pecorino Romano cheese, for serving

DIRECTIONS
Preheat the water bath to 182°F/83°C. Add polenta, stock, butter and a pinch of sea salt to a resealable plastic bag and seal. Immerse the bag in the water bath and cook for 1 hour. Remove from the water bath and add to a mixing bowl. Fold in cheese until well-incorporated and serve warm.

281. GLAZED CARROTS

Cal.: 67 | Fat: 2.1g | Protein: 0.8g   ⬛ 11 min | 🍲 60 min | ✖ Servings 4

INGREDIENTS
- 1 lb. baby carrots
- 2 teaspoons butter
- 2 teaspoons honey
- Salt and pepper

DIRECTIONS
Preheat the Sous Vide machine to 185°F/85°C. Place all the ingredients in the bag including salt and pepper to taste. Seal and place the bag in your preheated container and set your timer for 1 hour. When the carrots are cooked, put them on a plate to cool for a few minutes, and drizzle with cooking juices. Serve with your main dish

283. TENDER DOENJANG-SPICED EGGPLANT

Cal.: 280 | Fat: 15.7g | Protein: 7.5g   6 min | 41 min | Servings 4

INGREDIENTS

- 4 large pieces of eggplant, cut into wedges
- 1/4 cup peanut oil
- 2 tablespoons Doenjang paste
- 2 tablespoons light soy sauce
- 1 tablespoon brown sugar
- 1 tablespoon sesame seeds

DIRECTIONS

Preheat the bath to 185°F/85°C. Whisk the Doenjang paste, peanut oil, soy sauce and sugar together in a mixing bowl. Add the eggplant and toss to coat evenly, then transfer to a bag and vacuum tight. Cook for 45 minutes. Drain the eggplant wedges from the cooking liquid. Sear the eggplants on a hot grilling pan. Top with sesame seeds and serve.

284. TANGY GARLIC CHILI TOFU

Cal.: 377 | Fat: 29.8g | Protein: 7g   11 min | 4 hours | Servings 2

INGREDIENTS

- 1 block of super firm tofu
- 1/4 cup brown sugar
- 1/4 cup soy sauce
- 1/4 cup toasted sesame oil
- 2 tablespoons chili garlic paste

DIRECTIONS

Preheat the water bath to 180°F/82°C. Press out liquid from tofu. Cut tofu into thick chunks, about 2 inches each. Preheat a frying pan on medium, spray with non-stick cooking spray, and cook until golden on each side. Mix soy sauce, brown sugar, toasted sesame oil, and chili garlic paste together until well-blended in a mixing bowl. Toss tofu in sauce to coat well. Transfer tofu and sauce to a bag and seal. Immerse in the bath and cook for 4 hours. Remove and serve immediately.

285. YUMMY STEAK FRIES

Cal.: 291 | Fat: 11.9g | Protein: 4.9g   11 min | 95 min | Servings 4

INGREDIENTS

- 5 russet Potatoes
- ½ stick unsalted butter
- For the seasoning mix:
- 1 teaspoon garlic powder
- 1 teaspoon chili powder
- ½ teaspoon smoked paprika
- ½ teaspoon sea salt
- ½ teaspoon black pepper

DIRECTIONS

Preheat the Sous Vide machine to 190°F/88°C. Cut potatoes in half and lengthwise into wedges. Melt butter in the microwave. Mix together seasonings in a separate bowl. Place potatoes in a resealable plastic bag, toss in butter until covered evenly. Toss in seasoning mix and toss to coat again. Seal and lower bag into the water bath. Cook for 90 minutes. Remove, place on a baking sheet broil for 2-3 minutes on each side. Serve hot!

286. TENDER LEEKS WITH HERBED BUTTER

Cal.: 130 | Fat: 11.7g | Protein: 0.8g   11 min | 60 min | Servings 4

INGREDIENTS

- 4 baby leeks (or 2 large)
- 4 tablespoons butter, salted
- 1 teaspoon Herbes de Provence

DIRECTIONS

Preheat the Sous Vide machine to 180°F/82°C. Wash leeks and cut off ends. If using large leeks, split down the middle, then cut again in half, making four sections per leek. Baby leeks can be left intact. Melt butter in the microwave, add herbs, and mix. Put leeks and butter into a large zipper-lock bag, swirl the butter mixture around to evenly coat the leeks. Remove excess air and seal shut. Place in the bath and cook for one hour. Serve as a tender side dish for any main course.

287. TANGY TENDER MUSHROOMS

Cal.: 90 | Fat: 7.3g | Protein: 4.1g   11 min | 30 min | Servings 4

INGREDIENTS

- 1 lb. button mushrooms cleaned, rinsed, and cut into bite-size pieces
- 2 tablespoons soy sauce
- 2 tablespoons extra-virgin olive oil
- 1 tablespoon balsamic vinegar
- ½ teaspoon black pepper
- ½ teaspoon sea salt, plus more to taste

DIRECTIONS

Preheat your water bath to 176°F/80°C. Combine the mushrooms with the rest of the ingredients, in a large mixing bowl, and toss to coat evenly. Place the mixture in a sealable plastic bag; seal using the water displacement method or use a vacuum sealer. Add mushrooms to the water bath and cook for 30 minutes. Remove the bag from the water bath and serve immediately with your favorite meal.

288. EASY FLAVOR-PACKED PICKLES

Cal.: 475 | Fat: 27.8g | Protein: 4.7g   11 min | 2 hours 30 min | Servings 10

INGREDIENTS

- 20 small cucumbers, stems removed
- 4 medium mason jars
- 20 black peppercorns
- 4 garlic cloves, smashed
- 4 teaspoons fresh dill

For the Pickling Brine:

- 2-½ cups white wine vinegar
- 2-½ cups water
- ½ cup sugar, granulated
- 2 tablespoons pickling salt

DIRECTIONS

Preheat the water bath to 140°F/60°C. Whisk brine ingredients together in a large mixing bowl until well-combined. Place 5 cucumbers, 5 peppercorns, 1 garlic clove and 1 teaspoon dill in each Mason jar. Fill each jar with brine and seal the lid tight. Immerse mason jars in the water bath and cook for 2 hours 30 minutes. Remove from the water bath and allow to cool to room temperature. Refrigerate overnight or up to 3 days to brine. Serve with your favorite meals or as a delicious snack.

289. HOT CHILI CHUTNEY

Cal.: 91 | Fat: 0.6g | Protein: 1.7g   11 min | 5 hours 50 min | Servings 6

INGREDIENTS

- 5 medium jalapeños
- 2 medium red bell peppers
- 1 medium red onion, chopped
- ½ tablespoon rosemary
- 1 bay leaf
- ½ teaspoon ground cinnamon
- 1/4 teaspoon sea salt
- 1/4 teaspoon black pepper
- ½ cup brown sugar
- 1 tablespoon balsamic vinegar

DIRECTIONS

Preheat the Sous Vide machine to 182°F/83°C. Roast the peppers under a broiler until the skins are completely charred. Transfer the peppers to a bowl, cover with plastic wrap, and let sit about 15 to 20 minutes or until cool enough to handle. Peel away the charred outer skins, cut the peppers in half, core, seed and finely chop the flesh. Add peppers and remaining ingredients to a cooking pouch and vacuum seal. Immerse the pouch in a water bath and cook for 5 hours. Remove from the water bath and quick chill by submerging in ice water for 30 minutes. Serve right away, or refrigerate in the pouch, unopened, for up to a week.

290. FRAGRANT TOMATO SAUCE

Cal.: 84 | Fat: 5.3g | Protein: 2g   11 min | 56 min | Servings 6

INGREDIENTS

- 2 tablespoons olive oil
- ½ cup onion, chopped
- 2 garlic cloves, minced
- 3 sprigs fresh oregano, stemmed
- 2 lbs. ripe tomatoes
- 6 large basil leaves, chopped
- 1 whole green pepper, seeded and cut into four large pieces

DIRECTIONS

Heat olive oil to medium in a sauté pan. Add onion, garlic, and oregano, and cook until fragrant, about 5 to 7 minutes, and set aside to cool. Preheat the water bath to 120°F/49°C. Add olive oil mix, tomatoes and remaining ingredients to a resealable plastic bag, and seal airtight. Cook for 50 minutes. Remove the bag from the water, open and let cool for a few minutes. Remove peppers and discard. Remove and peel the tomatoes. Add peeled tomatoes and the remaining contents of the bag to a food processor or blender and process until desired texture is achieved. Serve with your favorite dishes.

291. CREAMY BÉARNAISE SAUCE

Cal.: 205 | Fat: 6.4g | Protein: 5.7g   15 min | 30 min | Servings 4

INGREDIENTS

For the reduction:
- 1 bunch fresh tarragon, chopped
- 2 medium shallots, minced
- ½ cup white wine vinegar
- ½ cup dry white wine
- 6 whole black peppercorns

For the sauce:
- 3 egg yolks
- 2 cups, premium French butter
- 3-4 tablespoons reduction
- Sea salt and pepper, to taste

DIRECTIONS

Preheat the water bath for 140°F/60°C. In a small saucepan, combine tarragon, shallots, vinegar, pepper and wine over medium-high heat. Bring to simmer and cook until reduced by half. Remove from heat, strain liquid, and set it aside to cool. Place reduction, butter and egg yolks in a resealable plastic bag—DO NOT seal. Place the bag in the water bath to cook for 30 minutes. Pour the sauce into a food processor or blender, and process until thickened. Season with sea salt and pepper and serve immediately.

292. HOLIDAY CRANBERRY SAUCE

Cal.: 102 | Fat: 0.2g | Protein: 3g   3 min | 2 hours | Servings 8

INGREDIENTS

- 1 package frozen cranberries (or fresh)
- 1–2 tablespoons raw honey
- 1 cinnamon stick
- 2 fresh cloves
- 1 orange, sliced thin
- ½ tablespoon cinnamon
- ½ teaspoon nutmeg

DIRECTIONS

Preheat the water bath to 185°F/85°C. Place cranberries in a sealed bag along with the remaining ingredients and cook for about 2 hours. Remove and transfer to an ice bath for 5-10 minutes. Serve with your favorite meals; alternatively, you can refrigerate for up to 14 days.

293. GREEN BEANS ALMONDINE

Cal.: 209 | Fat: 17.5g | Protein: 5.5g   📐 15 min | 🍲 90 min | 🍴 Servings 4

INGREDIENTS

- 3 cups fresh green beans
- 2 tablespoons olive oil
- 1 tablespoon lemon zest
- 1 teaspoon salt
- 2 tablespoons lemon juice
- ½ cup toasted almonds

DIRECTIONS

Preheat your water bath to 180°F/82°C. Clean and trim the green beans and mix with lemon zest and olive oil. Roughly chop the almonds. Place the whole mixture in the bag, seal, and place in your preheated container. Set the timer for 1-½ hours. Put the cooked green beans on a plate, top with lemon juice, and season with salt. Mix in the almonds and serve.

294. APPLE BUTTERNUT SQUASH SOUP

Cal.:226 | Fat: 7.3g | Protein: 3.6g   📐 11 min | 🍲 2 hours | 🍴 Servings 4

INGREDIENTS

- 1 medium butternut squash,
- 1 large tart apple
- ½ yellow onion
- 1 teaspoon sea salt
- 3/4 cup light cream

DIRECTIONS

Preheat your bath to 185°F/85°C. Core and slice the apple, peel and slice the butternut squash, slice the onion. Place the butternut squash, apple and onion in a bag. Seal and place the bag in your preheated container and set your timer for 2 hours. Once cooked, place the ingredients in a blender and blend until smooth. Add the remaining ingredients and purée again.

295. SWEET POTATOES WITH COCONUT CHILI

Cal.: 164 | Fat: 7.1g | Protein: 2.4g   📐 11 min | 🍲 60 min | 🍴 Servings 4

INGREDIENTS

- 4 sweet potatoes
- 2 tablespoons coconut oil, melted
- ½ teaspoon chili powder
- ½ teaspoon cumin powder
- ¼ teaspoon salt
- 2 tablespoons chopped cilantro, for garnish

DIRECTIONS

Preheat the Sous Vide machine to 190°F/88°C. Peel and cut sweet potatoes into 1-inch-thick roundels. Mix melted coconut oil and spices in a bowl. Add sweet potato and mix well, making sure to cover the roundels in the oil and spice. Place in a large zipper-lock bag (or multiple smaller zipper-lock bags), remove excess air and seal. Place in the bath and cook for 60 minutes. Serve garnished with some chopped cilantro.

296. GARLIC AND ROSEMARY RISOTTO

Cal.: 228 | Fat: 3.2g | Protein: 7.9g   📐 11 min | 🍲 46 min | 🍴 Servings 4

INGREDIENTS

- 1 cup Arborio rice
- 1 teaspoon extra virgin olive oil
- 2 tablespoons jarred, roasted minced garlic
- 3 cups chicken or vegetable broth
- 1 sprig of fresh rosemary
- Salt and pepper
- 1/3 cup grated Romano cheese

DIRECTIONS

Preheat the Sous Vide machine to 185°F/85°C. Discard the stems from the rosemary and mince the leaves. Place all ingredients except for cheese in a resealable bag. Place the bag in your preheated container and set your timer for 45 minutes. When the rice is cooked, place it in a bowl and fluff with a fork. Mix in the cheese and serve immediately.

297. LEMON AND PARMESAN BROCCOLI

Cal.: 63 | Fat: 4.8g | Protein: 1.7g   11 min | 52 min | ✖ Servings 5

INGREDIENTS
- 1 head of broccoli
- 2 tablespoons butter
- Salt and pepper
- Parmesan cheese, for sprinkling
- 1 lemon

DIRECTIONS
Preheat the Sous Vide machine to 185°F/85°C. Cut the head of broccoli into large pieces. Put the broccoli and butter in a bag. Salt and pepper to taste. Place the bag in your preheated container and set your timer for 45 minutes. Transfer broccoli to a plate and add the lemon juice and top with cheese to serve.

298. OMELET WITH PARMESAN

Cal.: 303 | Fat: 17.39g | Protein: 21.85g   3 min | 20 min | ✖ Servings 1

INGREDIENTS
- 2 large eggs
- 1 Tbsp. butter, diced
- 1 Tbsp. Parmesan cheese, finely grated
- A pinch of salt and pepper

For Servings:
- Fresh parsley, chopped
- A pinch of basil

DIRECTIONS
Preheat a water bath to 73°C/164°F. In a large bowl, crack the eggs and whisk quickly. When they are well mixed, add butter, Parmesan, salt and pepper. Stir well. Pour the mixture into a medium vacuum pouch and seal. Put the bag in a water bath. Cook for 10 minutes. After 10 minutes remove the bag from the bath and shake it well. That way, the eggs will start to get that "omelet look." Put the bag back in the bath and cook for another 10 minutes. When the eggs are finally cooked, transfer them to a plate. Add a dash of basil and parsley and serve.

299. BACON 'N' CHEESE EGG BITES

Cal.: 212 | Fat: 13.55g | Protein: 16.32g   7 min | 60 min | ✖ Servings 6

INGREDIENTS
- 2 slices cooked bacon, split
- 6 eggs
- 55g/1.94oz. cream cheese
- 50g/1.77oz. Gruyere cheese, grated
- A pinch of salt and pepper

DIRECTIONS
Preheat a water bath to 78°C/172°F. Mix the eggs, salt, pepper and both kinds of cheese into a blender. You want a consistent and smooth texture. Put each piece of bacon into one jar. Then pour the egg mixture. Seal with the lids. Place the jars in the water bath and cook for about an hour. Remove the bits from jars with the help of a spoon or a knife. Serve with your favorite salad.

300. SOFT-POACHED EGGS

Cal.: 173 | Fat: 8.57g | Protein: 13.59g   2 min | 12 min | ✖ Servings 2

INGREDIENTS
- 2 slices cooked bacon, split
- 6 eggs
- 55g/1.94oz. cream cheese
- 50g/1.77oz. Gruyere cheese, grated
- A pinch of salt and pepper

DIRECTIONS
Preheat a water bath to 75°C/167°F. With a slotted spoon, lower the eggs into the bath. Be careful not to break them. Cook for 12 minutes straight, no more, no less. In the meantime, grab a large bowl and fill it with water and ice. When the eggs are done, transfer them to an ice bowl. Let them cool for 2 minutes. Serve with the salad of your choice or with toasts.

301. SOFT BOILED EGGS

Cal.: 109 | Fat: 5.39g | Protein: 9.02g   ⚖ 11 min | 🍲 46 min | 🍴 Servings 2

INGREDIENTS
- 4 large eggs

DIRECTIONS
Preheat a water bath to 63°C/145°F. Use a slotted spoon to kindly place the eggs in the bath. Cook for 45 minutes. When the cooking time is finished, smoothly remove the eggs from the bath (once again use a slotted spoon). Serve immediately.

302. TOAST WITH FLAWLESSLY POACHED EGGS

Cal.: 329 | Fat: 23.41g | Protein: 13.76g   ⚖ 11 min | 🍲 90 min | 🍴 Servings 4

INGREDIENTS
- 8 large eggs

For toast:
- 8 slices of toast
- 8 slices of smoked salmon/ham
- 8 slices of tomato
- A dash of basil or lettuce leaves, salt and pepper

DIRECTIONS
Preheat a water bath to 64°C/147°F. Put the eggs directly into the bath and cook for 90 minutes. In the meantime, prepare sandwiches, put a smoked salmon or ham on each toast. Top every toast with one slice of tomato and a dash of basil or lettuce leaves. When the eggs are done, remove them from the water bath. Crack each egg on a toast and sprinkle with seasonings. Serve.

303. POACHED EGGS WITH AVOCADO TOAST

Cal.: 281 | Fat: 9.54g | Protein: 19.61g   ⚖ 6 min | 🍲 35 min | 🍴 Servings 4

INGREDIENTS
- 4 Eggs

For avocado toast:
- 4 slices of toasted bread of your choice
- 1 Avocado, sliced
- Fresh chives
- A pinch of salt and pepper
- and pepper

DIRECTIONS
Preheat a water bath to 75°C/167°F. Gently lower all the eggs into the bath, making sure they don't crack. Cook for 15 minutes. Remove the eggs. Put the eggs in an ice bowl (half ice, half water) and hold them there for about 1 minute. Place avocado slices on every toast and crack one egg over each slice. Sprinkle it with chives, salt and pepper. Serve.

304. PERFECTLY COOKED MUSHROOMS

Cal.: 94 | Fat: 3.22g | Protein: 5.02g   ⚖ 11 min | 🍲 30 min | 🍴 Servings 4

INGREDIENTS
- 450g/1lb. mixed mushrooms, thoroughly washed and cut into tiny pieces
- 2 tbsp./1Fl.oz. Extra-virgin olive oil
- 2 tsp. fresh thyme leaves
- 1 tbsp./0.5Fl.oz. Balsamic vinegar
- 2 tbsp./1Fl.oz. Soy sauce
- ½ tsp. black pepper
- Salt to taste

DIRECTIONS
Preheat a water bath to 80°C/176°F. In the meanwhile, add mushrooms and all ingredients to a big bowl. Stir thoroughly so that the ingredients cover mushrooms. Place the mixture in the plastic bag and seal. Let it cook for 30 minutes. When done, remove the bag from the bath. Serve warm.

305. BRUSSELS SPROUTS

Cal.: 234 | Fat: 4.39g | Protein: 21.13g   9 min | 60 min | Servings 6

INGREDIENTS

- 6 cups Brussels sprouts, halved (don't forget to remove the outer leaves)
- 5 Garlic cloves, cut
- 227g/1 cup butter
- 1 tsp. Tabasco sauce (chipotle flavor)
- ¾ tbsp. Kosher salt

DIRECTIONS

Preheat a water bath to 85°C /185°F. In a large bowl, combine all ingredients and transfer them to a vacuum bag. Use a vacuum sealer to seal the bag. Put the pouch in a water bath and cook for an hour. When cooked, remove the vacuum bag from the water bath. Then, quickly Immerse it in an ice-water bath for 1–2 hours. Store in the fridge for up to 3 days. Serve with meat when you wish.

306. GOOD OLD FRIES

Cal.: 367 | Fat: 9.98g | Protein: 0.5g   16 min | 90 min | Servings 4

INGREDIENTS

- 5 Russet potatoes
- ¼ tsp. onion powder
- ¼ tsp. garlic powder
- ½ tsp. paprika
- ¼ tsp. cayenne pepper
- ½ stick butter
- ¼ tsp. salt

DIRECTIONS

Preheat a water bath to 87°C/190°F. Peel potatoes and cut them into ¼ thin pieces. In a saucepan stir butter until completely melted. Remove from fire and add seasonings. Put potatoes in a vacuum bag and add the butter mixture. Shake for a few seconds, so that all potatoes are covered with the mixture. Use a vacuum sealer to tightly seal the bag. Cook potatoes for 90 minutes. When done, transfer fries to a baking pan. Cook for 3 minutes on every side, so that fries become crispy. Serve with your favorite meat.

307. SIMPLE ARTICHOKES

Cal.: 260 | Fat: 8.41g | Protein: 14.83g   11 min | 90 min | Servings 2

INGREDIENTS

- 7 tbsp. /100ml olive oil
- 4 globe artichokes
- 16 tbsp. /250ml water
- 4 tbsp. /60ml white wine vinegar
- 16 tbsp. /250ml white wine
- 1 bay leaf
- 1 small stem of thyme
- 2 garlic cloves
- 1 tsp. white peppercorns
- 1 tsp. coriander seeds

DIRECTIONS

Preheat the water bath to 85°C/185°F. In the meantime, add all ingredients (excluding the olive oil) into a skillet. When they start to boil, set them aside. Let them cool. When the mixture is cooled, you need to pour it through a sieve. Then add the olive oil. Now, it's time to prepare the artichokes. Add the artichokes and the mixture into a vacuum bag and seal. Immerse the pouch in the water bath. Let it cook for 1 and a half hours. When done, remove the vacuum bag from the bath. Set aside to cool but don't remove the food from the bag. When finally cooled, divide artichokes and serve right away.

308. ROOT VEGETABLES WITH DELIGHTFUL BROWN BUTTER

Cal.: 244 | Fat: 4.3g | Protein: 9.65g   ✎ 16 min | 🍲 3 hours 15 min | 🍴 Servings 2

INGREDIENTS
- 1 small turnip
- 4 small carrots
- 1 small parsnip
- ½ small red onion
- 1 small rutabaga
- 1 sprig of fresh rosemary
- 2 garlic cloves, crushed
- A pinch of salt and pepper
- 1 Tbsp. butter
- 1 Tbsp. /0.5°Fl.oz. extra-virgin olive oil

DIRECTIONS
Preheat a water bath to 85°C/185°F. Add rosemary, vegetables and olive oil to a vacuum bag and seal. Cook for three hours. Then pour the mixture from the bag into a sauté pan and sprinkle with salt and pepper. Cook for 4 minutes at a high temperature—the liquid should turn into a sauce. Add butter and stir slowly. When the veggies turn brown, set aside. Serve warm.

309. EARTHY AND SWEET BEETS

Cal.: 64 | Fat: 1.67g | Protein: 0.26g   ✎ 9 min | 🍲 60 min | 🍴 Servings 4

INGREDIENTS
- 3 large beets
- 1 tsp. /5ml pure Maple syrup
- 3 slices fresh orange
- A sprinkle of salt and pepper
- 1 tbsp. goat cheese for serving

DIRECTIONS
Preheat a water bath to 83°C/181°F. Cut the tips and tops off the beets and peel their skin. Put all ingredients (excluding the goat cheese) in a vacuum bag and seal. Place in the bath and cook for 1 hour. When the beets are almost cooked, transfer them into a pan. Stop cooking when the glaze starts to form. Move the mixture to a serving dish and serve immediately with the goat cheese and orange slices or with the meat.

310. RISOTTO WITH GARLIC AND PARMESAN

Cal.: 168 | Fat: 8.22g | Protein: 11.06g   ✎ 9 min | 🍲 45 min | 🍴 Servings 4

INGREDIENTS
- 90g/1 cup Arborio rice
- 720 ml/3 cups chicken broth
- 5 ml/1 tsp. extra virgin olive oil
- 2 Tbsp. minced garlic
- Salt and pepper
- 1 sprig of rosemary leaves, powdered
- 50g/1.77oz. grated Parmesan cheese

DIRECTIONS
Preheat a water bath to 83°C/181°F. Put all ingredients, apart from the cheese, into a zipped cooking pouch. Immerse the pouch in the bath and cook for 45 minutes. When rice is cooked, transfer it to a serving bowl and add cheese. Stir well. Serve.

311. FRESH JULIENNED ONION

Cal.: 176 | Fat: 3g | Protein: 3g   15 min | 🍲 2 hours | 🍴 Servings 4

INGREDIENTS
- 2 brown onions, julienned
- 2 tablespoons olive oil
- 1 tablespoon balsamic vinegar
- 2 tablespoon brown sugar
- Salt and pepper to taste

DIRECTIONS
Prepare your water bath by submerging your immersion circulator and raise the temperature to 185°F/85°C. Add listed ingredients to a heavy duty zip bag. Seal using the immersion method. Immerse and let it cook for 2 hours. Transfer the container to your fridge and chill for 3 hours. Serve and enjoy!

312. SIMPLE AND APPEALING CARROTS AND POTATOES

Cal.: 439 | Fat: 10.34g | Protein: 5.32g   11 min | 60 min | Servings 8

INGREDIENTS

For Carrots:
- 1 bunch heirloom carrots
- 2 leaves fresh sage
- 1 Tbsp. browned butter
- 2 tsp. /10 ml Demerara sugar

For Potatoes:
- 11 baby potatoes, halved
- A sprig of fresh thyme
- 2 Tbsp. /30ml olive oil

DIRECTIONS

Preheat a water bath to 83°C/181°F. Prepare veggies, peel the carrots (don't forget to remove the tops and tips). Scrub the potato peel and cut each potato in half. For this recipe, you need two vacuum bags. In one put all the ingredients for the carrots, and in the second put all ingredients for the potatoes. Cook for 1 hour. After an hour, transfer the potatoes mixture to a heated skillet. When the potatoes get golden brown, transfer them to a serving dish. Do the same with the carrots; just remember to wipe the skillet with a paper towel first. Add the final touch—sprinkle parmesan on the potatoes and spray the carrots with your favorite glaze. Serve with beef, pork, or poultry.

313. SHALLOT AND CREAM PEAS

Cal.: 519 | Fat: 46g | Protein: 6g   15 min | 60 min | Servings 2

INGREDIENTS

- 1 pound frozen sweet peas
- 1 cup heavy cream
- ¼ cup butter
- 1 tablespoon cornstarch
- ¼ teaspoon ground nutmeg
- 4 cloves
- 2 bay leaves
- Fresh ground black pepper

DIRECTIONS

Prepare your water bath by submerging your immersion circulator and raise the temperature to 183°F/84°C. Add cream, nutmeg, cornstarch in a small bowl and mix well until cornstarch dissolves. Add listed ingredients to a zip bag and seal using the immersion method. Immerse and cook for 1 hour. Remove and garnish with pepper. Serve and enjoy!

314. PERFECT CACTUS

Cal.: 59 | Fat: 2g | Protein: 2g   16 min | 60 min | Servings 4

INGREDIENTS

- 2 tablespoons freshly squeezed lime juice
- 1 tablespoon canola oil
- 1 garlic clove, thinly sliced
- 1 teaspoon ground coriander
- 1 teaspoon ground cumin
- 1 teaspoon salt
- 4 cactus paddles, thorns removed

DIRECTIONS

Prepare your water bath by submerging your immersion circulator and raise the temperature to 175°F/79°C. Take a bowl and whisk in lime juice, garlic, oil, coriander, cumin, salt and mix well. Transfer the whole mixture alongside cactus to a zip bag and seal using the immersion method. Immerse and cook for 60 minutes. Remove and drain cactus, discard cooking liquid. Use a veggie peeler to remove the skin from the cactus into strips. Serve and enjoy!

315. BUTTER RADISH

Cal.: 248 | Fat: 1g | Protein: 1g   16 min | 44 min | ✗ Servings 4

INGREDIENTS

- 1 pound radish, halved
- 3 tablespoons unsalted butter
- 1 teaspoon salt
- ½ teaspoon freshly ground black pepper

DIRECTIONS

Prepare your water bath by submerging your immersion circulator and raise the temperature to 180°F/82°C. Add listed ingredients to a heavy-duty zip bag and seal using the immersion method. Immerse and cook for 45 minutes. Once done, remove the bag and transfer contents to a platter. Serve and enjoy!

316. BEEF STOCK WITH VEGGIES

Cal.: 326 | Fat: 41.41g | Protein: 15.57g   9 min | 12 hours | ✗ Servings 4

INGREDIENTS

- 600g/1.3 lb. beef bones
- 750 ml/3 cups water
- 1 white onion, chopped
- 1 celery stick, chopped
- 1 carrot, chopped

DIRECTIONS

Preheat a water bath to 90°C/194°F. Place all the ingredients in a zip lock cooking bag and seal. Lower the bag in the bath and let it cook for 12 hours. When cooked, pour the contents of the bag into a pot and bring to a boil. When the stock starts to boil, leave it that way for 5-10 minutes. When it reduces by 1/3, remove from the oven and strain.

317. SOUP WITH ONIONS

Cal.: 362 | Fat: 6.49g | Protein: 26.06g   11 min | 46 min | ✗ Servings 2

INGREDIENTS

- 240 ml/1 cup light cream
- 5 ml/1 tsp. olive oil
- 5 ml/1 tsp. soy sauce
- 2 garlic cloves, chopped
- 1 bunch spring onions, cleaned and trimmed
- 1 medium russet potato, diced
- Salt and black pepper, to taste

DIRECTIONS

Preheat a water bath to 82°C/180°F. Place the onions (both green and white part), olive oil, soy sauce, garlic, potato and seasonings in a zip lock pouch and seal. Immerse the bag in the water oven and cook for 45 minutes. When cooked, transfer the contents from the bag into a blender and blend. Then add half of the light cream and blend once again. If you want more consistency, add the remaining cream.

CHAPTER 7:
Seafood Recipes

🔪 Preparation Time | 🍲 Cooking Time | ✗ Servings

318. MAHI-MAHI TACOS

Cal.: 300 | Fat: 24g | Protein: 13g   15 min | 20 min | Servings 6

INGREDIENTS
- 1 ½ pound mahi-mahi strips
- 6 tortillas
- 1/4 cup cornstarch
- 1 teaspoon chili powder
- ½ teaspoon baking powder
- 1 1/4 cup flour
- 1 cup beer
- Salt, pepper, canola oil

DIRECTIONS
Make a mixture of cornstarch, baking powder, 1 cup flour, salt and chili powder with beer and stand for 10 minutes. Toss the fish strips first in flour and then in the above mixture. Preheat the Sous Vide machine to 195°F/91°C. Take a large Ziploc bag and place these fish strips side by side in it. Apply vacuum to remove the air. Place this bag in the water bath for 20 minutes. Sprinkle salt and pepper and serve on tortillas.

319. SHRIMP SOUP

Cal.: 127 | Fat: 8g | Protein: 23g   10 min | 60 min | Servings 1

INGREDIENTS
- 1 pound shrimps
- 1 onion
- 2 carrots
- 1 bell pepper
- 1 yellow zucchini
- 3 garlic cloves
- 3 celery stalks
- 2 teaspoon chili powder
- 1 tablespoon olive oil
- 1 cup chicken broth
- 1 cup tomato juice
- ½ cup corn kernels
- Salt, pepper, oregano as per taste

DIRECTIONS
Heat oil in a pan and cook all the vegetables for 3 minutes. Add all the spices, broth and tomatoes. Simmer for 20 minutes. Preheat the Sous Vide machine to 195°F/91°C. Take the shrimps in a Ziploc bag and apply a vacuum to remove the air. Place this bag in the water bath for 30 minutes. The shrimps should turn pink. Add the shrimps to the above pan and cook for 2 minutes. Garnish with the lime wheels and serve hot.

320. LEMON FLAVORED SCALLOPS

Cal.: 100 | Fat: 20g | Protein: 9g   5 min | 10 min | Servings 4

INGREDIENTS
- 1 ½ pound scallops
- 1 cup chicken broth
- 1 tablespoon capers
- 1 cup cornstarch
- 1 garlic clove
- 1 teaspoon lemon zest
- 1 tablespoon lemon juice
- 3 teaspoon butter
- 2 tablespoon parsley
- Salt, pepper as per taste

DIRECTIONS
Take a mixing bowl. Mix the cornstarch with broth, capers, salt, pepper, lemon juice, lemon zest, garlic until it dissolves. Preheat the Sous Vide machine to 195°F/91°C. Take the scallops in a Ziploc bag. Add butter and seal the bag. Place this bag in the water bath for 30 minutes. Boil the broth mixture until it thickens. Add butter and parsley. Place scallops on a serving plate. Add the hot broth and serve.

321. FRENCH MUSSELS

Cal.: 420 | Fat: 18g | Protein: 10g   10 min | 🍲 10 min | 🍴 Servings 4

INGREDIENTS
- 2 pounds mussels
- 1 slices fennel
- 4 chopped garlic cloves
- 2 chopped tomatoes
- ½ cup pastis
- 2 tablespoon olive oil
- Salt, pepper, baguette as per need

DIRECTIONS
Heat oil in a large saucepan. Add garlic, fennel, salt and cook for 5 minutes. Add the pastis, tomatoes and simmer for 3 minutes. Preheat the Sous Vide machine to 195°F/91°C. Take the mussels in a large Ziploc bag and apply a vacuum to remove the air. Place this bag in the water bath for 20 minutes. Add the cooked mussels and cover the vessel. Cook it for 5 minutes with continuous stirring. Serve hot with the baguette.

322. HONEY FLAVORED ROASTED SALMON

Cal.: 383 | Fat: 30g | Protein: 23g   15 min | 🍲 25 min | 🍴 Servings 4

INGREDIENTS
- 1 pound potatoes
- 1 tablespoon olive oil
- 1 pound salmon fillet
- 2 tablespoon whole rosemary
- 2 tablespoon whole-grain mustard
- 2 cup baby arugula
- 2 teaspoon honey
- 1 tablespoon red wine vinegar
- Salt, pepper as per taste

DIRECTIONS
Preheat the Sous Vide machine to 195°F/91°C. Toss the potatoes with oil, rosemary, salt, pepper. Place this mixture in a Ziploc bag and seal it. Sprinkle salt and pepper over the salmon. Take this in another Ziploc bag and seal. Place these bags in the water bath for 30 minutes. In a mixing bowl, make a mixture of mustard, honey, vinegar, oil, salt and pepper. Toss the potatoes with the above mixture, add arugula. Serve the salmon with the above mixture.

323. SALMON BURGER

Cal.: 138 | Fat: 6g | Protein: 18g   10 min | 🍲 30 min | 🍴 Servings 4

INGREDIENTS
- 2 cups salmon
- 2 ½ cup bread crumbs
- 3 eggs
- 3/4 cup celery
- 1 cup green onions
- 2 tablespoons oil
- 4 English muffins
- Salt, pepper, fries as per need

DIRECTIONS
Preheat the Sous Vide machine to 195°F/91°C. Take the salmon in a bag and apply a vacuum to remove the air. Place this bag in the water bath for 10 minutes. Take a large bowl and beat the eggs. Add the cooked salmon, bread crumbs, celery, green onions, salt, pepper and mix. Make 4 patties from the above dough and cook in oil for 10 minutes on medium flame. Flip and repeat. Place the patty on the toasted English muffin and garnish with favorite salads.

324. CRUNCHY COCONUT SHRIMPS

Cal.: 260 | Fat: 14g | Protein: 7g   ⬎ 5 min | 🍲 15 min | 🍴 Servings 4

INGREDIENTS

- 24 shrimps
- 1/4 cup skim milk
- 3 tablespoon flour
- ½ cup coconut
- 1/4 cup cornflakes

DIRECTIONS

Preheat the Sous Vide machine to 195°F/91°C. Take the shrimps in a Ziploc bag and apply a vacuum to remove the air. Place this bag in the water bath for 5 minutes. Make a mixture of milk and flour in a mixing bowl. Toss the above shrimps in it. In another mixing bowl, make a mixture of coconut and cornflakes crumbs. Add the shrimps to the above mixture and coat it uniformly. Preheat the oven to 450 ° F. Grease the baking tray with cooking spray. Place the shrimps on this tray and bake for 5 minutes. Flip and repeat. Serve hot.

325. SALMON CAKES

Cal.: 280 | Fat: 16g | Protein: 17g   ⬎ 25 min | 🍲 20 min | 🍴 Servings 6

INGREDIENTS

- 1 ½ pounds boiled potatoes
- 1 teaspoon lemon zest
- 1 teaspoon lemon juice
- 1 pound chopped salmon
- 4 tablespoon oil
- 1 onion
- 1 tablespoon grated ginger
- 1 egg
- 1 teaspoon soy sauce
- 6 lettuce leaves
- Salt, pepper, mayonnaise as per taste

DIRECTIONS

Preheat the Sous Vide machine to 195°F/91°C. Take salmon in the Ziploc bag and remove air. Place this bag in the water bath for 5 minutes. In a pan heat oil and cook the onions and ginger. Add boiled potatoes and mash the mixture. Add salmon, egg, pepper, salt and mix. Make 12 small cakes from this mixture. Heat oil in the skillet and cook these salmon cakes for 6 minutes until brown. Flip and repeat. In a small bowl add lemon juice, soy sauce, ginger, mayonnaise and mix. Serve the salmon cakes with the above mixture.

326. CRISPY CATFISH FINGERS

Cal.: 460 | Fat: 28g | Protein: 45g   ⬎ 10 min | 🍲 10 min | 🍴 Servings 4

INGREDIENTS

- 1 ½ pound catfish fillets
- 3 cups canola oil
- 1 cup cornmeal
- 1/4 cup cayenne pepper
- Salt as per taste

DIRECTIONS

Take a mixing bowl and toss the catfish with salt and cayenne pepper. Preheat the Sous Vide machine to 195°F/91°C. Take the catfish fillets in a Ziploc bag. Seal it. Place this bag in the water bath for 5 minutes. Spread the cornmeal in a place and keep aside. Coat the fish with cornmeal and fry them in oil at 350°F/176°C until golden. Transfer it to a baking sheet pat to remove excess oil. Serve hot.

327. SEAFOOD SALAD

Cal.: 318 | Fat: 23g | Protein: 25g   30 min | 30 min | Servings 4

INGREDIENTS

For seafood:

- ½ pound each of shrimp, salmon, red snapper fillet
- ½ cup lemon juice
- 1 teaspoon orange zest
- 1/4 cup orange juice
- 1/4 cup vinegar
- 1 tablespoon sugar
- 1 orange bell pepper
- ½ cup diced red onion
- 1 green scotch bonnet chili

For salad:

- ½ cup cilantro
- 1/4 cup olive oil
- 3 cup torn frisee
- 2 cup diced watermelon
- 1 avocado and mango

DIRECTIONS

Preheat the Sous Vide machine to 195°F/91°C. Take all the ingredients of the seafood in a large Ziploc bag. Apply vacuum to remove the air. Place this bag in the water bath for 30 minutes. In a mixing bowl combine all the salad ingredients. Add the salad to the serving plate and top with seafood.

328. SEAFOOD NOODLES

Cal.: 287 | Fat: 32g | Protein: 19g   25 min | 40 min | Servings 6

INGREDIENTS

- 12 shrimps
- 12 sea scallops
- 8 cup chicken broth
- 1 cup cooked noodles
- 2 tablespoon grated ginger
- 3 tablespoon soy sauce
- 4 mushrooms
- 4 cabbage leaves
- 12 snow peas
- 3 scallions
- Salt, pepper, cilantro as per need

DIRECTIONS

Set the machine to 195°F/91°C. Take all the ingredients of the seafood in a large Ziploc bag. In another Ziploc bag take all the required vegetables and seal the bag. Apply vacuum to remove the air. Place these bags in the water bath for 30 minutes. Take a large cooking pan. Add broth, soy sauce and boil for 10 minutes. Take the serving bowl. Add the noodles, cooked seafood, vegetables and broth. Sprinkle cilantro, salt, pepper and serve.

329. CARAMEL SHRIMP CHILI

Cal.: 340 | Fat: 31g | Protein: 29g   ⟍ 15 min | 🍲 30 min | ✗ Servings 4

INGREDIENTS
- 1 cup cooked rice noodles
- 1 pound cooked broccoli
- 1 chopped green onion
- 3 tablespoon sugar
- 1 tablespoon water
- 1 tablespoon oil
- 3 garlic cloves
- 1/4 teaspoon crushed red pepper
- 1 tablespoon fish sauce
- 1 pound shrimp
- 1/4 cup cilantro
- Salt, pepper

DIRECTIONS
In a bowl, toss broccoli, green onion and salt. In a saucepan, cook water and sugar until it starts to caramelize. Add ginger, oil, pepper, fish sauce. Add cilantro and pepper. Preheat the Sous Vide machine to 195°F/91°C. Take the shrimps in a bag and seal it. Place this bag in the water bath for 20 minutes. In a serving bowl, add the noodles, shrimps and top with broccoli. Add the shrimps with sauce and serve.

330. MEDITERRANEAN TILAPIA STEW

Cal.: 359 | Fat: 39g | Protein: 21g   ⟍ 10 min | 🍲 30 min | ✗ Servings 4

INGREDIENTS
- 1 pound tilapia fillets
- 2 teaspoons olive oil
- 4 red potatoes
- 2 garlic cloves
- 1 cup marinara sauce
- 1/4 cup sliced green olives
- 2 tablespoon chopped cilantro
- Salt, pepper, water as per need

DIRECTIONS
Preheat the Sous Vide machine to 195°F/91°C. Take the fish in a Ziploc bag and apply vacuum to remove the air. Place this bag in the water bath for 20 minutes. Take a large non-stick skillet and heat oil. Add the potatoes, pepper, garlic and cook for 5 minutes. Add water and cook until potatoes are tender. Then, add marinara sauce and bring it to boil. Add cooked fish and simmer for 5 minutes. Garnish with cilantro, olives and serve.

331. TOMATOES STUFFED WITH TUNA

Cal.: 162 | Fat: 32g | Protein: 18g   ⟍ 15 min | 🍲 15 min | ✗ Servings 5

INGREDIENTS
- 4 tomatoes
- 2 cups white tuna
- 2 celery stalks
- 2 tablespoons capers
- 1 tablespoon olive oil
- 1 tablespoon red wine vinegar
- ½ cup parsley
- Salt, pepper as per need

DIRECTIONS
Preheat the Sous Vide machine to 195°F/91°C. Take tuna is a Ziploc bag. Place this bag in the water bath for 10 minutes. Cut off the top and bottom thin slices of tomatoes. Remove the seeds and pulp using the spoon. Take the seeds and pulp in a mixing bowl. To this, add tuna, oil vinegar, celery, salt, pepper, capers, parsley and mix. Cook this mixture for 5 minutes. Add the tuna mixture into the tomato cavities and serve.

332. WALNUT COATED HALIBUT

Cal.: 453 | Fat: 29g | Protein: 10g 15 min | 25 min | Servings 4

INGREDIENTS

- 1 egg white
- 1 cup walnut
- 4 halibut fillets
- 2 tablespoons all-purpose flour
- 3 oranges
- ½ tablespoon red onion
- 2 tablespoon cilantro
- 1 jalapeno pepper
- 1 teaspoon vinegar
- Salt, pepper, mashed potatoes

DIRECTIONS

Add flour, salt and pepper in one bowl. Beat the egg with water in another bowl. Take crushed walnut in the third bowl. Coat the fish with flour mixture, dip it in egg mixture and coat it with the crushed walnut. Preheat the Sous Vide machine to 195°F/91°C. Place these fish pieces in a large Ziploc bag in a side by side manner. Apply vacuum to remove the air. Place this bag in the water bath for 30 minutes. In a bowl toss onion, oranges, cilantro, vinegar and jalapeno. Serve the above salad with the cooked fish.

333. POACHED HALIBUT

Cal.: 575 | Fat: 45g | Protein: 32g 10 min | 30 min | Servings 2

INGREDIENTS

- 2 5oz. halibut fillets
- 1/3 cup sea salt
- 1/3 cup sugar
- ¼ cup Vin Jaune

Sauce:

- ½ cup Vin Jaune
- ¾ cup chicken stock
- 1 cup unsalted butter
- 2 tablespoon chopped chives
- Salt, to taste

DIRECTIONS

Preheat the Sous Vide machine to 132°F/56°C. Sprinkle the fish fillets with salt and sugar. Place aside minutes. Place the halibut fillets into separate bags. Add Vin Jaune. Vacuum seal the bags and Immerse in water. Cook the fish for 30 minutes. Make the sauce; simmer Vin Jaune and chicken stock in a saucepan until reduced by half. Add the butter and whisk until sauce-like consistency. Season to taste. Remove the fish from the bags and arrange on a plate. Drizzle with sauce and sprinkle with chives. Serve.

334. ASIAN STYLE SALMON

Cal.: 394 | Fat: 21g | Protein: 24g 10 min | 30 min | Servings 4

INGREDIENTS

- 4 5oz. salmon fillets
- 2 tablespoons rice wine
- 2 tablespoons sweet rice wine
- 2 tablespoons miso paste
- 1 tablespoon Sriracha
- 2 tablespoon unsalted butter
- 1 tablespoon vegetable oil
- 2 spring onions, chopped
- 1 tablespoon toasted sesame seeds

DIRECTIONS

Preheat the Sous Vide machine to 105°F/40°C. Combine rice wine, sweet rice wine, miso paste, Sriracha and butter in a bowl. Spread the miso paste over salmon. Place the salmon into sous-vide bags and vacuum seal. Immerse in water and cook for 30 minutes. Remove the salmon from a bag. Heat vegetable oil in a large skillet. Sear salmon on both sides, 1 minute per side. Serve on a plate. Top with chopped spring onion and sesame seeds.

335. PERFECT SCALLOPS IN CITRUS SAUCE

Cal.: 279 | Fat: 2g | Protein: 37g   15 min | 30 min | Servings 4

INGREDIENTS
- 2lb. scallops, cleaned
- 2 lemons (1 quartered, 1 zest and juiced)
- 2 tablespoons ghee
- 2 shallots, chopped
- ¼ cup pink grapefruit juice
- ¼ cup orange juice
- 2 tablespoons acacia honey
- Salt and pepper, to taste

DIRECTIONS
Preheat the Sous Vide machine to 122°F/50°C. Rinse scallops and drain. Season scallops with salt and pepper. Divide scallops between two bags. Place 2 quarters lemon in each bag and vacuum seal. Cook the scallops for 30 minutes. Make the sauce; heat ghee in a saucepan. Add the chopped shallots and cook until tender for 4 minutes. Remove the scallops from the bag and sear on both sides in a lightly greased skillet. Remove the scallops from the skillet. Deglaze the pan with orange juice. Pour in pink grapefruit juice and lemon juice. Add shallots and lemon zest. Simmer until half reduces the sauce. Stir in honey and simmer until thickened. Serve scallops with sauce.

336. HADDOCK ON VEGETABLE SAUCE

Cal.: 349 | Fat: 19g | Protein: 27g   10 min | 70 min | Servings 4

INGREDIENTS
- 4 6oz. haddock fillets

Marinade:
- 1 pinch curry
- 1 pinch brown sugar
- 1 pinch fine sea salt
- 5 tablespoons olive oil
- 1 sprig thyme, chopped
- 1 teaspoon lemon juice

Vegetables:
- 1 pinch chili powder
- 1 cucumber
- 3 carrots
- 1 leek, chopped
- 1 tablespoon olive oil
- 3 bell peppers, red, yellow, and green
- 1 sweet potato
- Salt, and pepper, to taste

DIRECTIONS
Preheat the Sous Vide machine to 130°F/55°C. In a bag, combine marinade ingredients. Add haddock fillets and shake to coat the fish. Vacuum seal the bag and cook for 30 minutes. In a separate bag, combine all vegetables, with seasonings and olive oil. Vacuum seal the bag and cook the veggies at 185°F/85°C for 40 minutes. Open the bags carefully. Heat some olive oil in a large skillet. Cook the fish fillets for 2 minutes per side. Serve fish with vegetables.

337. TROUT

Cal.: 459 | Fat: 49g | Protein: 31g   7 min | 53 min | Servings 4

INGREDIENTS
- 2 trout portions, each weighing 150g
- Pinch of sea salt
- Sprigs of thyme
- 4-6 fresh basil leaves
- 1 tbsp. olive oil

DIRECTIONS
Preheat the water bath to 113°F /45°C. Salt the trout portions. Lay both trout pieces flat inside a vacuum bag. Add the olive oil, thyme, and basil. Seal the bag and place in the water bath. Cook for 45 minutes. Remove trout from the vacuum bag and pat dry. Heat a dash of oil in a skillet on high heat. When the oil is hot, sear the skin side of the trout until it turns golden brown and crispy. Serve.

338. TERIYAKI SALMON

Cal.: 291 | Fat: 12g | Protein: 33g

 10 min | 15 min | Servings 2

INGREDIENTS

- ½ cup plus 1 teaspoon teriyaki sauce
- 2 (5 oz.) skinless salmon fillets
- 4 oz. Chinese egg noodles
- 1 tablespoon sesame oil
- 2 teaspoons soy sauce
- 2 teaspoons thinly sliced scallions, plus 4 (1-inch pieces) scallion greens, for serving
- 1-inch fresh ginger, peeled and sliced into thin strips
- 4 oz. lettuce, chopped
- 1/8 small red onion, thinly sliced
- 1 tablespoon Japanese roasted sesame dressing
- 1 tablespoon sesame seeds, toasted

DIRECTIONS

Divide ½ cup teriyaki sauce between 2 Ziploc bags. Place 1 salmon fillet in each bag and seal bags using the water immersion method. Do not place salmon fillets, but place aside to marinate at room temperature for 15 minutes. Meanwhile, preheat the Sous Vide machine to 131°F/55°C. Place the bags in a water bath and cook for 15 minutes. While salmon is cooking, prepare egg noodles according to package instructions. Drain well, return to the cooking pot and stir in sesame oil and soy sauce, reserving one teaspoon. Divide pasta between serving plates. Prepare the dipping sauce; combine scallions, ginger, remaining teriyaki sauce and one teaspoon soy sauce. Also, prepare the salad by combining lettuce and onion with one tablespoon of roasted sesame dressing. When the timer goes off, remove salmon from the water bath, reserving cooking liquid. Top the pasta with salmon fillets and drizzle all with reserved cooking liquid. Garnish salmon with sesame seeds and serve with prepared salad and dipping sauce.

339. HALIBUT

Cal.: 359 | Fat: 39g | Protein: 21g

 11 min | 30 min | Servings 4

INGREDIENTS

- 2 Halibut Fillets
- 2 tbsp. Butter
- Fresh dill, to taste
- Lemon, to taste
- Salt, to taste
- Pepper, to taste
- Olive oil, to taste

DIRECTIONS

Generously salt both sides of the halibut and refrigerate for 30 minutes to 24 hours. Preheat the water bath to 122°F/50°C. Gently place the halibut fillets in a vacuum bag. Add a bit of oil and fresh dill to the bag. Seal the bag and place into the water bath. Cook for 20/30 minutes depending on the thickness of the filet. We want to finish the Halibut in the pan. Remove from the water bath and pat dry with paper towels. Preheat a skillet pan with avocado oil on medium-high/high heat. Add halibut, followed by a tablespoon or two of butter and fresh herbs. Baste the halibut with butter as it cooks, 1–2minutes. You only need to sear one side. Remove and serve!

340. MEZCAL-LIME SHRIMP

Cal.: 389 | Fat: 32g | Protein: 16g

 9 min | 45 min | Servings 4

INGREDIENTS

- 1 ½ pounds shell-on jumbo shrimp
- 1 oz. mezcal
- Zest and juice of 1 lime
- 1 Tbsp. olive oil
- 1 tbsp. ancho chili powder
- 2 tsp. ground cumin
- 2 tsp. kosher salt
- 1 garlic clove, minced
- Fresh cilantro, for serving

DIRECTIONS

Preheat the water bath to 135°F/57°C. Combine the shrimp, mezcal, olive oil, chili powder, lime zest, lime juice, cumin, salt and garlic in a large zipper-lock bag. Seal the bag using the water displacement method and place in the water bath. Cook for 30 minutes, or up to 45 minutes. Remove the bag from the water bath. Pour the contents of the bag into a serving bowl and garnish with cilantro. Serve.

341. SCARLET SHRIMP WITH SAUTÉED ARTICHOKES

Cal.: 429 | Fat: 33g | Protein: 20g   8 min | 39 min | Servings 4

INGREDIENTS

- 6 pieces of scarlet shrimp
- 2-3 Tbsp. extra virgin olive oil
- Salt, to taste
- 4 pieces of artichokes

DIRECTIONS

Preheat the water bath to 149°F/65°C. Peel the shrimp, leaving the head, the last link and the tail. Place shrimp into the vacuum bag, salt to taste, and drizzle with extra virgin olive oil. Seal bag and place in a water bath. Cook for 6 minutes. Remove from the water bath and set aside. Preheat the water bath to 190°F/90°C. Clean and peel the artichokes. Cut artichokes into quarters and place them in a vacuum bag. Salt to taste and drizzle with extra virgin olive oil, then seal the bag. Place the bag in a water bath for 30 minutes. When finished cooking, remove the bag from the water bath. Heat a drizzle of extra virgin olive oil in a skillet on high heat. Sauté the artichokes until they start to brown. Serve shrimp and artichokes.

342. COD

Cal.: 329 | Fat: 38g | Protein: 16g   18 min | 3 hours | Servings 4

INGREDIENTS

- 2 cod filets
- 2 Tbsp. butter
- 1 sprig fresh dill
- Lemon and Capers (Optional)
- Salt, to taste
- Pepper, to taste

DIRECTIONS

Preheat the water bath to 131°F/55°C. Place cod filets in a vacuum bag. Add 2 tbsp. butter and sprig of fresh dill. Optionally you may also add a few slices of lemon and capers. Seal the bag and cook for 30 minutes. When finished cooking, remove from the bag. Serve.

343. SHRIMP COCKTAIL

Cal.: 399 | Fat: 31g | Protein: 12g   18 min | 30 min | Servings 4

INGREDIENTS

- 1 pound jumbo shrimp (16-20), peeled and deveined, with tails left on
- Cocktail sauce, for serving

DIRECTIONS

Preheat the water bath to 135°F/57°C. Place the shrimp in a large vacuum seal bag. Seal the bag using the vacuum sealer on the moist setting. Place the bag in the water bath and cook for 30 minutes. When finished cooking, remove the bag from the water bath. Transfer bag to an ice bath. When the shrimp are cooled to room temperature, transfer to the refrigerator. Refrigerate for at least 1 hour before serving with the cocktail sauce.

344. DUNGENESS CRAB

Cal.: 309 | Fat: 45g | Protein: 20g   8 min | 50 min | Servings 4

INGREDIENTS

- 1 Dungeness crab

DIRECTIONS

Preheat the water bath to 154°F/68°C. Bring a large pot of water to a boil. Fully Immerse crab in boiling water for 1 minute to blanch. Transfer crab to the Supreme. Cover with lid, and steam for 45 minutes. Serve hot, or chill in an ice bath for 10 minutes to serve cold.

345. LOBSTER TAIL

Cal.: 368 | Fat: 38g | Protein: 23g   ✎ 11 min | 🍲 3 hours | ✖ Servings 2

INGREDIENTS

- 2 Lobster tails (frozen)
- 10 Tbsp. butter
- 1 Tbsp. fresh parsley

DIRECTIONS

Preheat the water bath to 134°F/56°C. Defrost lobster tails in a bowl of water for approximately 30 minutes. Cut the shell down the middle with kitchen shears and slowly but firmly pull the shell apart, ensuring not to rip the meat. Remove lobster meat from the shell and devein, if necessary. Place lobster tails, fresh parsley and 2-3 tbsp. of butter into a heavy duty Ziploc bag. Use the water displacement method to remove the air from the bag and seal it. Place the bag in the water bath and cook for 1 hour. Melt 6-8 tbsp. of butter in a saucepan over medium heat. When melted, pour the butter into a serving bowl. Serve.

346. MISO BUTTER COD

Cal.: 429 | Fat: 42g | Protein: 30g   ✎ 17 min | 🍲 51 min | ✖ Servings 2

INGREDIENTS

- 1 large Atlantic Cod filet
- 2 Tbsp. miso paste
- 1.5 Tbsp. brown sugar
- 2 Tbsp. soy sauce
- 2 Tbsp. mirin
- 2 Tbsp. butter
- Sesame seeds and green onions for garnish
- Rice for serving

DIRECTIONS

Marinate the cod with the miso paste, brown sugar, soy sauce and mirin for 24 hours in the refrigerator. Preheat the water bath to 131°F/55°C. Place the cod and marinade in a Ziploc bag and seal using the water displacement method. Place in the water bath for 30 minutes. Take the bag out of the water bath. Melt 1 tbsp. of butter in a non-stick pan on medium-high heat. Sear cod 1 minute on each side, and set aside. Take the sauce from the bag and pour it onto the pan. Reduce the sauce until thickened. Add 1 tbsp. of butter and stir. Drizzle the sauce on the cod and garnish with sesame seeds and green onions. Serve with hot steamed rice.

347. KING PRAWNS WITH GINGER AND CARAMELIZED ONION

Cal.: 359 | Fat: 39g | Protein: 21g   ✎ 14 min | 🍲 30 min | ✖ Servings 4

INGREDIENTS

For King Prawns:
- 8 king prawns, skinned with their heads and tails
- 20 g ginger juice

For Caramelized Onions:
- 2 onions, thinly sliced
- 2 Tbsp. butter
- 2 Tbsp. balsamic vinegar
- Pinch of sugar
- Pinch of salt
- 1 Tbsp. thyme, finely sliced

DIRECTIONS

Peel and cut the onions in half. Then cut each half into thin slices. Add the butter, balsamic vinegar, sugar, salt and thyme to a pot and put over high heat. As soon as the butter and sugar melts, add the onions. Stir to combine and sauté for 5 minutes. When all the liquid has evaporated (about 5 minutes), lower the heat. Continue to cook, stirring more often, until the onions turn golden brown (about 15-20 minutes). Set aside to cool. Preheat your water bath to 149°F/65°C. Place the king prawns, caramelized onion and ginger juice into a Ziploc bag and seal using the water displacement method. Cook for 6 min at 149°F/65°C. When finished cooking, remove the bag from the water bath. Open the bag and spread the caramelized onion out on a plate and stagger the king prawns on top, drizzling with the cooking juices.

348. SWORDFISH

Cal.: 361 | Fat: 38g | Protein: 18g   🔪 8 min | 🍲 50 min | 🍴 Servings 2

INGREDIENTS

- 2 (6-ounce) swordfish steaks
- 2 tbsp. extra virgin olive oil
- Zest and juice of 2 lemons
- 4 sprigs fresh thyme
- Kosher salt and freshly ground black pepper to taste

DIRECTIONS

Preheat the water bath to 130°F /55°C. Season the swordfish with salt and pepper to taste. Place in a large vacuum seal bag with olive oil, lemon zest, lemon juice and thyme. Seal the bag using the moist setting. Place in the water bath and cook for 30 minutes, or up to 45 minutes. When it is finished cooking, remove the bag from the water bath. Carefully remove the swordfish from the bag and pat dry with paper towels. Reserve cooking liquid. Heat a skillet to high heat and then sear the swordfish for 1 to 2 minutes on each side. Transfer to a plate and let rest for 5 minutes. Divide the swordfish between two serving plates and drizzle with some of the cooking liquid from the bag. Serve.

349. SALMON WITH HOLLANDAISE SAUCE

Cal.: 419 | Fat: 37g | Protein: 17g   🔪 14 min | 🍲 76 min | 🍴 Servings 2

INGREDIENTS

For Salmon:
- 2 fresh salmon filets
- Salt for brining

For Hollandaise:
- 4 Tbsp. butter
- 1 Egg yolk
- 1 tsp. Lemon Juice
- 1 tsp. Water
- ½ Shallot, diced
- Pinch of cayenne
- Salt, to taste

DIRECTIONS

Dry brine salmon by generously salting both sides and place in the refrigerator for a minimum of 30 minutes. Preheat the water bath to 148°F/64°C. Add all of the ingredients for Hollandaise sauce into a large Ziploc bag and seal it using the water displacement method. It will be blended later, so no need to mix it. Immerse and cook for 45 minutes. Decrease your water bath temperature to 130°F/55°C. (Note: Add ice or a few cups of cold water to speed this up. Place salmon in a Ziploc bag and seal it using the water displacement method). Cook salmon for 30-45 minutes. Remove your Hollandaise mixture from the water bath and pour it into your blender. Blend on a medium speed until the mixture is a smooth light yellow. Remove salmon, pat dry, and sear (if desired). Serve with hollandaise sauce.

350. SALMON MARINATED IN MAPLE SYRUP

Cal.: 469 | Fat: 34g | Protein: 18g   🔪 8 min | 🍲 51 min | 🍴 Servings 4

INGREDIENTS

- One salmon loin of approximately 150 g, around 2.5 cm thick
- Salt, to taste
- Pepper, to taste
- 1 sprig of dill
- 25 g maple syrup
- 1 potato
- 1 small aubergine (eggplant)
- ½ a red pepper
- 50 ml white wine
- Extra virgin olive oil to taste

DIRECTIONS

Preheat the water bath to 149°F/65°C. Salt and pepper the salmon to taste and put it into a vacuum bag together with the dill and maple syrup. Seal the bag and place in a water bath. Cut the aubergine, potato and pepper into small cubes and toss it with a drop of oil and the white wine. When the salmon is finished, take it out and open the bag. Reserve the cooking liquids.

To serve: place the vegetables on the plate and the salmon on top, dress it and finish it off with a dash of extra virgin olive oil.

351. SCALLOPS WITH LEMON HERB SALSA VERDE

Cal.: 459 | Fat: 34g | Protein: 16g   15 min | 60 min | Servings 2

INGREDIENTS

- 8 Sea scallops, side muscle removed
- Pink Himalayan salt and pepper, to taste
- 1 tbsp. olive oil
- 1 tbsp. ghee or butter
- ¼ cup fresh cilantro, parsley, chives and basil, roughly chopped
- Juice from ½ Lemon
- ¼ cup olive oil
- 1 small shallot, minced
- 1 garlic clove, minced

DIRECTIONS

Preheat the water bath to 123.8°F/51°C. Salt and pepper scallops on both sides and place in a Ziploc bag in a single layer. Pour in 1 tbsp. olive oil. Place the scallops into your water bath using the water displacement method. Cook for 30 minutes. While scallops are cooking, prepare your salsa Verde. Add your chopped herbs into a bowl with the shallot, garlic and lemon juice and stir to combine. Let sit for 5 minutes and then mix in the ¼ cup olive oil and set aside. When the scallops are finished cooking, remove from the water bath. Remove them from the bag and carefully place them on a plate and pat dry. Heat the ghee/butter on high heat in a cast-iron skillet. When the ghee is melted, add the Scallops, one at a time and cook for 45 seconds on each side. Serve with salsa Verde.

352. SEA BASS

Cal.: 362 | Fat: 36g | Protein: 16g    18 min | 30 min | Servings 2

INGREDIENTS

- 2 sea bass portions, each weighing 120g
- 2 lemon wedges
- Dash of olive oil
- Pinch of sea salt

DIRECTIONS

Preheat the water bath to a temperature of 122°F/50°C. Sprinkle the sea salt over the sea bass and seal in a vacuum bag with olive oil and lemon wedges. Place the bag in the water bath and cook for 15 minutes. When it is finished cooking, carefully slide the cooked fish out of the vacuum bag, and pat dry. Heat a skillet on high heat. Sear on the skin side until the skin is crisp and golden. Serve.

353. SALMON FILLETS

Cal.: 329 | Fat: 32g | Protein: 14g    12 min | 43 min | Servings 4

INGREDIENTS

- 4 salmon fillets, each weighing approx. 130g
- 1 tsp. flaky sea salt
- 1 tsp. sugar
- ½ tsp. fennel seeds
- ½ tsp. coriander seeds
- 3 Tbsp. olive oil

DIRECTIONS

Preheat the water bath to 122°F/50°C. Lightly toast the seeds in a dry frying pan then transfer to a pestle and mortar. Roughly grind the seeds down a little. Place each salmon fillet in a vacuum bag with the seeds, salt, sugar and a dash of oil. Seal bag and cook for 15 minutes. Once ready, remove the fillets from the bags and drain on a paper towel. Heat a non-stick pan with a dash of oil until hot then add the salmon skin-side down. Cook until the skin is lightly golden. Serve.

354. WHITE WINE CLAMS AND ARTICHOKE HEARTS

Cal.: 419 | Fat: 41g | Protein: 18g   12 min | 60 min | ✗ Servings 5

INGREDIENTS
- 24 clams, cleaned
- 1 cup Marinated artichoke hearts, halved
- 3 garlic cloves, sliced
- 2 tbsp. extra virgin olive oil
- 1 tbsp. cornstarch
- 1 cup veggie or fish stock
- 3 tbsp. white wine
- Salt and pepper to taste
- Parsley for garnish

DIRECTIONS
Preheat the water bath to 133°F/56°C. Pour stock and white wine into a big pot on high heat until boiling. Clean clams and quickly blanch them in the pot until they open up, about 1 minute. Quickly remove clams using a colander reserving the white wine and stock soup. Allow soup and clams to cool for 15 minutes. Add clams, garlic, extra virgin olive oil and stock-wine mixture into a zip bag, remove air through the water displacement method. Immerse and cook in a water bath for 10 minutes. When finished cooking, remove the bag from the water bath. Heat up a skillet on medium and pour the liquid from the bag in. Stir in cornstarch to thicken the sauce. Toss in artichoke hearts to warm. Add in clams to mix quickly. Serve immediately and garnish with parsley.

355. TILAPIA WITH PEACH MANGO SALSA

Cal.: 359 | Fat: 39g | Protein: 21g   8 min | 55 min | ✗ Servings 4

INGREDIENTS
- 1 Tilapia filleted
- Sea salt, to taste
- Black pepper, to taste
- 2 tbsp. butter
- Peach Mango Salsa
- 2 peaches, peeled and diced
- 1 mango, peeled and diced
- 1 red bell pepper, diced
- 2 tbsp. fresh cilantro, chopped
- 1 medium shallot, diced
- 2 tbsp. jalapeños, diced (remove seeds and white pith if you like it less spicy)
- 4 tsp. apple cider vinegar
- 2 tsp. lime juice
- 1 tsp. honey
- 1/8 tsp. black pepper
- 2 tsp. extra virgin olive oil

DIRECTIONS
In a medium bowl, add peaches, mango, pepper, cilantro, shallot, and jalapeños. Pour the vinegar, lime juice, honey, pepper and olive oil over the mixture. Mix well and refrigerate for at least an hour before using. Preheat the water bath to 140°F/60°C. Place tilapia and salsa into a vacuum bag and seal. Place the bag in a water bath and cook for 25 minutes. When finished cooking, remove tilapia and pat dry. Pour contents of the bag into a bowl for serving. Heat a skillet on high heat and sear each side of the tilapia. Serve with steamed vegetables or over white rice using all the juices and the salsa fruit.

356. SCALLOPS

Cal.: 344 | Fat: 39g | Protein: 21g   11 min | 29 min | ✗ Servings 4

INGREDIENTS
- 4 large scallops, shucked and washed
- Sea salt, to taste
- 1 Tbsp. olive oil

DIRECTIONS
Preheat the water bath to a temperature of 125.6°F/52°C. Sprinkle the scallops with salt. With the vacuum sealer set on medium pressure, seal the scallops in a vacuum bag with olive oil. Place the vacuum bag in the water bath and cook for 20 minutes. Take the scallops out of the bag and gently pat them dry. Using a non-stick frying pan over a heat high, pan-fry the scallops until golden and caramelized on both sides. Approximately 1–2minutes per side. Remove from the pan and serve.

357. MARINATED KING PRAWNS WITH LIME MAYONNAISE

Cal.: 428 | Fat: 38g | Protein: 20g   �’ 11 min | 🍲 61 min | 🍴 Servings 8

INGREDIENTS

- 16 fresh king prawns
- 30 g of fish sauce
- 2 fresh green chilies
- Sesame
- 2 limes in juice
- 5 g of ginger
- 5 g of garlic
- 1 mini lime
- Soya
- Egg white
- Rice noodles
- Flour

For Mayonnaise:

- 10 units of lime leaves
- 250 g of sunflower oil
- 1 egg
- Salt, to taste
- Juice of a mini lime

DIRECTIONS

First, mix the ingredients for the marinade: the fish sauce, the chopped chilies, lime and mini lime juice, chopped ginger, garlic and soya. Peel the king prawns leaving the tail and removing the head. Marinate the king prawns by vacuum packing for 20 minutes, which will accelerate the marinating. Preheat the water bath to 140°F/60°C. Once the king prawns are marinated, remove the solid elements and put them aside. For the mayonnaise, place oil and lime leaves in a Ziploc bag and seal using the water displacement method. Immerse the bag, and cook for 1 hour. When the oil is finished cooking, make a basic mayonnaise with the egg, the lime oil, the mini lime juice and salt. Meanwhile, break up the rice noodles by hand leaving pieces of 1–2cm. To finish, cover the king prawns with flour, beaten egg white and finally the broken rice noodles. Fry in an abundance of hot oil. Serve with the mayonnaise.

358. SOLE FISH WITH BACON

Cal.: 298 | Fat: 29g | Protein: 24g   �’ 10 min | 🍲 25 min | 🍴 Servings 2

INGREDIENTS

- 2 5oz. sole fish fillets
- 2 tablespoons olive oil
- 2 slices bacon
- ½ tablespoon lemon juice
- Salt and pepper, to taste

DIRECTIONS

Preheat the Sous Vide machine to 132°F/56°C. Cook the bacon in a non-stick skillet and cook bacon until crispy. Remove the bacon and place aside. Season fish fillets with salt, pepper and lemon juice. Brush the fish with olive oil. Place the fish in a bag. Top the fish with the bacon. Vacuum seal the bag. Immerse in a water bath and cook for 25 minutes. Remove the fish from the bag. Serve while warm.

359. SALMON WITH LEMON AND DILL

Cal.: 366 | Fat: 21.2g | Protein: 44g   �’ 11 min | 60 min | 🍴 Servings 2

INGREDIENTS

- 1 (1-lb) salmon fillet
- Kosher salt
- 1 tablespoon coarsely chopped dill
- 1 tsp. finely grated lemon zest
- ½ tsp. crushed red pepper flakes
- 1 tablespoon extra-virgin olive oil
- 1 tablespoon vegetable oil

DIRECTIONS

Preheat the Sous Vide machine to 125°F/52°C. Chop the dill coarsely and finely zest the lemon. Salt the salmon to taste and mix the remaining spices in a bowl. Coat both sides of the salmon with the mixed herbs. Place the salmon in the bag and add the oil before sealing. Place the bag in your preheated container and set your timer for 1 hour. Heat a skillet with the vegetable oil over medium-high heat. Remove the salmon from the bag and sear, skin side down for 3 to 4 minutes. Serve crispy skin side up.

360. POACHED TUNA WITH BASIL BUTTER

Cal.: 746 | Fat: 61.6g | Protein: 30.3g   15 min | 27 min | Servings 2

INGREDIENTS

- 1 stick (½ cup) softened unsalted butter
- 1/3 cup fresh basil
- 2 garlic cloves
- Zest of 1 lemon
- Sea salt and freshly ground black pepper
- 2 7- ounce fresh tuna steaks, 1-inch thick
- 1-1 ½cups extra virgin olive oil
- Sea salt and freshly ground black pepper
- 2 tablespoons vegetable oil

DIRECTIONS

Preheat the Sous Vide machine to 110°F/43°C. Finely mince the garlic and basil, and finely zest the lemon. Mash together the butter with basil, garlic and lemon zest until well mixed. Add salt and pepper to taste. Put each piece of tuna in a separate bag and pour in ½-3/4 cups of oil in each bag. Place the bag in your preheated container and set your timer for 25 minutes. While the salmon is cooking, place the butter on one side of a piece of plastic wrap. Roll the butter in the plastic wrap to create a log. Place the butter in the refrigerator. When the tuna is almost cooked, heat the vegetable oil in a skillet over high heat. Remove the tuna from the bag and sear for 30 seconds per side. Top with at least ½-inch-thick piece of basil butter to serve.

361. CLAMS WITH WHITE WINE AND ARTICHOKE HEARTS

Cal.: 158 | Fat: 10.3g | Protein: 8.6g   31 min | 11 min | Servings 4

INGREDIENTS

- 24 clams
- 1 cup marinated artichoke hearts
- 3 garlic cloves
- 2 tbsp. extra virgin olive oil
- 1 tablespoon cornstarch
- 1 cup veggie or fish stock
- 3 tbsp. white wine
- Salt and pepper to taste
- Parsley for garnish

DIRECTIONS

Preheat the Sous Vide machine to 133°F/56°C. Rinse the clams, slice the garlic, and cut the hearts in half. Place the stock and wine in a pot and heat it on high heat until it boils. Place the clams in the boiling pot until they open. Remove the clams from the pot and allow to cool for 15 minutes. Place the cooled ingredients in a bag with the garlic and olive oil and place the bag in your preheated container for 3 minutes. While the clams are cooking, heat a skillet over medium heat. When the clams are cooked, transfer the liquid to the heated skillet. Mix in the cornstarch until the sauce thickens. Add in the artichoke heart until they're warm. Then mix in the clams for a few seconds before removing from heat. Serve in bowls topped with parsley.

362. LIME SHRIMP WITH CILANTRO AVOCADO SAUCE

Cal.: 388 | Fat: 19g | Protein: 48.5g   9 min | 30 min | Servings 4

INGREDIENTS

- 1 lb. shrimp, peeled and deveined
- Salt and pepper
- 2 tbsp. lime juice (juice of 2 limes)
- 3 tbsp. butter, cut into rough chunks
- ½ avocado, roughly diced
- 1/4 cup sour cream
- 1 tablespoon lime juice
- ½ tsp. kosher salt

DIRECTIONS

Preheat the Sous Vide machine to 140°F/60°C. Peel and devein the shrimp, dice the avocado roughly, and cut the butter into chunks. Salt and pepper the shrimp to taste. Place it in the bag with the lime juice. Place the bag in your preheated container and set your timer for 15 minutes. Meanwhile, place the avocado, sour cream, lime juice and kosher salt in a blender or food processor, and blend until they become a smooth sauce. Once the shrimp is cooked, top them with the sauce and serve.

363. LOBSTER TAIL WITH CHIMICHURRI BUTTER

Cal.: 415 | Fat: 25g | Protein: 43.7g   ➘ 11 min | 🍲 36 min | 🍴 Servings 2

INGREDIENTS

- 4 tbsp. softened unsalted butter
- 2 tbsp. parsley
- 2 tsp. fresh lemon juice
- 1 small garlic clove, finely minced
- 2 lobster tails, about 8 oz. each
- 1 lemon, halved
- Parsley for garnish

DIRECTIONS

Preheat the Sous Vide machine to 135°F/57°C. Chop the parsley, mince the garlic, and cut the lemon in half. Mix the parsley, lemon juice, garlic and butter in a bowl until well combined. Place the lobster in the bag with half of the butter and cook for 30 minutes. When the lobster is almost finished cooking, preheat your grill so half the grill is on high heat and the other half is medium-low. When the lobster is cooked put them under cold water until cool and cut them in half lengthwise. Place the tails on the hot side of the grill with the flesh side down for 2 minutes. Flip the tails and baste with remaining butter, cooking another 2-3 minutes. Remove the tails from the grill. Allow the lemon pieces to cook on the hot side of the grill with the flesh side down for 2-3 minutes. Garnish the tails with parsley and serve with the grilled lemon.

364. LOBSTER TAIL IN BUTTER WITH TARRAGON

Cal.: 461 | Fat: 46.6g | Protein: 11.4g   ➘ 11 min | 🍲 30 min | 🍴 Servings 2

INGREDIENTS

- Pinch of salt and pepper
- 8 tbsp. butter
- Sprig of tarragon
- 2 lobster tails, about 8 oz. each
- 2 lemon wedges

DIRECTIONS

Preheat the Sous Vide machine to 135°F/57°C. Bring a pot of water to a boil. Place the lobster in the boiling water for 1 minute. Cut the lobster shell lengthwise. Put the tails in the bag of your choice with 6 tbsp. butter and tarragon and place the bag in your preheated container for 30 minutes. When the lobster is almost done cooking, melt the remaining butter in a pan on medium heat. Serve the lobster with a side of melted butter and lemon wedges.

365. SCALLOPS WITH BROWN BUTTER

Cal.: 208 | Fat: 12.4g | Protein: 20.3g   ➘ 6 min | 🍲 36 min | 🍴 Servings 2

INGREDIENTS

- 16 oz. scallops
- 4 tsp. brown butter
- Salt and pepper

DIRECTIONS

Preheat the Sous Vide machine to 140°F/60°C. Use a paper towel to gently dry the scallops. Place the scallops in the bag with 2 tsp. brown butter and salt and pepper to taste. Place the bag or bags in your preheated container and set your timer to 35 minutes. Heat the remaining brown butter in a skillet on high heat. When the scallops are cooked, take them out of the bag and place them in the skillet. Sear them for 30 seconds a side. They should have a golden color on both sides when seared.

366. CHARRED CALAMARI WITH MISO AND MIRIN

Cal.: 438 | Fat: 23.2g | Protein: 19.1g   ➘ 15 min | 🍲 2 hours 30 min | ✖ Servings 2

INGREDIENTS
- 2 tbsp. cooking sake
- 2 tbsp. miso paste
- 2 tbsp. mirin
- 2 tbsp. light brown sugar
- 3 tbsp. chili oil
- 8 oz. squid bodies
- 1 medium lemon

DIRECTIONS
Preheat the Sous Vide machine to 138°F/59°C. Clean and cut the calamari into thin rings and juice the lemon. Mix the sake, sugar, miso and mirin in a bowl. Add in the calamari and toss until well coated. Place the calamari and marinade in the bag and cook for 2 hours. In the last couple minutes of cooking, heat a grill pan on high heat. When the calamari are cooked, gently pat it dry using a paper towel. Sear the calamari in batches for 30 seconds. Place seared calamari in a bowl. Mix in the lemon juice and the chili oil. Serve immediately.

367. CAJUN SPICED TILAPIA

Cal.: 188 | Fat: 7.3g | Protein: 22.9g   ➘ 11 min | 🍲 30 min | ✖ Servings 4

INGREDIENTS
- 4 tilapia fillets
- 1 tablespoon black pepper
- 1 tablespoon kosher salt
- 1 tablespoon smoked paprika
- 2 tbsp. Italian seasoning
- 2 tbsp. cayenne pepper
- 2 tbsp. garlic powder
- 2 tbsp. dried onion granules or onion powder
- 1 tablespoon vegetable oil

DIRECTIONS
Preheat the Sous Vide machine to 138°F/59°C. Pat the fish dry using a paper towel. Mix together all the spices in a bowl and rub the spice mixture on the fish. Place the fish in the bag and cook for 30 minutes. Heat the oil in a skillet over medium-high heat and add the fish to the pan-searing for 1 minute per side.

368. SWORDFISH WITH BALSAMIC BROWN BUTTER SAUCE

Cal.: 634 | Fat: 34.5g | Protein: 64.3g   ➘ 21 min | 🍲 34 min | ✖ Servings 4

INGREDIENTS
- 2 lbs. swordfish steaks
- Salt and pepper
- Zest from ½ lemon
- 1 stick unsalted butter
- 3 tbsp. balsamic vinegar
- 3 tbsp. honey
- 1 tablespoon Dijon mustard

DIRECTIONS
Preheat the Sous Vide machine to 126°F/52°C.
Salt and pepper your steaks to taste and season with lemon zest. Place the steaks in the bag and place in the water bath for 30 minutes. Add the butter in a saucepan over medium heat until it foams. Once it stops foaming and turns a golden brown, whisk in the balsamic vinegar, Dijon and honey. Lower the heat to a simmer and allow the sauce to thicken. Remove the steaks from the bag and top with the sauce to serve.

369. COD WITH LEMON AND CAPERS

Cal.: 265 | Fat: 15.7g | Protein: 30.9g   ⟍ 11 min | 🍲 30 min | ✕ Servings 2

INGREDIENTS

- 2 (6-ounce) cod fillets
- Salt and freshly ground black pepper
- ½ lemon, sliced into 4 rounds
- 1/4 cup plus 1 tablespoon extra-virgin olive oil
- 12 tsp. capers
- Fresh dill

DIRECTIONS

Preheat the Sous Vide machine to 120°F/49°C. Slice the lemon into four pieces and chop the dill. Salt and pepper the cod to taste. Place the cod in the bag and add 2 pieces of lemon. Pour in 1/4 cup oil and the capers. Place your bag in the preheated container and set your timer for 30 minutes. When the cod is done, top with olive oil and the dill.

370. HALIBUT WITH ROSEMARY AND KAFFIR LIME LEAVES

Cal.: 214 | Fat: 5g | Protein: 37.1g   ⟍ 16 min | 🍲 16 min | ✕ Servings 4

INGREDIENTS

- 4 halibut fillets, each 6 oz. and 1 ½ inches-thick
- Kosher salt
- ½ cup milk
- 3 fresh rosemary sprigs
- 4 kaffir lime leaves

DIRECTIONS

Preheat the Sous Vide machine to 125°F/52°C. Slice the lime leaves thinly. Salt the halibut and place it in the bag with the remaining ingredients. Place the bag in your preheated container and set your timer for 15 minutes. Remove and serve immediately.

371. RED SNAPPER WITH FENNEL SEEDS AND CHILI FLAKES

Cal.: 462 | Fat: 21.9g | Protein: 60.7g   ⟍ 16 min | 🍲 28 min | ✕ Servings 2

INGREDIENTS

- 1 lb. red snapper, bones removed
- 3 tbsp. butter
- 1.5 tbsp. fennel seeds
- 1 tsp. chili flakes
- 1 tablespoon kosher salt
- ½ lemon

DIRECTIONS

Preheat the Sous Vide machine to 131°F/55°C. Use a paper towel to pat the snapper dry. Juice the lemon. Use mortar and pestle or a spice grinder to combine the chili, salt and fennel sides. Season the snapper with the spice mixture. Place the snapper in the bag with half the butter, and place in the water bath for 25 minutes. When the snapper is done, put the juices from the bag in a saucepan over medium heat while adding in the butter and lemon juice. Whisk until the sauce comes together, around 3 minutes. Serve the snapper with the sauce on top.

372. BRINED SALMON

Cal.: 399 | Fat: 28.8g | Protein: 24g   5 hours 11 min | 28 min | Servings 4

INGREDIENTS

- 4 salmon fillets
- 6 tbsp. unsalted butter
- 3 tbsp. sugar
- Fresh ground pepper
- 5 tablespoon coarse salt, plus more for taste
- ½ cup olive oil or melted, cooled butter

DIRECTIONS

Place 4 ½ cups of water in a large bowl. Pour in the 5 tbsp. salt and 3 tbsp. sugar. Stir the mixture until all solids dissolve. Place the salmon in the mixture and Immerse. Place the bowl in the refrigerator for 5 hours. Preheat the Sous Vide machine to 115°F/46°C. Take the salmon out of the bowl and place it in separate bags along with 2 tbsp. olive oil. Place the bags in your preheated container and set your timer for 24 minutes. In the last few minutes of cooking, place the 6 tbsp. butter in a skillet and melt it over medium-low heat. When the salmon is cooked, salt and pepper to taste. Place the salmon in the skillet and allow it to cook for 30 seconds per side. Serve immediately.

373. KING CRAB LEGS WITH HERBED BUTTER

Cal.: 205 | Fat: 13g | Protein: 20.2g   26 min | 51 min | Servings 4

INGREDIENTS

- 2 lbs. king crab legs
- 8 tbsp. unsalted butter
- 2 tsp. grated lemon zest
- 4 tsp. parsley
- 2 tsp. thyme
- 2 garlic cloves
- ½ tsp. salt
- Freshly ground black pepper

DIRECTIONS

Preheat the Sous Vide machine to 115°F/46°C. Finely chop the parsley and thyme, soften the butter, and peel and finely chop the garlic. Mix together all of the ingredients except for the crab. Allow it to rest for 15 minutes. Carefully cut open one side of the crab legs to expose the flesh. Pack the exposed side with the herbed butter. Place the remaining butter in the refrigerator and put the legs in the bag. You may need to double bag them to avoid punctures. Place the bag in your preheated container and set your timer for 45 minutes. When the legs are cooked, place any leftover juice in a serving container with the remaining herbed butter. Serve the legs with the butter on the side for dipping.

374. EAST ASIAN MARINATED CATFISH

Cal.: 463 | Fat: 38.3g | Protein: 23.7g   11 min | 30 min | Servings 4

INGREDIENTS

- 4 catfish filets
- 1/3 cup vegetable oil
- 1/4 cup low sodium soy sauce
- 2 garlic cloves minced
- 2 tbsp. rice wine vinegar
- 2 tbsp. sesame seeds
- 1 tablespoon sesame oil
- 1/4 tsp. black pepper
- 1/4 tsp. red pepper flakes

DIRECTIONS

Preheat the Sous Vide machine to 150°F/66°C. Combine all the ingredients in a bowl except for the catfish. Place the catfish in a bag, and pour the mixture in. Place the bag in your preheated container and set your timer for 20 minutes. When the catfish is cooked, serve it with the leftover sauce.

375. SPANISH SPICED SHRIMP

Cal.: 456 | Fat: 21.2g | Protein: 52.6g   12 min | 30 min | Servings 3

INGREDIENTS
- 1 ½ lbs. shrimp
- Kosher salt and pepper
- 2 tbsp. olive oil
- 6 garlic cloves
- 1 tablespoon Spanish hot smoked paprika
- 1 tablespoon sweet smoked paprika
- 4 tbsp. sherry
- 2 tbsp. butter
- 6 lemon wedges

DIRECTIONS
Preheat the Sous Vide machine to 120°F/49°C. Peel and devein the shrimp and mince the garlic. Salt and pepper the shrimp to taste. Put the olive oil in a skillet and heat it over medium-low heat. Add the garlic and paprika and allow it to cook for 2-3 minutes. Add the sherry and raise the temperature to high, cooking for 2-3 minutes. Remove from the heat and mix in the butter and add salt. Allow the sauce to cool for 15 minutes. Place the shrimp in the bag and pour in the sauce and cook for 20 minutes. Serve the shrimp with lemon wedges.

376. SAVORY HALIBUT

Cal.: 341 | Fat: 26.9g | Protein: 22g   20 min | 45 min | Servings 4

INGREDIENTS
- 1 tablespoon fresh ginger
- 1 teaspoon oregano
- 1 teaspoon ground white pepper
- 1 teaspoon paprika
- ½ teaspoon soy sauce
- 1 teaspoon chili flakes
- ½ cup fresh basil
- ¼ lemon
- 3 tablespoon butter
- 2-pound halibut

DIRECTIONS
Grate the fresh ginger and combine it with oregano, ground white pepper, and paprika, soy sauce and chili flakes in a large bowl. Stir to combine. Slice the lemon. Rub the halibut with the fresh ginger mixture and put sliced lemon over the halibut. Wrap the halibut in the fresh basil and put it in the plastic bag. Preheat the water bath to 142°F/61°C and put the halibut there. Cook fish for 45 minutes. When ready, remove fish from the bag and serve. Don't forget to discard the lemon and the basil.

377. PICKLED SHRIMPS

Cal.: 120 | Fat: 4.5g | Protein: 13g   15 min | 30 min | Servings 8

INGREDIENTS
- 1 tablespoon fennel seeds
- 1 teaspoon coriander seeds
- 1 teaspoon thyme
- 1 teaspoon cilantro
- ½ teaspoon oregano
- ½ tablespoon mustard seeds
- 2 tablespoon olive oil
- 1 teaspoon lemon zest
- 1-pound shrimps
- 2 oz. garlic cloves, peeled
- 1 tablespoon bay leaf
- 3 tablespoon vinegar
- ¼ cup lime juice
- 1 white onion
- 1 teaspoon salt

DIRECTIONS
Peel the onion and grate it. Combine the grated onion, lemon zest, lime juice and vinegar in a large bowl. Add peeled shrimps. Season with fennel seeds, coriander seeds, thyme, cilantro, oregano, mustard seeds, salt and olive oil. Stir to combine well. Transfer the mixture to a plastic bag and seal it. Preheat the Sous Vide machine to 149°F/65°C and cook the shrimps for 30 minutes. When ready, Serve and enjoy!

CHAPTER 8:
Vegetable Recipes

✎ Preparation Time | 🍲 Cooking Time | ✗ Servings

378. SNOW PEAS WITH MINT

Cal.: 117 | Fat: 0.6g | Protein: 8g   ⬛ 10 min | 🍲 15 min | ✖ Servings 2

INGREDIENTS

- 1 tbsp. Butter
- ½ cup Snow Peas
- 1 tbsp. Mint Leaves, chopped
- A pinch Salt
- Sugar to taste

DIRECTIONS

Make a water bath, place a cooker in it, and set it at 183°F/84°C. Place all the ingredients in a vacuum-sealable bag. Release air by the water displacement method, seal the bag and Immerse in the water bath. Set the timer for 15 minutes. Once the timer has stopped, remove and unseal the bag. Transfer the ingredients to a serving plate. Serve as a condiment.

379. HERBED ASPARAGUS MIX

Cal.: 190 | Fat: 0.1g | Protein: 2.2g   ⬛ 15 min | 🍲 12 min | ✖ Servings 3

INGREDIENTS

- 1 ½ lb. medium Asparagus
- 5 tbsp. butter
- 2 tbsp. lemon juice
- ½ tsp. lemon zest
- 1 tbsp. chives, sliced
- 1 tbsp. parsley, chopped
- 1 tbsp. + 1 tbsp. fresh dill, chopped
- 1 tbsp. + 1 tbsp. tarragon, chopped

DIRECTIONS

Make a water bath, place the cooker in it, and set to 183°F/84°C. Cut off and discard the tight bottoms of the asparagus. Place the asparagus in a vacuum-sealable bag. Release air by the water displacement method, seal and Immerse the bag in the water bath and set the timer for 10 minutes. Once the timer has stopped, remove the bag and unseal it. Place a skillet over low heat, add the butter and steamed asparagus. Season with salt and pepper and toss continually. Add lemon juice and zest and cook for 2 minutes. Turn heat off and add parsley, 1 tablespoon dill, and 1 tablespoon tarragon. Toss evenly. Garnish with remaining dill and tarragon. Serve warm as a side dish.

380. BALSAMIC BRAISED CABBAGE

Cal.: 129 | Fat: 6g | Protein: 2g   15 min | 🍲 1 hour 30 min | ✖ Servings 3

INGREDIENTS

- 1 lb. red cabbage, quartered and core removed
- 1 shallot, thinly sliced
- 2 garlic cloves, thinly sliced
- ½ tbsp. balsamic vinegar
- ½ tbsp. unsalted butter
- Salt to taste

DIRECTIONS

Make a water bath, place the cooker in it, and set to 183°F/84°C. Divide cabbage and remaining ingredients into 2 vacuum-sealable bags. Release air by the water displacement method and seal the bags. Immerse them in the water bath and set the timer to cook for 1 hour 30 minutes. Once the timer has stopped, remove and unseal the bag. Transfer the cabbage with juices into serving plates. Season with salt and vinegar to taste. Serve as a side dish.

381. NUTS, BEETROOT AND CHEESE SALAD

Cal.: 127 | Fat: 7g | Protein: 7g   ⟋ 15 min | 🍲 2 hours 30 seconds | ✗ Servings 3

INGREDIENTS

- 1 lb. Beetroot, peeled
- ½ cup Almonds, blanched
- 2 tbsp. Hazelnuts, skinned
- 2 tsp. Olive Oil
- 1 garlic clove, finely minced
- 1 tsp. Cumin Powder
- 1 tsp. Lemon Zest
- Salt to taste
- ½ cup Goat Cheese, crumbled
- Fresh Mint Leaves to garnish

Dressing:

- 2 tbsp. Olive Oil
- 1 tbsp. Apple Cider Vinegar

DIRECTIONS

Make a water bath, place the cooker in it, and set at 183°F/84°C. Cut the beetroots into wedges and bag in a vacuum-sealable bag. Release air by the water displacement method, seal and Immerse the bag in the water bath and set the timer for 2 hours. Once the timer has stopped, remove and unseal the bag. Place the beetroot aside. Put a pan over medium heat, add almonds and hazelnuts, and toast for 3 minutes. Transfer to a cutting board and chop. Add oil to the same pan, add garlic and cumin. Cook for 30 seconds. Turn heat off. In a bowl, combine the goat cheese, almond mixture, and lemon zest and garlic mixture. Mix. Whisk olive oil and vinegar and place aside. Serve as a side dish.

382. CREAMY CAULIFLOWER BROCCOLI SOUP

Cal.: 102 | Fat: 5.9g | Protein: 3g   ⟋ 5 min | 🍲 2 hours 3 min | ✗ Servings 2

INGREDIENTS

- 1 medium cauliflower, cut into small florets
- ½ lb. Broccoli, cut into small florets
- 1 Green Bell Pepper, chopped
- 1 medium White Onion, diced
- 1 tsp. Olive Oil
- 1 garlic clove, crushed
- ½ cup Vegetable Stock
- ½ cup Skimmed Milk

DIRECTIONS

Make a water bath, place the machine in it, and set it to 185°F/85°C. Place the cauliflower, broccoli, bell pepper and white onion in a vacuum-sealable bag and pour olive oil into it. Release air by the water displacement method and seal the bag. Immerse the bag in the water bath. Set the timer for 50 minutes and cook. Once the timer has stopped, remove the bag and unseal it. Transfer the vegetables to a blender, add garlic and milk, and purée to smooth. Place a pan over medium heat, add the vegetable purée and vegetable stock and simmer for 3 minutes. Season with salt and pepper. Serve warm as a side dish.

383. SPEEDY POACHED TOMATOES

Cal.: 180 | Fat: 16g | Protein: 34g   ⟋ 5 min | 🍲 30 min | ✗ Servings 3

INGREDIENTS

- 4 cups Cherry Tomatoes
- 5 tbsp. Olive Oil
- ½ tbsp. Fresh Rosemary Leaves, minced
- ½ tbsp. Fresh Thyme Leaves, minced
- Salt to taste
- Pepper to taste

DIRECTIONS

Make a water bath, place the machine in it, and set to 131°F/55°C. Divide the listed ingredients into 2 vacuum-sealable bags, season with salt and pepper. Release air by the water displacement method and seal the bag. Immerse them in the water bath and set the timer to cook for 30 minutes. Once the timer has stopped, remove the bag and unseal it. Transfer the tomatoes with the juices into a bowl. Serve as a side dish.

384. MEDITERRANEAN EGGPLANT LASAGNA

Cal.: 25 | Fat: 0.2g | Protein: 1g   20 min | 2 hours | Servings 3

INGREDIENTS

- 1 lb. eggplant, peeled and thinly sliced
- 1 tsp. salt
- 1 cup tomato sauce, divided into 3
- 2 oz. fresh mozzarella, thinly sliced
- 1 oz. parmesan cheese, grated
- 2 oz. Italian blend cheese, grated
- 3 tbsp. fresh basil, chopped

For Mayonnaise:

- ½ tbsp. Macadamia nuts, toasted and chopped
- 1 oz. parmesan cheese, grated
- 1 oz. Italian blend cheese, grated

DIRECTIONS

Make a water bath, place the cooker in it, and set at 183°F/84°C. Place eggplants in a colander, toss with salt and let drain for 15 minutes. While water heats, peel eggplants, slice into thin rounds and toss with salt. Lay a vacuum-sealable bag on its side, make a layer of half the eggplant, spread one portion of tomato sauce, layer mozzarella, then parmesan, then cheese blend, then basil. Top with the second portion of tomato sauce. Seal the bag carefully by the water displacement method, keeping it flat as possible. Immerse the bag flat in the water bath. Set the timer for 2 hours and cook. Release air 2 to 3 times within the first 30 minutes as eggplant releases gas as it cooks. Once the timer has stopped, remove the bag gently and poke one corner of the bag using a pin to release liquid from the bag. Lay the bag flat on a serving plate, cut open the top of it and gently slide the lasagna onto the plate. Top with remaining tomato sauce, macadamia nuts, cheese blend and Parmesan cheese. Melt and brown the cheese using a torch.

385. TRADITIONAL RATATOUILLE

Cal.: 200 | Fat: 20g | Protein: 3g   30 min | 1 hour 50 min | Servings 3

INGREDIENTS

- 2 medium zucchini, cut into ¼ inch dices
- 2 medium tomatoes, cut into ¼ inch dices
- 2 red capsicums, seeded and cut into 2-inch dices
- 1 small eggplant, cut into ¼ inch dices
- 1 onion, cut into 1-inch dices
- Salt to taste
- ½ red pepper flakes
- 8 garlic cloves, crushed
- 2 ½ tbsp. olive oil
- 5 sprigs + 2 sprigs basil leaves

DIRECTIONS

Make a water bath, place a cooker in it, and set it at 185°F/85°C. Place the tomatoes, zucchini, onion, bell pepper and eggplant, each in 5 separate vacuum-sealable bags. Put garlic, basil leaves and 1 tablespoon olive oil in each bag. Release air by the water displacement method, seal and Immerse the bags in the water bath and set the timer for 20 minutes. Once the timer has stopped, remove the bag with the tomatoes. Place aside. Reset the timer for 30 minutes. Once the timer has stopped, remove the bags with the zucchinis and red bell peppers. Place aside. Reset the timer for 1 hour. Once the timer has stopped, remove the remaining bags and discard the garlic and basil leaves. In a bowl, add tomatoes and use a spoon to mash them lightly. Roughly chop the remaining vegetables and add to the tomatoes. Season with salt, red pepper flakes, remaining olive oil, and basil. Serve.

386. SIMPLE HARD-BOILED EGGS

Cal.: 78 | Fat: 5.3g | Protein: 6.3g   10 min | 60 min | Servings 6

INGREDIENTS

- 6 large Eggs
- Ice bath

DIRECTIONS

Make a water bath, place a cooker in it, and set it at 165°F/74°C. Place the eggs in the water bath and set the timer for 1 hour. Once the timer has stopped, transfer the eggs to the ice bath. Peel eggs. Serve as a snack or in salads.

387. CHILI BRUSSELS SPROUTS IN SWEET SYRUP

Cal.: 43 | Fat: 0.3g | Protein: 3.4g　　　 20 min | 🍲 56 min | 🍴 Servings 3

INGREDIENTS

- 4 lb. Brussels sprouts, stems trimmed and halved
- 3 tbsp. olive oil
- ¾ cup fish sauce
- 3 tbsp. water
- 2 tbsp. sugar
- 1 ½ tbsp. rice vinegar
- 2 tsp. lime juice
- 3 red chilies, sliced thinly
- 2 garlic cloves, minced

DIRECTIONS

Make a water bath, place a cooker in it, and set it at 183°F/84°C. Pour Brussels sprouts, salt, and oil in a vacuum-sealable bag, release air by the water displacement method, seal and Immerse the bag in the water bath. Set the timer for 50 minutes. Once the timer has stopped, remove the bag, unseal it, and transfer the Brussels sprouts to a foiled baking sheet. Preheat a broiler to high, place the baking sheet in it, and broil for 6 minutes. Pour the Brussels sprouts in a bowl. Make the sauce: in a bowl, add the remaining listed cooking ingredients and stir. Add the sauce to the Brussels sprouts and toss evenly. Serve as a side dish.

388. AROMATIC BRAISED BEETROOTS

Cal.: 43 | Fat: 0.3g | Protein: 1.7g　　　 15 min | 🍲 60 min | 🍴 Servings 3

INGREDIENTS

- 2 beets, peeled and sliced into 1 cm inches
- 1/3 cup balsamic vinegar
- ½ tsp. olive oil
- 1/3 cup toasted walnuts
- 1/3 cup grana padano cheese, grated
- Salt to taste
- Pepper to taste

DIRECTIONS

Make a water bath, place a cooker in it, and set it at 183°F/84°C. Place the beets, vinegar and salt in a vacuum-sealable bag. Release air by the water displacement method, seal and Immerse the bag in the water bath. Set the timer for 1 hour. Once the timer has stopped, remove and unseal the bag. Transfer the beets to a bowl, add olive oil and toss. Sprinkle walnuts and cheese over it. Serve as a side dish.

389. POMODORO SOUP

Cal.: 270 | Fat: 4g | Protein: 18g　　　 10 min | 🍲 50 min | 🍴 Servings 3

INGREDIENTS

- 2 lb. tomatoes, halved
- 1 onion, diced
- 1 celery stick, chopped
- 3 tbsp. olive oil
- 1 tbsp. unsweetened tomato purée
- A pinch of Sugar
- 1 bay leaf

DIRECTIONS

Make a water bath, place a cooker in it, and set it at 185°F/85°C. Place all the listed ingredients, except salt, in a bowl and toss. Put them in a vacuum-sealable bag. Release air by the water displacement method, seal and Immerse the bag into the water bath. Set the timer for 40 minutes. Once the timer has stopped, remove the bag and unseal it. Purée the ingredients using a blender. Pour the blended tomato into a pot and set it over medium heat. Season with salt and cook for 10 minutes. Dish soup into bowls and cool.

390. SIMPLE MUSHROOM SOUP

Cal.: 22 | Fat: 0.3g | Protein: 3.1g   4 min | 40 min | Servings 3

INGREDIENTS

- 1 lb. mixed mushrooms
- 2 onions, diced
- 3 garlic cloves
- 2 sprigs parsley leaves, chopped
- 2 tbsp. thyme powder
- 2 tbsp. olive oil
- 2 cups cream
- 2 cups vegetable stock

DIRECTIONS

Make a water bath, place a cooker in it, and set it at 185°F/85°C. Place the mushrooms, onion and celery in a vacuum-sealable bag. Release air by the water displacement method, seal and Immerse the bag in the water bath. Set the timer for 30 minutes. Once the timer has stopped, remove and unseal the bag. Blend the ingredients in the bag in a blender. Put a pan over medium heat, add the olive oil. Once it starts to heat, add the pureed mushrooms and the remaining listed ingredients except for the cream. Cook for 10 minutes. Turn off heat and add cream. Stir well. Serve with a side of bread.

391. EASY MIXED VEGETABLE SOUP

Cal.: 150 | Fat: 0.3g | Protein: 1.2g   10 min | 40 min | Servings 3

INGREDIENTS

- 1 sweet onion, sliced
- 1 tsp. garlic powder
- 2 cups zucchini, cut in small dices
- 3 oz. parmesan rind
- 2 cups baby spinach
- 2 tbsp. olive oil
- 1 tsp. red pepper flakes
- 2 cups vegetable stock
- 1 sprig rosemary
- Salt to taste

DIRECTIONS

Make a water bath, place a cooker in it, and set it at 185°F/85°C. Toss all the ingredients with olive oil, except the garlic and salt, and place them in a vacuum-sealable bag. Release air by water displacement method, seal and Immerse the bag in the water bath. Set the timer for 30 minutes. Once the timer has stopped, remove and unseal the bag. Discard the rosemary. Pour the remaining ingredients into a pot and add the salt and garlic powder. Once the timer has stopped, remove and unseal the bag. Discard the rosemary. Pour the remaining ingredients into a pot and add the salt and garlic powder. Put the pot over medium heat and simmer for 10 minutes. Serve as a light dish.

392. POWER GREEN SOUP

Cal.: 153 | Fat: 1g | Protein: 6g   10 min | 40 min | Servings 3

INGREDIENTS

- 4 cups vegetable stock
- 1 tbsp. olive oil
- 1 garlic clove, crushed
- 1-inch ginger, sliced
- 1 tsp. coriander powder
- 1 large zucchini, diced
- 3 cups kale
- 2 cups broccoli, cut into florets
- 1 lime, juiced and zest

DIRECTIONS

Make a water bath, place a cooker in it, and set it at 185°F/85°C. Place the broccoli, zucchini, kale and parsley in a vacuum-sealable bag. Release air by the water displacement method, seal and Immerse the bag in the water bath. Set the timer for 30 minutes. Once the timer has stopped, remove and unseal the bag. Add the steamed ingredients to a blender with garlic and ginger. Purée to smooth. Pour the green purée into a pot and add the remaining listed ingredients. Put the pot over medium heat and simmer for 10 minutes. Serve as a light dish.

393. COLORFUL BELL PEPPER MIX

Cal.: 31 | Fat: 0.4g | Protein: 1g   20 min | 15 min | Servings 2

INGREDIENTS
- 1 red bell pepper, chopped
- 1 yellow bell pepper, chopped
- 1 green bell pepper, chopped
- 1 large orange bell pepper, chopped
- Salt to taste

DIRECTIONS
Make a water bath, place a cooker in it, and set it at 183°F/84°C. Place all the bell peppers with salt in a vacuum-sealable bag. Release air by the water displacement method, seal and Immerse in the water bath. Set the timer for 15 minutes. Once the timer has stopped, remove and unseal the bag. Serve bell peppers with its juices as a side dish.

394. CILANTRO CURRIED ZUCCHINIS

Cal.: 17 | Fat: 0.3g | Protein: 1.2g   10 min |  25 min | Servings 3

INGREDIENTS
- 3 small zucchinis, diced
- 2 tsp. curry powder
- 1 tbsp. olive oil
- Salt to taste
- Pepper to taste
- ¼ cup cilantro

DIRECTIONS
Make a water bath, place a cooker in it, and set it at 185°F/85°C. Place the zucchinis in a vacuum-sealable bag. Release air by the water displacement method, seal and Immerse the bag in the water bath. Set the timer for 20 minutes. Once the timer has stopped, remove and unseal the bag. Place a skillet over medium, add olive oil. Once it has heated, add the zucchinis and the remaining listed ingredients. Season with salt and stir-fry for 5 minutes. Serve.

395. PAPRIKA BELL PEPPER PURÉE

Cal.: 20 | Fat: 0.2g | Protein: 0.9g   20 min | 23 min | Servings 4

INGREDIENTS
- 8 Red Bell Peppers, cored
- 1/3 cup Olive Oil
- 2 tbsp. Lemon Juice
- 3 garlic cloves, crushed
- 2 tsp. Sweet Paprika

DIRECTIONS
Make a water bath and place a cooker in it and set it at 183°F/84°C. Put the bell peppers, garlic, and olive oil in a vacuum-sealable bag. Release air by the water displacement method, seal and Immerse the bags in the water bath. Set the timer for 20 minutes and cook. Once the timer has stopped, remove the bag and unseal it. Transfer the bell pepper and garlic to a blender and purée to smooth. Place a pan over medium heat; add bell pepper purée and the remaining listed ingredients. Cook for 3 minutes. Serve warm or cold as a dip.

396. CHILI AND GARLIC SAUCE

Cal.: 25 | Fat: 0.2g | Protein: 0.9g   7 min | 30 min | Servings 15

INGREDIENTS
- 2 lb. red chili peppers
- 4 garlic cloves, crushed
- 2 tsp. smoked paprika
- 1 cup cilantro leaves, chopped
- ½ cup basil leaves, chopped
- 2 lemons' juice

DIRECTIONS
Make a water bath, place a cooker in it, and set it at 185°F/85°C. Place the peppers in a vacuum-sealable bag. Release air by the water displacement method, seal and Immerse the bag in the water bath. Set the timer for 30 minutes. Once the timer has stopped, remove and unseal the bag. Transfer the pepper and the remaining listed ingredients to a blender and purée to smooth. Store in an airtight container, refrigerate and use for up to 7 days.

397. ARTICHOKE HEARTS WITH GREEN CHILIES

Cal.: 47 | Fat: 0.2g | Protein: 3.3g　　　　🔪 1 hour 15 min | 🍲 33 min | 🍴 Servings 6

INGREDIENTS

- 2 onions, quartered
- 3 garlic cloves, minced
- 15 oz. artichoke hearts, soaked for 1 hour, drained and chopped
- 18 oz. frozen spinach, thawed
- 5 oz. green chilies
- 3 tbsp. olive oil mayonnaise
- 3 tbsp. whipped cream cheese

DIRECTIONS

Make a water bath, place a cooker in it, and set it at 181°F/82°C. Divide the onions, garlic, artichoke hearts, spinach and green chilies into 2 vacuum-sealable bags. Release air by the water displacement method, seal and Immerse the bags in the water bath. Set the timer for 30 minutes to cook. Once the timer has stopped, remove and unseal the bag. Purée the ingredients using a blender. Place a pan over medium heat and add the butter. Once it has melted, add the vegetable purée, lemon juice, olive oil mayonnaise, and cream cheese. Season with salt and pepper. Stir and cook for 3 minutes. Serve warm with a side of vegetable strips.

398. PARMESAN GARLIC ASPARAGUS

Cal.: 85 | Fat: 1g | Protein: 0.9g　　　　🔪 6 min | 🍲 16 min | 🍴 Servings 4

INGREDIENTS

- 1 bunch green asparagus, trimmed
- 4 tbsp. unsalted butter, cut into cubes
- Sea salt
- 1 tbsp. pressed garlic
- 1/4 cup shaved Parmesan cheese

DIRECTIONS

Preheat the Sous Vide machine to 185°F/85°C. Use paper towels to pat the salmon dry. Place the asparagus in a single layer row in the bag or bags you're going to use to sous. Put a tbsp. butter in each of the corners, the pressed garlic in the middle, salt to taste, and seal the bag. Move the bag around to get garlic to disperse evenly. Place the bag in your preheated water and set the timer for 14 minutes. Top the cooked asparagus with some of the liquid from the bag and the parmesan cheese. Serve immediately.

399. BLACKENED BRUSSELS SPROUTS WITH GARLIC AND BACON

Cal.: 105 | Fat: 6g | Protein: 9g　　　　🔪 16 min | 🍲 85 min | 🍴 Servings 8

INGREDIENTS

- 2 lbs. Brussels sprouts
- 3 garlic cloves, chopped
- 3 strips bacon
- Bacon fat, from cooking the bacon
- Salt and pepper

DIRECTIONS

Preheat the Sous Vide machine to 183°F/83.9°C. Wash the Brussels sprouts and use paper towels to pat them dry. Heat a skillet on medium heat for a few min. When it's hot, add in the bacon. Cook the bacon until crispy, flipping halfway through. Remove the bacon and add in the garlic. Cook the garlic in the pan with the bacon fat until fragrant, about 1 minute. Then place the bacon fat and garlic in a bowl. Put the Brussels sprouts in the bag or bags you're going to use to sous, along with the bacon fat, a little fresh ground pepper and garlic. Shake the bag around so everything is well mixed and seal the bag. Place the bag in your preheated water and set the timer for 50 minutes. At the 35-minute mark preheat your oven to 400°F/205°C and line a large rimmed baking sheet with parchment paper. Place the cooked mixture on the baking sheet, making sure the Brussels sprouts are in a single layer. Put the baking sheet in the oven and cook the Brussels sprouts for 5 to 7 min. The sprouts should blacken a little bit when they're ready. Serve immediately.

400. ASIAN INSPIRED BOK CHOY

Cal.: 98 | Fat: 1g | Protein: 9g   11 min | 30 min | Servings 4

INGREDIENTS

- 1 tbsp. ginger, minced
- 2 garlic cloves, minced
- 1 tbsp. toasted sesame oil
- 1 tbsp. canola oil
- 1 tbsp. soy sauce
- 1 tbsp. fish sauce
- 1 tsp. red pepper flake
- 1 lb. baby bok choy, cut in half lengthwise
- 1 tbsp. toasted sesame seed
- 1 tbsp. cilantro leaves

DIRECTIONS

Preheat the Sous Vide machine to 176°F/80°C. Put the garlic and ginger in a large heat-proof container. Put the sesame oil and canola oil in a small pot and heat it on medium heat. You want the oil to get so hot that it just starts to smoke. Take the pot off the heat and pour it into the container with the garlic and ginger. Mix in the bok choy, red pepper flakes, fish sauce and soy sauce. Place the entire mixture in the bag you're going to use to sous and seal the bag. Place the bag in your preheated water and set the timer for 20 minutes. Place the cooked bok choy on a plate or in a bowl, and top with the cilantro and sesame seeds. Serve immediately.

401. ROSEMARY AND GARLIC POTATOES

Cal.: 65 | Fat: 5g | Protein: 11g   6 min | 60 min | Servings 4

INGREDIENTS

- 8 to 10 red-skinned new potatoes, scrubbed, rinsed, and quartered
- Olive oil
- Coarse salt
- Freshly ground black pepper
- Garlic powder
- 2 tsp. fresh rosemary, finely minced
- 1 tbsp. olive oil
- 1 tbsp. rendered bacon or duck fat, or unsalted butter (optional)

DIRECTIONS

Preheat the Sous Vide machine to 183°F/83.9°C. Place the potatoes in a bowl and drizzle them with a little olive oil, just enough to coat them. Toss the potatoes to ensure every part is coated with oil. Season with the 2 tsp. Rosemary, salt, pepper and garlic powder to taste. Toss the potatoes again. Place the butter or bacon or duck fat with the potatoes in a ziploc bag and seal it. Place the bag in your preheated water and set the timer for 1 hour. Place the cooked potatoes in a bowl or on a plate. Serve immediately.

402. CANDIED SWEET POTATOES

Cal.: 115 | Fat: 11g | Protein: 9g   6 min | 90 min | Servings 6

INGREDIENTS

- 4 cups sweet potatoes, peeled and cubed into ½ inch pieces
- 4 tbsp. unsalted butter, cut into small pieces
- 4 tbsp. brown sugar
- 1 tsp. ginger root, finely minced
- 1 pinch cinnamon
- 1 pinch cayenne pepper
- 1 pinch ground clove
- Salt and pepper to taste
- 1 cup mini marshmallows
- 1 to 2 tbsp. brown sugar, optional addition for topping

DIRECTIONS

Preheat the Sous Vide machine to 183°F/83.9°C. Put the sweet potatoes in the bag you're going to use to sous vide along with the butter, ginger, cinnamon, cayenne, clove and salt and pepper. Massage the bag to evenly disperse the butter and seal the bag. Place the bag in your preheated water and set the timer for 1 hour 30 minutes. Place the cooked sweet potatoes in a bowl and top with brown sugar and marshmallows. Serve immediately.

403. PICKLED ASPARAGUS

Cal.: 145 | Fat: 19g | Protein: 10g   21 min | 30 min | Servings 4

INGREDIENTS

- 12 oz. asparagus, woody ends trimmed
- 2/3 cup white wine vinegar
- 2/3 cup water
- 3 tbsp. sugar
- 1 tbsp. sea salt
- ½ tsp. whole peppercorns
- ½ tsp. yellow or brown mustard seeds
- ¼ tsp. coriander seeds
- 2 garlic cloves, peeled and sliced in half lengthwise
- 1 bay leaf
- Fresh chili pepper, sliced in half

DIRECTIONS

Preheat the Sous Vide machine to 190°F/87.8°C. Place everything but the asparagus in a small pot and heat on high heat until it boils. Carefully stir the mixture until the sugar dissolves. Place the asparagus in a single layer row in the bag(s) you're going to use to sous, along with the heated mixture and seal the bag. Place the bag in your preheated water and set the timer for 10 min. While asparagus is cooking, prepare an ice bath (half ice half water). Place the cooked asparagus, still in the bag in the ice bath and let it chill for 15 minutes before serving.

404. SPICY PICKLED VEGETABLE MEDLEY

Cal.: 145 | Fat: 17g | Protein: 9g   11 min | 30 min | Servings 6

INGREDIENTS

- 1 cup apple cider vinegar
- ½ cup sriracha
- ¼ cup granulated sugar
- 4 tsp. kosher salt
- 4 tsp. red pepper flake
- 1 cup baby beets, cut into quarters lengthwise
- 1 cup carrot, sliced ¼ inch
- 1 cup Persian cucumbers, sliced ¼ inch thick
- 1 cup shallot, sliced ¼ inch thick

DIRECTIONS

Preheat the Sous Vide machine to 176°F/80°C. Mix together everything but the vegetables in a measuring cup. Place the beets in a bag, the carrots in a bag, and the cucumbers and shallots in a bag. Pour and an equal amount of the liquid in each bag. Place the beets bag in your preheated water. Set the timer for 30 min. Add the carrots bag and cook the carrots bag for 15 minutes. Add the cucumber and shallots bag and cook for 5 minutes. While the vegetables are cooking, prepare an ice bath, which is half ice half water. Place the cooked vegetables, still in the bag in the ice bath and let it chill for 15 minutes before serving.

405. TURMERIC PICKLED CAULIFLOWER

Cal.: 125 | Fat: 21g | Protein: 11g   11 min | 3 hours | Servings 6

INGREDIENTS

- 4 cups Cauliflower Florets
- 1 cup White Wine Vinegar
- 1 cup Water
- 1/4 cup Sugar
- 1 tbsp. Salt
- 1 Thumb-Sized Piece Turmeric sliced
- A few Sprigs Dill
- 1 tbsp. Black Peppercorns

DIRECTIONS

Preheat the Sous Vide machine to 140°F/60°C. Place everything but the dill and cauliflower in a small pot and bring to a simmer on medium heat. Stir the mixture carefully until the sugar dissolves. Place the cauliflower and dill in the bag you're going to use to sous along with the heated mixture and seal the bag. Place the bag in your preheated water and set the timer for 3 hours. Towards the end of the cooking process, prepare an ice bath, which is half ice half water. Place the cooked cauliflower, still in the bag in the ice bath and let it chill for 15 minutes before serving.

406. SIMPLE HONEY GLAZED CARROTS

Cal.: 145 | Fat: 24g | Protein: 16g   6 min | 50 min | Servings 3

INGREDIENTS

- 6-8 Medium to Large Sized Carrots, Washed and Peeled
- 3 tbs. Unsalted Butter
- 2 tbs. Honey
- 1 Cinnamon Stick
- Sea Salt to Taste

DIRECTIONS

Preheat the Sous Vide machine to 185°F or 85°C. Place all the ingredients in the bag you're going to use to sous and seal the bag. Place the bag in your preheated water and set the timer for 45 minutes. Towards the end of the cooking process, heat a skillet on high heat until it's hot. Place the cooked carrots in the skillet and sear for a total of 1 to 2 minutes, making sure to sear both sides. Top the carrots with a little more honey to serve.

407. TOMATOES

Cal.: 125 | Fat: 2g | Protein: 0.9g   7 min | 47 min | Servings 4

INGREDIENTS

- 4 medium on-the-vine tomatoes
- Kosher salt and freshly ground black pepper
- 2 tbsp. extra virgin olive oil
- 2 tbsp. balsamic vinegar, plus more for serving
- 1 sprig of fresh rosemary, plus more for serving

DIRECTIONS

Preheat the Sous Vide machine to 140°F/60°C. Bring water to a boil in a big pot on high heat. Prepare an ice bath. Slice a small X in the top of each tomato and put them in the water. Allow the tomatoes to cook for around 1 minute, until the skin starts to peel off. Then quickly put the tomatoes in the prepared ice bath. When the tomatoes cool down, take off the skins. Season the tomatoes with salt and pepper to taste. Place the tomatoes in the bag you're going to use to sous along with the olive oil, balsamic vinegar, and rosemary. Then seal the bag. Place the bag in your preheated water and set the timer for 45 minutes. Place the cooked tomatoes on a plate, sprinkle with a little more balsamic vinegar and top with more rosemary to serve.

408. GARLIC CHEESE RISOTTO

Cal.: 165 | Fat: 23g | Protein: 9g   6 min | 43 min | Servings 4

INGREDIENTS

- 1 cup Arborio rice
- 1 tsp. extra virgin olive oil
- 2 tbsp. roasted minced garlic (jarred)
- 3 cups chicken or vegetable broth
- 1 sprig fresh rosemary, leaves only, minced
- Salt and pepper to taste
- 1/3 cup grated Romano cheese

DIRECTIONS

Preheat the Sous Vide machine to 183°F/83°C. Place the first 6 ingredients in the bag you're going to use to sous. Place the bag in your preheated water and set the timer for 45 minutes. Place the cooked risotto in 4 bowls and fluff it with a fork. Mix in the cheese and serve.

409. ARTICHOKE AND ROASTED RED PEPPER RISOTTO

Cal.: 142 | Fat: 12g | Protein: 8g   11 min | 60 min | Servings 4

INGREDIENTS

- 1 cup Arborio rice
- 3 cups vegetable or chicken broth
- 1, 14 oz. can artichoke hearts, drained and chopped
- 1,12 oz. jar roasted red peppers, drained and chopped
- 1 tbsp. extra virgin olive oil
- 4 garlic cloves, peeled and pressed or finely chopped
- 1 tsp. Italian seasoning
- Ground black pepper, to taste
- ½ cup grated Parmesan cheese

DIRECTIONS

Preheat the Sous Vide machine to 183°F/83°C. Place the first 8 ingredients in the bag you're going to use to sous. Place the bag in your preheated water and set the timer for 1 hour. Place the cooked risotto in 4 bowls and fluff it with a fork. Mix in the cheese and serve.

410. TURKEY AND MUSHROOM RISOTTO

Cal.: 129 | Fat: 13g | Protein: 5g   6 min | 60 min | Servings 4

INGREDIENTS

- 1 cup Arborio rice
- 1 tsp. extra virgin olive oil
- 1 small yellow onion, peeled and diced
- 8 to 10 crimini mushrooms, wiped clean and sliced
- 8 oz. cooked turkey or chicken, diced (leftovers work well!)
- 2 tbsp. roasted minced garlic (jarred)
- 720 ml turkey or chicken broth
- 1 sprig fresh rosemary, leaves only, minced
- Salt and pepper to taste
- 1/3 cup grated Romano cheese

DIRECTIONS

Preheat the Sous Vide machine to 183°F/83°C. Heat up the olive oil in a frying pan on medium heat. Cook the onion and mushrooms until they become tender, about 5 min. Place the first 9 ingredients in the bag you're going to use to sous. Place the bag in your preheated water and set the timer for 1 hour. Place the cooked risotto in 4 bowls and fluff it with a fork. Mix in the cheese and serve.

411. PARMESAN AND SCALLION OMELET

Cal.: 25 | Fat: 0.2g | Protein: 0.9g   6 min | 30 min | Servings 1

INGREDIENTS

- 2 large eggs
- 1 tbsp. minced scallion greens
- 1 tbsp. finely grated Parmesan cheese
- 1 tbsp. unsalted butter, diced
- Salt and pepper
- Chopped fresh parsley, for serving

DIRECTIONS

Preheat the Sous Vide machine to 165°F/73°C. Whisk the eggs in a medium bowl. Then whisk in the parmesan, butter, scallions, and salt and pepper to taste. Place the mixture in the bag that you're going to use to sous and seal it. Place the bags in your preheated water and set the timer for 10 min. After 10 minutes, gently fold the eggs into the shape of an omelet and cook for 10 more minutes. Place the cooked omelet on a plate and top with the parsley to serve.

412. SPRING VEGETABLE RISOTTO

Cal.: 135 | Fat: 17g | Protein: 9g   11 min | 50 min | Servings 4

INGREDIENTS

Risotto:
- 1 cup Arborio rice
- 3 cups vegetable or mushroom broth
- ½ tsp. butter
- 2, 4 oz. cans mushroom stems and pieces, chopped
- 1 sprig fresh rosemary, leaves minced
- Salt and pepper to taste

Spring Vegetables:
- 1 lb. spring vegetables like asparagus, broccoli, peppers, summer squash, cut into bite-sized pieces, peeled if necessary
- Salt and pepper to taste
- 1 to 2 tbsp. butter
- Fresh or dried herbs of choice

DIRECTIONS

Preheat the Sous Vide machine to 183°F/83°C. Place the risotto ingredients in the bag you're going to use to sous and the spring vegetable ingredients in a separate bag and seal them. Place the bags in your preheated water and set the timer for 45 min. Place the cooked risotto in 4 bowls and fluff it with a fork. Mix in the cheese and vegetables, and serve.

413. FENNEL RISOTTO

Cal.: 136 | Fat: 9g | Protein: 4g   15 min | 46 min | Servings 4

INGREDIENTS

- 1 cup Arborio rice
- 3 cups vegetable broth
- 1 glass white wine
- 1 tbsp. olive oil
- Salt and pepper
- 4 fennel bulbs, trimmed cut in half
- A little butter
- Freshly grated Parmesan cheese, for serving

DIRECTIONS

Preheat the Sous Vide machine to 183°F/83°C. Place the first 5 ingredients in the bag you're going to use to sous and the fennel and a little butter in a separate bag, and seal them. Place the bags in your preheated water and set the timer for 45 min. Place the cooked risotto in 4 bowls and fluff it with a fork. Mix in the cheese and fennel, and serve.

414. FANTASTIC EARLY MORNING ARTICHOKE

Cal.: 370 | Fat: 22g | Protein: 14g   15 min | 30 min | Servings 2

INGREDIENTS

- 1 whole artichoke
- 2 tablespoons vegan butter
- 1 garlic clove, sautéed
- 1 teaspoon sea salt

DIRECTIONS

Preheat your water bath by submerging the immersion circulator and set the temperature at 180°F/82°C. Peel outer leaves and stems of the artichokes. Then cut up the artichokes in half from the bloom end to the stem end. Season it with salt and garlic. Add all the listed ingredients into a heavy-duty resealable zip bag. Seal bag using the immersion method, Immerse it. Cook for 30 minutes. Serve and enjoy!

415. ROASTED RED PEPPER EGG WHITE BITES

Cal.: 134 | Fat: 19g | Protein: 9g   11 min | 60 min | Servings 6

INGREDIENTS

- 6 egg whites
- 1/4 cup cream cheese
- ½ cup cottage cheese
- 1/4 tsp. salt
- 1/4 tsp. pepper
- 2 tbsp. finely chopped roasted red pepper
- 2 green onions, green parts only, finely chopped
- Butter or oil

DIRECTIONS

Preheat the Sous Vide machine to 172°F/77.8°C. Place the first 5 ingredients in a blender or food processor and blend until smooth. Use butter or oil to grease 6, 4 oz. mason jars. Pour in an equal amount of the egg mixture and place an equal amount of roasted red pepper in the mason jars. Use a butter knife to stir the mixture. Use your fingertips to tighten the lids. Place the jars in your preheated water and set the timer for 1 hour. Allow the cooked egg bites to cool for a few minutes. Serve the cooked egg bites in the jars or use a knife to remove them and put them on plates.

416. CARAMELIZED ONION AND BROCCOLI PALEO EGG BITES

Cal.: 125 | Fat: 22g | Protein: 8g   21 min | 60 min | Servings 6

INGREDIENTS

- 6 eggs
- 1/4 tsp. salt
- 1 cup broccoli florets cut pieces
- ½ cup yellow onion, minced
- 1 tbsp. olive oil
- 1/4 tsp. garlic powder
- 2 tbsp. water
- 2 tbsp. finely chopped roasted red pepper

DIRECTIONS

Preheat the Sous Vide machine to 172°F/77.8°C. Place the first 2 ingredients in a blender and blend on medium-high speed. Blend until the mixture turns to a creamy color and the mixture is homogenized. Pour the olive oil into a small frying pan and heat it on medium-high heat until the oil moves around the pan freely. Put in the onions, a pinch of salt, garlic powder and broccoli in the pan and mix until the vegetables are coated with oil. Reduce the temperature to medium heat and cook for 3 to 4 minutes. Pour the water into the pan and stir the mixture. Cook for another minute, until all the water evaporates. Take the pan off the heat and allow the mixture to cool. Pour in an equal amount of the egg mixture. Place an equal amount of roasted red pepper and the onion mixture in the mason jars. Use a butter knife to stir the mixture. Use your fingertips to tighten the lids. Place the jars in your preheated water and set the timer for 1 hour. Allow the cooked egg bites to cool for a few minutes. Serve the cooked egg bites in the jars or use a knife to remove them and put them on plates.

417. BALSAMIC MUSHROOMS AND MIXED HERBS

Cal.: 405 | Fat: 18g | Protein: 12g   15 min | 60 min | Servings 4

INGREDIENTS

- 1 pound cremini mushrooms, stems removed
- 1 tablespoon extra-virgin olive oil
- 1 tablespoon apple balsamic vinegar
- 1 teaspoon black pepper, freshly ground
- 1 teaspoon fresh thyme, minced
- 1 garlic clove, minced
- 1 teaspoon kosher salt

DIRECTIONS

Preheat your water bath by submerging the immersion circulator and set the temperature at 140°F/60°C. Add all the listed ingredients into a heavy-duty resealable zip bag. Seal bag using the immersion method, Immerse it. Cook for 1 hour. Serve and enjoy!

CHAPTER 9:
Soup and Stew Recipes

🔪 Preparation Time | 🍲 Cooking Time | 🍴 Servings

418. CREAM OF CELERY SOUP

Cal.: 372 | Fat: 23g | Protein: 14g   🥄 18 min | 🍲 60 min | 🍴 Servings 2

INGREDIENTS

- 2 cups celery, diced into large pieces
- ½ cup russet potatoes, peeled, diced into small pieces
- ½ cup leek, diced into large pieces
- ½ cup stock (vegetable or chicken
- ½ cup heavy cream
- 1 tablespoon butter
- 1 bay leaf
- 1 teaspoon kosher salt or to taste
- White pepper powder to taste

DIRECTIONS

Set your machine to 180°F/82°C. Place all the ingredients in a Ziploc or a vacuum-seal bag. Remove the air by using the water displacement method or a vacuum-sealed one. Seal and then immerse in the water bath. Cook for 1 hour or until the vegetables are tender. When done, remove the bay leaf and purée the soup. Strain through a wire mesh strainer and discard the solids. Serve hot.

419. CARROT AND CORIANDER SOUP

Cal.: 260 | Fat: 27g | Protein: 12g   🥄 13 min | 🍲 1 hour 45 min | 🍴 Servings 4

INGREDIENTS

- 1 lb. carrots
- 1 cup coconut cream
- 2 teaspoons ground coriander
- 1 teaspoon ground cumin
- 1 garlic clove, crushed
- Fresh coriander, chopped, to serve

DIRECTIONS

Set your Sous Vide machine to 190°F/88°C. Put carrots, coconut cream, coriander, cumin and garlic into a Ziploc or vacuum-seal bag and remove all the air. Seal and immerse the bag in the water bath and cook for 1 hour and 45 minutes. Transfer the ingredients to a blender, breaking up the carrots as you remove them, and blend until smooth. Serve warm, topping with chopped coriander to taste.

420. SPRING ONION SOUP

Cal.: 368 | Fat: 28g | Protein: 10g   🥄 14 min | 🍲 60 min | 🍴 Servings 2

INGREDIENTS

- 2 bunches of spring onions, rinsed, trimmed, chopped
- 4 garlic cloves, peeled, chopped
- 1 large russet potato, peeled, diced
- 2 teaspoons olive oil plus extra for serving
- 2 teaspoons soy sauce
- Salt to taste
- Pepper powder to taste
- 2-3 tablespoons fresh parsley leaves for garnishing

DIRECTIONS

Set your Sous Vide machine to 180°F/82°C. Add all the ingredients into a ziplock or a vacuum-seal bag and remove all the air. Seal and immerse the bag in the water bath and cook for 45 minutes to 1 hour. Remove the pouch and transfer into a blender and blend until smooth and creamy. Ladle into individual soup bowls. Garnish with parsley and serve.

421. CHICKEN AND VEGETABLE SOUP

Cal.: 369 | Fat: 26g | Protein: 14g   ➘ 12 min | 🍲 68 min | ✗ Servings 2

INGREDIENTS

- ½ cup zucchini, diced
- ½ cup red bell pepper, diced
- ½ cup cauliflower, chopped
- 3 baby carrots, chopped
- 1 medium onion, chopped
- 2 cups fresh spinach leaves
- ½ teaspoon garlic powder or to taste
- ½ teaspoon onion powder
- Sea salt to taste
- Black pepper powder to taste
- Cayenne pepper to taste
- 1 cup chicken, diced, cooked
- ½ tablespoon olive oil
- 2 cups chicken broth

DIRECTIONS

Set your Sous Vide machine to 180°F/82°C. Place all the vegetables and spices in a bowl. Mix well and place into a zip lock or a vacuum-seal bag. Remove all the air. Seal and Immerse the bag in the water bath and cook for 1 hour or until the vegetables are tender. To make the soup, heat olive oil in a soup pot over medium heat. Add broth and bring to a boil. Lower heat and add chicken and cooked vegetables along with their juices. Simmer for 5–7 minutes. Serve hot.

422. CAULIFLOWER SOUP

Cal.: 370 | Fat: 22g | Protein 14g   ➘ 9 min | 🍲 70 min | ✗ Servings 2

INGREDIENTS

- 1 large head cauliflower, break into florets
- 2 shallots, chopped
- 4 cups of vegetable stock
- ½ cup white wine
- ½ cup sour cream
- 1 ½ cups cream
- Juice of a lemon
- 1 teaspoon Ras el Hanout
- Zest of 2 lemons, grated
- A few slices of roasted caraway bread
- 1 teaspoon ground cumin
- Cooking spray
- 1 cup grated cauliflower to serve
- Extra virgin olive oil to serve

DIRECTIONS

Place a skillet over medium heat. Spray with cooking spray. Add shallot and sauté for a couple of minutes. Set your machine to 167°F/75°C. Place shallots, cauliflower, stock, and wine, sour cream, cream and lemon juice into a Ziploc or a vacuum-seal bag and remove all the air with the water displacement method or a vacuum-sealed. Seal and immerse the bag in the water bath. Meanwhile mix together the grated cauliflower, Ras el Hanout and half of the lemon zest. Remove the pouch from the cooker and transfer into the blender and blend until smooth. Season with salt and pepper. Pulse a couple of times to mix well. Place the grated cauliflower mixture on bread slices. Drizzle some oil over it. Sprinkle salt, cumin and the remaining lemon zest. Ladle into individual soup bowls. Serve with the garnished bread slices.

423. BUTTERNUT SQUASH AND APPLE SOUP

Cal.: 372 | Fat: 26g | Protein: 11g   🔪 12 min | 🍲 60 min | 🍴 Servings 2

INGREDIENTS

- 1 small butternut squash, peeled, sliced
- 1 medium apple like Granny Smith, peeled, cored, sliced
- 3 green onions, trimmed, sliced
- ½ teaspoon sea salt or to taste.
- ½ cup light cream

DIRECTIONS

Set your Sous Vide machine to 185°F/85°C. Place all the vegetables and apples into a ziplock or a vacuum-seal bag and remove all the air. Seal and Immerse the bag in the water bath, cook for 2 hours or until the vegetables are cooked through. When done, purée the soup. Add salt and cream and blend again. Serve hot.

424. CHICKEN NOODLE SOUP

Cal.: 366 | Fat: 29g | Protein: 15g   🔪 13 min | 🍲 60 min | 🍴 Servings 2

INGREDIENTS

- 3 pounds whole chicken, trussed
- 3 cups carrots, finely diced
- 9 cups chicken stock
- 3 cups white onion, finely diced
- 3 cups celery, finely diced
- Salt to taste
- Pepper to taste
- 2 bay leaves
- 1 ½ pounds dried egg noodles

DIRECTIONS

Set your Sous Vide machine to 150°F/65°C. Add all the ingredients, except noodles, into a large Ziploc bag or a vacuum-seal bag. Remove all the air with the water displacement method or a vacuum-sealed. Seal and Immerse the bag in the water bath and cook for 6 hours or until the vegetables and chicken are cooked. Cover the cooker with plastic wrap so that the evaporation is kept to the minimum. When done, remove from the cooker. Transfer into a large pot. Place the pot over medium heat. Cook for around 20 minutes. Remove the chicken with a slotted spoon. Add noodles and cook until al dente. Shred the chicken with a pair of forks and add it back into the pot. Heat thoroughly and serve.

425. SLOW CHICKEN STOCK

Cal.: 379 | Fat: 21g | Protein 16g   🔪 11 min | 🍲 71 min | 🍴 Servings 12

INGREDIENTS

- 2 pounds chicken bones
- 2 cups diced carrots
- 2 cups diced celery
- 2 cups diced leeks
- 2 tablespoons extra virgin olive oil
- 8 cups water
- 1 tablespoon whole black peppercorns
- 2 bay leaves

DIRECTIONS

Set your Sous Vide machine to 180°F/82°C and preheat your oven to 450°F/230°C. In a large bowl, mix together the chicken bones, carrots, celery, and leeks with olive oil. Place the ingredients onto a sheet pan and roast until golden brown, about 20 minutes. Transfer all of the bones and vegetables, along with any accumulated juices and brown bits on the sheet pan, into a large ziplock or vacuum-seal bag. Add the water, peppercorns and bay leaves. Seal the bag using the water displacement method or a vacuum-sealed. Immerse the bag in the water bath and set the timer for 12 hours. Cover the water bath with plastic wrap to minimize water evaporation. Continuously top off the pot with more water to keep the bag fully Immersed under water. When ready, strain the ingredients and then portion out the stock into airtight containers. Store in the refrigerator for up to 1 week or freeze up to 2 months.

426. CREAMY TOMATO SOUP

Cal.: 362 | Fat: 26g | Protein: 12g   18 min | 60 min | ✖ Servings 2

INGREDIENTS

- ¼ cup butter
- 3 tablespoons flour
- 2 ¼ cups milk
- ½ cup heavy cream
- 1 ½ cans whole or diced tomatoes, peeled
- 1 fresh onion, chopped
- 1 small green pepper, chopped
- 1 garlic clove, chopped
- 1 tablespoon dried basil leaves
- A pinch of cayenne pepper
- Tabasco sauce to taste
- ½ teaspoon salt or to taste
- ½ teaspoon black pepper powder or to taste

DIRECTIONS

Place a saucepan over medium heat. Add half the butter. When the butter starts melting, add flour and sauté for a couple of minutes stirring constantly. Slowly add milk and continue stirring until the mixture thickens. Add cream and continue stirring. Do not boil. Remove from heat and keep aside. Place another saucepan over medium heat. Add the remaining butter. When butter melts, add onions, garlic and green pepper and sauté until the onions are translucent. Add tomatoes and basil and simmer for a few minutes. Lower heat and add the white sauce, cayenne pepper, Tabasco, salt and pepper. Set your machine to 172-175°F/78-79°C. Place all the vegetables into a ziplock or a vacuum-seal bag and remove all the air. Seal and Immerse the bag in the water bath and cook for 45 minutes. When done, purée the soup. Serve hot.

427. CHILLED PEA AND CUCUMBER SOUP

Cal.: 381 | Fat: 30g | Protein 22g   9 min | 75 min | ✖ Servings 4

INGREDIENTS

- 10 oz. peas
- 1 onion, diced
- 1 garlic clove, crushed
- 2 Lebanese cucumbers, seeded, roughly chopped
- ¼ cup mint leaves
- 2 cups vegetable stock, chilled

DIRECTIONS

Set your Sous Vide machine to 180°F/82°C. Put the peas, onion and garlic into a large ziplock or vacuum-seal bag. Seal the bag using the water displacement method or a vacuum-sealed. Cook peas for 1 hour. When done, Immerse in an ice bath for 15 minutes. Purée the contents of the bag, with the cucumber and mint. Slowly add the stock until ingredients are well-combined and you reach a smooth consistency. Serve chilled, giving the soup a stir if there is any separation.

428. BORSCHT

Cal.: 384 | Fat: 28g | Protein: 11g   9 min | 60 min | ✖ Servings 4

INGREDIENTS

- 2 large beets, peeled and sliced
- 2 large carrots, peeled and sliced
- ½ large onion, peeled and sliced
- 1 small potato, peeled and sliced
- ¼ head red cabbage, thinly sliced
- 2 quarts stock of your choice
- ½ cup chopped fresh dill
- 3 tablespoons red wine vinegar
- Salt and pepper to taste
- Sour cream, to serve
- Fresh dill, to serve

DIRECTIONS

Set your Sous Vide machine to 182°F/83°C. Put the beets, carrots, potato and onions into a Ziploc or a vacuum-seal bag and remove all the air. Do the same with the cabbage in a separate pouch. Place the bags in the cooker for at least 1 hour. They can stay in for up to. Remove the vegetables. Purée the beets, carrots and onions. Leave the cabbage to the side. Bring the stock to the boil, adding the pureed vegetables, cabbage, dill, vinegar, salt and pepper. Let the soup simmer until you are ready to eat. Serve the soup with a spoonful of sour cream and some fresh dill.

429. CORNISH HEN SOUP

Cal.: 370 | Fat: 22g | Protein: 14g   🍴 13 min | 🍲 62 min | 🍴 Servings 4

INGREDIENTS

- 2 tablespoons coconut oil
- 4 medium shallots, smashed and peeled
- 3 garlic cloves, smashed and peeled
- 2 lemongrass stalks, roughly chopped
- Piece fresh ginger, thinly sliced
- 5 dried red Thai chilies
- 2 teaspoons dried green peppercorns, coarsely ground
- 1 teaspoon ground turmeric cups water
- 2 whole Cornish game hens
- ½ cup chopped cilantro
- 2 scallions, coarsely chopped
- 2 tablespoons Asian fish sauce
- 1 teaspoon finely grated lime zest
- Kosher salt and freshly ground black pepper

DIRECTIONS

Set your Sous Vide machine to 150°F/65°C. In a large skillet, melt the coconut oil over medium heat. When hot, add the shallots, garlic, lemongrass, ginger, chilies, peppercorns and turmeric. Cook, stirring occasionally, until shallots begin to soften, about 5 minutes. Add the water to the skillet and stir, making sure to scrape the bottom of the pan. Carefully transfer to a large ziplock or vacuum-seal bag. Add the game hens to the bag and then seal using the water displacement method. Place the bag in the water bath and set the timer for 4 hours. When ready, remove the bag from the water bath and take out the hens. Let the hen rest until cool enough to handle. Separate the legs, wings, and breast meat. Add the cooking liquid to a large pot and bring it to a simmer over medium-high heat. Stir in the cilantro, scallions, fish sauce, lime juice and game hen meat. Season to taste with salt and pepper.

430. CHICKEN CURRY SOUP

Cal.: 379 | Fat: 34g | Protein: 15g   🍴 16 min | 🍲 70 min | 🍴 Servings 8

INGREDIENTS

- 1 (4-pound whole chicken, trussed
- 6 cups water
- 2 cups diced carrots
- 2 cups diced celery
- 2 cups diced white onion
- Kosher salt and freshly ground black pepper
- 1 tablespoon coconut oil
- 1 cup thinly sliced shallots
- 2 tablespoons red curry paste
- 1 tablespoon curry powder
- 2 garlic cloves, minced
- 1 teaspoon ground turmeric
- 1 teaspoon ground coriander
- 1 teaspoon sugar
- ½ teaspoon crushed red pepper
- 4 cups fresh spinach leaves
- 1/4 cup thinly sliced scallions
- 1 tablespoon fish sauce
- Cilantro and lime wedges, for serving

DIRECTIONS

Preheat the Sous Vide machine to 150°F/65°C. In a large ziplock or vacuum-seal bag, combine the chicken, water, carrots, celery, and onion. Season with salt and pepper. Seal the bag by using the water displacement technique or a vacuum-seal. Set a timer for 6 hours. Cover the water bath with plastic wrap to minimize water evaporation. Continuously top up the pot of water to keep the chicken fully Immersed. When the timer goes off, remove the bag from the water bath. Remove the chicken from the bag and then strain the soup with a fine mesh strainer. Discard the rest of the vegetables. Let the chicken rest until cool to the touch, then remove and shred the meat. Heat the coconut oil in a stockpot or Dutch oven over medium heat. Add the shallots and cook until softened. Stir in the curry paste, curry powder, garlic, turmeric, coriander, sugar, and crushed red pepper. Continue to cook for 5 minutes, and then add in the reserved chicken cooking liquid and bring to a simmer. Continue to simmer for 30 minutes to allow the flavors to meld. Near the end of the cooking process, add the spinach, scallions, fish sauce and shredded chicken. Simmer until heated through and the spinach has wilted, about 2 minutes. Season to taste with salt and pepper. Serve topped with cilantro and lime wedges.

431. STRACCIATELLA ALLA ROMANA SOUP

Cal.: 391 | Fat: 36g | Protein: 14g   📐 11 min 63 min | ✗ Servings 8

INGREDIENTS

- 1 (4-pound whole chicken, trussed
- 6 cups water
- 2 cups diced carrots
- 2 cups diced celery
- 2 cups diced white onion
- Kosher salt and freshly ground black pepper
- ½ cup grated Parmesan cheese
- 4 large eggs, beaten
- 1/4 cup thinly sliced scallion
- 2 tablespoons freshly squeezed lemon juice
- 2 tablespoons minced fresh parsley
- 2 cups baby spinach

DIRECTIONS

Preheat the Sous Vide machine to 150°F/65°C. In a Ziploc or vacuum-seal bag, combine the chicken, water, carrots, celery and onion. Season with salt and pepper. Seal the bag using the water displacement technique and then place the bag into the hot water bath. Set a timer for 6 hours. Cover the water bath with plastic wrap to minimize water evaporation. Continuously top off the pot with water to keep the chicken fully Immersed. When the timer goes off, remove the bag from the water bath and carefully remove the chicken from the bag. Strain the cooking liquid through a fine-mesh strainer into a stockpot. Discard the rest of the ingredients. Let the chicken rest for about 20 minutes or until cool to the touch. Remove and shred the meat. Bring the cooking liquid to a simmer over medium-high heat. In a medium bowl, whisk together the Parmesan, eggs, scallion, lemon juice and parsley. While stirring the stock, slowly pour in the egg mixture in a thin ribbon. Let the eggs cook undisturbed for 1 minute, and then stir. Add the spinach and shredded chicken and simmer until heated through and the spinach has wilted. Season and serve.

432. OYSTER STEW

Cal.: 376 | Fat: 26g | Protein 12g   📐 9 min | 🍲 62 min | ✗ Servings 4

INGREDIENTS

- 4 tablespoons unsalted butter
- 1 cup thinly sliced leeks
- 1 small garlic clove, minced
- 2 cups shucked oysters with liquid
- 2 cups whole milk
- 2 cups heavy cream
- 1 bay leaf
- Kosher salt and freshly ground black pepper

DIRECTIONS

Preheat the Sous Vide machine to 120°F/49°C. Melt the butter in a large skillet over medium heat and then add the leeks and garlic. Sauté while stirring until the vegetables are tender. Set aside to cool. In a large ziplock or vacuum-seal bag, combine the oysters, milk, cream, bay leaf, and leek mixture. Seal the bag using the water displacement method or a vacuum-sealed and then place in the water bath. Set the timer for 1 hour. When the timer goes off, remove the bag from the water bath. Divide the stew into bowls and remove the bay leaf. Season with salt and pepper to taste and serve.

433. CHICKEN STOCK

Cal.: 83 | Fat: 137g | Protein 173g   📐 18 min | 8 hours | ✗ Servings 8

INGREDIENTS

- 10 lbs. chicken bones
- 1 lb. yellow onion peeled and cut in half
- 8 oz. carrots, chopped
- 8 oz. celery, chopped
- ½ teaspoon black peppercorn
- 10 sprigs of fresh thyme
- Small handful parsley stem
- 1-piece bay leaf

DIRECTIONS

Roast your chicken bones for about 1 ½ hours at 400°F/205°C in your oven. Add the roasted chicken bones, onion and the rest of the ingredients to a resealable zipper bag. Add the water (reserve 1 cup) and seal using the immersion method. Prepare the water bath to a temperature of 194°F/90°C. using your immersion circulator. Immerse underwater and cook for 6-8 hours. Strain the mixture from the zip bag through a metal mesh into a large-sized bowl. Cool the stock using an ice bath and place it in your oven overnight. Scrape the surface and discard fat. Use as needed.

434. SPRING MINESTRONE SOUP

Cal.: 330 | Fat: 7g | Protein: 7g   🔪 10 min | 🍲 40 min | 🍴 Servings 4

INGREDIENTS

- 2 chopped carrots
- 1 sliced leek
- Sprigs thyme
- 3 chopped red potatoes
- 2 tablespoons olive oil
- Cups vegetable broth
- 1 bunch sliced asparagus
- 2 cups navy beans
- 2 tablespoons chopped dill
- Salt

DIRECTIONS

Take a large mixing pan and combine the carrots, thyme, leek and salt. Preheat the Sous Vide machine to 165°F/74°C. Take the above mixture in a Ziploc bag and seal it. Place the bag in and cook for 8 minutes. Take a large skillet and take the cooked vegetables, add red potatoes, vegetable broth and cook for 25 minutes until they turn tender. Then add asparagus and cook for 3 more minutes. Remove thyme and add navy beans, chopped dill, salt and pepper. Serve hot.

435. MUSHROOM ORZO GREEN SOUP

Cal.: 230 | Fat: 8g | Protein: 7g   🔪 5 min | 🍲 35 min | 🍴 Servings 6

INGREDIENTS

- 1 cup sliced mushroom
- 1 cup orzo
- 3 cups sliced spinach
- 3 cups broccoli
- Cups vegetable broth
- 2 tablespoons olive oil
- 1 1/4 cup celery
- ½ cup shallots
- 1/4 cup garlic
- Salt, pepper and basil pesto

DIRECTIONS

In a large cooking pan mix the celery, shallots, garlic, salt and oil. Preheat the Sous Vide machine to 175°F/79°C. Take the above mix in a Ziploc pouch. Seal it under vacuum or under water. Place the bag in and cook for 8 minutes. Take the cooked vegetables in a skillet and add vegetable broth and broccoli. Simmer for 15 minutes. Add mushroom, orzo, spinach and simmer again for 10 minutes until all vegetables soften. Sprinkle salt, pepper, basil pesto and serve hot.

436. SQUASH AND LENTIL STEW

Cal.: 325 | Fat: 4g | Protein: 19g   🔪 15 min | 🍲 35 min | 🍴 Servings 6

INGREDIENTS

- 1 pound green lentils
- 2 sliced shallots
- 1 butternut squash
- Cups baby spinach
- Cups vegetable broth
- 1 tablespoon chopped ginger
- 1 teaspoon coriander powder
- ½ teaspoon cardamom powder
- 1 tablespoon vinegar
- Salt and pepper

DIRECTIONS

Take the squash and peel it. Cut it into 1 ½" pieces. Preheat the Sous Vide machine to 165°F/74°C. Take the lentils, squash in the bag.
Place the bag in and cook for 5 minutes. Transfer it to a cooking pan. Add shallot, ginger, oil, cardamom powder, coriander powder, salt and vegetable broth. Cook on high flame for 12 minutes. Add spinach, vinegar, salt, pepper and serve hot.

437. CHICKEN DILL AND LEMON SOUP

Cal.: 366 | Fat: 3g | Protein: 5g   ✎ 20 min 🍲 50 min | ✗ Servings 8

INGREDIENTS

- 3 boneless chicken breasts
- 3 carrots
- 2 tablespoon olive oil
- 3 celery stalks
- ½ onion
- 3 garlic cloves
- Cup chicken broth
- 3 thyme sprigs
- 4 cup spinach
- 3 tablespoon dill
- 1 tablespoon lemon zest
- 2 tablespoon lemon juice
- Salt and pepper

DIRECTIONS

Heat oil in a large Dutch oven and cook carrots, onion, garlic, celery for 6 minutes. Add the broth, thyme and bring it to boil. Simmer for 30 minutes. Preheat the Sous Vide machine to 195°F/91°C. Place the chicken, salt and pepper in the Ziploc bag and seal. Place this bag in the water bath for 20 minutes. Remove chicken and cut into small bite-size pieces. Add this to the soup and cook for 10 minutes. Add spinach, lemon zest, lemon juice, dill and season with salt and pepper. Serve with garlic toast.

438. BOUILLABAISSE

Cal.: 273 | Fat: 5.1g | Protein 45.1g   ✎ 20 min | 🍲 2 hours 30 min | ✗ Servings 6

INGREDIENTS

- 1 ½ lb. clams (cleaned, rinsed)
- 1 ½ lbs. grouper
- ½ lb. octopus
- 1 tablespoon parsley (fresh)
- 3 teaspoons olive oil
- 2 garlic cloves
- Black pepper (to taste)
- Salt (to taste)
- 1 red bell pepper (chopped)
- 1 green bell pepper (chopped)
- 2 jalapeno peppers (minced)
- 10 ounces tomatoes (canned)
- ½ teaspoon dill weed (dried)
- ½ teaspoon lemon rind (freshly grated is better)
- 1 teaspoon rosemary (dried)
- ½ teaspoon basil (dried)
- 3 cups water

DIRECTIONS

Grab your water bath and preheat it to 140°F/60°C. Season your clams to your taste with salt and pepper. Put the clams, garlic, parsley and a teaspoon of olive oil into a Ziploc bag. Seal the bag nice and tight. Immerse the Ziploc bag into your water bath, making sure it's below the ping pong balls. Allow this to cook for 10 minutes, then you can take it out. Now, preheat your water bath to 149°F/65°C. Now, you're going to season your octopus with pepper and salt to taste. After seasoning the octopus, put it in a Ziploc bag. Add a teaspoon of olive oil to the bag, and then seal it nice and tight. Put it in the water bath and allow it to cook for an hour and fifty minutes. Take it out when the time elapses. Now, preheat your water bath to 137°F/58°C. Grab another Ziploc bag, and then add in the rest of the olive oil, as well as the peppers, grouper, tomatoes and seasonings. Immerse the Ziploc bag into your water bath, and let it cook for just 20 minutes. Once done, take all the ingredients out of their Ziploc bags, and then move them to a stock pot on medium-high heat. Add in three cups of water, and then allow your stew to simmer, until it's all nicely heated up. Ladle this glorious stew into your serving bowls.

439. COCONUT COD STEW

Cal.: 400 | Fat: 18g | Protein: 40g   📐 30 min | 🍲 30 min | 🍴 Servings 6

INGREDIENTS

- 2 lbs. fresh cod, cut into fillets
- Salt and freshly ground black pepper, to taste
- 1 can (15 ounces) coconut milk (divided
- 1 tablespoon olive oil
- 1 sweet onion, julienned
- 1 red bell pepper, julienned
- 4 garlic cloves, minced
- 1 can (15 ounces) crushed tomatoes
- 1 teaspoon fish sauce
- 1 teaspoon lime juice
- Sriracha hot sauce, to taste
- 2 tablespoon chopped fresh cilantro leaves

DIRECTIONS

Preheat water to 130°F/55°C in a cooker or with an immersion circulator. Season cod fillets with salt and pepper and vacuum-seal with 1/4 cup coconut milk in a bag (or use a plastic zip-top freezer bag), removing as much air as possible from the bag before sealing. Immerse the bag in water and cook for 30 minutes. Immediately begin preparing the sauce. Heat olive oil in a nonstick skillet over medium-high heat and sauté onion and bell pepper until softened, 3 to 4 minutes, stirring frequently. Add garlic and sauté about 1 minute more, stirring constantly. Add undrained tomatoes, fish sauce, lime juice, sriracha sauce, and remaining coconut milk and stir until thoroughly combined. Season sauce to taste with salt and pepper, reduce heat to low, and simmer until the end of the cooking time for the cod, stirring occasionally. Remove cod from a cooking bag, add to sauce and turn gently to coat with sauce. Let stew stand for about 5 minutes. Garnish the stew with cilantro leaves to serve. Enjoy!

440. CORNISH HEN STEW

Cal.: 82 | Fat: 7g | Protein: 0.9g   📐 20 min | 🍲 4 hours | 🍴 Servings 4

INGREDIENTS

- 2 tablespoons coconut oil
- 4 medium shallots, smashed and peeled
- 3 garlic cloves, smashed and peeled
- 2 lemongrass stalks, roughly chopped
- Piece fresh ginger, thinly sliced
- 5 dried red Thai chilies
- 2 teaspoons dried green peppercorns, coarsely ground
- 1 teaspoon ground turmeric cups water
- 2 whole Cornish game hens
- ½ cup chopped cilantro
- 2 scallions, coarsely chopped
- 2 tablespoons Asian fish sauce
- 1 teaspoon finely grated lime zest
- Kosher salt and freshly ground black pepper

DIRECTIONS

Preheat the Sous Vide machine to 150°F/65°C. In a large skillet, melt the coconut oil over medium heat. When hot, add the shallots, garlic, lemongrass, ginger, chilies, peppercorns and turmeric. Cook, stirring occasionally, until shallots begin to soften, about 5 minutes. Add the water to the skillet and stir, making sure to scrape the bottom of the pan. Carefully transfer to a large ziplock or vacuum-seal bag. Add the game hens to the bag and then seal using the water displacement method. Place the bag in the water bath and set the timer for 4 hours. When ready, remove the bag from the water bath and take out the hens. Let the hen rest until cool enough to handle. Separate the legs, wings and breast meat. Add the cooking liquid to a large pot and bring it to a simmer over medium-high heat. Stir in the cilantro, scallions, fish sauce, lime juice and game hen meat. Season to taste with salt and pepper.

441. CURRIED CHICKEN SOUP

Cal.: 514 | Fat: 6.5g | Protein: 67.6g   20 min | 6 hours 30 min | Servings 8

INGREDIENTS

- 1 (4-lb whole chicken, trussed
- 6 cups water
- 2 cups diced carrots
- 2 cups diced celery
- 2 cups diced white onion
- Kosher salt and freshly ground black pepper
- 1 tablespoon coconut oil
- 1 cup thinly sliced shallots
- 2 tablespoons red curry paste
- 1 tablespoon curry powder
- 2 garlic cloves, minced
- 1 teaspoon ground turmeric
- 1 teaspoon ground coriander
- 1 teaspoon sugar
- ½ teaspoon crushed red pepper
- 4 cups fresh spinach leaves
- 1/4 cup thinly sliced scallions
- 1 tablespoon fish sauce
- Cilantro and lime wedges, for serving

DIRECTIONS

Preheat the Sous Vide machine to 150°F/65°C. In a large ziplock or vacuum-seal bag, combine the chicken, water, carrots, celery and onion. Season with salt and pepper. Seal the bag by using the water displacement technique or a vacuum-seal. Set a timer for 6 hours. Cover the water bath with plastic wrap to minimize water evaporation. Continuously top up the pot of water to keep the chicken fully Immersed. When the timer goes off, remove the bag from the water bath. Remove the chicken from the bag and then strain the soup with a fine mesh strainer. Discard the rest of the vegetables. Let the chicken rest until cool to the touch, then remove and shred the meat. Heat the coconut oil in a stockpot or Dutch oven over medium heat. Add the shallots and cook until softened. Stir in the curry paste, curry powder, garlic, turmeric, coriander, sugar and crushed red pepper. Continue to cook for 5 minutes, and then add in the reserved chicken cooking liquid and bring to a simmer. Continue to simmer for 30 minutes to allow the flavors to meld. Near the end of the cooking process, add the spinach, scallions, fish sauce and shredded chicken. Simmer until heated through and the spinach has wilted, about 2 minutes. Season to taste with salt and pepper. Serve topped with cilantro and lime wedges.

442. STRACCIATELLA SOUP

Cal.: 497 | Fat: 19.5g | Protein 69.8g   20 min | 6 hours 20 min | Servings 8

INGREDIENTS

- 1 (4-lb whole chicken, trussed
- 6 cups water
- 2 cups diced carrots
- 2 cups diced celery
- 2 cups diced white onion
- Kosher salt and freshly ground black pepper
- ½ cup grated Parmesan cheese
- 4 large eggs, beaten
- 1/4 cup thinly sliced scallion
- 2 tablespoons freshly squeezed lemon juice
- 2 tablespoons minced fresh parsley
- 2 cups baby spinach

DIRECTIONS

Preheat the Sous Vide machine to 150°F/65°C. In a Ziploc or vacuum-seal bag, combine the chicken, water, carrots, celery and onion. Season with salt and pepper. Seal the bag using the water displacement technique and then place the bag into the hot water bath. Set a timer for 6 hours. Cover the water bath with plastic wrap to minimize water evaporation. Continuously top off the pot with water to keep the chicken fully Immersed. When the timer goes off, remove the bag from the water bath and carefully remove the chicken from the bag. Strain the cooking liquid through a fine-mesh strainer into a stockpot. Discard the rest of the ingredients. Let the chicken rest for about 20 minutes or until cool to the touch. Remove and shred the meat. Bring the cooking liquid to a simmer over medium-high heat. In a medium bowl, whisk together the parmesan, eggs, scallion, lemon juice and parsley. While stirring the stock, slowly pour in the egg mixture in a thin ribbon. Let the eggs cook undisturbed for 1 minute, and then stir. Add the spinach and shredded chicken and simmer until heated through and the spinach has wilted. Season and serve.

443. MUSHROOM SOUP

Cal.: 254 | Fat: 21.7g | Protein: 3.6g   50 min | 40 min | Servings 3

INGREDIENTS
- 1 lb. mixed mushrooms
- 2 onions, diced
- 3 garlic cloves
- 2 sprigs parsley leaves, chopped
- 2 tbsp. thyme powder
- 2 tbsp. olive oil
- 2 cups cream
- 2 cups vegetable stock

DIRECTIONS
Make a water bath, place it, and set to 185°F/85°C. Place the mushrooms, onion, and celery in a vacuum-sealable bag. Release air by the water displacement method, seal and Immerse the bag in the water bath. Set the timer for 30 minutes. Once the timer has stopped, remove and unseal the bag. Blend the ingredients in the bag in a blender. Put a pan over medium heat, add the olive oil. Once it starts to heat, add the pureed mushrooms and the remaining listed ingredients, except for the cream. Cook for 10 minutes. Turn off heat and add cream. Stir well. Serve.

444. VEGETARIAN PARMESAN RISOTTO

Cal.: 433 | Fat: 10.5g | Protein: 16.6g   65 min | 50 min | Servings 5

INGREDIENTS
- 2 cups Arborio rice
- ½ cup plain white rice
- 1 cup veggie stock
- 1 cup water
- 6–8 ounces Parmesan cheese, grated
- 1 onion, chopped
- 1 tbsp. butter
- Salt and black pepper to taste

DIRECTIONS
Prepare a water bath and place it. Set to 185°F/85°C. Melt the butter in a saucepan over medium heat. Add onions, rice and spices and cook for a few minutes. Transfer to a vacuum-sealable bag. Release air by the water displacement method, seal and immerse the bag in a water bath. Set the timer for 50 minutes. Once the timer has stopped, remove the bag and stir in the Parmesan cheese.

445. GREEN SOUP

Cal.: 129 | Fat: 5.3g | Protein: 5.8g   55 min | 40 min | Servings 3

INGREDIENTS
- 4 cups vegetable stock
- 1 tbsp. olive oil
- 1 garlic clove, crushed
- 1-inch ginger, sliced
- 1 tsp. coriander powder
- 1 large zucchini, diced
- 3 cups kale
- 2 cups broccoli, cut into florets
- 1 lime, juiced and zested

DIRECTIONS
Make a water bath, place it, and set to 185°F/85°C. Place the broccoli, zucchini, kale and parsley in a vacuum-sealable bag. Release air by the water displacement method, seal and Immerse the bag in the water bath. Set the timer for 30 minutes. Once the timer has stopped, remove and unseal the bag. Add the steamed ingredients to a blender with garlic and ginger. Purée to smooth. Pour the green purée into a pot and add the remaining listed ingredients. Put the pot over medium heat and simmer for 10 minutes. Serve as a light dish.

446. FALL SQUASH CREAM SOUP

Cal.: 101 | Fat: 5.8g | Protein: 1.2g 20 min 🍲 2 hours | ✕ Servings 6

INGREDIENTS

- ¾ cup heavy cream
- 1 winter squash, chopped
- 1 large pear
- ½ yellow onion, diced
- 3 fresh thyme sprigs
- 1 garlic clove, chopped
- 1 tsp. ground cumin
- Salt and black pepper to taste
- 4 tbsp. crème fraîche

DIRECTIONS

Prepare a water bath and place it. Set to 186°F/85°C. Combine the squash, pear, onion, thyme, garlic, cumin and salt. Place it in a vacuum-sealable bag. Release air by the water displacement seal and immerse the bag in the water bath. Cook for 2 hours. Once the timer has stopped, remove the bag and transfer all the contents into a blender. Purée until smooth. Add the cream and stir well. Season with salt and pepper. Transfer the mix into serving bowls and top with some crème fraiche. Garnish with pear chunks.

447. CREAM OF CORN SOUP

Cal.: 105 | Fat: 3g | Protein 4g 10 min | 🍲 40 min | ✕ Servings 4

INGREDIENTS

- Kernels of 4 corn ears
- 6 cups still water
- 1 cup heavy cream
- 1 tbsp. olive oil
- Salt and pepper to taste

DIRECTIONS

Preheat the Sous Vide machine to 183°F/84°C. Place the kernels, salt, pepper and olive oil into the plastic bag, and seal it, removing the air. Set the cooking time for 25 minutes. Transfer the cooked kernels with the liquid to a pot. Add the cream and still water (if needed and simmer on a medium heat for about 10 minutes). Blend the soup with an immersion blender, add salt and pepper if needed and serve with chopped parsley.

448. COLD PEA AND YOGURT SOUP

Cal.: 135 | Fat: 1g | Protein 7g 📐 10 min | 🍲 1 hour | ✕ Servings 4

INGREDIENTS

- 1 onion, chopped
- 2 garlic cloves, minced
- 1 carrot, peeled and grated
- 1 ½ cups frozen peas
- 2 cups vegetable stock
- Salt and pepper to taste
- Greek yogurt for serving
- Chopped dill or cilantro for serving

DIRECTIONS

Preheat the Sous Vide machine to 183°F/84°C. Place the onion, garlic and carrot into the vacuum bag, and seal it, removing the air. Set the cooking time for 50 minutes. Blend the cooked vegetable with the stock using an immersion blender, and salt and pepper to taste. Serve refrigerated with yogurt and chopped dill or cilantro.

449. POTATO AND CURRY SOUP

Cal.: 355 | Fat: 17g | Protein: 11g   ⎐ 10 min | 🍲 60 min | ✗ Servings 4

INGREDIENTS
- 1 onion, chopped
- 2 garlic cloves, minced
- 1 carrot, peeled and grated
- 1 ½ cup potato, peeled and cubed
- 2 cups vegetable stock
- Salt and pepper to taste
- 2 tbsp. curry powder
- Chopped cilantro for serving

DIRECTIONS
Preheat the Sous Vide machine to 183°F/84°C. Put the vegetables and curry powder into the vacuum bag, and seal it, removing the air. Set the cooking time for 50 minutes. Transfer the cooked vegetables to a pot, add the vegetable stock and blend everything together using an immersion blender. Bring the soup to a boil and simmer for 2–3 minutes. Add salt and pepper to taste. Serve with yogurt and chopped dill or cilantro.

450. CARROT AND CELERY SOUP

Cal.: 80 | Fat: 1g | Protein: 5g   ⎐ 10 min | 🍲 2 hours 30 min | ✗ Servings 4

INGREDIENTS
- 2 medium carrots, peeled and chopped
- 1 celery stalk, chopped
- 1 yellow onion, peeled and chopped
- 2 garlic cloves, minced
- 1 tsp. dried rosemary
- 2 bay leaves
- 6 cups vegetable stock
- Salt and pepper to taste

DIRECTIONS
Preheat the Sous Vide machine to 183°F/84°C. Put the ingredients into the vacuum bag, and seal it, removing the air. Set the cooking time for 2 hours 10 minutes. Transfer the cooked vegetables with the liquid into a pot. Add the vegetable stock, bring to boil, and simmer for 10 more minutes. Blend everything together using an immersion blender. Serve with yogurt and chopped dill or cilantro.

451. WARM BEEF SOUP WITH GINGER

Cal.: 214 | Fat: 1g | Protein: 35g   ⎐ 15 min | 🍲 4 hours | ✗ Servings 8

INGREDIENTS
- 2 lbs. chopped beef
- ¼ cup chopped onion
- ½ cup chopped celery
- ¼ tsp. pepper
- ½ tsp. nutmeg
- ½ tsp. ginger
- 2 quarts water

DIRECTIONS
Preheat an oven to 450°F/232° then line a baking sheet with parchment paper. Set aside. Place the beef in a bowl together with chopped onion, celery, pepper, nutmeg and ginger. Mix well. Place all on the prepared baking sheet and bake for about 10 minutes. Meanwhile, preheat the Sous Vide machine to 145°F/63°C and wait until it reaches the targeted temperature. Next, remove the beef from the oven and transfer all to a big plastic bag. Pour water into the bag then seal it properly and cook for 4 hours. Once it is done, transfer to a serving bowl and enjoy immediately.

452. KALE SOUP WITH ROASTED CHICKPEAS

Cal.: 260 | Fat: 9g | Protein: 12g   5 min | 🍲 30 min | ✗ Servings 4

INGREDIENTS
- 1 cup chickpeas
- 1 tbsp. olive oil
- 1 tsp. paprika
- 1 tsp. cayenne powder
- 2 cups chopped kale
- 1 tsp. minced garlic
- 2 tbsp. lemon juice
- 1 cup low sodium vegetable broth
- 1 cup chopped onion
- 1 tsp. vegetable oil

DIRECTIONS
Preheat an oven to 400°F/204° then line a baking sheet with aluminum foil. Set aside. Pour olive oil into a bowl then add chickpeas to it. Sprinkle paprika and cayenne over the chickpeas and mix well. Transfer the chickpeas to the prepared baking sheet and spread evenly in a single layer. Bake until the chickpeas are completely golden and crispy. Remove from the oven and set aside. Next, preheat the Sous Vide machine to 183°F/84°then wait until the machine achieves the targeted temperature. Place the chopped kale in a plastic bag then add minced garlic and lemon juice to it. Vacuum seal the plastic bag properly then place it in the water bath. Cook for 30 minutes then remove from the machine. Cut the plastic bag then transfer the kale to a blender along with the cooking liquid. Preheat a saucepan over medium heat then pour vegetable oil in it. Once the oil is hot, stir in chopped onion then sauté until wilted and aromatic. Transfer the onion to the blender then blend all together until smooth. Pour the kale soup into a soup bowl then sprinkle roasted chickpeas on top. Serve and enjoy immediately.

453. CHILI SHRIMP SOUP

Cal.: 127 | Fat: 8g | Protein: 23g   10 min 🍲 60 min | ✗ Servings 1

INGREDIENTS
- 1 lb. shrimps
- 1 onion
- 2 carrots
- 1 bell pepper
- 1 yellow zucchini
- 3 garlic cloves
- 3 celery stalks
- 2 teaspoon chili powder
- 1 tablespoon olive oil
- 1 cup chicken broth
- 1 cup tomato juice
- ½ cup corn kernels
- Salt, pepper, oregano as per taste

DIRECTIONS
Heat oil in a pan and cook all the vegetables for 3 minutes. Add all the spices, broth and tomatoes. Simmer for 20 minutes. Preheat the Sous Vide machine to 195°F/91°C. Take the shrimps in a Ziploc bag and apply a vacuum to remove the air. Place this bag in the water bath for 30 minutes. The shrimps should turn pink. Add the shrimps to the above pan and cook for 2 minutes. Garnish with the lime wheels and serve hot.

454. CHEESY BROCCOLI SOUP

Cal.: 200 | Fat: 3g | Protein: 4g   🔪 15 min | 🍲 30 min | 🍴 Servings 4

INGREDIENTS

- 5 tablespoons butter
- 1 chopped onion
- 1 cup chopped celery
- 3 minced garlic cloves
- ¼ cup flour
- 8 cup vegetable broth
- 5 cup broccoli florets
- 1 chopped carrot
- 3 cups shredded cheddar cheese
- Salt and pepper

DIRECTIONS

In a cooking bowl, melt butter and cook the onion and garlic. Add broth, salt, pepper and boil until thicken. Preheat the Sous Vide machine to 175°F/79°C. Take the broccoli florets and chopped cabbage in the Ziploc bag and vacuum seal it. Place the bag in and cook for 20 minutes. Add the cooked broccoli and cook for 2 minutes. Make a purée of this mixture. Take this purée in a bowl, add cheese and heat for 1 minute. Serve hot.

455. CHICKEN STEW WITH MUSHROOMS

Cal.: 242 | Fat: 8g | Protein: 33g   🔪 20 min | 🍲 4 hours | 🍴 Servings 2

INGREDIENTS

- 2 medium-sized chicken thighs, skinless
- ½ cup fire-roasted tomatoes, diced
- ½ cup chicken stock
- 1 tablespoon tomato paste
- ½ cup button mushrooms, chopped
- 1 medium-sized celery stalk
- 1 small carrot, chopped
- 1 small onion, chopped
- 1 tablespoon dried basil, finely chopped
- 1 garlic clove, crushed
- ½ teaspoon salt
- ¼ teaspoon black pepper, ground
- Serve with:
- Sour cream and basil

DIRECTIONS

Rinse the thighs and remove the skin. Rub with salt and pepper. Set aside. Clean the vegetables. Peel and chop the onion, slice the carrot. Chop the celery stalk into half-inch long pieces. Now place the meat in a large Ziploc bag along with onion, carrot, mushrooms, celery stalk and fire roasted tomatoes. Cook them for 2-4 hours at 141°F/60.5°C Remove from the water bath and open the bag. The meat should be falling off the bone easily, so remove the bones. Heat up some oil in a medium-sized saucepan and add garlic. Briefly fry, for about 3 minutes, stirring constantly. Now add chicken along with cooked vegetables, chicken stock, tomato paste and basil. Bring it to a boil and reduce the heat to medium. Cook for 5 more minutes, stirring occasionally.

456. ZUCCHINI BEEF STEW

Cal.: 383 | Fat: 15g | Protein: 53g   ⬎ 25 min 🍲 6 hours | ✖ Servings 4

INGREDIENTS

- 1 lb. lean ground beef
- ½ cup button mushrooms, sliced
- 1 cup stew beef, chopped into bite-sized pieces
- 1 small zucchini, peeled and chopped
- 1 small onion, chopped
- 1 cup tomato sauce
- 1 small carrot, chopped
- 2 cups beef broth
- 1 tablespoon extra-virgin olive oil
- 1 teaspoon salt
- ¼ teaspoon black pepper, ground

Serve with:
- Steamed kale

DIRECTIONS

In a large skillet, heat up the oil over medium-high heat. Add chopped onion and stir-fry until translucent. Now add ground beef and continue to cook for 10 more minutes, stirring a couple of times. Remove from the heat and set aside. Place stew beef in a large colander and rinse well. Season with salt and pepper and transfer to a large Ziploc bag along with mushrooms, chopped zucchini, tomato sauce, carrot, and broth. Seal the bag and cook them for 6 hours at 140°F/60°C.

457. CHILI PORK STEW WITH FRESH CILANTRO

Cal.: 427 | Fat: 23g | Protein: 34g   ⬎ 10 min 🍲 1 hour | ✖ Servings 5

INGREDIENTS

- 5 lb. pork shoulder, cut into 1-inch thick pieces
- 1 small onion, sliced
- ¾ cup beef stock
- 4 tablespoon vegetable oil
- ½ cup green tomatillo salsa
- ½ teaspoon pink Himalayan salt
- ¼ teaspoon black pepper, freshly ground

Serve with:
- A handful of fresh cilantro, roughly chopped

DIRECTIONS

Heat up the oil in a large skillet over a medium-high heat. Add onions and stir-fry until translucent, stirring constantly. Add meat and brown for 4 minutes. Remove from the heat and transfer to a large Ziploc bag along with onions, beef stock, tomatillo salsa, salt and pepper. Seal the bag and cook them for 1 hour at 144°F/62°C.

CHAPTER 10:
Vegan Recipes

⟍ Preparation Time | 🍲 Cooking Time | ✖ Servings

458. VEGAN STEEL CUT OATS

Cal.: 141 | Fat: 6g | Protein: 5g   6 min | 3 hours | Servings 5

INGREDIENTS
- 2 cups water
- ½ cup steel cut oats
- ½ teaspoon salt
- Cinnamon and maple syrup for topping

DIRECTIONS
Prepare the water bath by using your immersion circulator and raise the temperature to 180°F/82°C. Take a heavy-duty resealable zipper bag and add all the listed ingredients except the cinnamon and maple syrup Seal the bag using the immersion method and Immerse underwater. Cook for about 3 hours. Once cooked, remove it and transfer the oats to your serving bowl. Serve with a sprinkle of cinnamon and some maple syrup.

459. HONEY ROASTED CARROTS

Cal.: 174 | Fat: 1g | Protein: 2g  6 min | 75 min | Servings 4

INGREDIENTS
- 1-pound baby carrots
- 4 tablespoons vegan butter
- 3 tablespoons honey
- ¼ teaspoon kosher salt
- ¼ teaspoon ground cardamom

DIRECTIONS
Prepare the sous-vide water bath using your immersion circulator and increase the temperature to 185°F/85°C. Add the carrots, honey, whole butter, kosher salt and cardamom to a resealable bag. Seal using the immersion method. Cook for 75 minutes and once done, remove it from the water bath. Strain the glaze by passing through a fine mesh. Set it aside. Take the carrots out from the bag and pour any excess glaze over them. Serve with a few seasonings.

460. FENNEL PICKLE WITH LEMON

Cal.: 156 | Fat: 5g | Protein: 1g  31 min | 30 min | Servings 5

INGREDIENTS
- 1 cup white wine vinegar
- 2 tablespoons beet sugar
- Juice and zest from 1 lemon
- 1 teaspoon kosher salt
- 2 medium bulb fennels, trimmed up and cut into ¼ inch thick slices

DIRECTIONS
Prepare the water bath using your immersion circulator and raise the temperature to 180°F/82°C. Take a large bowl and add the vinegar, sugar, lemon juice, salt, lemon zest and whisk them well. Transfer the mixture to your resealable zip bag. Add the fennel and seal using the immersion method. Immerse underwater and cook for 30 minutes. Transfer to an ice bath and allow the mixture to reach the room temperature. Serve!

461. HONEY TRUFFLE SUNCHOKES

Cal.: 255 | Fat: 10g | Protein: 5g  16 min | 90 min | Servings 4

INGREDIENTS
- 8 ounces peeled Sunchokes, sliced into ¼ inch thick pieces
- 3 tablespoons unsalted vegan butter
- 2 tablespoons agave nectar
- 1 teaspoon truffle oil
- Kosher salt, and black pepper, to taste

DIRECTIONS
Prepare the water bath using your immersion circulator and raise the temperature to 180°F/82°C. Take a heavy-duty resealable zip bag and add the butter, nectar, sunchokes and truffle oil and mix them well. Sprinkle some salt and pepper, and then seal using the immersion method. Immerse it underwater and cook for 1 ½ hour. Once cooked, transfer the contents to a skillet. Put the skillet over medium-high heat and cook for 5 minutes more until the liquid has evaporated. Season with pepper and salt to adjust the flavor if needed. Serve!

462. GARLIC CITRUS ARTICHOKES

Cal.: 408 | Fat: 20g | Protein: 12g 　　　　🔪 31 min 🍲 90 min | 🍴 Servings 4

INGREDIENTS

- 4 tablespoons freshly squeezed lemon juice
- 12 pieces' baby artichokes
- 4 tablespoons vegan butter
- 2 fresh garlic cloves, minced
- 1 teaspoon fresh lemon zest
- Kosher salt, and black pepper, to taste
- Chopped up fresh parsley for garnishing

DIRECTIONS

Prepare the water bath using your immersion circulator and raise the temperature to 180°F/82°C. Take a large bowl and add the cold water and 2 tablespoons of lemon juice. Peel and discard the outer tough layer of your artichoke and cut them into quarters. Transfer to a cold water bath and let it sit for a while. Take a large skillet and put it over medium-high heat. Add in the butter to the skillet and allow the butter to melt. Add the garlic alongside 2 tablespoons of lemon juice and the zest. Remove from heat and season with a bit of pepper and salt. Allow it to cool for about 5 minutes. Then, drain the artichokes from the cold water and place them in a large resealable bag. Add in the butter mixture as well. Seal it up using the immersion method and immerse underwater for about 1 and a ½ hour. Once cooked, transfer the artichokes to a bowl and serve with a garnish of parsley.

463. ITALIAN PICKLED VEGETABLES

Cal.: 245 | Fat: 7g | Protein 4g 　　　　🔪 31 min | 🍲 60 min | 🍴 Servings 8

INGREDIENTS

- 2 cups white wine vinegar
- 1 cup water
- ½ cup beet sugar
- 3 tablespoons kosher salt
- 1 tablespoon whole black peppercorns
- 1 cup cauliflower, cut up into ½-inch pieces
- 1 stemmed and seeded bell pepper, cut up into ½-inch pieces
- 1 cup carrots, cut up into ½-inch pieces
- ½ thinly sliced white onion
- 2 seeded and stemmed Serrano peppers, cut up into ½-inch pieces

DIRECTIONS

Prepare the sous-vide water bath using your immersion circulator and raise the temperature to 180°F/82°C. Take a large bowl and mix in vinegar, sugar, salt, water and peppercorns. Transfer the mixture to a large resealable zipper bag and add the cauliflower, onion, serrano peppers, vinegar mixture, bell pepper, and carrots. Seal it up using the immersion method and immerse underwater, cook for about 1 hour. Once cooked, take it out from the bag and serve.

464. ALFREDO VEGAN CAULIFLOWER

Cal.: 160 | Fat: 11g | Protein: 8g　　　　　📐 16 min | 🍲 90 min | 🍴 Servings 6

INGREDIENTS

- 4 cups chopped cauliflower
- 2 cups water
- 2/3 cup cashews
- 2 garlic cloves
- ½ teaspoon dried oregano
- ½ teaspoon dried basil
- ½ teaspoon dried rosemary
- 4 tablespoons nutritional yeast
- Salt, and pepper to taste

DIRECTIONS

Prepare the sous-vide water bath using your immersion circulator and increase the temperature to 170°F/76°C. Take a heavy-duty resealable zip bag and add the cashews, cauliflower, oregano, water, garlic, rosemary and basil. Seal using the immersion method. Immerse underwater and cook for 90 minutes. Transfer the cooked contents to a blender and purée. Use Alfredo over your favorite pasta.

465. MARINATED MUSHROOMS

Cal.: 440 | Fat: 28g | Protein: 19g　　　　📐 21 min | 🍲 60 min | 🍴 Servings 2

INGREDIENTS

- 10 large button mushrooms
- 3 tablespoons truffle oil
- 3 tablespoons olive oil
- 1 tablespoon chopped fresh thyme
- 1 thinly sliced garlic clove
- Salt, and pepper to taste

DIRECTIONS

Prepare the sous-vide water bath using your immersion circulator and raise the temperature to 185°F/85°C. Take a large bowl and add the truffle oil, mushrooms, olive oil, garlic, and thyme. Season with some pepper and salt. Transfer the mushroom mixture to a large sous-vide resealable zip bag and add the mixture to the bag. Seal it up using the immersion method. Immerse underwater and cook for 1 hour. Once cooked, drain the mushrooms and discard the cooking liquid. Take a large skillet and put it over medium heat for 3 minutes. Add the mushrooms and sear for about 1 minute to brown it. Transfer the cooked mushroom to a serving plate and season with pepper and salt. Top it up with thyme. Serve!

466. CANNELLINI BEANS WITH HERBS

Cal.: 578 | Fat: 18g | Protein: 31g　　　　📐 16 min | 🍲 3 hours | 🍴 Servings 5

INGREDIENTS

- 1 cup cannellini beans (dried) soaked overnight in salty cold water
- 1 cup water
- ½ cup extra-virgin olive oil
- 1 peeled carrot, cut up into 1-inch dice
- 1 celery stalk, cut up into 1-inch dice
- 1 quartered shallot
- 4 crushed garlic cloves
- 2 fresh rosemary sprigs
- 2 bay leaves
- Kosher salt, and pepper to taste

DIRECTIONS

Prepare the water bath using your sous-vide immersion circulator and raise the temperature to 190°F/88°C. Drain the soaked beans and rinse them. Transfer to a heavy-duty resealable zip bag and add the olive oil, celery, water, carrot, shallot, garlic, rosemary and bay leaves. Season with pepper and salt. Seal using the immersion method and cook for 3 hours. Once cooked, remove the beans and check for seasoning. Discard the rosemary and serve!

467. BUDDHA'S DELIGHT

Cal.: 186 | Fat: 6g | Protein: 10g   21 min | 60 min | Servings 8

INGREDIENTS
- 1 cup vegetable broth
- 2 tablespoons tomato paste
- 1 tablespoon grated ginger
- 1 tablespoon rice wine
- 1 tablespoon rice wine vinegar
- 1 tablespoon agave nectar
- 2 teaspoons Sriracha sauce
- 3 minced garlic cloves
- 2 boxes of cubed tofu

DIRECTIONS
Prepare your water bath using your immersion circulator and raise the temperature to 185°F/85°C. Take a medium bowl and add all the listed ingredients except the tofu. Mix well. Transfer the mixture to a heavy-duty resealable zipper bag and top with the tofu. Seal it up using the immersion method. Cook for 1 hour. Pour the contents into a serving bowl. Serve!

468. NAVY BEANS

Cal.: 210 | Fat: 2g | Protein 14g    15 min | 3 hours | Servings 8

INGREDIENTS
- 1 cup dried and soaked navy beans
- 1 cup water
- ½ cup extra-virgin olive oil
- 1 peeled carrot, cut up into 1-inch dices
- 1 stalk celery, cut up into 1-inch dices
- 1 quartered shallot
- 4 cloves crushed garlic
- 2 sprigs of fresh rosemary
- 2 pieces' bay leaves
- Kosher salt, to taste
- Freshly ground black pepper, to taste

DIRECTIONS
Prepare your sous-vide water bath using your immersion circulator and raise the temperature to 190°F/88°C. Carefully drain and rinse your beans and add them alongside the rest of the ingredients to a heavy-duty zip bag. Seal using the immersion method and immerse it underwater. Cook for about 3 hours. Once cooked, taste the beans. If they are firm, then cook for another 1 hour and pour them in a serving bowl. Serve!

469. BUTTERED RADISHES

Cal.: 134 | Fat: 0.3g | Protein 1g   6 min | 46 min | Servings 4

INGREDIENTS
- 1 pound radishes, cut up in half lengthwise
- 3 tablespoons vegan butter
- ½ teaspoon sea salt

DIRECTIONS
Prepare your water bath using your immersion circulator and raise the temperature to 190°F/88°C. Add your radish halves, butter and salt in a resealable zipper bag and seal it up using the immersion method. Immerse underwater and cook for 45 minutes. Once cooked, strain the liquid and discard. Serve the radishes in a bowl!

470. RHUBARB

Cal.: 111 | Fat: 0.2g | Protein: 111g   🔪 16 min | 🍲 40 min | 🍴 Servings 4

INGREDIENTS
- 2 cups rhubarb
- 1 tablespoon Grand Marnier
- 1 teaspoon beet sugar
- ½ teaspoon kosher salt
- ½ a teaspoon freshly ground black pepper

DIRECTIONS
Prepare the sous-vide water bath to a temperature of 140°F/60°C. using your immersion circulator. Take a large heavy-duty resealable zip bag and add all the listed ingredients. Whisk everything well. Seal the bag using the immersion method/water displacement method. Place it under your preheated water and cook for about 40 minutes. Once cooked, take the bag out from the water bath, take the contents out and place it on a serving plate. Serve warm!

471. CHINESE BLACK BEAN SAUCE

Cal.: 375 | Fat: 12g | Protein: 12g   🔪 21 min | 🍲 90 min | 🍴 Servings 4

INGREDIENTS
- 4 cups halved green beans
- 3 minced garlic cloves
- 2 teaspoons rice wine vinegar
- 1½ tablespoons prepared black bean sauce
- 1 tablespoon olive oil

DIRECTIONS
Prepare the sous-vide water bath using your immersion circulator and raise the temperature to 170°F/76°C. Add all the listed ingredients into a large mixing bowl alongside the green beans. Coat everything evenly. Take a heavy-duty zip bag and add the mixture. Zip the bag using the immersion method and immerse it underwater. Cook for about 1 hour and 30 minutes. Once cooked, take it out and serve immediately!

472. CHIPOTLE AND BLACK BEANS

Cal.: 466 | Fat: 37g | Protein: 20g   🔪 21 min | 🍲 6 hours | 🍴 Servings 6

INGREDIENTS
- 1 cup dry black beans
- 2 2/3 cup water
- 1/3 cup freshly squeezed orange juice
- 2 tablespoons orange zest
- 1 teaspoon salt
- 1 teaspoon cumin
- ½ teaspoon chipotle chili powder

DIRECTIONS
Prepare the sous-vide water bath using your immersion circulator and raise the temperature to 194°F/90°C. Take a heavy-duty resealable plastic bag and add the listed ingredients into the bag. Immerse it underwater and cook for 6 hours. Once cooked, take the bag out from the water bath. Pour the contents into a nice sauté pan and place it over medium heat. Simmer until the amount has been reduced. Once your desired texture is achieved, remove from the heat and serve!

473. PICKLED MIXED VEGGIES

Cal.: 174 | Fat: 2g | Protein: 4g   🔪 11 min | 🍲 40 min | 🍴 Servings 4

INGREDIENTS
- 12 oz. beets, cut up into ½-inch slices
- ½ Serrano pepper, seeds removed
- 1 garlic clove, diced
- 2/3 cup white vinegar
- 2/3 cup filtered water
- 2 tablespoons pickling spice

DIRECTIONS
Prepare the sous-vide water bath using your immersion circulator and raise the temperature to 190°F/88°C. Take 4–6 ounces' mason jar and add the Serrano pepper, beets and garlic cloves Take a medium stock pot and add the pickling spice, filtered water, white vinegar and bring the mixture to a boil. Remove the stock and strain the mix over the beets in the jar. Fill them up. Seal it loosely and immerse it underwater. Cook for 40 minutes. Allow the jars to cool and serve!

474. ROOT VEGETABLES MIX

Cal.: 268 | Fat: 10g | Protein: 6g   15 min | 3 hours | ✗ Servings 4

INGREDIENTS

- 1 peeled turnip, cut up into 1-inch pieces
- 1 peeled rutabaga, cut up into 1-inch pieces
- 8 pieces petite carrots peeled up and cut into 1-inch pieces
- 1 peeled parsnip, cut up into 1-inch pieces
- ½ red onion, cut up into 1-inch pieces and peeled
- 4 pieces' garlic, crushed
- 4 sprigs of fresh rosemary
- 2 tablespoons extra-virgin olive oil
- Kosher salt, and black pepper to taste
- 2 tablespoons unsalted vegan butter

DIRECTIONS

Prepare the sous-vide water bath using your immersion circulator and raise the temperature to 185°F/85°C. Take two large heavy-duty resealable zipper bags and divide the vegetables and the rosemary between the bags. Add 1 tablespoon oil to the bag and season with some salt and pepper. Seal the bags using the immersion method. Immerse underwater and cook for 3 hours. Take a skillet and place it over high heat and add in the oil. Once done, add the contents of your bag to the skillet. Cook the mixture for about 5–6 minutes until the liquid comes to a syrupy consistency. Add the butter to your veggies and toss them well. Keep cooking for another 5 minutes until they are nicely browned. Serve!

475. PICKLED CARROTS

Cal.: 127 | Fat: 2g | Protein 1g   31 min | 90 min | ✗ Servings 1

INGREDIENTS

- 1 cup white wine vinegar
- ½ cup beet sugar
- 3 tablespoons kosher salt
- 1 teaspoon black peppercorns
- 1/3 cup ice-cold water
- 10–12 pieces' petite carrots, peeled with the stems trimmed
- 4 sprigs of fresh thyme
- 2 peeled garlic cloves

DIRECTIONS

Prepare the sous-vide water bath using your immersion circulator and raise the temperature to 190°F/88°C. Take a medium-sized saucepan and add the vinegar, salt, sugar and peppercorns and place it over medium heat. Then, let the mixture reach the boiling point and keep stirring until the sugar has dissolved alongside the salt. Remove the heat and add the cold water. Allow the mixture to cool down to room temperature. Take a resealable bag and add the thyme, carrots and garlic alongside the brine solution and seal it up using the immersion method. Immerse underwater and cook for 90 minutes. Once cooked, remove the bag from the water bath and place into an ice bath. Carefully take the carrots out from the bag and serve.

476. GARLIC TOMATOES

Cal.: 289 | Fat: 8g | Protein 11g   11 min | 45 min | ✗ Servings 4

INGREDIENTS

- 4 pieces cored and diced tomatoes
- 2 tablespoons extra-virgin olive oil
- 3 minced garlic cloves
- 1 teaspoon dried oregano
- 1 teaspoon fine sea salt

DIRECTIONS

Prepare the sous-vide water bath using your immersion circulator and raise the temperature to 145°F/63°C. Add all the listed ingredients to the resealable bag and seal using the immersion method. Immerse underwater and let it cook for 45 minutes. Once cooked, transfer the tomatoes to a serving plate. Serve with some vegan French bread slices.

477. SWEET CURRIED WINTER SQUASH

Cal.: 185 | Fat: 9g | Protein: 2g   ⟋ 21 min | 🍲 90 min | ✗ Servings 6

INGREDIENTS
- 1 medium winter squash
- 2 tablespoons unsalted vegan butter
- 1 to 2 tablespoons Thai curry paste
- ½ teaspoon kosher salt
- Fresh cilantro for serving
- Lime wedges for serving

DIRECTIONS
Prepare the sous-vide water bath using your immersion circulator and raise the temperature to 185°F/85°C. Slice up the squash into half lengthwise and scoop out the seeds alongside the inner membrane. Keep the seeds for later use. Slice the squash into wedges of about 1 ½-inch thickness. Take a large heavy-duty bag resealable zip bag and add the squash wedges, curry paste, butter and salt and seal it using the immersion method. Immerse it underwater and let it cook for 1 ½ hour. Once cooked, remove the bag from water and give it a slight squeeze until it is soft. If it is not soft, then add to the water once again and cook for 40 minutes more. Transfer the cooked dish to a serving plate and drizzle with a bit of curry butter sauce from the bag. Top your squash with a bit of cilantro, lime wedges and serve!

478. VEGAN CAULIFLOWER ALFREDO

Cal.: 350 | Fat: 9g | Protein: 20g   ⟋ 9 min | 🍲 1 hour 30 min | ✗ Servings 6

INGREDIENTS
- 4 tablespoons nutritional yeast
- Salt and pepper
- ½ teaspoon dried rosemary
- 4 cups chopped cauliflower
- ½ teaspoon dried oregano
- ½ teaspoon dried basil
- 2 garlic cloves
- 2 cups water
- ¼ cup cashews

DIRECTIONS
Level the Sous Vide Machine to 185°F/85°C. Transfer the cauliflower, liquid cashews, cloves, oregano, herbs and rosemary to a thick plastic-seal bag and cover. Place the bag in the vacuum and cook for 1½ hours. In a bowl, add in the contents. Mix and serve.

479. VEGAN CARROT-CURRY SOUP

Cal.: 322 | Fat: 6g | Protein: 12g   ⟋ 9 min | 🍲 1 hour 45 min | ✗ Servings 4

INGREDIENTS
- 1 garlic clove, minced
- 1-pound carrots, peeled and sliced
- 2 teaspoons yellow curry powder
- 1 teaspoon ground turmeric
- 1 stalk lemongrass, sliced
- 1 cup unsweetened coconut milk
- 1 tablespoon Thai red chili paste
- 1 shallot, thinly sliced
- 2 teaspoons kosher salt

DIRECTIONS
Adjust the Sous Vide Machine to 190°F/88°C. In a big zipper-lock package, combine all the ingredients. Use the water immersion method to close the bag and put it in the water bath. For 1 hour and 45 minutes, adjust the clock. Remove the pack from the boiling water when the effects go off. Discard bits of lemongrass. Move the contents of the package to a processor and purée for around 2 minutes, until smooth. To achieve the desired consistency, add extra coconut milk or water. As required, sprinkle with salt.

480. CRUNCHY BALSAMIC ONIONS

Cal.: 757 | Fat: 13g | Protein: 29g   6 min | 2 hours | Servings 10

INGREDIENTS
- 2 tbsp. brown sugar
- Salt and pepper
- 2 brown onions (julienned)
- 1 tbsp. balsamic vinegar
- 2 tbsp. olive oil

DIRECTIONS
In a jar, combine all of the components, lock and cook for 2 hours at 185°F/85°C. For 3 hours or night, move to a jar and chill in the fridge.

481. VEGETABLE STOCK

Cal.: 335 | Fat: 19g | Protein 31g   11 min | 13 hours | Servings 12

INGREDIENTS
- 1 tablespoon whole black peppercorns
- 2 bay leaves
- 2 cups (diced) carrots
- 2 cups white button mushrooms
- 1 bunch parsley
- 2 tablespoons (extra-virgin) olive oil
- 8 cups of water
- 1 cup (chopped) fennel
- 6 garlic cloves (crushed)
- 2 cups (chopped) celery
- 2 cups (chopped) leeks

DIRECTIONS
Adjust the Sous Vide Machine to 180°F/82°C. Heat the boiler to 450°F/230°C. Toss the olive oil with the carrot, leeks, celery, fennel and cloves in a large bowl. Switch to a baking tray and roast for about 20 minutes, until lightly browned. Move to a whole zipper-locking bag with steamed veggies, any leftover juices and golden-brown parts. Add water, coriander, peppercorns, mushroom and bay leaves. Close the package using the method of water immersion. Place the package and press the button for 12 hours in the boiling water. To prevent water evaporation, protect the water bath with plastic wrap. To keep the veggies covered, apply water occasionally.

482. TURMERIC TOFU WITH SUMAC AND LIME

Cal.: 95 | Fat: 5g | Protein 12g   13 min | 2 hours 45 min | Servings 4

INGREDIENTS
- 2 limes, cut into wedges
- Sumac, for serving
- 1 package firm tofu, drained and sliced
- 1 teaspoon ground turmeric
- 1 teaspoon kosher salt
- 2 teaspoons freshly ground black pepper
- 2 tablespoon extra-virgin olive oil
- 4 garlic cloves, roughly minced

DIRECTIONS
Put the tofu planks on a baking tray that is a wash cloth-lined. Add a separate towel and a separate baking sheet to the middle. To measure the tofu, put a large pot or many canned goods on it. Leave it to stay at room temperature for thirty minutes. Level the Sous Vide Machine, meanwhile, to 180°F/82°C. Stir together the olive oil, cloves, pepper, turmeric and salts in a small cup. In a large zipper-locking or vacuum lock package, put the tofu in a single sheet. With the garlic-turmeric paste, rub all edges of the tofu. Use the water immersion method or a vacuum adhesive on the wet setting to close the container. In the boiling water, put the bag and set the timer for 2 hours. Warm the broiler heavy for about 5 minutes until the tofu is done. Remove the package from the boiling water when the timer goes off. Remove the tofu carefully from the bag and put it on a baking tray lined with foil. Sprinkle over the tofu with any leftover oil from the packet. Roast until golden brown on either edge, 3 minutes. Shift to a tray for serving. Squeeze over the tofu with lemon juice and scatter with cilantro. Serve hot.

483. TOMATO-BASIL PASTA SAUCE

Cal.: 67 | Fat: 5g | Protein: 19g   ✎ 8 min | 🍲 75 min | 🍴 Servings 7

INGREDIENTS
- 3 bay leaves
- 1 teaspoon red pepper flakes
- 1 can (crushed) tomatoes
- 1 tablespoon (extra-virgin) olive oil
- 1 tablespoon garlic salt
- 2 cups fresh basil leaves
- 1 carrot (peeled and finely diced)
- ½ white onion (finely chopped)

DIRECTIONS
Preheat the Sous Vide machine to 185°F/85°C. In a big zipper-locking package, mix all the ingredients. Wrap the package using the method of water immersion. Set the timer for 1 hour or up to 2 hours and put the package in the water bath. Take the package from the boiling water when the timer goes off. Shift the entire stock of the package to a food processor. Discard the bay leaves and purée for about 30 seconds until creamy. Eat with pasta. It is also possible to cool and chill in the fridge for up to 2 days or preserve for up to a month.

484. CONFIT GARLIC

Cal.: 105 | Fat: 6g | Protein: 18g   ✎ 11 min | 🍲 4 hour 10 min | 🍴 Servings 8

INGREDIENTS
- 1 tablespoon kosher salt
- ¼ cup (extra-virgin) olive oil
- 1 cup (peeled) garlic cloves

DIRECTIONS
Level the Sous Vide Machine to 190°F/88°C. In a complete zipper-locking or vacuum sealing container, mix all the ingredients. Use the water immersion method or a vacuum adhesive on the wet setting to seal the container. Place the package in the water bath and set a timer for 4 hours. Take the bag from the boiling water when the timer goes off. Move the confit to an enclosed storage container and cool for up to one month.

485. QUINOA

Cal.: 156 | Fat: 8g | Protein: 21g   ✎ 6 min | 🍲 1 hour 5 min | 🍴 Servings 6

INGREDIENTS
- Kosher salt
- 1 ½ cups water
- 1 cup quinoa (rinsed)
- 1 small sprig of fresh basil
- 2 garlic cloves (peeled)

DIRECTIONS
Adjust the Sous Vide Machine to 180°F/82°C. In a complete sealed bag, mix the quinoa, cloves, basil and ½ teaspoon salt. Use the water immersion method, add the water and close the package. In the boiling water, put the bag then set the timer for 1 hour. Remove the package from the boiling water as soon as the timer goes off. To a medium cup, move the entire contents of the package and remove the basil and cloves. Fluff the quinoa using a spoon and season with salt.

486. STRAWBERRY-RHUBARB JAM

Cal.: 36 | Fat: 18g | Protein: 9g   ✎ 8 min | 🍲 1 hour 45 min | 🍴 Servings 12

INGREDIENTS
- 2 tablespoons powdered pectin
- 2 tablespoons (freshly squeezed) lemon juice
- 1 cup granulated sugar
- 1 cup (diced) strawberries
- 1 cup (chopped) rhubarb

DIRECTIONS
Level the Sous Vide Machine to 180°F/82°C. In a big zipper-locking package, mix all the ingredients. Use the water immersion method to close the bag and put it in the boiling water. For 2 hours, set the timer. Remove the package from the boiling water when the timer goes off. Move the pack's entire contents to an enclosed jar and let it cool down to room temperature. For up to 1 month, put it in the fridge.

487. SUNCHOKES WITH TOASTED MARCONA ALMONDS

Cal.: 120 | Fat: 6g | Protein: 17g 13 min | 1 hour 40 min | Servings 4

INGREDIENTS
- 2 tablespoons (chopped) Marconi almonds
- (Minced) fresh chives
- 1 ½ pounds sunchokes (scrubbed)
- 4 tablespoons (extra-virgin) olive oil
- Kosher salt
- (freshly ground) black pepper

DIRECTIONS
Level the Sous Vide Machine to 194°F/90°C. Put the sunchokes, salt and black pepper in a vacuum seal package or large zipper-locking. Pour one tablespoon olive oil. Use the water immersion method or a vacuum adhesive on the wet setting to seal the container. In the boiling water, put the bag and set a timer for one hour. Heat the oven to 450°F about ten minutes until the timer goes off. Cover with foil on a rimmed baking dish. Use one tablespoon olive oil to brush the baking dish. Take the bag from the boiling water when the timer goes off. Pick the sunchokes and hold the dry ones from the package. Let them cool. Crush each one with the palm of your hand when they are about half-inch thick and when sunchokes are easy enough to manage. Position the sunchokes and drizzle with the leftover two tablespoons of olive oil on the baking dish and season with pepper and salt. Roast sunchokes, tossing half-way back, 20 to 25 minutes until the sides are crispy and fresh. Toss the almonds on the tops of the sunchokes, then proceed to roast for 2 minutes till the almonds are brown. Move sunchokes and seasoning with chives onto a serving tray. Serve immediately.

488. TURMERIC AND DILL PICKLED CAULIFLOWER

Cal.: 320 | Fat: 14g | Protein 27g 13 min | 6 hours 10 min | Servings 4

INGREDIENTS
- A few sprigs dill
- 1 tablespoon black peppercorns
- 1 tablespoon salt
- 1 (thumb-sized piece) turmeric (sliced)
- 1 cup water
- ¼ cup sugar
- 4 cups cauliflower florets
- 1 cup white wine vinegar

DIRECTIONS
Preheat the Sous Vide machine to 140°F/60°C. In a pan, combine the water, salt, vinegar, black peppercorn, sugar and turmeric. Simmer to remove the sugar. Load the florets and dill sprigs of cauliflower into pureeing pots. Through the pots, pour the pickling liquid. Keep the jars sealed. Cook for 3 hours. Carry out the pot of water and leave overnight on your kitchen table.

489. DOENJANG-SPICED EGGPLANT

Cal.: 243 | Fat: 14g | Protein 26g 9 min |  1 hours 35 min | Servings 2

INGREDIENTS
- 1 tablespoon brown sugar
- 1 tablespoon sesame seeds
- 2 tablespoons Doenjang paste
- 2 tablespoons soy sauce
- ¼ cup peanut oil
- 4 pieces Thai eggplants (cut into wedges)

DIRECTIONS
In a cup, whisk together the Doenjang mixture, peanut oil, soya sauce and sugar. In the cup, add the eggplants and mix to fill uniformly. In a Sous Vide pack, position the eggplants and sauces. Set your Sous Vide machine to 185°F/85°C, simmer for 45 minutes. Wash the wedges of the eggplant from the water for frying. Cook in a frying skillet with the eggplants. While eating, fill with sesame seeds.

490. HARISSA MARINATED TOFU AND KALE BOWL

Cal.: 321 | Fat: 11g | Protein: 20g   20 min | 3 hours | Servings 12

INGREDIENTS

- 1 package firm or extra-firm tofu, about 14 ounces
- 3 tablespoons harissa or other chile-garlic sauce
- 1 tablespoon soy sauce
- 1 tablespoon sesame oil
- 3 cups coarsely chopped kale
- 3 cloves garlic, minced
- 2 tablespoons minced ginger
- 2 tablespoons soy sauce
- 1 tablespoon rice wine vinegar
- 1 cup cooked farro
- 1 1/2 cups cooked lentils
- 1/2 cup roasted red peppers
- 1/4 cup chopped fresh basil leaves

DIRECTIONS

Preheat a water bath to 180°F (82.2°C). Drain the tofu and cut into slabs 3/4" to 1" thick (19mm to 25mm). Place the slabs on paper towels, top with more paper towels and a sheet pan lightly weighted down. Let sit for 20 to 30 minutes. Mix the harissa and soy sauce together. Remove the sheet pan from the tofu and brush the tofu with the harissa mixture. Place the tofu in a sous vide bag then lightly seal it. Place the bag in the water bath and cook for 3 hours. Heat the sesame oil in a pan over medium heat. Add the kale, garlic, ginger, soy sauce and vinegar then cover and let cook until the kale is tender, about 10 to 20 minutes. Remove the cooked tofu from the sous vide bag and dry thoroughly using paper towels or a dish cloth. Sear the tofu with a torch or under a broiler until it starts to brown. Remove from the heat and cut into bite-sized chunks. Place the farro and lentils in a bowl and top with the kale and its juices. Add the tofu and the roasted red peppers. Sprinkle with the basil then serve.

491. SMOKY BBQ BUTTER CORN

Cal.: 242 | Fat: 9g | Protein: 28g   11 min | 1 hour 5 min | Servings 3

INGREDIENTS

- 2 tablespoons smoky BBQ spice blend
- ½ stick butter
- 3 ears corn husked (ends trimmed)

DIRECTIONS

Add the melted butter and BBQ seasoning together. Rub corn with BBQ butter all across. In a Sous Vide jar, place the buttered corn and the leftover butter. Heat at 183°F/84°C for thirty minutes.

492. CHILI-GARLIC TOFU

Cal.: 421 | Fat: 19g | Protein: 32g   9 min | 8 hours 10 min | Servings 3

INGREDIENTS

- ¼ Cup sesame oil
- 2 tablespoons chili-garlic (paste)
- 1 block firm tofu (cut into slices)
- ½ cup brown sugar
- ¼ cup soy sauce

DIRECTIONS

Hot skillet-fry pieces of tofu until they are nicely browned. In a pan, mix all the remaining ingredients. Toss in the sauce with the tofu pieces. In a Sous Vide packet, bring the tofu along with the sauce. Heat at 180°F/82°C for 4 hours.

493. GLAZED CARROTS AND PEPPER

Cal.: 70 | Fat: 6g | Protein: 11g   9 min | 1 hour | Servings 6

INGREDIENTS

- Freshly ground black pepper
- 1 tablespoon chopped parsley
- 1 tablespoon granulated sugar
- 2 tablespoons unsalted butter
- Kosher salt
- 1 pound of baby carrots (medium to large carrots)

DIRECTIONS

Preheat the Sous Vide machine to 183°F/84°C. In a vacuum bag, put the vegetables, butter, sugar, and 1 tablespoon kosher salt and seal as instructed by the supplier. In boiling water, boil the carrot until absolutely tender, for around 1 hour. At this stage, carrots can be kept for up to 1 week in the refrigerator. Load the entire contents of the package into a high-bottomed 12-inch oven and bake over medium temperature, stirring vigorously for about 2 minutes, until the liquid is reduced to a glossy glaze. Season with salt to taste, whisk in the parsley, and prepare. If glaze cracks and becomes greasy, apply water about 1 tablespoon at a time, shake the pot to re-form coating.

494. FRENCH FRIES

Cal.: 85 | Fat: 9g | Protein 2g   11 min | 55 min | Servings 4

INGREDIENTS

- Vegetable oil for frying
- Salt to taste
- ¼ teaspoon sugar
- ¼ teaspoon baking soda
- 500 grams of potatoes, peeled
- ½ tablespoon salt
- ½ cup water

DIRECTIONS

Combine the water, sugar, salt, and baking soda together. Place potatoes in the pocket with the salted water. Cook in the Sous Vide at 194°F/90°C for 15 minutes. Let potatoes dry. Fry for 7 minutes at 266°F/130°C. Let it soak and cool. Fry for 2 minutes at 374°F/190°C.

495. THYME-INFUSED MUSHROOMS

Cal.: 125 | Fat: 22g | Protein 20g   9 min | 45 min | Servings 4

INGREDIENTS

- 2 large garlic cloves, sliced
- Salt to taste
- 1 pinch freshly, ground black, pepper
- 2 tablespoons olive oil
- 1 tablespoon chopped, fresh, flat-leaf parsley
- 1 tablespoon olive oil
- 1 tablespoon chopped, fresh thyme
- 1 pound of sliced mushrooms

DIRECTIONS

In a plastic storage jar, mix the mushrooms, parsley, thyme and one tablespoon of olive oil. To spread the seasonings, apply fresh peppers and lift. To clear the air and close the container, please use a vacuum sealer. Preheat the Sous Vide machine to 175°F/79°C. Lower the sealable bag and drench it in the water. Set a 30-minute timer. Use stainless steel tweezers to keep the package in position if you don't have a Sous Vide stand. In the meantime, prepare 2 tablespoons of olive oil on medium heat in a casserole dish and insert minced garlic. To infuse the oil, cook it for 10 minutes. Remove from the heat until the mushrooms are fully cooked. When the mushrooms are fully cooked, on medium-high heat, heat the garlic oil. Use a rubber spatula to pick the mushrooms out of the package and sauté them in garlic oil for 3 minutes. Season with salt and pepper.

496. FLAN

Cal.: 120 | Fat: 9g | Protein: 2g   ⬟ 8 min | 🍲 95 min | ✗ Servings 8

INGREDIENTS
- 3 large eggs
- 1 tablespoon vanilla extract
- 1 can (sweetened) condensed milk
- 1 can evaporated milk
- ¾ cup white sugar
- 4-ounce jars with lids

DIRECTIONS
In a wide heat-proof bowl full of water, put a Sous Vide cook within. Preheat medium 179°F/81°C. water tank. Melt the sugar in a small saucepan for around 5 minutes, until golden brown. Load 8 4-ounce Mason jars of hot molten sugar, enough to hit the end of each. In a separate cup, combine the condensed milk, evaporated milk, eggs and vanilla extract separately. Add to the bottles and seal. In the water bath, put the jars and set a timer for 1one hour. Replace the boiling water jars. Let cool for about 20 minutes, before safe to touch. Uncover the jars and run along the edges of the flan with a thin rubber spatula. Use a plate to cover each flan; turn the side and shake thoroughly.

497. STEEL CUT OATMEAL

Cal.: 141 | Fat: 6g | Protein: 5g   ⬟ 5 min | 🍲 3 hours | ✗ Servings 2

INGREDIENTS
- 2 cups water
- ½ cup steel cut oats
- ½ teaspoon salt
- Cinnamon and maple syrup for topping

DIRECTIONS
Prepare the water bath by using your immersion circulator and raise the temperature to 180°F/82°C. Take a heavy-duty resealable zipper bag and add all the listed ingredients except the cinnamon and maple syrup. Seal the bag using the immersion method and immerse underwater. Cook for about 3 hours. Once cooked, remove it and transfer the oats to your serving bowl. Serve with a sprinkle of cinnamon and some maple syrup.

498. HONEY DRIZZLED CARROTS

Cal.: 174 | Fat: 1g | Protein: 2g   ⬟ 5 min | 🍲 1 hour 15 min | ✗ Servings 4

INGREDIENTS
- 1-pound baby carrots
- 4 tablespoons vegan butter
- 1 tablespoon agave nectar
- 3 tablespoons honey
- ¼ teaspoon kosher salt
- ¼ teaspoon ground cardamom

DIRECTIONS
Prepare the sous-vide water bath using your immersion circulator and increase the temperature to 185°F/85°C. Add the carrots, honey, whole butter, kosher salt and cardamom to a resealable bag. Seal using the immersion method. Cook for 75 minutes and once done, remove it from the water bath. Strain the glaze by passing through a fine mesh. Set it aside. Take the carrots out from the bag and pour any excess glaze over them. Serve with a few seasonings.

499. PICKLED FENNEL

Cal.: 156 | Fat: 1g | Protein: 5g   ⬟ 30 min | 🍲 30 min | ✗ Servings 5

INGREDIENTS
- 1 cup white wine vinegar
- 2 tablespoons beet sugar
- Juice and zest from 1 lemon
- 1 teaspoon kosher salt
- 2 medium bulb fennels, trimmed up and cut into ¼ inch thick slices

DIRECTIONS
Prepare the water bath using your immersion circulator and raise the temperature to 180°F/82°C. Take a large bowl and add the vinegar, sugar, lemon juice, salt, lemon zest and whisk them well. Transfer the mixture to your resealable zip bag. Add the fennel and seal using the immersion method. Immerse underwater and cook for 30 minutes. Transfer to an ice bath and allow the mixture to reach the room temperature. Serve!

500. LEMON AND GARLIC ARTICHOKES

Cal.: 408 | Fat: 20g | Protein: 12g   ⬎ 30 min | 🍲 90 min | 🍴 Servings 4

INGREDIENTS

- 4 tablespoons freshly squeezed lemon juice
- 12 pieces' baby artichokes
- 4 tablespoons vegan butter
- 2 fresh garlic cloves, minced
- 1 teaspoon fresh lemon zest
- Kosher salt, and black pepper, to taste
- Chopped up fresh parsley for garnishing

DIRECTIONS

Prepare the water bath using your immersion circulator and raise the temperature to 180°F/82°C. Take a large bowl and add the cold water and 2 tablespoons of lemon juice. Peel and discard the outer tough layer of your artichoke and cut them into quarters. Transfer to a cold water bath and let it sit for a while. Take a large skillet and put it over medium-high heat. Add in the butter to the skillet and allow the butter to melt. Add the garlic alongside 2 tablespoons of lemon juice and the zest. Remove from heat and season with a bit of pepper and salt. Allow it to cool for about 5 minutes. Then, drain the artichokes from the cold water and place them in a large resealable bag. Add in the butter mixture as well. Seal it up using the immersion method and Immerse underwater for about 1 and a ½ hour. Once cooked, transfer the artichokes to a bowl and serve with a garnish of parsley.

501. TRUFFLE SUNCHOKES

Cal.: 255 | Fat: 10g | Protein 5g   ⬎ 15 min | 🍲 1 hour 30 min | 🍴 Servings 4

INGREDIENTS

- 8 ounces peeled Sunchokes, sliced into ¼ inch thick pieces
- 3 tablespoons unsalted vegan butter
- 2 tablespoons agave nectar
- 1 teaspoon truffle oil
- Kosher salt, and black pepper, to taste

DIRECTIONS

Prepare the water bath using your immersion circulator and raise the temperature to 180°F/82°C. Take a heavy-duty resealable zip bag and add the butter, nectar, sunchokes and truffle oil and mix them well. Sprinkle some salt and pepper, and then seal using the immersion method. Immerse it underwater and cook for 1 ½ hour. Once cooked, transfer the contents to a skillet. Put the skillet over medium-high heat and cook for 5 minutes more until the liquid has evaporated. Season with pepper and salt to adjust the flavor if needed. Serve!

502. SPICY GIARDINIERA

Cal.: 245 | Fat: 7g | Protein 4g   ⬎ 30 min | 🍲 60 min | 🍴 Servings 8

INGREDIENTS

- 2 cups white wine vinegar
- 1 cup water
- ½ cup beet sugar
- 3 tbs kosher salt
- 1 tbs whole black peppercorns
- 1 cup cauliflower, cut up into ½-inch pieces
- 1 stemmed and seeded bell pepper, cut up into ½-inch pieces
- 1 cup carrots, cut up into ½-inch pieces
- ½ thinly sliced white onion
- 2 seeded and stemmed Serrano peppers, cut up into ½-inch pieces

DIRECTIONS

Prepare the sous-vide water bath using your immersion circulator and raise the temperature to 180°F/82°C. Take a large bowl and mix in vinegar, sugar, salt, water and peppercorns. Transfer the mixture to a large resealable zipper bag and add the cauliflower, onion, serrano peppers, vinegar mixture, bell pepper and carrots. Seal it up using the immersion method and Immerse underwater, cook for about 1 hour. Once cooked, take it out from the bag and serve.

503. VEGAN ALFREDO

Cal.: 160 | Fat: 11g | Protein: 8g   15 min | 90 min | Servings 6

INGREDIENTS
- 4 cups chopped cauliflower
- 2 cups water
- 2/3 cup cashews
- 2 garlic cloves
- ½ teaspoon dried oregano
- ½ teaspoon dried basil
- ½ teaspoon dried rosemary
- 4 tablespoons nutritional yeast
- Salt, and pepper to taste

DIRECTIONS
Prepare the sous-vide water bath using your immersion circulator and increase the temperature to 170°F/76°C. Take a heavy-duty resealable zip bag and add the cashews, cauliflower, oregano, water, garlic, rosemary and basil. Seal using the immersion method. Immerse underwater and cook for 90 minutes. Transfer the cooked contents to a blender and purée. Use the Alfredo sauce over your favorite pasta.

504. MUSHROOM AND TRUFFLE OIL

Cal.: 440 | Fat: 19g | Protein: 28g   20 min | 60 min | Servings 2

INGREDIENTS
- 10 large button mushrooms
- 3 tablespoons truffle oil
- 3 tablespoons olive oil
- 1 tablespoon chopped fresh thyme
- 1 clove thinly sliced garlic
- Salt, and pepper to taste

DIRECTIONS
Prepare the sous-vide water bath using your immersion circulator and raise the temperature to 185°F/85°C. Take a large bowl and add the truffle oil, mushrooms, olive oil, garlic and thyme. Season with some pepper and salt. Transfer the mushroom mixture to a large sous-vide resealable zip bag and add the mixture to the bag. Seal it up using the immersion method. Immerse underwater and cook for 1 hour. Once cooked, drain the mushrooms and discard the cooking liquid. Take a large skillet and put it over medium heat for 3 minutes. Add the mushrooms and sear for about 1 minute to brown it. Transfer the cooked mushroom to a serving plate and season with pepper and salt. Top it up with thyme. Serve!

505. WHITE CANNELLINI BEANS

Cal.: 578 | Fat: 18g | Protein: 31g   15 min | 180 min | Servings 5

INGREDIENTS
- 1 cup cannellini beans, dried, soaked overnight in salty cold water
- 1 cup water
- ½ cup extra-virgin olive oil
- 1 peeled carrot, cut up into 1-inch dice
- 1 celery stalk, cut up into 1-inch dice
- 1 quartered shallot
- 4 crushed garlic cloves
- 2 fresh rosemary sprigs
- 2 bay leaves
- Kosher salt, and pepper to taste

DIRECTIONS
Prepare the water bath using your sous-vide immersion circulator and raise the temperature to 190°F/88°C. Drain the soaked beans and rinse them. Transfer to a heavy duty resealable zip bag and add the olive oil, celery, water, carrot, shallot, garlic, rosemary and bay leaves. Season with pepper and salt. Seal using the immersion method and cook for 3 hours. Once cooked, remove the beans and check for seasoning. Discard the rosemary and serve!

506. TOFU DELIGHT

Cal.: 186 | Fat: 6g | Protein: 10g   20 min | 🍲 1 hour | ✕ Servings 8

INGREDIENTS
- 1 cup vegetable broth
- 2 tablespoons tomato paste
- 1 tablespoon grated ginger
- 1 tablespoon rice wine
- 1 tablespoon rice wine vinegar
- 1 tablespoon agave nectar
- 2 teaspoons Sriracha sauce
- 3 minced garlic cloves
- 2 boxes of cubed tofu

DIRECTIONS
Prepare your water bath using your immersion circulator and raise the temperature to 185°F/85°C. Take a medium bowl and add all the listed ingredients except the tofu. Mix well. Transfer the mixture to a heavy-duty resealable zipper bag and top with the tofu. Seal it up using the immersion method. Cook for 1 hour. Pour the contents into a serving bowl. Serve!

507. WHITE BEANS

Cal.: 210 | Fat: 2g | Protein 14g   15 min | 🍲 3-4 hours | ✕ Servings 8

INGREDIENTS
- 1 cup dried and soaked navy beans
- 1 cup water
- ½ cup extra-virgin olive oil
- 1 peeled carrot, cut up into 1-inch dices
- 1 stalk celery, cut up into 1-inch dices
- 1 quartered shallot
- 4 crushed garlic cloves
- 2 sprigs of fresh rosemary
- 2 pieces' bay leaves
- Kosher salt, to taste
- Freshly ground black pepper, to taste

DIRECTIONS
Prepare your sous-vide water bath using your immersion circulator and raise the temperature to 190°F/88°C. Carefully drain and rinse your beans and add them alongside the rest of the ingredients to a heavy-duty zip bag. Seal using the immersion method and immerse it underwater. Cook for about 3 hours. Once cooked, taste the beans. If they are firm, then cook for another 1 hour and pour them in a serving bowl. Serve!

508. RADISHES WITH "VEGAN" BUTTER

Cal.: 134 | Fat: 0.2g | Protein 1g   5 min | 🍲 45 min | ✕ Servings 4

INGREDIENTS
- 1 pound radishes, cut up in half lengthwise
- 3 tablespoons vegan butter
- ½ teaspoon sea salt

DIRECTIONS
Prepare your water bath using your immersion circulator and raise the temperature to 190°F/88°C. Add your radish halves, butter and salt in a resealable zipper bag and seal it up using the immersion method. Immerse underwater and cook for 45 minutes. Once cooked, strain the liquid and discard. Serve the radishes in a bowl!

509. SPICY EGGPLANT

Cal.: 65 | Fat: 1.5g | Protein: 2.8g   10 min | 25 min | Servings 4

INGREDIENTS
- 1 pound eggplants, sliced
- ¼ cup lemon juice
- 2 tablespoons olive oil
- ½ teaspoon hot paprika
- 1 red chili pepper, minced
- 1 tablespoon chili powder
- A pinch of salt and black pepper

DIRECTIONS
In a large bag, mix the eggplants with the lemon juice, oil and the other ingredients, seal the bag, Immerse in the water bath, cook at 170°F/76°C. for 25 minutes, divide the mix between plates and serve.

510. PESTO TOMATO MIX

Cal.: 25 | Fat: 1.9g | Protein: 1.4g   10 min | 20 min | Servings 4

INGREDIENTS
- 1 pound cherry tomatoes, halved
- 2 tablespoons olive oil
- 2 tablespoons basil pesto
- ½ teaspoon sweet paprika
- 1 teaspoon garlic, minced
- A pinch of salt and black pepper
- 1 tablespoon chives, chopped

DIRECTIONS
In a bag, mix the tomatoes with the pesto, oil and the other ingredients, seal the bag, cook in the water bath at 167°F/75°C for 20 minutes, divide the mix between plates and serve.

511. CABBAGE SAUTÉ

Cal.: 36 | Fat: 1.4g | Protein: 2g   10 min | 25 min | Servings 4

INGREDIENTS
- 1 pound red cabbage, shredded
- 1 tablespoon lime juice
- 2 tablespoons olive oil
- 1 teaspoon sweet paprika
- A pinch of salt and black pepper
- ¼ cup chicken stock
- 1 tablespoon dill, chopped

DIRECTIONS
In a bag, mix the cabbage with the lime juice, oil and the other ingredients, seal the bag, cook in the water bath at 170°F/76°C for 25 minutes, divide the mix between plates and serve.

512. ZUCCHINI AND TOMATO MIX

Cal.: 41 | Fat: 1.2g | Protein: 2.4g   10 min | 30 min | Servings 4

INGREDIENTS
- 2 cups zucchinis, sliced
- 1 cup cherry tomatoes, halved
- 2 tablespoons olive oil
- 2 tablespoons balsamic vinegar
- A pinch of salt and black pepper
- 2 tablespoons parsley, chopped

DIRECTIONS
In a bag, mix the zucchinis with the tomatoes and the other ingredients, seal the bag, Immerse in the water bath, cook at 160°F/71°C for 30 minutes, divide the mix between plates and serve.

513. PAPRIKA OKRA

Cal.: 26 | Fat: 1.2g | Protein: 1.4g   10 min | 25 min | Servings 4

INGREDIENTS

- 2 cups okra
- 1 teaspoon sweet paprika
- 1 tablespoon olive oil
- 1 tablespoon lemon juice
- A pinch of salt and black pepper
- 1 tablespoon balsamic vinegar
- 1 tablespoon chives, chopped

DIRECTIONS

In a bag, mix the okra with the lemon juice, paprika and the other ingredients, seal the bag, cook in the water bath at 160°F/71°C for 25 minutes, divide the mix between plates and serve.

514. CHILI COLLARD GREENS

Cal.: 151 | Fat: 12.2g | Protein: 4g   10 min | 20 min | Servings 4

INGREDIENTS

- 1 pound collard greens, trimmed
- 2 tablespoons balsamic vinegar
- ½ teaspoon chili powder
- 1 red chili pepper, minced
- 2 tablespoons olive oil
- 1 tablespoon sweet paprika
- A pinch of salt and black pepper
- 1 tablespoon cilantro, chopped

DIRECTIONS

In a bag, mix the collard greens with the vinegar, chili powder and the other ingredients, seal the bag, cook in the water bath at 160°F/71°C for 20 minutes, divide the mix between plates and serve.

515. BEET AND RADISH MIX

Cal.: 61 | Fat: 1.3g | Protein: 3.2g   10 min | 35 min | Servings 4

INGREDIENTS

- 1 pound radishes, halved
- ½ pound beets, peeled and cut into wedges
- 2 tablespoons olive oil
- 2 tablespoons balsamic vinegar
- 1 tablespoon chives, chopped
- A pinch of salt and black pepper

DIRECTIONS

In a bag, mix the radishes with the beets, oil and the rest of the ingredients, seal the bag, cook in the water oven at 167°F/75°C for 35 minutes, divide the mix between plates and serve.

516. CILANTRO HOT ARTICHOKES

Cal.: 141 | Fat: 1.5g | Protein: 7.3g ⟋ 10 min | 🍲 30 min | 🍴 Servings 4

INGREDIENTS

- ½ cup canned artichoke hearts, drained and chopped
- 2 red chilies, minced
- ½ teaspoon hot paprika
- 1 tablespoon cilantro, chopped
- 2 tablespoons olive oil
- 2 tablespoons balsamic vinegar
- A pinch of red pepper flakes, crushed
- A pinch of salt and black pepper

DIRECTIONS

In a large bag, mix the artichoke hearts with the chilies and the other ingredients, seal the bag, cook in the water bath at 170°F/76°C. for 30 minutes, divide the mix between plates and serve.

517. CRISP CORN WITH BUTTER AND FRESH HERBS

Cal.: 179 | Fat: 20g | Protein: 11g ⟋ 18 min | 🍲 30 min | 🍴 Servings 4

INGREDIENTS

- 2.8g black pepper
- Fresh herbs
- 57g butter
- 5 fresh thyme, sprigs
- 60 ml of olive oil
- 383g corn
- 2.8g salt
- 3 garlic cloves (peeled)

DIRECTIONS

Preheat the Sous Vide Machine to 194 °F / 90 °C. On the grill, pour oil into a pan. Add sliced garlic cloves. Keep frying on medium-high heat, spooning oil on the garlic until the cloves become brown and roasted for about 10 minutes. Move the oil and leave to cool down for 15 minutes in a shallow dish. Using your fingertips, pull at the corn packaging the blob and linen to extract them from the sides of the corn. A few at a time, horizontally tilt each cob over a bowl. Then, remove corn from cob by slicing directly downwards with a sharp knife. Transfer the corn kernels to the vacuum sealer bag and add salt, butter, roasted garlic, and thyme. Seal the bag. Lower the vacuum-sealed bag into the water. If the bag floats, use tongs to weigh it down. Cook for 20 minutes. Transfer corn to a serving dish and garnish with pepper, infused garlic oil, fresh herbs, edible flowers, or whatever you like.

CHAPTER 11:
Dessert Recipes

 Preparation Time | 🍲 Cooking Time | ✗ Servings

518. BUTTERED SPICED APPLES

Cal.: 229 | Fat: 12g | Protein: 0.9g   21 min | 2 hours | Servings 6

INGREDIENTS

- Zest and juice from 1 lemon
- 6 small apples
- 6 tbsp. unsalted butter
- ½ tsp. salt
- ½ tsp. ground cinnamon
- 1/4 tsp. ground nutmeg
- 1 heaping tsp. dark brown sugar
- 1 heaping tablespoon dark or golden raisins
- Dollops of crème fraiche, whipped cream or ice cream

DIRECTIONS

Preheat your Sous Vide Machine to 170°F or 77°C. Peel and core the apples, soften the butter, and completely zest the lemon. Coat the apples with lemon juice. Place the lemon zest in a bowl and combine with the cinnamon, sugar, nutmeg, raisins, butter and salt. Place an equal amount of the mixture in the hollowed-out center of each apple. Put 2 apples in each bag and set your timer for 2 hours. Remove apples from the bag and serve immediately with cooking liquid.

519. STRAWBERRIES

Cal.: 80 | Fat: 12g | Protein: 0.6g   11 min | 16 min | Servings 4

INGREDIENTS

- 12 oz. strawberries trimmed
- 2 tbsp. champagne
- 2 tsp. sugar

DIRECTIONS

Preheat your Sous Vide Machine to 185°F or 85°C. Place all the ingredients in a bag and place the bag in the preheated container and set your timer for 15 minutes. Meanwhile, prepare an ice bath. When the strawberries are cooked, put them directly in the ice bath until they're cold.

520. RED WINE POACHED PEARS

Cal.: 299 | Fat: 0.3g | Protein: 1g   9 min | 6 hours | Servings 4

INGREDIENTS

- 4 ripe Bosc pears
- 1 cup red wine
- ½ cup granulated sugar
- 1/4 cup sweet vermouth
- 1 tsp. salt
- 3 (3-inch pieces) orange zest
- 1 vanilla bean
- Vanilla ice cream

DIRECTIONS

Preheat your Sous Vide Machine to 175°F/79°C. Peel the pear and scrape the vanilla bean seeds. Put everything, except the ice cream in a bag. Then, place the bag in the preheated container and set your timer for 1 hour. When the pears are cooked, slice them up and core them. Reserve the juices from the bag. Place the sliced pears in 4 bowls and add a scoop of ice cream. Top with the reserved juices and serve.

521. ROSE WATER APRICOTS

Cal.: 17 | Fat: 0.2g | Protein: 0.5g   11 min | 1 hour | Servings 8

INGREDIENTS

- 8 apricots
- 1 tsp. rosewater
- ½ cup water

DIRECTIONS

Preheat your Sous Vide Machine to 180°F/82°C. Cut the apricots in half and remove the pit. Place all the ingredients in a bag. Then, place the bag in your preheated container and set your timer for 1 hour. When the peaches are cooked, serve in a small bowl or plate.

522. DOLCE DE LECHE

Cal.: 91 | Fat: 2.5g | Protein: 2.2g   6 min | 13 hours | Servings 8

INGREDIENTS
- 12 oz. sweetened condensed milk

DIRECTIONS
Preheat your Sous Vide Machine to 185°F/85°C. Put the milk in a bag or a pint size mason jar. Put the bag or Mason jar in your preheated container and set your timer for 13 hours. When the dolce de Leche is cooked, pour it into 4 bowls to serve.

523. CHAMPAGNE ZABAGLIONE

Cal.: 231 | Fat: 10.3g | Protein 3.5g   21 min | 1 hour | Servings 4

INGREDIENTS
- 4 large egg yolks
- ½ cup superfine sugar
- ½ cup champagne
- ½ cup heavy whipping cream
- ½-pint fresh raspberries

DIRECTIONS
Preheat your Sous Vide Machine to 165°F/74°C. Place the eggs in a bowl and slowly whisk in the sugar. Continue to whisk until ingredients become thick. Add the champagne and continue to lightly whisk until you have dissolved the sugar. Place the mixture in a bag. Then, place the bag in the preheated container. Set your timer for 20 minutes. vMeanwhile, prepare an ice bath. Once cooked, put the bag in the ice bath until cold. Whip the cream and fold the whipped cream into the cold zabaglione. Place a layer of the mixture in a glass and then top with some berries. Add another layer of the mixture and top with a couple more berries. Repeat the process with 3 more glasses. Serve immediately.

524. MEXICAN POT DE CRÈME

Cal.: 332 | Fat: 22.3g | Protein 5.6g   2 hours 20 min | 30 min | Servings 5

INGREDIENTS
- 1 cup heavy whipping cream
- ½ cup whole milk
- 1 cup bittersweet chocolate, chopped
- ½ tsp. cinnamon
- 1 tablespoon sugar
- 3 egg yolks
- 2 tsp. cocoa powder
- ½ tsp. vanilla extract
- 1/8 tsp. salt
- Flakey sea salt for garnish
- 5 (4-oz) mason jars

DIRECTIONS
Preheat your Sous Vide Machine to 180°F/82°C. Chop the chocolate and put it in a large bowl with the sugar and cinnamon. Heat a pan on medium heat with cream and milk. Allow the mixture to come to a boil and then pour it over the chocolate. Let the mixture rest for 5 minutes. While the mixture is resting, whisk together the vanilla, salt, cocoa powder, and eggs. Stir the chocolate mixture. Whisk in the cocoa powder mixture into the chocolate mixture. Pour an equal amount of the mixture into the mason jars. Place the mason jars in your preheated container and set your timer for 30 minutes. When the jars are cooked, place them on top of a kitchen towel on the counter to cool for 20 minutes. Place the cooled jars in the refrigerator for at least 2 hours. Sprinkle the jars with a little sea salt to serve.

525. LAVENDER SPICED CRÈME BRÛLÉE

Cal.: 321 | Fat: 24.4g | Protein: 8.5g   ⟍ 2 hours 20 min | 🍲 60min | ✕ Servings 6

INGREDIENTS

- 8 jumbo egg yolks
- ½ cup sugar plus more for topping
- 1 tsp. salt
- 1 tsp. culinary lavender
- 2 ½ cups heavy whipping cream

DIRECTIONS

Preheat your Sous Vide Machine to 176°F/80°C. Combine the eggs, sugar, lavender and salt, in a bowl and whisk them together. Heat the cream on medium heat until simmering. Carefully and slowly mix the cream into the lavender mixture using a whisk. Otherwise, the eggs will curdle. Strain the ingredients and discard the lavender. Pour an equal amount of the mixture into 6 mason jars. Tighten the lids so they're finger tight. You don't want to tighten the lids as tight as possible, because the trapped air may crack the jars. Place the jars in your preheated container and set your timer for 1 hour. Once cooked, place the jars on a kitchen towel on the counter. Let the jars come down to room temperature. Prepare an ice bath. Put the cooled jars in the ice bath until cold, top the crème Brulée with a layer of sugar and use a kitchen torch to caramelize it. Allow it to harden for 5 minutes
Serve immediately.

526. CRÈME BRÛLÉE

Cal.: 444 | Fat: 45.3g | Protein: 7g   ⟍ 2 hours 20 min| 🍲 60 min | ✕ Servings 6

INGREDIENTS

- 11 egg yolks
- Granulated sugar, plus more for dusting
- 3 g salt
- 600 g heavy cream
- 6 (6-oz) mason jars

DIRECTIONS

Preheat your Sous Vide Machine to 176°F/80°C. Place the eggs, sugar and salt, in a bowl and whisk them together. Carefully and slowly mix the cream into the egg mixture using a whisk. Otherwise, the eggs will curdle. Strain the new mixture and allow it to rest for 20–30 minutes. The goal is to get rid of all the bubbles. Take off any removing bubbles. Slowly pour an equal amount of the mixture from a low height into the mason jars. You want to make sure you don't create more bubbles. Tighten the lids so they're finger tight. You don't want to tighten the lids as tight as possible, because the trapped air may crack the jars.
Place the jars in your preheated container and set your timer for 1 hour. Once cooked, place the jars on a kitchen towel on the counter. Let the jars come down to room temperature. Prepare an ice bath and place the cooled jars in the ice bath until cold. Top the crème brulée with a layer of sugar using a sieve and use a kitchen torch to caramelize it. Allow it to harden for 5 minutes Serve immediately.

527. WINE AND CINNAMON POACHED PEARS

Cal.: 173 | Fat: 0.4g | Protein: 1g   ⟍ 9 min | 🍲 90 min | ✕ Servings 4

INGREDIENTS

- 4 pears, peeled
- 2 cinnamon sticks
- 2 cups red wine
- 1/3 cup sugar
- 3-star anise

DIRECTIONS

Preheat the Sous Vide machine to 175°F/79°C. Combine the pears, wine, anise, sugar and cinnamon in a Ziploc bag. Seal and immerse in the preheated water. Cook for 1 hour. Serve the pears drizzle with the wine sauce.

528. LECHE FLAN GLAZE

Cal.: 665 | Fat: 26.6g | Protein: 19.9g   ⟋ 21 min | 🍲 1 hour | ✖ Servings 4

INGREDIENTS
- 3/4 cups granulated sugar
- 12 egg yolks
- 1 (14-oz can) of condensed milk
- 1 (12-oz can) evaporated milk
- 1 tsp. vanilla extract
- 4 (½ pint) mason jars

DIRECTIONS
Preheat your Sous Vide Machine to 180°F/82°C. Heat the sugar in a saucepan on medium-high heat. Stir constantly until the sugar melts and turns a caramel color. Pour equal portions of the caramel into the 4 mason jars and allow it cool Lightly mix together the remaining ingredients and strain through cheesecloth. Pour an equal amount into the mason jars. Place the jars in the preheated container and set your timer for 2 hours. When the flan is cooked, place the jars on a kitchen towel on the counter. Allow the jars to cool down to room temperature. Place the jars in the refrigerator for at least 2 hours before serving. Serve directly in the jar or remove and put the flan on a plate.

529. CINNAMON CLOVE BANANA BOWLS

Cal.: 241 | Fat: 1.8g | Protein: 2g   ⟋ 11 min | 🍲 35 min | ✖ Servings 6

INGREDIENTS
- 7 ripe bananas
- 2 cinnamon sticks
- 1-1/4 cup brown sugar
- 6 cloves, whole

DIRECTIONS
Preheat your Sous Vide Machine to 176°F/80°C. Peel the banana and slice it into chunks Combine all the ingredients in a bag. Place the bag in your preheated container and set your timer for 35 minutes. When the bananas are cooked, place them in 6 bowls and let them cool slightly. Remove the cinnamon and cloves and serve alone or with ice cream.

530. CREAMY SWEET CORN CHEESECAKE

Cal.: 241 | Fat: 1.8g | Protein: 2g   ⟋ 31 min | 🍲 40 min | ✖ Servings 6

INGREDIENTS
- 1 cup frozen sweet corn
- ½ cup heavy cream
- ½ cup whole milk
- 4 eggs
- 1 cup sugar
- 1 tablespoon lemon juice
- 2 lemon peels
- ½ cup butter
- 3/4 cups cream cheese
- 3 gingerbread cookies
- 6 (6-oz) mason jars

DIRECTIONS
Preheat your Sous Vide Machine to 176°F/80°C. Defrost the corn. Place the first 6 ingredients in a blender and blend on high speed until smooth. Add the mixture and the lemon peels to a bag. Place the bag in your preheated container and set your timer for 40 minutes. When the mixture is cooked, discard the peels and place the mix back in the blender. Add in the cream cheese and butter and blend on high until smooth. Allow the mixture to cool completely. Pour an equal amount of the mixture in each Mason jar. Crumble up the cookies and top each Mason jar with the crumbs before serving.

531. SWEET CORN CHEESECAKE

Cal.: 443 | Fat: 34.5g | Protein: 11g   ⟍ 15 min | 🍲 90 min | ✗ Servings 5

INGREDIENTS

- 2 (8-oz) packages of cream cheese
- 100 grams granulated sugar
- 2 grams kosher salt
- 3 whole eggs
- 5 grams vanilla extract
- 130 grams buttermilk, or heavy whipping cream
- 5 (8-oz) mason jars

DIRECTIONS

Preheat your Sous Vide Machine to 176°F/80°C. Allow the cream cheese to rise to room temperature. Put the cream cheese, salt and sugar in a food processor. Process until smooth, making sure you scrape the sides of the bowl throughout to ensure all ingredients are mixed. Put in the eggs and vanilla and follow the same process as last time. While the food processor is running, pour in the buttermilk. Continue to process until smooth. Strain the mixture through a fine-mesh sieve for the smoothest texture. Pour an equal amount of mixture into each jar. Tighten the lids so they're finger tight, but not fully airtight to prevent cracking of the jars. Put the jars in your preheated container and set your timer for 90 minutes. When the cheesecake is cooked, place the jars on a kitchen towel on the counter. Let the jars come to room temperature. Refrigerate overnight. Serve with your favorite toppings.

532. BANANAS FOSTER

Cal.: 722 | Fat: 40.4g | Protein: 5.4g   ⟍ 15 min 🍲 26 min | ✗ Servings 2

INGREDIENTS

- 2 tbsp. dark rum
- 4 tbsp. butter
- 1 tsp. vanilla
- ½ cup brown sugar
- 2 bananas
- 1 tsp. cinnamon
- ½ cup pecans
- 2 scoops of vanilla ice cream

DIRECTIONS

Preheat your Sous Vide Machine to 145°F/63°C. Peel and cut the bananas into 1-inch pieces. Place the vanilla, butter, brown sugar and rum in a pan over high heat. Bring the mixture to a boil and remove from heat. Season the bananas with cinnamon and put them in the bag of your choice with 3 tbsp. of the sauce. Place the bag in your preheated container and set your timer for 25 minutes. When the bananas are cooked, plate them with a scoop of vanilla ice cream and top with the remaining sauce. Serve immediately.

533. MAPLE RAISIN RICE PUDDING WITH GINGER

Cal.: 311 | Fat: 3.2g | Protein: 6.5g   ⟍ 6 min | 2 hours| ✗ Servings 8

INGREDIENTS

- 3 cups skim milk
- 2 tbsp. butter
- 2 cups Arborio rice
- ½ cup golden raisins
- ½ cup maple syrup
- 2 tsp. ground cinnamon
- ½ tsp. ground ginger

DIRECTIONS

Preheat Sous Vide Machine to 180°F/82°C. Put all the ingredients in a bag and place the bag in your preheated container and set your timer for 2 hours. Once cooked, place equal portions in 8 bowls. Top each bowl with a little extra cinnamon to serve.

534. CARAMELIZED YOGURT WITH GRILLED BERRIES

Cal.: 101 | Fat: 3.5g | Protein: 5.4g   1 hour | 12 hours | Servings 8

INGREDIENTS

- 1 lb. natural yogurt plus 3.5 oz. natural yogurt
- 12 oz. blueberries
- 12 oz. raspberries
- Mint for garnish

DIRECTIONS

Preheat your Sous Vide Machine to 162°F/72°C. Place the yogurt in a bag and place the bag in the preheated container and set your timer for 12 hours. When nearly finished cooking, prepare an ice bath. Once cooked, place the bag in a bowl, and put the bowl in the ice bath. Allow the yogurt to cool. Open the bag and pour the yogurt into a colander or sieve that's lined with the muslin cloth. Position the sieve over a bowl and let strain for about an hour. Slowly whisk in the 3.5 ounces of yogurt. Grill the berries on a very hot grill for a short time or heat with a kitchen torch. Garnish with mint to serve.

535. CARAMELIZED YOGURT WITH GRILLED BERRIES

Cal.: 259 | Fat: 7.7g | Protein: 3.6g   21 min | 1 hour | Servings 4

INGREDIENTS

- 4 Bartlett pears, peeled
- ½ cup Marsala wine
- 1 ½ tsp. honey
- 2 tbsp. Demerara sugar
- 1/3 cup mascarpone cheese
- 1/3 cup 35% whipping cream or coconut cream
- 1/4 tsp. ground cinnamon
- 1 tablespoon maple syrup or honey

DIRECTIONS

Preheat your Sous Vide Machine to 185°F/85°C. Place the first 4 ingredients in a bag. Then, place the bag in your preheated container and set your timer for 1 hour. Towards the end of the cooking process, chill a bowl and place the cheese and cream in it. Whip the mixture until soft peaks appear. Whisk in the cinnamon and maple syrup until the peaks hold their shape. When the pears are cooked, place them in a bowl and pour the juices into a pan. Heat on medium-high heat until it reduces by half. Pipe or place a dollop of whip cream on a plate with each pear. Top the pears with the warm sauce. Enjoy!

536. SWEET AND SMOKY BUTTERNUT SQUASH

Cal.: 202 | Fat: 10.7g | Protein: 10g   16 min | 1 hour | Servings 4

INGREDIENTS

- ½ lb. butternut squash
- 12 oz. cooked bacon bits
- 1/4 cup brown sugar
- 1 tablespoon paprika
- 1 tsp. liquid smoke
- 1 tsp. vanilla extract
- Salt and black pepper

DIRECTIONS

Preheat your Sous Vide Machine to 185°F/85°C. Remove the seeds from the squash peel it and cut it into cubes. Mix all the ingredients in a bowl, adding salt and pepper to taste. Place the mixture in a bag. Place the bag in your preheated container and set your timer for 1 hour and serve immediately.

537. SWEETENED CARROTS

Cal.: 67 | Fat: 2.1g | Protein: 0.8g   11 min | 30 min | Servings 4

INGREDIENTS

- 1 lb. baby carrots
- 2 tsp. butter
- 2 tsp. honey
- Salt and pepper

DIRECTIONS

Preheat your Sous Vide Machine to 185°F/84°C. Place all the ingredients in the bag including salt and pepper to taste. Place the bag in your preheated container and set your timer for 1 hour. When the carrots are cooked, put them on a plate to cool for a few minutes. Serve with your main dish.

538. MAPLE ORANGE BEETS

Cal.: 18 | Fat: 0.1g | Protein: 0.7g   ⬕ 16 min | 🍲 70 min | ✕ Servings 4

INGREDIENTS
- 1 large beet
- 1 orange slice
- ½ tsp. maple syrup
- Salt and pepper
- Goat cheese for garnish

DIRECTIONS
Preheat your Sous Vide Machine to 183°F/84°C. Cut the top and bottom off the beet and peel it. Slice the beet into medium size chunks. Place the beets in the bag with the other ingredients, and salt and pepper to taste. Place the beets in your preheated container and set your timer for 1 hour. When the beets are cooked, heat a skillet on medium heat and pour in the beets and any liquid in the bag. Allow them to cook until the liquids thicken into a glaze. Pour everything onto a plate and top with goat cheese to serve.

539. CHOCOLATE PUDDING

Cal.: 850 | Fat: 79g | Protein: 19g   ⬕ 9 min | 🍲 45 min | ✕ Servings 4

INGREDIENTS
- ½ cup Milk
- 1 cup Chocolate Chips
- 3 Egg Yolks
- ½ cup Heavy Cream
- 4 tbsp. Cocoa Powder
- 3 tbsp. Sugar
- ¼ tsp. Salt

DIRECTIONS
Whisk the yolks along with the sugar, milk, heavy cream, and salt. Stir in the cocoa powder and chocolate chips. Divide the mixture between 4 jars. Preheat the Sous Vide machine to 185°F/85°C. Seal and immerse the jars in the water. Cook for 40 minutes. Let cool before serving.

540. APPLE PIE

Cal.: 205 | Fat: 11g | Protein: 2g   ⬕ 9 min | 🍲 80 min | ✕ Servings 8

INGREDIENTS
- 1 pound Apples, cubed
- 6 ounces Puff Pastry
- 1 Egg Yolk, whisked
- 4 tbsp. Sugar
- 2 tbsp. Lemon Juice
- 1 tbsp. Cornstarch
- 1 tsp. ground Ginger
- 2 tbsp. Butter, melted
- ¼ tsp. Nutmeg
- ¼ tsp. Cinnamon

DIRECTIONS
Preheat the Sous Vide machine to 180°F/82°C. Preheat your oven to 365°F/185°C. Roll the pastry into a circle. Brush it with the butter and place in the oven. Cook for 15 minutes. Combine all the remaining ingredients in a Ziploc bag. Seal and immerse in the water bath. Cook for 45 minutes. Top the cooked pie crust with the apple mixture. Return to the oven and cook for 15 more minutes.

541. SUGAR-FREE CHOCOLATE CHIP COOKIES

Cal.: 276 | Fat: 10g | Protein: 5g   12min | 3 hours 35 min | Servings 6

INGREDIENTS
- 1/3 cup sugar-free Chocolate Chips
- 7 tbsp. Heavy Cream
- 2 Eggs
- ½ cup Flour
- ½ tsp. Baking Soda
- 4 tbsp. Butter, melted
- ¼ tsp. Salt
- 1 tbsp. Lemon Juice

DIRECTIONS
Beat the eggs along with the cream, lemon juice, salt, and baking soda. Stir in the flour and butter. Fold in the chocolate chips.
Preheat the Sous Vide machine to 194°F/90°C. Divide the dough between 6 ramekins. Wrap them well with plastic foil.
Place the ramekins in the water bath. Cook for 3 ½ hours.
Remove the ramekins from the bath. Let cool slightly before serving.

542. VANILLA ICE CREAM

Cal.: 290 | Fat: 20g | Protein: 7g   18 min | 5 hour | Servings 4

INGREDIENTS
- 6 Egg Yolks
- ½ cup Brown Sugar
- 1 ½ tsp. Vanilla Extract
- 2 cups Half and Half

DIRECTIONS
Preheat the Sous Vide machine to 180°F/82°C. In your food processor, whisk all of the ingredients together until smooth and creamy, and place in a Ziploc bag. Seal the bag and immerse in the preheated. Cook for 1 hour. Make sure there are no clumps before transferring the mixture to a container with a lid. Remove and unseal the bag. Let cool in an ice bath. Pour the mixture into an ice cream machine, and process according to the maker's instructions. Place in the freezer for 4 hours until firm. Scoop into bowls and serve.

543. RICE PUDDING WITH RUM CRANBERRIES

Cal.: 202 | Fat: 10.7g | Protein: 10g   11 min | 4 hour 10 min | Servings 4

INGREDIENTS
- 2 cups rice
- 3 cups milk
- ½ cup dried cranberries soaked in ½ cup rum overnight and drained
- 1 tsp. cinnamon
- ½ cup brown sugar

DIRECTIONS
Preheat the Sous Vide machine to 170°F/76°C. Combine all of the ingredients in a bowl. Divide the mixture among 6 small jars. Seal them and immerse in the water. Cook for 4 hours. Once the timer has stopped, remove the jars from the bath. Serve warm or chilled.

544. CRÈME BRULÉE WITH BLUEBERRIES

Cal.: 493 | Fat: 48g | Protein: 5g   9 min | 2 hour 35 min | Servings 4

INGREDIENTS
- 2 cups heavy cream
- 4 egg yolks
- ¼ cup sugar
- 1 tsp. vanilla extract
- Zest from 1 orange
- 1 cup fresh blueberries

DIRECTIONS
Set your cooker to 180°F/82°C. Whisk together all the ingredients and pour the mixture into 4 shallow jars. Seal the jars and Immerse in the preheated water bath. Cook for 30 minutes. Once the timer has stopped, remove the jars and refrigerate for 2 hours. Unseal the jars and sprinkle sugar on top of each custard. Place under the broiler until they become caramelized. Serve garnished with fresh raspberries

545. SAVORY BREAD PUDDING

Cal.: 265 | Fat: 15g | Protein: 10g   12 min | 2 hours 15 min | Servings 8

INGREDIENTS

- 1 cup milk
- 1 cup heavy cream
- 10 ounces white bread
- 4 eggs
- 2 tbsp. butter, melted
- 1 tbsp. flour
- 1 tbsp. corn starch
- 4 tbsp. sugar
- 1 tsp. vanilla extract
- ¼ tsp. salt

DIRECTIONS

Preheat the water in the bath to 170°F/76°C. Chop the bread into small pieces and place in a Ziploc bag. Beat the eggs along with the remaining ingredients in a large bowl until smooth. Pour the egg mixture over the bread and let soak for 15 minutes. Distribute the mixture between 8 canning jars. Seal and immerse the jars in the water bath. Cook for 2 hours. Remove the jars and refrigerate for 2 hours.

546. LEMONY MUFFINS

Cal.: 303 | Fat: 21g | Protein: 6g   8 min | 3 hours 45 min | Servings 6

INGREDIENTS

- 2 eggs
- 1 cup flour
- 4 tbsp. sugar
- 1 tbsp. lemon juice
- 1 tbsp. lemon zest
- 1/3 cup heavy cream
- 2 eggs
- 1 tsp. baking soda
- ½ cup butter

DIRECTIONS

Beat the eggs and sugar until creamy. Gradually beat in the remaining ingredients. Divide the batter between 6 mason jars. Preheat the water to 190°F/88°C. Seal the jars and immerse them in the water. Cook for 3 ½ hours. Let cool before serving.

547. LIGHT COTTAGE CHEESE BREAKFAST PUDDING

Cal.: 426 | Fat: 24.6g | Protein: 27g   12 min | 3 hours 15 min | Servings 3

INGREDIENTS

- 1 cup Cottage Cheese
- 5 Eggs
- 1 cup Milk
- 3 tbsp. Sour Cream
- 4 tbsp. Sugar
- 1 tsp. Cardamom
- 1 tsp. Orange Zest
- 1 tbsp. Cornstarch
- ¼ tsp. Salt

DIRECTIONS

With an electric mixer, beat the eggs and sugar. Beat in the zest, milk and cornstarch. Add the remaining ingredients and beat on medium for 5 minutes. Grease 3 mason jars with cooking spray and divide the mixture between them. Seal. Preheat the Sous Vide machine to 175°F/79°C and place the jars inside. Cook for 3 hours. Let cool before serving.

548. CITRUS CURD

Cal.: 341 | Fat: 30g | Protein: 4g   12 min | 1 hour 35 min | Servings 8

INGREDIENTS
- 1 cup butter, melted
- 1 cup sugar
- 12 egg yolks
- 2 lemons
- 3 oranges
- ¼ tsp. salt

DIRECTIONS
Preheat the Sous Vide machine to 180°F/82°C. Grate the zest from the lemons and oranges and place in a bowl. Squeeze the juice and add to the bowl as well. Whisk the yolks, sugar, butter and salt. Transfer to a Ziploc bag. Seal the bag and immerse in the preheated water. Cook for 1 hour. Once the timer has stopped, remove and unseal the bag. Transfer the cooked citrus curd to a bowl, cover with a plastic wrap and place in an ice bath. Let chill thoroughly before serving.

549. RASPBERRY MOUSSE

Cal.: 216 | Fat: 13g | Protein: 5g   13 min | 75 min | Servings 6

INGREDIENTS
- 1 cup raspberries
- 1 cup milk
- 1 cup cream cheese
- 2 tbsp. cornstarch
- ½ cup sugar
- 1 tbsp. flour
- 1 tsp. ground ginger
- 1 tbsp. cocoa powder

DIRECTIONS
Preheat the Sous Vide machine to 170°F/76°C. Place all of the ingredients in a blender. Blend until smooth and pale. Divide between 6 small jars. Seal the jars and immerse in the water. Cook for 1 hour. Serve chilled.

550. CHOCOLATE CUPCAKES

Cal.: 211 | Fat: 11g | Protein: 4g   9 min | 3 hour 10 min | Servings 6

INGREDIENTS
- 5 tbsp. butter, melted
- 1 egg
- 3 tbsp. cocoa powder
- 1 cup flour
- 4 tbsp. sugar
- ½ cup heavy cream
- 1 tsp. baking soda
- 1 tsp. vanilla extract
- 1 tsp. apple cider vinegar
- Pinch of sea salt

DIRECTIONS
Whisk together the wet ingredients in one bowl. Combine the dry ingredients in another bowl. Combine the two mixtures gently. Divide the batter between 6 small jars. Preheat the Sous Vide machine to 194°F/90°C. Seal the jars and place in the water. Cook for 3 hours.

551. RAISIN-STUFFED SWEET APPLES

Cal.: 325 | Fat: 19g | Protein: 2.8g   ⬎ 12 min | 🍲 2 hours 15 min | ✗ Servings 4

INGREDIENTS
- 4 small apples, cored
- 1 ½ tbsp. raisins
- 4 tbsp. butter, softened
- ¼ tsp. nutmeg
- ½ tsp. cinnamon
- 1 tbsp. sugar

DIRECTIONS
Preheat the Sous Vide machine to 170°F/76°C. Combine the raisins, sugar, butter, cinnamon and nutmeg.Stuff the apples with the raisin mixture. Divide the apples between 2 Ziploc bags. Seal the bags and immerse them in the water. Cook for 2 hours.

552. APPLE COBBLER

Cal.: 170 | Fat: 2g | Protein: 2.4g   ⬎ 9 min | 🍲 3 hours 40 min | ✗ Servings 6

INGREDIENTS
- 1 cup milk
- 2 green apples, cubed
- 1 tsp. butter
- 7 tbsp. flour
- 4 tbsp. brown sugar
- 1 tsp. ground Cardamom

DIRECTIONS
Preheat the Sous Vide machine to 190°F/88°C. Whisk together the butter, sugar, milk and cardamom. Stir in the flour gradually. Fold in the apples. Divide the mixture between 6 small jars. Seal the jars and place them in the water bath. Cook for 3 ½ hours.

553. MINI STRAWBERRY CHEESECAKE JARS

Cal.: 308 | Fat: 19g | Protein: 15g   ⬎ 8 min | 🍲 90 min | ✗ Servings 4

INGREDIENTS
- 4 eggs
- 2 tbsp. milk
- 3 tbsp. strawberry jam
- ½ cup sugar
- ½ cup cream cheese
- ½ cup cottage cheese
- 1 tbsp. flour
- 1 tsp. lemon zest

DIRECTIONS
Preheat the Sous Vide machine to 180°F/82°C. Beat together the cheeses and sugar until fluffy. Beat in the eggs, one by one. Add the remaining ingredients and beat until well combined. Divide between 4 jars. Seal and place in the water. Cook for 75 minutes. Chill and serve.

554. MINI CHEESECAKES

Cal.: 380 | Fat: 19g | Protein: 16g   ⬎ 7 min | 1 hour 40 min | ✗ Servings 3

INGREDIENTS
- 3 eggs
- 5 tbsp. cottage cheese
- ½ cup cream cheese
- 4 tbsp. sugar
- ½ tsp. vanilla extract

DIRECTIONS
Place all of the ingredients in a mixing bowl. Beat with an electric mixer for a few minutes, until soft and smooth. Divide the mixture between 3 mason jars. Seal. Preheat the Sous Vide machine to 175°F/79°C. Immerse the jars inside the bath. Cook for 90 minutes. Chill until ready to serve.

555. COFFEE BUTTERY BREAD

Cal.: 410 | Fat: 35g | Protein: 5g    11 min | 3 hours 10 min | Servings 4

INGREDIENTS
- 6 ounces white bread
- ¾ cup butter
- 6 tbsp. coffee
- ½ tsp. cinnamon
- 1 tsp. brown sugar

DIRECTIONS
Slice the bread into strips and place in a Ziploc bag. Whisk the other ingredients in a bowl and pour the mixture over the bread. Get rid of the excess air and seal the bag. Preheat the Sous Vide machine to 195°F/91°C. Place the bag inside. Cook for 3 hours.

556. CARROT MUFFINS

Cal.: 173 | Fat: 12g | Protein: 4g   11 min | 3 hour 20 min | Servings 10

INGREDIENTS
- 1 cup Flour
- 3 Eggs
- ½ cup Butter
- ¼ cup Heavy Cream
- 2 Carrots, grated
- 1 tsp. Lemon Juice
- 1 tbsp. Coconut Flour
- ¼ tsp. Salt
- ½ tsp. Baking Soda

DIRECTIONS
Whisk the wet ingredients in one bowl and combine the dry ones in another. Gently combine the 2 mixtures together. Preheat the Sous Vide machine to 195°F/91°C. Divide the mixture between 5 mason jars (do not fill more than halfway. Use more jars if needed). Seal and immerse in the water. Cook for 3 hours. Cut into halves and serve.

557. UNBELIEVABLE FLOURLESS CHOCOLATE CAKE

Cal.: 375 | Fat: 29.3g | Protein: 4.4g   11 min | 7 hour 15 min | Servings 10

INGREDIENTS
- 4 large eggs, cold
- ½ lb. semisweet chocolate chips
- 4 ounces butter
- 6 (4 ounces) mason jars
- Powdered sugar, for dusting cakes

DIRECTIONS
Preheat the Sous Vide machine to 115°F/46°C. Place chocolate and butter in a resealable freezer bag and place in the water bath for 15 minutes to melt chocolate; massage the bag every 5 minutes to ensure the mixture is well blended.Remove the bag and set the machine to 170°F/76°C. Spray mason jars with non-stick spray or grease with butter. Beat the eggs with a standing mixer at high speed until the volume doubles. Turn the mixer to low, cut the corner off the freezer bag, and drizzle the melted chocolate mixture in slowly until the mixture is totally homogeneous. Scrape the batter into canning jars and smooth the surface by tapping the jar firmly but gently on a flat surface. Screw each lid on tight and add jars carefully to your water bath for 60 minutes. Cool jars on a wire rack to room temperature. Place jars in the refrigerator, cover with a kitchen towel, and leave to set for 6 hours. Garnish with powdered sugar to serve.

558. PUMPKIN PIE

Cal.: 183 | Fat: 22g | Protein: 9g   11 min | 8 hours | Servings 8

INGREDIENTS

- 1 cup dark brown sugar
- 2 cups of canned pumpkin
- 2/3 cups of heavy cream plus extra for serving
- 4 large eggs
- 2 tsp. ground ginger
- 2/3 cup whole milk
- 1 tsp. ground nutmeg
- 2 tsp. ground cinnamon
- ¼ tsp. ground cloves
- ½ tsp. salt
- 2 tbsp. granulated sugar
- 9 honey graham crackers, broken to medium pieces
- 5 tbsp. unsalted butter, melted and warm

DIRECTIONS

Preheat the Sous Vide machine to 176°F/80°C and the oven to 325°F/162°C. In a food processor, combine the eggs, brown sugar, and pumpkin. Blend for 1 minute or until the mixture becomes smooth. Transfer the mixture into a large bowl with a spout. Clean the blade and bowl of the food processor. Add the cloves, salt, nutmeg, cinnamon, ginger, milk, and cream into the bowl with the pumpkin mixture. Stir well until completely combined. Pour the mixture into a zip-lock freezer bag and seal using the water immersion method. Place the freezer bag into the water bath. Cook in the cooker for 90 minutes. Meanwhile, start making the crust by combining sugar and graham crackers in the food processor. Ground the graham crackers for 1 minute or until it turns into fine crumbs. Turn on the food processor and slowly pour the melted butter through the feed tube. Process for 20 seconds or until the texture becomes that of wet sand. Place the graham cracker mixture onto a 9-inch pie plate. Spread the mixture to evenly cover the bottom and sides of the pie plate. Using the bottom of a clean drinking glass, press the mixture to make a compact layer. Place the pie plate in the oven and bake for 15-18 minutes or until the crust is golden brown. Once done, place the pie plate on a wire rack to cool completely. Once the cooker timer goes off, remove the freezer bag from the water bath. Place the bag on a plate and let cool at room temperature for 15 minutes. Once cool, cut one corner and pipe the mixture into the cooled pie crust. Smooth the top using a spatula. Place the pie in the refrigerator and chill for at least 8 hours. To serve, let the pie cool down to room temperature before slicing. Serve with freshly whipped cream.

559. KEY LIME PIE

Cal.: 213 | Fat: 22g | Protein: 8g   7 min | 1 hour | Servings 6

INGREDIENTS

- ½ cup key lime juice
- 14 ounces of sweetened condensed milk
- A pinch of kosher salt
- 6 large egg yolks
- 3 cups of whipped cream
- 1 baked graham cracker crust
- 1 tbsp. key lime zest

DIRECTIONS

Preheat the Sous Vide machine to 180°F/82°C. In a blender, add in the salt, egg yolks, lime juice and condensed milk. Blend for 30 seconds or until frothy and smooth. Transfer the mixture into a Ziploc bag and seal using the water immersion method. Place the Ziploc bag into the water bath. Cook in the cooker for 30 minutes. While cooking, make sure to agitate the bag several times to prevent clumps from forming. Once done, remove the bag from the water bath and place on a bowl with water and ice. Once the mixture has cooled down, remove from the bag and pour into the crust. Top with whipped cream and garnish with lime zest. Place in the refrigerator to chill for at least 30 minutes then serve.

560. PECAN PIE

Cal.: 199 | Fat: 19g | Protein: 8g   9 min | 2 hours 25 min | ✕ Servings 8

INGREDIENTS

- 1 cup maple syrup
- 2 cups of whole pecans
- ½ cup heavy cream
- 1 cup light brown sugar
- 4 tbsp. unsalted butter
- 6 large egg yolks
- ½ tsp. salt
- Freshly whipped cream

DIRECTIONS

Preheat the Sous Vide machine to 195°F/91°C and preheat the oven to 350°F/176°C. Prepare 8 ½-pint jars and grease the insides with butter or spray with cooking spray. Place the pecan on a rimmed baking sheet and spread to make a single layer. Toast the pecans in the oven for 7–10 minutes. Once done, set aside until cool enough to handle. Roughly chop the pecans and set aside. In a medium saucepan, combine the molasses, heavy cream, sugar, and maple syrup. Set the saucepan over medium heat and stir the mixture until the sugar melts. Heat the mixture for 5 minutes while stirring continuously. Once done, remove the saucepan from the heat and let stand for 5 minutes. Once the sugar mixture has cooled down, whisk the salt and butter into the saucepan until completely melted. Add in the egg yolks and whisk together until smooth. Add in the pecans and stir until evenly combined. Divide the mixture evenly among the prepared jars, filling each jar halfway full. Clean the sides and tops of the jars using a damp towel. Cover the jars with the lids as tight as you can with just using your fingertips to let a little bit of pressure escape and prevent the jars from exploding while cooking. Place the jars in the water bath. Cook in the cooker for 2 hours. Once done, remove the jars from the water bath and set on a wire rack. Remove the lids carefully and let cool to room temperature. To serve, top each pecan pie with whipped cream.

561. FUDGY BROWNIES

Cal.: 173 | Fat: 22g | Protein: 6g   13 min |  3 hours 20 min | ✕ Servings 16

INGREDIENTS

- 3 ounces of bittersweet chocolate, chopped
- 1 stick of unsalted butter
- 2 large eggs
- ¾ cup plus 2 tablespoons of granulated sugar
- 2/3 cup all-purpose flour
- 1 tsp. vanilla extract
- ¼ tsp. salt

DIRECTIONS

Preheat the Sous Vide machine to 195°F/91°C. Prepare 4 ½-pint canning jars and grease the insides with butter or spray with cooking spray. Set a double boiler by placing a large bowl over a medium saucepan with 1 inch of water. Set over medium heat and bring the water to a simmer. Once the water is simmering, place the chocolate and butter into the bowl. Stir frequently to mix the melting butter and chocolate. Once completely melted, place the bowl on the counter and place a towel underneath. Add in the sugar and whisk until combined. Whisk in the eggs, one at a time, until the mixture is smooth. Add in the vanilla and whisk again. Add in the salt and flour and gently fold until just combined. Divide the batter equally among the prepared jars, filling each jar about halfway full. Clean the tops and sides of the jars using a damp towel. Tap the jars to remove the excess bubbles. Cover the jars with the lids and screw only as tight as you can with just using your fingertips. Place the jars into the water bath. Cook in the cooker for 3 hours. Once done, carefully remove the jars from the cooker and set on a cooling rack. Remove the lids to let the brownies cool. Once the brownies have completely cooled down, run a knife around the edges of the jars to un-mold. Divide each brownie into 4 horizontal slices to make individual servings. Serve immediately.

562. RASPBERRY CREAM TART

Cal.: 173 | Fat: 12g | Protein: 4g   ⟋ 11 min | 🍲 9 hours | ✖ Servings 4

INGREDIENTS
- ½ cup heavy cream
- 12 large egg yolks
- 5 tbsp. granulated sugar
- ½ cup whole milk
- 1/8 tsp. salt
- 1/8 tsp. vanilla extract
- ½ cup Nutella
- Pie dough
- Confectioner's sugar
- 1 pint of raspberries

DIRECTIONS
Preheat the Sous Vide machine to 176°F/80°C and set the oven to 350°F/176°C. Whisk the egg yolks and transfer to a large zip-lock freezer bag and seal using the water immersion method. Place the freezer bag into the cooker water bath and cook for 30 minutes. Meanwhile, prepare the tart shells by rolling out the pie dough until it measures 1/8-inch thick. Press the pie dough into 4 small tart pans. Line the tart pans with greased aluminum foil and put in pie weights. Cover and bake in the oven for 10 minutes. Once done, take off the pie weights and aluminum foil and resume baking for 5 more minutes or until the crust is firm and light brown in color. Set aside to cool. Once the egg yolks are finished cooking, remove the freezer bag from the water bath and transfer the egg yolks into a blender. Add in the salt, vanilla, sugar, milk and heavy cream and blend for 2–3 minutes or until smooth. Pour the mixture through a fine-mesh strainer set over a large bowl. Press the cream through the strainer using a spatula to remove any lumps. Pour the pastry cream into the tart shells. Place the tarts into the refrigerator and chill for at least 8 hours. Once the tarts are set, place the Nutella in a microwave-safe bowl. Place the bowl in the microwave and set on high. Heat the Nutella for 30 seconds. Pour the Nutella over the pastry cream. To serve, top with raspberries and a sprinkling of powdered sugar.

563. DOCE DE BANANA

Cal.: 273 | Fat: 32g | Protein: 18g   ⟋ 10 min | 🍲 45 min | ✖ Servings 4

INGREDIENTS
- 1 cup brown sugar
- 5 small bananas, peeled and cut to chunks
- 6 whole cloves
- 2 cinnamon sticks
- Whipped cream

DIRECTIONS
Preheat the Sous Vide machine to 176°F/80°C. Combine the cloves, cinnamon sticks, brown sugar and banana. Place the mixture into a Ziploc bag and seal using the water immersion method. Place the bag into the water bath. Cook in the cooker for 40 minutes. Once done, remove the bag from the water bath and set aside to cool slightly. Remove the cloves and cinnamon sticks and pour the remaining contents in a bowl. Top with whipped cream before serving.

564. BERRY COULIS

Cal.: 223 | Fat: 21g | Protein: 9g   ⟋ 12 min | 🍲 30 min | ✖ Servings 1

INGREDIENTS
- 1 cup fresh blueberries, stemmed and washed
- 1 cup ripe strawberries, stemmed and washed then quartered
- Juice of 1 lemon
- ½ cup granulated sugar

DIRECTIONS
Preheat the Sous Vide machine to 180°F/82°C. Combine the blueberries, strawberries, sugar and lemon juice in a bowl. Place the mixture in a Ziploc bag. Seal the bag using the water immersion method. Place the bag into the water bath and cook in the cooker for 30 minutes. Once done, remove the bag from the water bath and pour the contents into a blender. Purée the berries and chill. Serve over cakes or ice cream.

565. BLUEBERRY YOGURT PIE

Cal.: 273 | Fat: 32g | Protein: 14g   ✎ 12 min | 🍲 27 hours 30 min | 🍴 Servings 8

INGREDIENTS

- 3 tbsp. yogurt with live active cultures
- 4 ½ cups plus 3 tbsp. whole milk
- 8 tbsp. unsalted butter
- 10 ounces of gingersnap cookies
- 2 tsp. unflavored powdered gelatin
- 1 tsp. kosher salt
- 1 tsp. finely grated lemon zest
- ½ cup packed light brown sugar
- ¼ cup granulated sugar
- 3 cups of fresh blueberries
- 2 tbsp. minced fresh mint, plus extra for garnish
- ¼ cup freshly squeezed lemon juice

DIRECTIONS

Preheat the Sous Vide machine to 115°F/46°C. Set a medium saucepan of medium heat. Add in 4 cups of milk and heat to 180°F/82°C. Then, pour the heated milk into a large canning jar and cool to 100-120°F/37-49°C. Add the yogurt into the jar and stir. Seal the jar with a lid and place into the water bath. Cook in the cooker for 24 hours. Cover the water bath with cling wrap to prevent water evaporation. Add a little bit of water from time to time to keep the jar Immersed. Once done, remove the jar carefully from the water bath and place into a bowl filled with ice water to chill. Preheat the oven to 350°F/176°C. Place the salt, butter and gingersnaps in a food processor and pulse until finely ground. Transfer the mixture into a 9-inch pie plate and press the mixture into the bottom and sides to make an even layer of crust. Bake in the oven for 25 minutes or until set. Once done, set aside to cool completely. Whisk together the 3 tablespoons of milk and gelatin in a small bowl. Set aside for 10 minutes. Meanwhile, place the remaining ½ cup milk into a small saucepan set over medium heat. Bring the milk to a simmer then remove from the heat. Whisk in the gelatin mixture into the saucepan. Add in the yogurt, lemon zest and brown sugar. Whisk together until well-combined. Pour the mixture into the cooled pie crust and smooth the top. Place the pie in the refrigerator and chill for 2 hours. Place the lemon juice, granulated sugar and blueberries in a medium saucepan and mix until combined. Bring the mixture to boil then reduce the heat to low. Simmer until the mixture is reduced to half. Remove the saucepan from the heat and stir in the fresh mint. To serve, top the pie with the blueberry sauce and the extra mint leaves.

566. BANANA BREAD

Cal.: 243 | Fat: 9g | Protein: 6g   ✎ 31 min | 🍲 3 hours 30 min | 🍴 Servings 9

INGREDIENTS

- ½ cup butter
- ½ cup brown sugar
- ½ cup white sugar
- 2 eggs
- 1 teaspoon vanilla
- 1 teaspoon salt
- 3 tablespoons milk
- 3 very ripe mashed bananas
- ½ teaspoon baking soda
- 2 cups all-purpose flour

DIRECTIONS

Set up your immersion circulator to a temperature of 190°F/88°C. and prepare your water bath. Put the butter, white and brown sugar in a warm skillet and mix them well. Remove the heat and allow the mixture to cool, add the egg, vanilla, milk, and sugar. Stir well until the sugar has dissolved. Put the bananas, flour, baking soda, and salt and whisk them well. Transfer the mixture into 4-ounce mason jars and gently tighten the lid. Cook for 3 and a ½ hours underwater. Open the lid and enjoy!

567. BLUEBERRY MAPLE PIE

Cal.: 283 | Fat: 42g | Protein: 26g   ⬛ 9 min | 🍲 2 hours 30 min | ✕ Servings 8

INGREDIENTS

For the crust:
- 1/8 tsp. cinnamon
- 2 ¾ cups of all-purpose flour
- 1 tsp. salt
- 1 tbsp. maple sugar
- 4 tbsp. cold shortening
- ¼ tsp. baking powder
- 2 tsp. cider vinegar
- 12 tbsp. unsalted butter, cubed
- 6 tbsp. cold water

For the Filling:
- 1 Granny Smith apple
- 6 cups of blueberries
- 1/8 tsp. salt
- 2 tbsp. minute tapioca
- ½ cup sugar
- 1/8 tsp. cinnamon
- ¾ tsp. maple extract
- 1/3 cup maple syrup
- 1 egg yolk
- 1 tbsp. lemon juice
- 1 tbsp. heavy cream

DIRECTIONS

Preheat the Sous Vide machine to 150°F/65°C. Start making the dough by placing the baking powder, salt, maple sugar, cinnamon and flour into a food processor. Pulse to mix. Add in the shortening and process until evenly combined. Add the butter and pulse until combined. Add in the water and vinegar and pulse until the dough starts holding together. Make 2 discs of equal size using the mixture. Then, wrap in plastic and place in the refrigerator to chill overnight. To make the filling, place the blueberries into a Ziploc bag. Peel and remove the core of the apple and grate. Squeeze the grated apple to remove the liquid. Place the grated apple into the bag. Place the sugar, cinnamon, salt and tapioca in a food processor. Grind until the tapioca is fine in texture. Place the mixture into the bag. Combine the lemon juice, maple extract and maple syrup in a bowl and pour the mixture into the bag. Seal the bag using the water immersion method. Place the bag into the water bath. Cook in the cooker for 1 hour. Once done, remove the bag from the water bath and let cool for 5 minutes. Start assembling the pie by rolling out one of the dough disk on a flat and floured surface. Cut the dough into 4 large strips then place on a silicone mat and freeze. Roll out the second dough disk and place it on a 9-inch pie plate. Pour the blueberry filling into the crust. Place the 4 strips of dough over the pie and make a pattern by alternately placing one strip over another. Crimp the edges of the pie and trim if necessary. Place the pie in the freezer and chill. Preheat the oven to 425°F/218°C. Whisk together the heavy cream and egg yolk. Brush the mixture over the strips of dough. Reduce the oven temperature to 400°F/205°C and place the pie on the bottom rack. After 15 minutes, cover the pie with strips of foil and rotate. Bake for another 40 minutes. Allow the pie to cool slightly before serving.

568. POACHED PEARS

Cal.: 273 | Fat: 12g | Protein: 8g   ⬛ 11 min | 🍲 3 hour 30 min | ✕ Servings 4

INGREDIENTS
- 4 ounces of gorgonzola cheese, softened
- 2 firm and ripe pears, peeled and cored then halved
- ½ cup tawny port
- ½ cup dried cherries, chopped
- 1 tsp. pure vanilla extract
- 2 tsp. honey
- 4 sprigs of mint for garnish
- ½ cup toasted pecans, chopped then lightly toasted

DIRECTIONS

Preheat the Sous Vide machine to 165°F/74°C. Combine the dried cherries and cheese in a bowl. Take half of the mixture and use it to fill the cavity of each half of the pear. Set the remaining mixture aside. In another bowl, combine the vanilla, honey and port. Place ½ of a pear into each ramekin then divide the sauce equally among the ramekins. Place each ramekin in a Ziploc bag and seal using the water immersion method. Place the bags into the water bath and cook in the cooker for 3 ½ hours. Once finished, remove the ramekins from the bags. Make the remaining cherry mixture into balls. To serve, top each ramekin with the cherry cheese balls and pecans. Use the mint sprigs for garnish.

569. BUTTERMILK SAFFRON LEMON TART

Cal.: 188 | Fat: 10g | Protein: 29g   🥄 8 min | 🍲 5 hours | 🍴 Servings 6

INGREDIENTS

For the crust:

- 1 tbsp. sugar
- 1 ¼ cups of all-purpose flour
- ½ cup chilled unsalted butter, cut to pieces
- ½ tsp. kosher salt
- ¼ cup buttermilk

For the filling and servings:

- 6 large egg yolks
- 2 tbsp. all-purpose flour, plus extra
- 1 ¼ cups of buttermilk
- 3 large eggs
- 1 tbsp. finely grated lemon zest
- 1 ¼ cups of sugar
- ¼ tsp. kosher salt
- 1/3 cup fresh lemon juice
- 2 tbsp. unsalted butter, melted and slightly cooled
- A pinch of saffron threads
- Whipped cream

DIRECTIONS

Start making the dough by placing the salt, sugar and flour in a food processor. Pulse until combined. Add in the butter and pulse until the mixture resembles a coarse meal. Transfer the mixture into a bowl and pour in the buttermilk. Once a ragged dough starts to form, knead the mixture very lightly until there are no more dry spots. Set the oven to 325°F/162°C. Roll out the dough on a flat and floured surface. Place the dough into a 9-inch pie plate, crimp the edges and use a fork to perforate the bottom. Preheat the Sous Vide machine to 179°F/81°C. Cover the crust with aluminum foil and fill with pie weights. Bake in the oven for 20–25 minutes or until the crust is dry around the edges. Remove the pie weights and foil and bake for another 10–12 minutes. Meanwhile, make the filling by placing the saffron, salt, lemon juice, lemon zest, sugar, buttermilk, eggs and egg yolks in a blender. Blend until smooth. While mixing, add in the butter and 2 tablespoons of flour. Tap the blender jar on the counter to remove air bubbles from the mixture. Pour the mixture into a Ziploc bag and seal using the water immersion method. Place the bag into the water bath. Cook in the cooker for 30 minutes. Halfway through cooking, agitate the bag to mix the ingredients around. Once done, pour the custard into the pie crust and place in the refrigerator to chill for 4 hours. Whip 1 ½ cups of whipped cream with powdered sugar. Top each serving with the cream and garnish with lemon zest and mint leaf before serving.

570. APPLE CRANBERRY PIE

Cal.: 197 | Fat: 26g | Protein: 10g   🥄 9 min | 🍲 90 min | 🍴 Servings 18

INGREDIENTS

- 8 ounces of fresh cranberries
- 2lbs of Granny Smith apples, peeled and cored then diced to ¼-inch cubes
- 2 tbsp. cornstarch
- ¾ cup brown sugar
- 2 tbsp. butter
- 2 tsp. chai spice
- 1 pack of puff pastry
- 2 tsp. granulated sugar
- 2 tsp. whole milk

DIRECTIONS

Preheat the Sous Vide machine to 160°F/71°C. Combine the butter, chai spice, cornstarch, brown sugar, cranberries and apples and place the mixture in a zip-lock freezer bag. Seal using the water immersion method. Place the bag into the water bath. Cook in the cooker for 90 minutes. Once done, place the bag into a bowl with ice water. To assemble the pie, roll one sheet of puff pastry to fit a 9 x 13-inch pan. Place the pastry into the pan and pour in the filling. Roll out the second sheet of puff pastry and place over the filling. Crimp the edges to seal the pie. Brush the surface of the pastry with milk and sprinkle the granulated sugar on top. Cut slits on the surface for ventilation. Set the oven to 375°F/190°C and bake for 35 minutes or until the pastry puffs are golden brown. Let cool before slicing and serving.

571. HOMEMADE APPLE PIE

Cal.: 263 | Fat: 42g | Protein: 31g   🔪 12 min | 🍲 6 hours | 🍴 Servings 12

INGREDIENTS

- ¾ cup sugar, plus extra for sprinkling
- 5 lbs. of apples, peeled and cored then sliced to make ½-inch thick pieces
- ½ tsp. ground cinnamon
- 2 tbsp. cornstarch
- 1 egg white

For the dough:

- 2 tbsp. sugar
- 2 ½ cups of all-purpose flour
- 2 ½ sticks of unsalted butter, cut to make 1/-4 inch pats
- 1 tsp. kosher salt
- 6 tbsp. cold water

DIRECTIONS

To make the dough for the crust, combine the salt, sugar and 2/3 of the flour in a food processor. Pulse to combine. Add in the butter and pulse 25 times or until the dough starts to clump together and no dry flour remains. Add the remaining flour and pulse 5 times or until the dough is just broken up. Place the dough in a large bowl. Add in the water and fold the dough to form a ball. Divide the dough ball in half and roll each half to a 4-inch disk. Wrap each disk in plastic and refrigerate to chill for 2 hours. Place the oven rack to the middle position and place a rimmed baking sheet on top. Set the oven to 425°F/218°C. In a bowl, toss together the lemon zest, lemon juice, cinnamon, cornstarch, sugar and apple slices. Set aside for 10 minutes. Preheat the Sous Vide machine to 160°F/71°C. Place the apple mixture into a zip-lock freezer bag and seal using the water immersion method. Place the bag into the water bath. Cook in the cooker for 1 hour. Once done, transfer the contents into a Dutch oven and set over medium-high heat. Cook while stirring frequently for 10 minutes. Place the mixture into a baking sheet, not the one in the oven, and spread out to a single layer. Set aside for 1 hour to cool completely. When the apples are completely cool, take the dough disks from the refrigerator and roll one disk to make a 12-inch circle. Place the dough into a 9-inch pie plate and add in the apple filling. Roll the remaining dough disk to make another 12-inch circle and place on top of the pie to cover. Trim and crimp the edges of the crust. Using a sharp knife, cut 5 slits on top. Lightly beat the egg white and brush over the surface of the pie. Sprinkle the remaining sugar on top and place the pie plate on the baking sheet in the oven. Bake for 20 minutes then reduce the heat to 375°F/190°C. Bake for another 25 minutes. Once done, remove the pie plate from the oven and let cool for 4 hours before serving.

572. JUICY CANDIED POTATOES

Cal.: 320 | Fat: 5g | Protein: 3g   🔪 9 min | 🍲 2 hours | 🍴 Servings 4

INGREDIENTS

- 2 pounds' sweet potatoes, peeled up and cut into ¼ slices
- ½ cup unsalted butter
- ¼ cup maple syrup
- 2 oranges, juice, and zest
- 1 teaspoon kosher salt
- 1 cup chopped walnuts
- 1 cinnamon stick
- ¼ cup brown sugar

DIRECTIONS

Prepare your water bath by dipping the immersion circulator and increasing the temperature to 155°F/68°C. Take a heavy-duty zip bag and add ¼ cup butter and sweet potatoes. Seal using the immersion method and cook for 2 hours. Preheat your oven to 350°F/176°C. Remove the potatoes from the bag and pat dry. Arrange the potatoes evenly in a baking dish. Take a medium saucepan and bring ¼ cup butter, brown sugar, maple syrup, orange zest and juice, walnuts, salt and cinnamon stick to a boil. Remove from heat and pour over sweet potatoes; discard the cinnamon stick. Bake for 30 minutes and serve warm!

573. LEMON TART

Cal.: 273 | Fat: 12g | Protein: 4g 13 min |  6 hours | Servings 1

INGREDIENTS

For the crust:
- 2 tbsp. cold water
- 1 egg yolk
- 1 cup all-purpose flour
- 1 tsp. vanilla extract
- 1/3 cup sugar
- ¼ cup almond flour
- 1/8 tsp. baking powder
- ¼ tsp. salt
- ½ cup unsalted butter, cold and cubed

For the custard:
- 1 ½ cups of sugar
- 8 egg yolks, beaten
- 2 tbsp. lemon zest
- ½ cup freshly squeezed lemon juice
- 1 ¾ cups of unsalted butter, at room temperature and cubed

DIRECTIONS

To make the crust, set the oven to 375°F/190°C. Mix together the vanilla, cold water and egg yolk in a bowl. Add in the baking powder, salt, sugar, almond flour and all-purpose flour into the bowl and use an electric mixer to combine. While mixing, add in the butter cubes and continue to beat until smooth. Form the dough into a bowl and cover using a plastic wrap. Chill in the refrigerator for 30 minutes. Once done, roll out the dough to make a thin sheet then place in a tart pan. Poke holes at the bottom using a fork. Bake the tart shell in the oven for 12 minutes or until the crust starts to brown. Once done, set aside to cool completely. To make the custard, preheat the Sous Vide machine to 149°F/65°C. Place the egg yolks in a Ziploc bag and seal using the water immersion method. Place the bag into the water bath. Cook in the cooker for 35 minutes. In a medium saucepan, combine the lemon juice and sugar and boil for 3 minutes or until the sugar is completely dissolved. Remove the saucepan from the heat and set aside to cool. Once the eggs are done cooking, place the freezer bag into a bowl with ice and cold water. Then, pour the contents into a blender. While blending, gradually add in the lemon syrup. Add in the butter and lemon zest and blend until completely combined. Pour the mixture into the tart shell and refrigerate for at least 4 hours. Serve with a dollop of whipped cream.

574. FEISTY KIWI AND VANILLA

Cal.: 148 | Fat: 5g | Protein: 5g 8 min |  20 min | Servings 4

INGREDIENTS
- 2 kiwis, peeled and sliced
- 2 tablespoons granulated sugar
- 1 tablespoon fresh lemon, squeezed
- Fresh mint leaves

DIRECTIONS

Prepare your water bath by dipping the immersion circulator and increasing the temperature to 176°F/80°C. Take a medium bowl and add kiwi slices, sugar, lemon juice and stir. Transfer the mixture to a zip bag and seal using the immersion method. Cook for 20 minutes and remove the bag from the water. Divide the mixture between 2 serving plates. Scoop yogurt/vanilla ice cream onto the plate next to your kiwi and garnish with some mint leaves. Serve!

575. PEACH COBBLER

Cal.: 524 | Fat: 19g | Protein: 6g 15 min | 3 hours | Servings 6

INGREDIENTS
- 1 cup self-rising flour
- 1 cup granulated sugar
- 1 cup whole milk
- 1 teaspoon vanilla extract
- 8 tablespoons unsalted melted butter
- 2 cups roughly chopped peaches

DIRECTIONS

Set up your immersion circulator to a temperature of 195°F/91°C. and prepare your water bath. Prepare 6 half-pint canning jars by greasing the jars with melted butter. Mix the flour and sugar in a large bowl. Then mix in milk and vanilla. Stir in butter and peaches. Divide the batter between jars and wipe sides, seal gently. Immerse underwater and cook for 3 hours. Transfer the jars to a cooling rack, allow them to cool and serve!

576. CHOCOLATE CHIP COOKIES

Cal.: 199 | Fat: 22g | Protein: 9g   ✎ 9 min | 🍲 4 hours 30 min | ✗ Servings 24

INGREDIENTS

- 1 tsp. baking powder
- 1 cup all-purpose flour
- 6 tbsp. unsalted butter, at room temperature
- ¼ tsp. salt
- 1 large egg
- 2/3 cup packed dark brown sugar
- 1 cup chocolate chip cookies
- 2 tsp. vanilla extract

DIRECTIONS

Preheat the Sous Vide machine to 195°F/91°C. Prepare 5 ½-pint canning jars and grease the insides with butter or spray with cooking spray. Whisk together the salt, baking powder and flour in a medium bowl. Set aside. In another bowl, combine the sugar and butter. Using an electric mixer set on medium-high speed, beat the mixture for 3–5 minutes or until fluffy and light. Add in the egg and beat until combined. Then, add in the vanilla and beat again for 3 minutes or until the mixture is very fluffy and light. Add in the flour mixture into the bowl with the egg mixture and fold gently until just combined. Add in the chocolate chips and fold until evenly distributed. Divide the dough evenly between the greased jars. Grease your fingers and pat the dough to the bottom of the jars. Clean the tops and sides of the jars using a damp towel. Cover the jars with the lids and seal as tight as you can with just using your fingers to allow some air to escape. Place the jars into the water bath. Cook in the cooker for 3 hours. Once done, carefully remove the jars from the water bath. Set the jars on a wire rack. Remove the lids to let the cookies cool. Once the cookies are cool, carefully run a knife along the sides of the jars to unmold. Place the cookies on a plate and refrigerate to chill for 1 hour. To serve, take a sharp knife to slice each cookie to make ¼-inch thick pieces. Serve immediately.

577. DELICIOUS POACHED APPLE

Cal.: 160 | Fat: 3g | Protein: 1g   ✎ 10 min | 🍲 60 min | ✗ Servings 4

INGREDIENTS

- 3 gala apples, peeled
- 3 cups hard apple cider
- 1 cup granulated sugar
- 1 lemon, zest
- 1 vanilla bean, split
- 1 cinnamon ice cream
- Ice cream for serving

DIRECTIONS

Prepare your water bath by dipping the immersion circulator and increasing the temperature to 175°F/79°C. Add the listed ingredients to your zip bag and seal using the immersion method. Immerse underwater and cook for 1 hour. Remove the apples and transfer to a plate. Strain the liquid through a metal mesh into a saucepan. Bring it to a simmer over medium heat. Simmer for 10 minutes. Cut the apples in half lengthwise and scoop out the seed. Serve the apple with your desired ice cream topping.

578. BLUEBERRY AND LEMON COMPOTE

Cal.: 182 | Fat: 1g | Protein: 1g   ✎ 11 min | 🍲 60 min | ✗ Servings 4

INGREDIENTS

- ½ cup ultrafine sugar
- 1 tablespoon freshly squeezed lemon juice
- 1 tablespoon lemon zest
- 1 tablespoon cornstarch
- 1 pound blueberries

DIRECTIONS

Prepare your water bath by dipping the immersion circulator and increasing the temperature to 180°F/82°C. Take a medium-sized bowl and whisk in sugar, lemon zest, lemon juice and cornstarch. Mix well and add blueberries, toss to coat the berries. Transfer the whole to a zip bag and seal using the immersion method. Cook for 1 hour. Remove the bag and transfer to your serving dish. Enjoy!

579. STRAWBERRY MOUSSE

Cal.: 265 | Fat: 17g | Protein: 4g   ➘ 11 min | 🍲 46 min | ✖ Servings 4

INGREDIENTS
- 1 pound strawberries, stemmed and halved
- ¼ cup packed light brown sugar
- 3 tablespoons freshly squeezed lemon juice
- ½ teaspoon kosher salt
- ¼ teaspoon ground cinnamon
- 1 cup heavy cream
- 1 teaspoon vanilla extract
- 1 cup crème Fraîche

DIRECTIONS
Prepare your water bath by dipping the immersion circulator and increasing the temperature to 180°F/82°C. Add the strawberries, brown sugar, lemon juice, salt and cinnamon to a large-sized zip bag Seal using the immersion method and cook for 45 minutes. Remove the bag and transfer contents to a food processor. Purée for a few seconds until you have a smooth mixture. Take a large chilled mixing bowl and add heavy cream and vanilla; mix well until stiff peaks form. Fold in strawberry purée and crème Fraiche. Mix well and divide it among 8 serving bowls. Serve chilled!

580. CINNAMON APPLES

Cal.: 250 | Fat: 12g | Protein: 1g   ➘ 11 min | 🍲 70 min | ✖ Servings 4

INGREDIENTS
- 4 red apples, cored, peeled and sliced
- 4 tbsp. butter
- 2 tsp. ground cinnamon
- 2 tsp. liquid honey
- Juice of 1 lemon

DIRECTIONS
Preheat the Sous Vide machine to 180°F/82°C. Put the ingredients into the plastic bag, and seal it, removing the air. Put the bag into the chamber and set the cooking time for 1 hour 10 minutes. Serve warm in bowls with a spoon of vanilla ice cream (optionally).

581. LEMON CURD

Cal.: 66 | Fat: 4g | Protein: 1g   ➘ 11 min | 🍲 70 min | ✖ Servings 4

INGREDIENTS
- ½ cup white sugar
- 1/4 cup lemon juice
- 1 tbsp. lemon zest
- 4 tbsp. unsalted butter
- 1 ½ tbsp. gelatin
- 3 fresh eggs
- 1 tsp. cinnamon for sprinkling

DIRECTIONS
Preheat the Sous Vide machine to 165°F/74°C. Put the ingredients into the plastic bag; and seal it, removing the air. Set the timer for 1 hour. When the time is up, blend the mixture with an immersion blender. Wait until it cools down and refrigerate in portions. Serve sprinkled with cinnamon.

582. ALMOND VANILLA PUDDING

Cal.: 159 | Fat: 4g | Protein: 4g   ➘ 11 min | 🍲 70 min | ✖ Servings 4

INGREDIENTS
- 1/4 cup white sugar
- 1/4 cup vanilla sugar
- 1/4 cup almond milk
- 4 tbsp. unsalted butter
- 1 ½ tbsp. gelatin
- 3 fresh eggs
- 1 tsp. cinnamon for sprinkling

DIRECTIONS
Preheat the Sous Vide machine to 165°F/74°C. Put the ingredients into the plastic bag, and seal it, removing the air. Set the timer for 1 hour. When the time is up, blend the mixture with an immersion blender. Wait until it cools down and refrigerate in portions.

583. PEAR AND LINGBERRY PIE

Cal.: 272 | Fat: 16g | Protein: 3g   📐 11 min | 🍲 2 hours 20 min | 🍴 Servings 4

INGREDIENTS
- 2 pounds sweet pears, cored, peeled and sliced
- ½ pound lingberries
- 3/4 cup sugar
- 2 tbsp. cornstarch
- 2 tbsp. butter
- 1 pack puff pastry
- 2 tbsp. milk
- 2 tbsp. sugar

DIRECTIONS
Preheat the Sous Vide machine to 160°F/71°C. Put sliced pears, lingberries, cornstarch, sugar and butter in the vacuum bag and set the cooking time for 1 hour 30 minutes. When the time is up, cool down the filling to the room temperature. In the meantime, preheat the oven to 375°F/190°C, grease a baking pan, and roll out 1 sheet of the pastry. Pour the filling over the sheet, and cover it with another sheet, seal the sheets on the edges with your fingers. Bake in the preheated oven for 35 minutes.

585. APPLE AND CINNAMON PIE

Cal.: 272 | Fat: 16g | Protein: 3g   📐 11 min | 🍲 2 hours 20 min | 🍴 Servings 4

INGREDIENTS
- 2 pounds green, cored, peeled and sliced
- 3/4 cup sugar
- 2 tbsp. cornstarch
- 2 tbsp. butter
- 2 tsp. ground cinnamon
- 1 pack puff pastry
- 2 tbsp. milk
- 2 tbsp. sugar

DIRECTIONS
Preheat the Sous Vide machine to 160°F/71°C. Put the sliced apples, cornstarch, sugar, cinnamon and butter in the vacuum bag and set the cooking time for 1 hour 30 minutes. When the time is up, cool down the filling to the room temperature. In the meantime, preheat the oven to 375°F/190°C, grease a baking pan, and roll out 1 sheet of the pastry. Pour the filling over the sheet, and cover it with another sheet, seal the sheets on the edges with your fingers. Bake in the preheated oven for 35 minutes.

584. SPICY CUSTARD CRÈME

Cal.: 60 | Fat: 3g | Protein: 0.7g    11 min | 🍲 90 min | 🍴 Servings 3

INGREDIENTS
- 2 cups heavy cream
- 1 cup milk
- 3 tsp. ginger root, sliced
- 4 fresh egg yolks
- ½ cup brown sugar
- A pinch of salt

DIRECTIONS
Before preheating the water bath, arrange the ramekins: install the rack half-inch below the water surface. Place 4 ramekins on the rack. Make sure the water level is not higher than 2/3 of the ramekins. Remove the ramekins and set aside. Preheat the Sous Vide machine to 179°F/82°C. Combine the heavy cream, milk and sliced ginger in a small saucepan and heat the mixture but do not bring it to boil. Cover the pan and set aside for 30 minutes. In 30 minutes, strain the liquid, return it to the pan, and reheat again. Whisk the egg yolks with salt and sugar, and carefully pour the cream mixture into the yolk mixture. Whisk well until even. Pour the custards into the 4 ramekins, wrap them with plastic and return back on the rack. Set the timer for 45 minutes. If the custards do not look set, cook for an additional 15 minutes. When the time is up, cool the ramekins to the room temperature then refrigerate until cold and serve.

586. APRICOT AND CRANBERRY PIE

Cal.: 272 | Fat: 16g | Protein: 3g   📐 11 min | 🍲 2 hours 20 min | 🍴 Servings 4

INGREDIENTS
- 2 pounds ripe apricots, bone removed, halved
- ½ pound cranberries
- 3/4 cup sugar
- 2 tbsp. cornstarch
- 2 tbsp. butter
- 2 tsp. ground cinnamon
- 1 pack puff pastry
- 2 tbsp. milk
- 2 tbsp. sugar

DIRECTIONS
Preheat the water bath to 160°F/71°C. Put the apricots, cornstarch, cranberries, sugar, cinnamon and butter in the vacuum bag and set the cooking time for 1 hour 30 minutes. When the time is up, cool down the filling to the room temperature. In the meantime, preheat the oven to 375°F/190°C, grease a baking pan, and roll out 1 sheet of the pastry. Pour the filling over the sheet, and cover it with another sheet, seal the sheets on the edges with your fingers. Bake in the preheated oven for 35 minutes.

587. ORANGE YOGURT

Cal.: 120 | Fat: 3g | Protein: 12g   📐 11 min | 🍲 4 hours | 🍴 Servings 4

INGREDIENTS
- 4 cups milk
- ½ cup Greek yogurt
- 1 tbsp. orange zest
- ½ tbsp. lemon zest

DIRECTIONS
Pour the milk into a pan and heat it to 180°F/82°C. Cool it down to the room temperature. Preheat the water bath to 113°F/45°C. Mix in the yogurt, add the orange and lemon zest and pour the mixture into canning jars. Cover the jars with the lids and cook in the water bath for 3 hours. When the time is up, cool down the jars to the room temperature and then refrigerate before serving.

588. RASPBERRY AND HONEY YOGURT

Cal.: 140 | Fat: 3g | Protein: 12g   📐 11 min | 🍲 4 hours | 🍴 Servings 4

INGREDIENTS
- 4 cups milk
- ½ cup Greek yogurt
- ½ cup fresh raspberries
- 2 tbsp. honey

DIRECTIONS
Pour the milk into a pan and heat it to 180°F/82°C. Cool it down to the room temperature. Preheat the water bath to 113°F/45°C. Mix in the yogurt, add the raspberries, honey and pour the mixture into canning jars. Cover the jars with the lids and cook in the water bath for 3 hours. When the time is up, cool down the jars to the room temperature and then refrigerate before serving.

589. APPLE YOGURT WITH RAISINS

Cal.: 120 | Fat: 3g | Protein: 12g   📐 11 min | 🍲 4 hours | 🍴 Servings 4

INGREDIENTS
- 4 cups milk
- ½ cup Greek yogurt
- ½ cup sweet apples, peeled, cored and chopped into small pieces
- 1 tsp. cinnamon
- 4 tsp. small raisins
- 2 tbsp. honey

DIRECTIONS
Pour the milk into a pan and heat it to 180°F/82°C. Cool it down to the room temperature. Preheat the water bath to 113°F/45°C. Mix in the yogurt, add the apples, cinnamon, honey, raisins and pour the mixture into canning jars. Cover the jars with the lids and cook in the water bath for 3 hours. When the time is up, cool down the jars to the room temperature and then refrigerate before serving.

590. WHITE CHOCOLATE MOUSSE

Cal.: 218 | Fat: 15g | Protein: 4g　　　　　⟋ 11 min | 🍲 31 hours | 🍴 Servings 4

INGREDIENTS

- 2/3 cup white chocolate, chopped
- ½ cup milk
- ½ cup double cream
- ½ tsp. gelatin powder
- 2 tbsp. cold water

DIRECTIONS

Preheat the Sous Vide machine to 194°F/90°C. Place the chopped white chocolate in the vacuum bag. Seal the bag, put it into the water bath and set the timer for 6 hours. When the time is up, pour the chocolate into a bowl and stir with a spoon. Pour the milk into a pan and warm it over medium heat. Soak the gelatin powder in 2 tbsp. cold water and dissolve it in the warm milk. Carefully stir the milk-gelatin mixture into the chocolate paste until even and refrigerate for 25 minutes. Remove from the fridge, stir again and refrigerate for another 25 minutes. Beat the cream to peaks and combine with a white chocolate mixture. Pour into single serve cups and refrigerate for 24 hours before serving.

591. DARK CHOCOLATE MOUSSE

Cal.: 218 | Fat: 15g | Protein: 4g　　　　　⟋ 11 min | 🍲 31 hours | 🍴 Servings 4

INGREDIENTS

- 2/3 cup dark chocolate, chopped
- ½ cup milk
- ½ cup double cream
- ½ tsp. gelatin powder
- 2 tbsp. cold water

DIRECTIONS

Preheat the Sous Vide machine to 194°F/90°C. Place the chopped dark chocolate in the vacuum bag. Seal the bag, put it into the water bath and set the timer for 6 hours. When the time is up, pour the chocolate into a bowl and stir with a spoon. Pour the milk into a pan and warm it over medium heat. Soak the gelatin powder in 2 tbsp. cold water and dissolve it in the warm milk. Carefully stir the milk-gelatin mixture into the chocolate paste until even and refrigerate for 25 minutes. Remove from the fridge, stir again and refrigerate for another 25 minutes. Beat the cream to peaks and combine with white chocolate mixture. Pour into single serve cups and refrigerate for 24 hours before serving.

592. TANGERINE ICE CREAM

Cal.: 144 | Fat: 8g | Protein: 3g　　　　　⟋ 11 min | 🍲 24 hours 30 min | 🍴 Servings 6

INGREDIENTS

- 1 cup mandarin (only juice and pulp)
- 2 cups heavy cream
- 6 fresh egg yolks
- ½ cup milk
- ½ cup white sugar
- 1/4 cup sweet condensed milk
- A pinch of salt

DIRECTIONS

Preheat the Sous Vide machine to 185°F/85°C. In a big bowl, combine all ingredients and whisk well until even. Carefully pour the mixture into the vacuum bag and seal it. Cook for 30 minutes in the water bath. When the time is up, quick chill the vacuum bag without opening it. To do this, put it into a big bowl or container, filled with ice and water. Refrigerate the vacuum bag with ice-cream for 24 hours. Carefully transfer the mixture to an ice-cream machine and cook according to the instructions.

593. CITRUS CONFIT

Cal.: 90 | Fat: 2g | Protein: 1g   11 min | 60 min | Servings 15

INGREDIENTS
- 2 lemons, sliced and cut into quarters
- 1 orange, sliced and cut into quarters
- 1 lime, sliced and cut into quarters
- ½ cup sugar
- ½ cup salt

DIRECTIONS
Preheat the Sous Vide machine to 185°F/85°C. In a big bowl, combine all ingredients and mix well, making sure that fruits are evenly covered with salt and sugar. Carefully put the mixture into the vacuum bag and seal it. Cook for 1 hour in the water bath. This confit is very rich in vitamins and can be stored in the fridge for at least 1 month.

594. RASPBERRY COMPOTE

Cal.: 106 | Fat: 1g | Protein: 2g   11 min | 60 min | Servings 4

INGREDIENTS
- 1 cups raspberries
- 1 lemon zest
- 1 orange zest
- 1 tbsp. white sugar

DIRECTIONS
Preheat the Sous Vide machine to 185°F/85°C. Put the ingredients into the vacuum bag and seal it. Cook for 1 hour in the water bath. Serve over ice cream or cake.

595. STRAWBERRY JAM

Cal.: 50 | Fat: 0.3g | Protein: 0.1g   11 min | 90 min | Servings 10

INGREDIENTS
- 2 cups strawberries, coarsely chopped
- 1 cup white sugar
- 2 tbsp. orange juice

DIRECTIONS
Preheat the Sous Vide machine to 180°F/82°C. Put the ingredients into the vacuum bag and seal it. Cook for 1 hour 30 min in the water bath. Serve over ice cream or cheese cake, or store in the fridge in an airtight container.

596. PEACH AND ORANGE JAM

Cal.: 50 | Fat: 0.1g | Protein: 0.5g   11 min | 2 hours | Servings 10

INGREDIENTS
- 2 cups peaches, coarsely chopped
- 1 ½ cup white sugar
- 1 cup water
- Zest and juice of 1 orange

DIRECTIONS
Preheat the Sous Vide machine to 190°F/88°C. Put the ingredients into the vacuum bag and seal it. Cook for 2 hours in the water bath. Serve over ice cream or cake, or store in the fridge in an airtight container.

597. BLUEBERRY JAM

Cal.: 50 | Fat: 0.2g | Protein: 0.6g   11 min | 2 hours | Servings 10

INGREDIENTS
- 2 cups blueberries
- 1 cup white sugar
- 2 tbsp. lemon juice

DIRECTIONS
Preheat the water bath to 180°F/82°C. Put the ingredients into the vacuum bag and seal it. Cook for 1 hour 30 min in the water bath. Serve over ice cream or cake, or store in the fridge in an airtight container.

598. STAR-ANISE PEARS

Cal.: 35 | Fat: 0.6g | Protein: 0.1g   11 min | 20 min | Servings 6

INGREDIENTS

- 3 ripe pears, peeled, halved and cored
- 1/5 cup water
- 1/5 cup sugar
- 1 vanilla pod, seeds removed
- 1 anise star

DIRECTIONS

Preheat the Sous Vide machine to 185°F/85°C. In a small saucepan, combine water and sugar, heat the mixture to dissolve the sugar and make the syrup. Bring the syrup to boil and then cool it down. Carefully pour the syrup into the vacuum bag, add the pear halves, vanilla pod and anise star, and cook in the preheated water bath for 20 minutes. When the time is up, remove the vanilla pod and anise star and serve the pears.

599. POACHED SUGAR PLUMS

Cal.: 35 | Fat: 8g | Protein: 2g 11 min | 30 min | Servings 4

INGREDIENTS

- 8 ripe plums, halved, stone removed
- 1/5 cup sugar
- 1 tsp. ground cinnamon

DIRECTIONS

Preheat the Sous Vide machine to 158°F/69°C. In a small bowl, mix the sugar with the cinnamon. Carefully put the halved plums into the vacuum bag, sprinkle them with the sugar-cinnamon mixture, and cook in the preheated water bath for 20 minutes. Serve the plums with vanilla ice-cream.

600. VANILLA PUDDING

Cal.: 148 | Fat: 5g | Protein: 5g 15 min | 47 min | Servings 6

INGREDIENTS

- 1 cup whole milk
- 1 cup heavy cream
- ½ cup ultrafine sugar
- 3 large eggs (2 additional egg yolks)
- 3 tablespoons cornstarch
- 1 tablespoon vanilla extract
- A pinch of kosher salt
- Strawberries for garnishing

DIRECTIONS

Prepare the water bath using your immersion circulator and raise the temperature to 180°F/82°C. Then, take a blender and add all the listed ingredients except the garnishing, purée for 30–40 seconds until you have a frothy texture. Place the mixture to a resealable zip bag and seal it using the immersion method. Immerse underwater and let it cook for 45 minutes. Shake the bag about halfway through to prevent the formation of clumps. Once done, remove the bag, and transfer it to the blender once again. Purée again until it gets smooth. Then, transfer it to a bowl and allow it to chill. Serve with a garnish of strawberries or your favorite topping.

601. BUTTER AND SEA SALT RADISH

Cal.: 302 | Fat: 12g | Protein: 9g   16 min | 45 min | Servings 4

INGREDIENTS

- 1 lb. halved radishes
- 3 tablespoons unsalted butter
- 1 teaspoon sea salt
- ½ teaspoon freshly ground black pepper

DIRECTIONS

Prepare your water bath using your immersion circulator and raise the temperature to 180°F/82°C. Take a medium-sized resealable bag and add all the listed ingredients to the bag. Seal it using the immersion method and let it cook underwater for about 45 minutes. Once cooked, remove the bag and transfer the contents to a platter. Serve!

602. LEMON AND BLUEBERRY CRÈME BRULÉE

Cal.: 298 | Fat: 10g | Protein: 11g 9 min | 45 min | Servings 6

INGREDIENTS

- 6 large egg yolks
- 1 1/3 cup superfine sugar
- 3 cups heavy whipping cream
- Zest of 2 lemons
- 4 tablespoons freshly squeezed lemon juice
- 1 teaspoon vanilla extract
- 1 cup fresh blueberries

DIRECTIONS

Set up your immersion circulator to a temperature of 195°F/91°C. and prepare your water bath. Take an electric mixer and mix in egg yolks and sugar until you have a creamy mixture. Set it aside. Take a medium-sized saucepan and place it over medium heat, add the cream and heat it. Add the lemon zest, juice, vanilla and simmer for 4–5 minutes over low heat. Remove the cream mixture from heat and allow it to cool. Once cooled, transfer a small amount into the egg mixture and mix well. Add in the remaining cream mixture to the egg and stir. Divide the blueberries among six mini mason jars and pour the egg-cream mixture evenly over the six jars filled with blueberries. Tightly seal the lid and Immerse underwater, cook for 45 minutes. Remove the jars from the water and chill for 5 hours. Caramelize a layer of sugar on top using a blowtorch and serve!

603. BANANA AND PEANUT BUTTER FROZEN BITES

Cal.: 296 | Fat: 18g | Protein: 7g 9 min | 30 min | Servings 6

INGREDIENTS

- 3 bananas
- 3 tablespoons peanut butter
- 3 tablespoons dark chocolate chips

DIRECTIONS

Set up your immersion circulator to a temperature of 140°F/60°C. and prepare your water bath. Slice the bananas into ½-inch slices and add to a resealable bag. Add the peanut butter and dark chocolate chips and seal using the immersion method. Immerse underwater and let it cook for 30 minutes. Stir the contents and chill in popsicle molds. Pop out of the molds and serve!

604. PUMPKIN PIE JARS

Cal.: 269 | Fat: 17g | Protein: 5g 11 min | 60 min | Servings 6

INGREDIENTS

- 1 large can pumpkin pie filling
- 1 egg + 3 egg yolks
- 2 tablespoons flour
- ½ teaspoon kosher salt
- 1 tablespoon pumpkin pie spice
- 1 can evaporated milk
- ½ cup white sugar
- ½ cup brown sugar
- Whipped cream and candied nuts for garnishing

DIRECTIONS

Set up your immersion circulator to a temperature of 175°F/79°C. and prepare your water bath. Add 1 large can of pumpkin pie filling, 2 tablespoons of flour, ½ teaspoon of kosher salt, 1 tablespoon of pumpkin pie spice, 1 egg and 3 egg yolks alongside 1 can of evaporated milk. Whisk them well. Pour the mixture into 6 4-ounce jars and seal them tightly. Immerse underwater and cook for 1 hour. Once done, remove the jars and chill for 8 hours. Garnish with whipped cream and candied nuts. Serve!

605. PUMPKIN CRÈME BRÛLÉE

Cal.: 148 | Fat: 5g | Protein: 5g   ⬒ 11 min | 🍲 60 min | 🍴 Servings 5

INGREDIENTS

- 1 cup milk
- 1 cup heavy whipping cream
- 3 whole eggs
- 3 egg yolks
- ½ cup pumpkin purée
- ¼ cup maple syrup
- ½ teaspoon pumpkin spice
- A pinch of kosher salt
- Granulated sugar

DIRECTIONS

Set up your immersion circulator to a temperature of 167°F/75°C. and prepare your water bath. Take a large bowl and add the milk, heavy cream, 3 whole eggs, 3 egg yolks, and ½ cup pumpkin purée, ¼ cup of maple syrup, ½ teaspoon of pumpkin spice and a pinch of kosher salt. Whisk them well and keep whisking until it is combined and smooth. Pour the mixture into 6 4-ounce mason jars. Place the lid loosely and cook for 1 hour underwater. Allow them to chill. Spread a thin layer of sugar on top of the custard and caramelize with a blowtorch. Serve!

606. AMARETTO CRÈME BRÛLÉE

Cal.: 457 | Fat: 31g | Protein: 6g   ⬒ 11 min | 🍲 60 min | 🍴 Servings 12

INGREDIENTS

- 12 egg yolks
- ¾ cup sugar
- ½ teaspoon salt
- 2 ounces Amaretto
- 1-quart heavy cream

DIRECTIONS

Set up your immersion circulator to a temperature of 181°F/82°C. and prepare your water bath. Add the salt, and egg yolks to a bowl and mix them well. Add the Amaretto liqueur to the egg mixture and combine them well. Add in the heavy cream and whisk. Then, strain the whole mixture into a bowl through a metal mesh strainer. Allow the mixture to rest. Then fill up the 4-ounce mason jars, making sure that there is ½ inch space at the top. Gently tighten the lid and Immerse underwater. Cook for 1 hour. Chill in your fridge for 2 hours and sprinkle sugar on top. Broil or caramelize the sugar using a blowtorch and serve!

607. CHEESECAKE

Cal.: 615 | Fat: 41g | Protein: 8g   ⬒ 11 min | 🍲 90 min | 🍴 Servings 6

INGREDIENTS

- 12 oz. cream cheese at room temperature
- ½ cup sugar
- ¼ cup creole cream cheese
- 2 eggs
- Zest of 1 lemon
- ½ tablespoon vanilla extract

DIRECTIONS

Set up your immersion circulator to a temperature of 176°F/80°C. and prepare your water bath. Take a bowl and add both cream cheeses and sugar, and whisk them well. Gradually add the eggs one by one and keep beating until well combined. Add the zest and vanilla and mix well. Pour the cheesecake mixture into 6 different jars of 6 ounces and distribute evenly. Seal the jars with a lid. Place the jars underwater and let them cook for 90 minutes. Once done, remove from the water bath and chill until they are cooled. Serve chilled with a topping of fresh fruit compote.

TEMPERATURE CHARTS

🥩 MEAT	°F🌡 TEMPERATURE	⏱ TIME
Beef Steak, rare	129 °F	1 hour 30 min.
Beef Steak, medium-rare	136 °F	1 hour 30min.
Beef Steak, well done	158 °F	1 hour 30min.
Beef Roast, rare	133 °F	7 hours
Beef Roast, medium-rare	140 °F	6 hours
Beef Roast, well done	158 °F	5 hours
Beef Tough Cuts, rare	136 °F	24 hours
Beef Tough Cuts, medium-rare	149 °F	16 hours
Beef Tough Cuts, well done	185 °F	8 hours
Lamb Tenderloin, Rib eye, T-bone, Cutlets	134 °F	4 hours
Lamb Roast, Leg	134 °F	10 hours
Lamb Flank Steak, Brisket	134 °F	12 hours
Pork Chop, rare	136 °F	1 hour
Pork Chop, medium-rare	144 °F	1 hour
Pork Chop, well done	158 °F	1 hour
Pork Roast, rare	136 °F	3 hours
Pork Roast, medium-rare	144 °F	3 hours
Pork Roast, well done	158 °F	3 hours
Pork Tough Cuts, rare	144 °F	16 hours
Pork Tough Cuts, medium-rare	154 °F	12 hours
Pork Tough Cuts, well done	154 °F	8 hours
Pork Tenderloin	134 °F	1 hour 30min
Pork Baby Back Ribs	165 °F	6 hours
Pork Cutlets	134 °F	5 hours
Pork Spare Ribs	160 °F	12 hours
Pork Belly (quick)	185 °F	5 hours
Pork Belly (slow)	167 °F	24 hours

🍗 POULTRY	°F TEMPERATURE	⏱ TIME
Chicken White Meat, super-supple	140 °F	2 hours
Chicken White Meat, tender and juicy	149 °F	1 hour
Chicken White Meat, well done	167 °F	1 hour
Chicken Breast, bone-in	146 °F	2 hours 30 min.
Chicken Breast, boneless	146 °F	1 hour
Turkey Breast, bone-in	146 °F	4 hours
Turkey Breast, boneless	146 °F	2 hours 30 min.
Duck Breast	134 °F	1 hour 30 min.
Chicken Dark Meat, tender	149 °F	1 hour 30 min.
Chicken Dark Meat, falling off the bone	167 °F	1 hour 30 min.
Chicken Leg or Thigh, bone-in	165 °F	4 hours
Chicken Thigh, boneless	165 °F	1 hour
Turkey Leg or Thigh	165 °F	2 hours
Duck Leg	165 °F	8 hours
Split Game Hen	150 °F	6 hours
🐟 FISH AND SEAFOOD	°F TEMPERATURE	⏱ TIME
Fish, tender	104 °F	40 min.
Fish, tender and flaky	122 °F	40 min.
Fish, well done	140 °F	40 min.
Salmon, Tuna, Trout, Mackerel, Halibut, Snapper, Sole	126 °F	30 min.
Lobster	140 °F	50 min.
Scallops	140 °F	50 min.
Shrimp	140 °F	35 min.

🥕 VEGETABLES	°F TEMPERATURE	⏱ TIME
Vegetables, root (carrots, potato, parsnips, beets, celery root, turnips)	183 °F	3 hours
Vegetables, tender (asparagus, broccoli, cauliflower, fennel, onions, pumpkin, eggplant, green beans, corn)	183 °F	1 hour
Vegetables, greens (kale, spinach, collard greens, Swiss chard)	183 °F	3 min.
🍎 FRUITS	°F TEMPERATURE	⏱ TIME
Fruit, firm (apple, pear)	183 °F	45 min.
Fruit, for purée	185 °F	30 min.
Fruit, berries for topping desserts (blueberries, blackberries, raspberries, strawberries, cranberries)	154 °F	30 min.

WHAT TEMPERATURE SHOULD BE USED?

The rule of thumb is that the thicker the piece, the longer it should cook. Higher temperatures shorten the cooking time. Lower temperatures may take longer.

	TEMPERATURE	MIN COOKING TIME	MAX COOKING TIME
EGGS			
Soft Yolk	140°F (60°C)	1 hour	1 hour
Creamy Yolk	145°F (63°C)	¾ hour	1 hour
GREEN VEGETABLES			
Rare	183°F (84°C)	¼ hour	¾ hour
ROOTS			
Rare	183°F (84°C)	1 hour	3 hours
FRUITS			
Warm	154°F (68°C)	1¾ hour	2½ hour
Soft Fruits	185°F (85°C)	½ hour	1½ hour

	TEMPERATURE	MIN COOKING TIME	MAX COOKING TIME
CHICKEN			
Rare	140°F (60°C)	1 hour	3 hours
Medium	150°F (65°C)	1 hour	3 hours
Well Done	167°F (75°C)	1 hour	3 hours
BEEF STEAK			
Rare	130°F (54°C)	1½ hours	3 hours
Medium	140°F (60°C)	1½ hours	3 hours
Well Done	145°F (63°C)	1½ hours	3 hours
ROAST BEEF			
Rare	133°F (54°C)	7 hours	16 hours
Medium	140°F (60°C)	6 hours	14 hours
Well Done	158°F (70°C)	5 hours	11 hours
PORK CHOP BONE-IN			
Rare	136°F (58°C)	1 hour	4 hours
Medium	144°F (62°C)	1 hour	4 hours
Well Done	158°F (70°C)	1 hour	4 hours
PORK LOIN			
Rare	136°F (58°C)	3 hours	5½ hours
Medium	144°F (62°C)	3 hours	5 hours
Well Done	158°F (70°C)	3 hours	3½ hours
FISH			
Tender	104°F (40°C)	½ hour	½ hour
Medium	124°F (51°C)	½ hour	1 hour
Well Done	131°F (55°C)	½ hour	1½ hours

COOKING CONVERSION

WEIGHT COVERSION	
½ oz.	15g
1 oz.	30g
2 oz.	60g
3 oz.	85g
4 oz.	110g
5 oz.	140g
6 oz.	170g
7 oz.	200g
8 oz.	225g
9 oz.	255g
10 oz.	280g
11 oz.	310g
12 oz.	340g
13 oz.	370g
14 oz.	400g
15 oz.	425g
1 lb.	450g

LIQUID VOLUME MEASUREMENTS			
TABLESPOONS	TEASPOONS	FLUID OUNCES	CUPS
16	48	8 fl. Oz.	1
12	36	6 fl. Oz.	¾
8	24	4 fl. Oz.	½
5 ½	16	2 2/3 fl. Oz.	1/3
4	12	2 fl. Oz.	¼
1	3	0.5 fl. Oz.	1/16

LIQUID VOLUME CONVERSION		
CUPS / TABLESPOONS	FL. OUNCES	MILLILITERS
1 cup	8 fl. Oz.	240 ml
¾ cup	6 fl. Oz.	180 ml
2/3 cup	5 fl. Oz.	150 ml
½ cup	4 fl. Oz.	120 ml
1/3 cup	2 ½ fl. Oz.	75 ml
¼ cup	2 fl. Oz.	60 ml
1/8 cup	1 fl. Oz.	30 ml
1 tablespoon	½ fl. Oz.	15 ml
TEASPOON (tsp.) / TABLESPOON (Tbsp.)		MILLILITERS
1 tsp.		5ml
2 tsp.		10ml
1 Tbsp.		15ml
2 Tbsp.		30ml
3 Tbsp.		45ml
4 Tbsp.		60ml
5 Tbsp.		75ml
6 Tbsp.		90ml
7 Tbsp.		105ml

TEMPERATURE CONVERSIONS

CELSIUS	FAHRENHEIT
54.5°C	130°F
60.0°C	140°F
65.5°C	150°F
71.1°C	160°F
76.6°C	170°F
82.2°C	180°F
87.8°C	190°F
93.3°C	200°F
100°C	212°F

CONCLUSION

Sous-vide method is all about the simplicity through perfect texture and exquisite aroma of your food. It was my deepest desire to create a cookbook that will transform your everyday recipes into a rich heavenly meal that will gather your family around the table and create some precious memories.

Well, one great advantage of using a Sous Vide cooker is that it gives a bigger cooking window. Since the Sous Vide machine cooks on relatively low heat and even temperatures, it hardly overcooks the food if left unchecked for 2–3 hours over the set cooking time. With the rise of recent Sous Vide technology now that window of error is also shut closed as the Sous Vide machines beep or indicate in some other way that the food is ready.

Adopting this type of cooking technique to your kitchen doesn't just make you a better chef. It provides many benefits that you'll enjoy.

For one, it allows you to retain the nutrients in the food that would normally be lost or damaged through traditional methods of cooking. In addition to this, your cutlery and appliances will last longer because they won't get as hot during normal use.

The best part is this type of cooking is the greatest way to prepare your food in perfect condition every time!

In regard to cooking, you can take different approaches to produce amazing results ranging from classical French cuisine to modern fusion fare. This is because of the special properties of our modern kitchen equipment and the ingredients that we can use.

It ought to come as no surprise that it is one of those methods that produces amazing results when executed properly.

This book was designed to cover a variety of foods in many different ways for a great variety of tastes and textures. The recipes here are all designed to standardize the way that those foods are cooked, so that you'll get the same results with every single piece of meat you serve in your restaurant or at home.

Once you've tried these recipes out, you'll develop your own personal preferences for how you like your food prepared and what you're looking for in terms of taste, texture and presentation. With this knowledge, you'll be able to create original dishes that will appeal to your own personal tastes, as well as those of your guests and customers.

There are several advantages, but some people start with the idea of how this new cooking method can be used to make a great tasting meal. It has quickly become more popular as word spreads about the benefits of this new method.

Now you can have tender juicy steak, even your Thanksgiving turkey cooked to perfection and all without the worry of undercooking or overcooking. This is also a great way to enjoy filet mignon and other red meats without any worry about it being dry or tough.

The possibilities are truly endless when it comes to the new cooking method. You can prepare all kinds of foods at home. The possibilities are endless for vegetarian dishes as well. You can even prepare some fantastic desserts, from fruit crisps to chocolate cakes.

Whether you're just getting started with this type of cooking or an experienced cook who wants to try new things, this cookbook has something here for everyone!

Have a wonderful time trying these recipes!

RECIPE INDEX

Made in the USA
Monee, IL
30 November 2021